RACE AND CLASS IN TEXAS POLITICS

RACE AND CLASS IN TEXAS POLITICS

Chandler Davidson

PRINCETON UNIVERSITY PRESS   PRINCETON, NEW JERSEY

Copyright © 1990 by Princeton University Press
Published by Princeton University Press, 41 William Street,
Princeton, New Jersey 08540
In the United Kingdom: Princeton University Press, Oxford

Library of Congress Cataloging-in-Publication Data

Davidson, Chandler.
Race and class in Texas politics / Chandler Davidson.
p.   cm.
Includes bibliographical references and index.
ISBN 0-691-07861-0 (acid-free paper)
1. Texas—Politics and government—1951–   2. Texas—Race
relations.   3. Social classes—Texas.   I. Title.
F391.D255   1990
305.8'009764—dc20   90-38556

This book has been composed in Linotron Caledonia

Princeton University Press books are printed on acid-free paper, and meet the
guidelines for permanence and durability of the Committee on Production Guidelines
for Book Longevity of the Council on Library Resources

Printed in the United States of America by Princeton University Press,
Princeton, New Jersey

10 9 8 7 6 5 4 3 2 1

For Ian and Seth _____

WITH LOVE AND ADMIRATION

Contents

List of Illustrations   ix

List of Figures   xi

List of Tables   xiii

Preface   xv

Acknowledgments   xxi

Prologue   xxiii

PART ONE: LIBERALS AND CONSERVATIVES

1. V. O. Key's Theory of Texas Politics   3

2. The Myth of Overwhelming Conservatism   17

3. The Basis of the Liberal Coalition   40

PART TWO: CLASS STRUCTURES

4. The Upper Class   63

5. Upper-Class Institutions   85

6. Blue-Collar Texans   109

7. Money and Politics   133

PART THREE: PARTY POLITICS

8. The Struggle for Control of the Democratic Party   155

9. The Year of the Liberal Breakthrough   180

10. The Rise of Right-Wing Republicanism   198

11. Race and Realignment   221

12. Race and Class in Texas Politics   240

Epilogue   261

Notes   273

Index   331

List of Illustrations

1.	Maury Maverick, Jr.	xvii
2.	Jim Wright	xix
3.	V. O. Key, Jr.	4
4.	Ralph W. Yarborough	31
5.	Progressive Activists Swap Stories	41
6.	Minority Senators Huddle	45
7.	Homer P. Rainey	47
8.	Henry B. Gonzalez	52
9.	Willie Velasquez	58
10.	Bill Clements and George Bush	74
11.	Oveta Culp Hobby	75
12.	Anne Armstrong	96
13.	The Texas Establishment at Its Zenith	99
14.	Jim Hightower and Henry Cisneros	119
15.	Mickey Leland	125
16.	Bob Eckhardt	127
17.	George and Herman Brown	129
18.	Don Yarborough	142
19.	On the Rubber-Chicken Circuit	143
20.	Creekmore Fath and Mrs. R. D. ("Frankie") Randolph	165
21.	The High Tide of Texas Liberalism	167
22.	John Connally	170
23.	Sarah Weddington	173
24.	Billie Carr	181
25.	Billy Clayton	185
26.	John Tower	203
27.	H. L. Hunt	211
28.	Phil Gramm	244
29.	Jim Mattox Campaigns	254
30.	Pleading the People's Cause	255
31.	William Wayne Justice	258
32.	Barbara Jordan	262
33.	Bill Hobby	265
34.	Lloyd Bentsen, Jr.	269

List of Figures

2.1 Texas Voting-Age Population Voting for Governor,
Democratic Primary and General Election, 1880–1986   24

2.2 Self-Described Ideology of Adults, Selected States
and Nation, 1968   38

3.1 Voter Turnout in Texas General Elections, Contests
for President and Governor, 1944–1986   55

7.1 Statewide Candidates' Share of Expenditures and
Share of Votes, 1972–1974   135

10.1 Republican Elected Officials, Texas, 1960–1986   200

List of Tables

2.1 Support for Liberal Gubernatorial or U.S. Senatorial
Candidates, Texas Primary Elections, 1946–1984   26
2.2 Ideology of Texas Voting-Age Adults, 1968   37
3.1 Average Percent of the Vote for Liberal Candidates by
Geographic Area of Texas, 1946–1980   42
3.2 Presidential Vote in Selected Texas Cities, 1936–1984   43
3.3 Democratic Primary Vote in Selected Texas Cities,
1946–1984   48
3.4 Relative Voter Turnout among Texas Minorities, General
Gubernatorial Elections, 1978 and 1982   57
4.1 Support From Major Texas Donors to Candidates
in Presidential and Texas Gubernatorial Races, 1972   81
6.1 Occupational Groups in the Employed Work Force, Texas,
1940–1980   113
6.2 Funding for Job Safety Programs, Selected States, 1981   123
6.3 National and Southern Union Data, 1977   130
6.4 Blue-Collar Employees Who Are Union Members or Who
Would Like to Be, 1977   131
7.1 Campaign Expenditures of Leading Candidates in Selected
Liberal-Conservative Races, 1962–1970   138
7.2 Individual Contributions of $500 or More, Gubernatorial
Contests, 1972   141
8.1 Income of Texas Delegates to National Conventions, 1968
and 1972   175
10.1 Liberal Voting Record on Twelve Key Votes, Texas House
of Representatives, 1985   219
10.2 Liberal Voting Record on Eight Key Votes, Texas Senate,
1985   219
10.3 Liberal Voting Record, Texas Congressional Delegation,
1985–1986   220
12.1 Realignment of Ideological Voting Patterns, Texas Congressional Delegation, 1960–1961 and 1985–1986   246

Preface

IMAGINE that Texas is once more a sovereign country, just as it was between 1836 and 1846. In natural wealth, population, the sweep of its geography, and the magnitude of its economy, it would be one of the major nations of the world.

In 1980 there were some two hundred nations and territories on the globe. In area, Texas would have ranked among the largest fifth of them, its 266,807 square miles dwarfing many of the major countries of Europe and Asia. Texas is larger than any country in Western Europe: larger than France, West Germany, or Sweden; almost three times as large as the United Kingdom.

Texas would be a formidable economic competitor. Its personal income in 1980—roughly equivalent to the gross domestic product of nation-states—was $135.2 billion, ranking fourteenth in the world. The 977 million barrels of Texas crude oil produced that year was exceeded by only four countries.

The scale of the state's urban development is impressive. At the beginning of the twentieth century, Texas was an impoverished rural state still struggling to overcome the ravages of the Civil War. As a nation in 1980, it would have been at the forefront of the urbanized world. Approximately 80 percent of its population of 14.2 million lived in metropolitan statistical areas (MSAs) surrounding a central city of at least fifty thousand inhabitants. More than half of the metropolitan population was concentrated in four such areas: Houston, Dallas–Fort Worth, San Antonio, and Austin.

Now consider Texas as what it is, one state among fifty. In area, it ranked second in 1980; in population, third; in aggregate personal income, third. Its aggregate income was greater than that of the six New England states combined. Texas was among the most urbanized states in the union, on a par with New York, Connecticut, and Michigan. Between 1980 and 1985, Texas added 2.2 million inhabitants, an increase larger than the entire population of one-third of the states in 1985.

At the beginning of the 1980s, 30 percent of the nation's proved liquid hydrocarbon reserves lay under Texas soil and 27 percent of the nation's oil-refining capacity sat on top of it. But not in oil alone was the economy preeminent. Texas also ranked first among the states in the number of cattle, sheep, and goats and second in receipts for farm and ranch marketing. It ranked first in capital investment in manufacturing, third in the size of nonagricultural employment, seventh in value added by manufacture.

It ranked first in cargo tonnage shipped from its thirteen deep-water ports.

In recent decades, the state has played a remarkable role in the nation's politics. Tied with Illinois for the fourth largest number of electoral votes in 1980 and having the third largest congressional delegation, which often votes as a bloc on energy matters, Texas is a key player in presidential election campaigns and the dramatic struggles over national legislation. Its political heft has been magnified by the fact that, as a one-party state throughout most of the present century, it contributed an unusually large proportion of congressional committee chairmen, thanks to the now-defunct seniority rule. From the New Deal to the 1970s, Congress often seemed to be run by aging, crusty Texans who dominated key committees.

A mere list of the names of Texans who have played noteworthy roles in national politics in the recent past underlines the state's importance: Edward M. House, Woodrow Wilson's able tutor and éminence grise; John Nance Garner, the banker and land baron who became the Speaker of the House and then the vice president, playing an important part in FDR's first New Deal and in the attempt by FDR's enemies to scuttle the second one; and banker-publisher Jesse Jones, who presided over the Reconstruction Finance Corporation during the Great Depression, then became the administrator of the powerful Federal Loan Agency, and then the secretary of commerce before he, too, fell out with Roosevelt's liberalism.

There was Sam Rayburn, Garner's protégé, the Speaker of the House longer than any man in history; Lyndon Johnson, the New Deal congressman who won a controversial election to the U.S. Senate, and then went on to become majority leader, vice president, and on a fateful day in Dallas, the president; and John Connally, one of Johnson's close friends and advisers, who, after service as multimillionaire oilman Sid Richardson's lawyer, moved easily among Washington's power cliques, first as the oil industry's champion in his role of secretary of the navy under John Kennedy, then as secretary of the treasury under Richard Nixon.

In Congress, from the New Deal forward, a number of Texans made their marks on the national scene: Maury Maverick, Sr., the fiery San Antonian who was one of FDR's "young turks"; Wright Patman, the scourge of the big banks; Martin Dies, whose antics as chairman of the House Un-American Activities Committee from 1938 to 1944 anticipated McCarthyism by a decade; Ralph Yarborough, the leader of the state's liberal movement throughout most of the 1950s and 1960s whose work in the Senate on education reform earned him the title of "Mr. Education"; Bob Eckhardt, who gained a reputation during the 1970s as a knowledgeable critic of the big oil companies in Congress, as he had been in the state legislature; Lloyd Bentsen, Jr., conservative congressman and later sena-

1. Maury Maverick, Jr. A liberal activist lawyer, newspaper columnist, and former state legislator, Maverick examines a caricature of his father, who was a New Deal congressman—one of Franklin Roosevelt's "young turks"—and later mayor of San Antonio. Courtesy of the Barker Texas History Center (Russell Lee Collection).

tor who defeated Ralph Yarborough in 1970 and ran unsuccessfully for the presidency in 1976 and the vice presidency in 1988; Barbara Jordan, Texas's first black state senator in this century and then congresswoman; and Henry B. Gonzalez, state senator and then congressman, who became chairman of the House Banking Committee in 1989, as Congress grappled with the unprecedented collapse of the savings-and-loan industry.

In the midst of the Watergate era, Connally's college friend, Robert Strauss, a wealthy corporate Dallas lawyer and politico, took over the national Democratic party following George McGovern's defeat in 1972; and after skirmishes with the party's reform wing, he took on a series of major jobs in the Carter administration. Meanwhile, Congressman Jim Wright from Fort Worth continued to move up the ladder, and when Thomas ("Tip") O'Neill of Massachusetts retired from the House in 1987, Wright became the new Speaker.

By the early 1970s, the Texas Republicans were moving confidently onto Democratic turf. By then Houston publisher Oveta Culp Hobby had already played a series of remarkable roles—as head of the Women's Army Corps during World War II and then as the first secretary of the newly created Department of Health, Education, and Welfare under President Eisenhower. John Tower, with his stunning victory in 1961, became the South's first Republican senator since Reconstruction. He held his seat until 1985 and ultimately chaired the Senate Armed Services Committee, which he used to expound his hawkish views. After Tower's retirement in 1985, Ronald Reagan appointed him head of the U.S. negotiating team in the strategic arms talks with Russia. Soon he would head the Tower Commission, which investigated Reagan's arms-for-hostages deal with Iran.

Connecticut-born George Bush, after successes in West Texas oil exploration, moved to Houston and plunged into Republican politics, where he ran against Senator Yarborough in 1964 as a Goldwater Republican and then won election to Congress in 1966. Before his 1980 presidential bid, which resulted in his election as vice president, Bush had been the head of the U.S. delegation to the United Nations, the U.S. diplomatic mission in Peking shortly before formal relations with China were established, the Central Intelligence Agency, and the Republican National Committee, where he confronted his counterpart Robert Strauss on the Democratic side. By 1989 he had become the second president from Texas in twenty-five years. His close friend James Baker, scion of the family connected to Houston's Baker & Botts law firm, was also active in the Texas Republican party and ran unsuccessfully for statewide office. Reagan made Baker the White House chief of staff during his first term and then named him treasury secretary during his second one. After running Bush's 1988 presidential campaign, Baker was appointed secretary of state.

Yet, in spite of Texas's economic might and political importance, American social scientists are much better acquainted with the mayoral politics of New Haven and Chicago, or even Muncie, Indiana, where the "Middletown" investigations were conducted, than with the politics of Texas or, for that matter, those of most other major states of the union.

This is unfortunate because each state is a complex political and social entity of its own. It has its particular governmental structure, myths and history, leading families, economic resources, ethnic cultures, and traditions of interaction with Washington and the other states. Yet in political sociology today, there is no worthy tradition of state or even regional studies.

In addition, a cultural chauvinism in America, as in France or England, defines what is important as whatever happens in Manhattan, Paris, or London. What goes on elsewhere is hardly worth studying. The long-term results of this "New Yorko-centric" view, as Richard F. Hamilton calls it, are easy to see.[1] Raymond E. Wolfinger and John Osgood Field make the point clearly. "Perhaps because so much of the best scholarly research on

2. Jim Wright. A moderate Democrat from Fort Worth
and longtime congressman, Wright was Speaker of the
U.S. House of Representatives from 1987 to 1989. Courtesy of Jim Rockwell and the *Texas Observer*.

local politics has been conducted close to the great universities of the
Northeast and perhaps also because most serious nonacademic writers
live in a few northeastern cities, political organizations in these cities have
been described at great length, while very little is known about existing
machines in other parts of the country."[2] If intellectuals who live in Manhattan "know more about Queens and Nassau counties than about Pittsburgh or Philadelphia (or Trenton or even Jersey City)," writes Hamilton,
"there is no great loss involved because the latter places are of no great
importance anyway. . . . One might call this the provincialism of the
cosmopolitans."[3]

Such provincialism, like provincialism everywhere, has the effect of
preventing insight into the way things work. If one would understand the
United States, one must become acquainted with its parts. This is impos-

sible if the parts—the states and the leading cities—are assumed to be no more than miniature clones of the nation. There are similarities among them, to be sure, as comparative studies have made clear. But there are also differences, which are sometimes crucial for grasping the impact a state's politicians or voters have in the national sphere, especially when that impact is considerable. Nothing better demonstrates this fact than the pioneering work of Neal R. Peirce, who has provided perhaps the most detailed, readable accounts of the fifty individual states' politics to date.[4]

This book examines one of the provinces. It also represents an effort to get beyond a popular regional approach, the trademark of which is often sentimentality or reverse provincial chauvinism. Texas deserves to be studied because it matters itself and because it is an important piece in the puzzle of modern American politics.

Acknowledgments _____

MANY people and institutions have helped me with this book, and I am deeply indebted to them. To the National Endowment for the Humanities, which provided me with a yearlong fellowship in 1976 and thereby enabled me to begin research on the book in earnest, I owe special thanks. I also wish to acknowledge the receipt of research funds from the office of Joseph Cooper, then dean of social sciences at Rice University.

The Rice Department of Sociology, with its unique brand of collegiality, provided friendship and encouragement throughout the project. The staff of Rice's Fondren Library, too numerous to name individually, gave me help whenever I asked for it and went out of their way to make my task easier. Several classes of Rice students over the years have listened and responded to the ideas that gradually found their way into this work, and I appreciate their comments and criticisms. Other Rice students worked assiduously for me as student assistants, and I thank them personally: Janice Gillette, Kathy Vanderbeck Smyser, Bill Newsome, Robert Lange, Laurie Kyle, Michael McKinney, Ron Lee, and Monique Shankle. The research assistance of Carole Leamon is also appreciated.

David M. Kovenock of the University of Maine at Orono was helpful in supplying data on the 1968 Texas elections gathered by the Comparative State Elections Project of the University of North Carolina's Institute for Research in Social Science. George N. Green and William R. Miller, historians at the University of Texas at Arlington, shared their knowledge of people active in the turn-of-the-century reform movement in Texas and helped me locate material on Joshua Hicks, the Abilene Populist. Roy Evans of the U.S. Department of Labor; Walter G. Martin, formerly with the Texas Department of Health; and Pat Honchar, of the National Institute of Occupational Safety and Health, helped me understand some of the problems of occupational health.

My colleague Stephen Klineberg generously shared data from his annual Houston Area Survey whenever I requested it. Massoud Mafid aided me with graphs. Louis Marchiafava, director of the Houston Metropolitan Archives, and Lawrence A. Landis, photographs archivist with the Barker Texas History Center, were most helpful in my search for photographs of Texas politicians. So was Cliff Olofson, business manager of the *Texas Observer*, who has been generous over the years in other ways too numerous to mention.

I have valued the conversation and encouragement of friends while working on the project, and I am especially grateful to three of them: Allen Matusow—who read versions of chapters 9 and 11—Donald Huddle, and Walter G. Hall. Other persons who have generously read all or parts of the manuscript, offering valuable suggestions, are James E. Anderson, Joe Feagin, Joe B. Frantz, Bernard Grofman, Celia Morris, Stephanie Shaw, and Donald S. Strong. I owe a special debt to Ronnie Dugger, who read the manuscript with scrupulous care and suggested many helpful changes.

Several people typed portions of the manuscript over the years, and I thank them for it: Alicia Mikula, Terri Pallack, Kathy Koch, Crystalin Williams, and Keith Heston.

For their contributions in the last stages of the project, I would like to thank Gail Ullman, Social Science Editor of Princeton University Press, and Esther M. Luckett, my copy editor. Two other people have earned my special gratitude. One is Cathy Monholland, whose superb editorial skills and dedication to the project in the months before the manuscript was sent to the publisher were extraordinary. The other is my wife, Sharon, whose sacrifices to the book have been considerable. I want her to know how much I appreciate her forbearance.

Finally, a very special acknowledgment must be made to Richard F. Hamilton, teacher, colleague, and friend. His deeply informed criticism of an earlier draft made the book much better than it would otherwise have been.

Quotations from Stanley H. Brown, *Ling: The Rise, Fall and Return of a Texas Titan* (New York: Atheneum, 1972), are reprinted with permission of the Sterling Lord Literistic, Inc. The reproduction of a chart in V. O. Key, Jr., *Southern Politics in State and Nation* (New York: Random House, 1949), is reprinted with the permission of the V. O. Key estate.

Prologue

In 1888 a columnist for the *Advance-Advocate*, a newspaper with a national readership, criticized a strategy proposed by northern Prohibitionists in the South to break down "the color line." "The color line is here," asserted the columnist, Dr. J. B. Cranfill, a Texas Baptist minister, "and [it] will stay as long as there is race caste. The negro is a negro; is below the white men in every essential regard, and the dream of our good northern friends about breaking down the color line is a species of optimism that will never be realized."[1] The minister was soon answered by one Joshua Hicks of Sulphur Springs, a small town in East Texas:

> I believe Dr. Cranfill has erred in his interpretation of the purpose of our friends in the North who would "break down the color line" in the South. He seems to understand them as wishing to wipe out all race distinction at the South *socially*. That, I think, is altogether foreign to their purpose. They want to break down the color line *in politics*. The two races being here together under one government, they want to see them united, *politically*, by a common interest and a common danger. They see no good reason why the two races should stand arrayed against each other at the ballot-box. That such is the case here in the south, no one can deny. And that it results from the war . . . cannot be seriously questioned.[2]

Cranfill offered a heated rejoinder, which concluded dramatically:

> There are three questions in this country, difficult of adjustment, that are at this moment knocking at the door for settlement—the liquor question, the race question and the question of foreign domination. To continue the liquor traffic is death; to amalgamate with the Negro is death; to allow a continual, unchecked influx of foreign anarchists and paupers is death. To do all these things is death still more speedy and direful. My remedy would be as follows: Kill the liquor traffic; Sepegate [*sic*] the Negro; Restrict the foreigner.[3]

Hicks's views might strike the modern reader as unique in someone of his color, region, and time. While he did not advocate social equality, a southern white man openly supported the abolition of the color line in politics only a few years before black disfranchisement. Even though he admitted the possibility that blacks were inferior, he revealed elsewhere in his letter his strong admiration for nationally known black leaders whose work, he implied, would liberate blacks and whites alike.

But Hicks was far from unique in 1888. As Lawrence Goodwyn has demonstrated in his path-breaking reinterpretation of the Populist movement of the 1890s, large numbers of whites would soon prove willing to join forces with blacks, sometimes for narrow tactical reasons, sometimes for more generous and egalitarian motives, to break the iron grip on southern politics of the Democrats—the party that, as the Populists saw it, was heavily implicated in the massive impoverishment of farmers in the generation following the Civil War.[4]

Not long after his exchange with the Reverend Cranfill, Hicks sold his farm near Sulphur Springs "at a ruinous sacrifice," as his son later recalled, and headed west to Abilene, Texas, in search of cheaper land and better soil.[5] Arriving there in 1890, he found neither. An inveterate writer of letters to editors, he soon opined in an Abilene newspaper that the city and its hinterland would develop slowly until farming lands were subdivided "so as to give the fifty acre man a chance. . . . Give the poor man a chance," he promised, "and he will do more for Abilene with his muscles than the rich man is doing with his money."[6]

Hicks's concerns were widely shared. Farm tenancy was making a mockery of the ideal of the American yeoman farmer in Texas. In surrounding Taylor County, more than half the farmers were reduced to tenancy at the time he wrote.[7] Only weeks after his letter appeared, the Texas People's party was founded, and Hicks was caught up in the Populist whirlwind.

The new party quickly made headway. In 1894 the Populist congressional candidate was defeated by a single percentage point in the Abilene district. Taylor County elected three Populist county commissioners out of five that year, as well as county treasurer and attorney. In the city itself, an alderman belonging to the Populist party was elected in 1892 and another in 1898.[8] Hicks, having become a printer, went to work for the Abilene *West Texas Sentinel*, the official organ of the Farmers Alliance and Industrial Union in the 13th Congressional District, and came to know some of the major Populist figures of the day.[9]

With the collapse of the People's party in the latter 1890s, Hicks, who was a Methodist, became a printer for the *West Texas Baptist*; he still wrote an occasional column for the *West Texas Sentinel* under the pen name of "Cosma." His themes were common ones among thinking people who had been influenced by populism. In various "advanced" newspapers, he attacked such things as American and British imperialism and the disfranchising nature of the poll tax proposed as a prerequisite for voting.[10]

American socialism, appearing on the political scene in the early years of the twentieth century, lacked the broad appeal of populism but registered some notable successes at the local level. From 1908 to 1916 neighboring Oklahoma ranked first or second in the nation in the percentage of its popular support for the Socialist presidential candidate.[11] Socialist protest in Texas, based on the farmers' continuing descent from land-ownership into tenancy, was also significant and spilled over into municipal politics.

Conservatives feared that a new radical movement, coming on the heels of populism, would sweep the masses before it. President Theodore Roosevelt warned in 1905 that "growth of the Socialist party in this country [is] far more ominous than any populist movement in times past." In the following year, Texas Governor Joseph Sayers complained in a letter to fellow Texan Edward House that "not only this country but the entire world is fast converging into Socialism."[12]

As the gospel of socialism spread, Hicks began to publish the *Farmer's Journal*, which dealt mostly with farming matters but also with political subjects. Two years later, he and some friends joined the Socialist party. About the same time, Hicks gave up his belief in the Methodist creed, although he continued to believe in an afterlife.[13]

In March 1908, an advertisement appeared in the *National Rip-Saw*, a Socialist paper, announcing that "THE FARMER'S JOURNAL, one of the biggest little journals in all America, published at Abilene, Texas, and edited by J. L. Hicks, and which has been purely a farmer's journal for many years, in its issue of January 13th, last, DELIBERATELY, CANDIDLY and UN-HESITATINGLY laid aside all of its Populistic ideas, which do not harmonize with the doctrines of Socialism, and like a man, that its editor is, boldly declared for Socialism." Paid for by an anonymous benefactor, the ad encouraged Socialists to help the *Farmer's Journal* by sending a dime for a three-month trial subscription. Circulation soon rose to its peak of ten thousand.[14]

Hicks's paper was not the only Socialist voice crying in the West Texas wilderness. The nearby hamlet of Anson published a Socialist paper called the *Frying Pan*, and the *Comanche Socialist* was published in Comanche County. In 1912 there were seventeen weekly Socialist newspapers in the state and nineteen in Oklahoma. Hicks's paper later merged with the largest and most militant one in Texas, Hallettsville's the *Rebel*.[15]

In 1910 the city fathers of Abilene began to prepare for a charter revision, thus paving the way for a referendum on commission government the next spring. This would have the effect of decreasing the size of the city council from nine members to five.[16]

As in most other Texas cities switching to a commission form of government, the business community and its spokesmen, including the *Abilene Daily Reporter* and the "25,000 Club"—the forerunner of the Chamber of Commerce—strongly favored the change. First introduced in Galveston a few years earlier as a superior form of municipal government that was "businesslike" in its structure, commission government was seen by the upper classes as a mechanism that, when used in combination with at-large elections, could diminish the power of the working classes and political minorities, who, for their part, favored the ward-based aldermanic system.

Abilene's mayor, a conservative businessman, appointed a citizens' committee to meet at the "25,000 Club" hall and discuss the charter. The committee included the current aldermen, the town's ministers, and thirty-three other individuals, all of whom—among the twenty-three whose occupations could be identified—were business or professional men.[17]

The mayor also published a letter in the paper that attacked a critic of the proposed commission; the mayor argued that it was "very much out of place for a man who owns no more property in Abilene . . . to come before our people and assume guardianship over their business." An editorial expressed the view that "men who annually pay taxes on hundreds of thousands of dollars worth of property within the city of Abilene are in favor of adoption of the charter."[18]

Hicks by then was fifty-four, and his penchant for politics had taken him far beyond prohibitionist leanings he had nurtured earlier. (He was still a teetotaler, however.) As a Populist turned Socialist and attuned to the nationwide debate over the merits of so-called municipal reform sponsored primarily by the business class, Hicks found it impossible to let pass the provocations of both the mayor and the editorialist.

> The *Reporter*'s course in asking the "heaviest taxpayers" and in not specially and personally asking some of the heaviest consumers and hardest workers, for their opinion on the proposed charter, is tantamount to a declaration of the principle that those who have wealth to acquire are less worthy to be consulted than those whose wealth has already been acquired. . . . The proposed charter itself is the negation of nearly all that is supposed to be meant by the term "People's government." . . . In the face of the present almost universal and seemingly spontaneous demand for a wider diffusion rather than a narrower concentration of governing power, the charter proposed for Abilene seems almost like an affront.[19]

The editor, in his reply, challenged Hicks's analysis with a dig at the aging radical newsman: "For years Mr. Hicks has stood as the champion of the laboring man, particularly the man whose taxes is [*sic*] confined to the amount of a poll tax receipt."[20]

In the days preceding the 1911 referendum, a major debate between a leading Socialist and a well-known Methodist minister was scheduled in Abilene. Three days before the election, according to a front-page story in the daily paper, "on all trains north, east and west delegations are coming in for the Clark-Hamilton debate. . . . Mr. Clark is a national committee-man of the Socialist party of Oklahoma and is regarded in socialist circles as the greatest orator that party has in the South. Nationally he is regarded as second only to Eugene V. Debs. Rev. G. G. Hamilton is regarded as one of the strongest men in the Methodist denomination in Texas."[21]

Curiously, given the potential drama of this confrontation, the Abilene daily paper failed to report the debate itself. Surely with a twinkle in his eye, Hicks later pasted in his scrapbook a newspaper article announcing that the Reverend Hamilton had converted to socialism.[22] When the votes in the city charter referendum a few days later were counted, Hicks was on the losing side, as he had been in so many other political battles over the previous quarter century. The new charter won in all four boxes by a total of almost four to one.[23]

Shortly thereafter Hicks moved to Waco, Texas, and founded a socialist paper, *Humanity*, which lasted about a year. The Socialist party was then reaching its apogee. In 1912 it polled the second largest vote after the Democrats, the Republicans having been thrown into disarray by the emergence of Theodore Roosevelt's Bull Moose party, a major aim of which was to create a lily-white party in the South to destroy the Democratic monopoly. Hicks ran on the statewide Socialist ticket in 1914 for the position of comptroller, along with Henry Faulk of Austin, a candidate for attorney general, and E. R. Meitzen of Hallettsville, the candidate for governor.[24]

In his last years, Hicks wrote articles for progressive journals and letters to local newspapers, championing women's suffrage and laws to increase voter turnout. He also managed to convince himself that his longtime dream of abolishing the color line was coming to pass, at least in the workplace. Writing in the *American Socialist* in 1915, Hicks stated that in Waco black and white "capitalists" worked easily together, just as did black and white laborers. He concluded that capitalism was dissolving race barriers and that class differences were taking their place. "But some people in the south, after seeing white and black workers rub against each other in the ditch, and white and black capitalists rub against each other in their meetings at the court house, are still afraid that Socialism will mean 'nigger equality.' "[25] Clearly Hicks was still arguing the position he had taken in his letter responding to Cranfill almost thirty years before: political equality and collaboration between the races.

Although there is no record of his feelings, Hicks's illusions about the gradual blurring of the color line must have been shattered the following year, 1916, when a lynching occurred that focused the entire nation's attention on Waco. Jesse Washington, a black "charged with assault and murder, was beaten, stabbed, and mutilated beyond recognition before [his body] was hanged and finally burned" by white citizens of the city,[26] who brought their children to the festivities and held them up high over their heads, to give them a better view of the spectacle. Nothing more on race seems to have been written by Hicks, who died in 1921.

Part One

LIBERALS AND CONSERVATIVES

1

V. O. Key's Theory of Texas Politics

IN 1908, the year in which Joshua Hicks's *Farmer's Journal* declared for socialism, V. O. Key, Jr., was born in Austin, Texas. V. O. Key, Sr., subsequently moved his family to the West Texas town of Lamesa, where he practiced law and farmed. The younger Key went to Abilene in the 1920s, where he spent two years at McMurray College, a Methodist institution. He then transferred to the University of Texas, where he received a B.A. degree in 1929 and an M.A. in 1930. He received a doctorate in political science from the University of Chicago in 1934.[1]

Twelve years later, the Rockefeller Foundation made a grant to the University of Alabama to study "the electoral process in the South." Fortunately for the project, Key, who was by then a thirty-eight-year-old professor of political science at Johns Hopkins University, became the research director. Assisted by two junior colleagues, Alexander Heard and Donald S. Strong, Key assembled a staff and in an amazingly short time produced a book.[2] When *Southern Politics in State and Nation* was published in 1949, Key's reputation, already influential among his peers, was established beyond question. The book was magisterial, a brilliant, sweeping survey of the eleven southern states that destroyed once and for all the myth of the "solid South." C. Vann Woodward opined that "Key's monumental work marks the beginning of the end of this age of obscurantism" in southern political science.[3] Ralph Bunche, the black scholar who had assisted the Swedish economist Gunnar Myrdal in his research for *An American Dilemma*, called it "an outstanding contribution to the literature on the American political system."[4]

The book was more than a descriptive survey; it was one of those reorienting works that challenge fundamental assumptions. Everyone knew racial conflict to be an essential element in southern politics, and Key deftly traced its ramifications throughout the region. But, in addition, he introduced the element of class conflict and set out a theory of the interworkings of these two variables that both explained a number of seemingly disparate phenomena and suggested a solution to the southern problem that, until then, had largely escaped the broad cross section of progressive opinion leaders—political scientists, journalists, activists.

Widely read during succeeding decades, *Southern Politics* became part of the conventional wisdom of Key's generation. Had Joshua Hicks been

3. V. O. Key, Jr. (1908–1963). Born in Austin, Texas, Key was the author of several influential works, including *Southern Politics in State and Nation*. He was a professor of government at Harvard University when he died. Courtesy of Harvard University News Office.

alive to read the work of fellow West Texan Key, he probably would have been astounded that ideas that were central to progressive Prohibitionists and Populists of his era, ideas he himself had advanced for most of his adult life, had been adopted by a later generation of academicians.[5]

At the theory's heart lay a simple proposition: "Politics generally comes down, over the long run, to a conflict between those who have and those who have less." At the state level, Key argued, "the crucial issues tend to turn around taxation and expenditure. What level of public education and what levels of other public services shall be maintained? How shall the burden of taxation for their support be distributed?" While admitting that such issues varied in importance with time and place and that the issue of democracy itself was also sometimes significant, he nonetheless asserted that "if there is a single grand issue it is that of public expenditure."[6] Although certainly not a Marxist, Key believed that the question of how to distribute the social surplus was central to politics and that under ordinary circumstances, the different interests of broad social classes generated conflict. This viewpoint was an essential aspect of *Southern Politics*. But why was class conflict so difficult to discern, and why did race conflict *seem* to be the essence of southern politics?

Key did not deny that race was tremendously important. "The hard core of the political South—and the backbone of southern political unity— is made up of those counties and sections of the southern states in which Negroes constitute a substantial proportion of the population. In these areas a real problem of politics, broadly considered, is the maintenance of control by a white minority."[7]

The situation of whites in the southern black belt counties, as Key portrayed it, foreshadowed the condition of South African whites today. Surrounded by an oppressed black majority, southern whites were deadly intent on maintaining their privileges through a system of brutal racial domination. They could not achieve this end without assistance. Only by convincing their fellow white southerners that all whites' interests were similar, whether they lived in counties with few blacks or with many, could the black belt's privileged status remain secure. Through this liaison, a small minority of southern whites, "in a sense, managed to subordinate the entire South to the service of their peculiar local needs."[8]

How was this accomplished? According to Key, the answer lay in the nature of the political economy of the black belt counties and in the outcome of the two fundamental crises of the South in the nineteenth century. In these counties were "located most of the large agricultural operators who supervise the work of many tenants, sharecroppers, and laborers, most of whom are colored. *As large operators they lean generally in a conservative direction in their political views*."[9]

The economic—and not simply the racial—conservatism of the ruling class in the black belt was the essential factor in shaping events surrounding the Civil War in the 1860s and the Populist revolt a generation later. The unity and political skill of the planter class enabled it to enlist the rest of the South in the war, which, along with Reconstruction, increased greatly the solidarity of southern whites in all regions and thus dampened the internal conflicts that had existed before the war.[10]

By the 1890s, however, even the South's hostility to the North could not hide the divisive conflict between poor farmers, black and white, on one side, and on the other the Bourbons, as the conservatives of the day were called. The radical forces consisted of "the upcountrymen, the small farmers of the highlands and other areas where there were few Negroes and where there was no basis for a plantation economy. And they were joined by many of the workers of the cities which were beginning to grow, as well as by many poor white farmers of other regions." Against the Populists were arrayed the black belt oligarchs, who presented the radicals with their "most consistent, . . . most intense rural resistance," and they formed alliances with "the merchants and bankers of the towns and . . . the new industrialists." It was a class struggle of significant proportions, one in which not only fundamental economic issues were to be decided but also the nature of southern politics in the next century.[11]

The black belt ruling class won the conflict with the Populists as it had won the controversy over whether the South should go to war to defend slavery: by "raising . . . a fearful specter of Negro rule," and, in the case of Populism, by "the ruthless application of social pressures against those who treasonably fused with the Republicans under Populist leadership." Redirecting discontent among the poor whites toward the "fearful specter," the black belt oligarchy triumphed once more, "impress[ing] on an entire region a philosophy agreeable to its necessities" and welding "a regional unity" for their defense in national politics.[12]

Key's theory challenged the explanation of the race problem that the southern aristocrats fobbed off on credulous outsiders—including not a few northern liberals. In this conventional view, the "poor whites" were to blame. But Key placed the responsibility primarily on the black belt oligarchs and their allies in the business class for using the bogey of black rule to divert attention from economic discontent.[13]

In a few words, this was Key's theory of southern politics. He fleshed it out with a broad array of evidence he and his colleagues had accumulated, on a state-by-state basis, to demonstrate how social and political structures allowed the upper class to consolidate its power and to maintain the status quo. The structures of domination consisted of Jim Crow institutions, a one-party system, a wide variety of barriers to voting that disadvantaged both blacks and poor whites, the manipulation of election structures to diminish their strength even when they did vote, a system of campaign financing that gave a net advantage to the wealthy, and the intentional insulation of state from national politics. In the course of demonstrating the interlocking nature of these phenomena, Key developed a complex institutional model for explaining the region's electoral structure.

Key was particularly fascinated by the effects of "one-partyism," which in many southern states, he observed, was equivalent to the absence of a party system altogether. The significance of this claim rests on Key's view of the role of a two-party system in a democracy characterized by persistent class conflict. Key set great store by this system. "As institutions," he admitted, "parties enjoy a general disrepute," but "most of the democratic world finds them indispensable as instruments of self-government, as means for the organization and expression of competing viewpoints on public policy."[14] In a two-party system, each party consisted "of little groups of leaders and subleaders bound together at least by the ambition to control the machinery of government." Typically the parties were both vital and stable, and the leaders were concerned for the party's welfare, which meant the welfare of its adherents, who reflected "sectional, class, or group interests."[15]

Platforms represented the different interests of the parties' constituent groups, and at election time, they provided the people with a choice of policies and enabled the parties to rally adherents to their cause. To the extent that elected officials belonged to a disciplined party organization, they could ratify "the people's choice" by pursuing policy programs modeled on the victorious party's platform.

If class interests created the grand issues of politics, then a two-party system was the mediator of the ensuing conflict. A healthy two-party system would provide leadership and a policy program for the conflicting classes. Parties that functioned competitively were thus vehicles for mobilizing and reconciling opposing class interests in a rational, nonviolent framework.

If only one party existed, then one class's interests were not fully articulated, and its political strength remained unrealized. This, according to Key, was precisely the case in the South following the demise of Populism. And because a one-party system was a no-party system, "the South really has no parties. Its factions differ radically in their organization and operation from political parties." Key's investigation of factional politics in the southern states revealed that in most of them, parties were displaced "by a veritable melee of splinter factions, each contending for control of the state somewhat after the fashion of a multiparty system."[16] And while a two-faction polarization along class lines within the Democratic party did sometimes develop, Key believed that such a conflict was a pale reflection of healthy class conflict in a genuine two-party system.

What were the results of this "politics of disorganization"? In two-party politics, "organization . . . is essential . . . for the promotion of a sustained program in behalf of the have-nots, although not all party or factional organization is dedicated to that purpose." It therefore followed that "over the long run the have-nots lose in a disorganized politics. They have no mechanism through which to act and their wishes find expression in fitful rebellions led by transient demagogues who gain their confidence but often have neither the technical competence nor the necessary stable base of political power to effectuate a program." Conversely, the upper classes were at least the short-term beneficiaries of the South's politics of disorganization, although Key argued that, in the long run, a lack of competitiveness hurt society as a whole, including the upper class. It was thus very much in the short-term interests of the southern ruling class to prevent the creation of a two-party system, in the hope of continuing to benefit from the politics of chaos.[17]

In conjunction with this effort were the ruling forces' attempts to isolate state from national politics. "It is difficult," Key wrote, "to build a well-organized politics solely around the issues of state government. Isolation of state politics from national politics inherent in the one-party system removes the opportunity for the easy projection into the state arena of national issues and national political organization. . . . Transfer of the great issues to the Federal sphere deprives state politics of many questions that form voters into antagonistic groups and compel the organization of politics."[18]

Multifarious disfranchising devices also enhanced the power of the oligarchy. Of course, no politically well-informed person in the 1940s could fail to be aware of the all-white primary, the poll tax, and the literacy test that prevented blacks from voting. But Key, along with contemporaries such as C. Vann Woodward, showed that the poll tax and the widespread use of violence when the tax was instituted were often aimed at poor whites as well and that these phenomena had had the intended effect. Key's investigation of populism and disfranchisement around the turn of the century revealed that class antagonisms as well as racial hatreds were behind the successful efforts to remove large numbers of people from the electorate. More often than not, the Bourbons spearheaded those efforts.[19]

Disfranchising the poor of both races made the actual voting electorate much more conservative. This was obvious where blacks were concerned. "Negro disfranchisement has about the same effect in the South as would result in Chicago, for example, if the entire population of from five to twenty-five of that city's least prosperous wards were removed from the electorate."[20] But much of the depressed voter turnout in the South was not the result of black nonparticipation. The lower-income whites failed to turn out too, not only because of the burdensome poll tax but because of the lack of competitive two-party politics and the isolation of state from national issues. For "a genuine competition for power is not likely to be maintained for state purposes unless the state is also a battleground between national parties in the presidential campaign."[21] In consequence, candidates were free to ignore the needs of the nonvoting population, whether black or white.

Discussing the suffrage crisis of the 1940s, Key observed in the same vein that "in a sense the issue of Negro suffrage is a question not of white supremacy but of the supremacy of which whites." The issue was really not whether blacks should be allowed to vote but whether people of whatever race (including poor whites) should be allowed or encouraged to vote.[22] Once more Key shifted the focus of the debate about the nature of southern politics from racial politics pure and simple to race combined with class conflict. And he reiterated the point that it was not poor whites but the Bourbons who were responsible for keeping blacks from the polls for reasons of class interest.

Key's Hopeful Prognosis

The enthusiasm that greeted *Southern Politics* did not result solely from its elegant and persuasive analysis. Equally important were the hopeful prospects for change that emerged in the book's concluding chapter, "Is There a Way Out?" While characteristically cautious, Key believed there was indeed a way out of the moral, political, and economic morass known as "the southern problem." His prescriptions followed closely from his analysis.

He admitted that the race question obviously was paramount, but he pointed out once more, as he had throughout the book, that "even on the question of race the unity of the region has been greatly exaggerated in the national mind. Nor do the conventional stereotypes of southern politics convey any conception of the diversity of political attitude, organization, and tradition among the southern states."[23] Emphasizing yet again the predominant role of black belt whites in setting the political agenda for the entire South, Key returned to his theme of their small numbers within particular states and in the region as a whole. He distinguished between states with heavy black population concentrations and the "rim states," particularly Florida, Texas, and Arkansas, which had proportionally fewer blacks. Along with Tennessee, Virginia, and North Carolina, they "manifest[ed] a considerably higher degree of freedom from preoccupation with the race question than [did] the states of the Deep South."[24]

Key also saw hopeful auguries in the sweeping demographic and economic changes that threatened to undercut the black belt's influence. Cities were growing rapidly. "It is in the cities that the obstacles to Negro political participation are least formidable. It is mainly in the cities that a Negro is now and then elected to a minor office. In the cities, too, the white vote is conditioned to a much less degree by the Negro than in the rural counties."[25] These facts were especially significant in light of Key's earlier finding that voter turnout was far lower in the cities than in the rural areas.[26] If turnout could be increased, thus bringing more blacks and poor whites into the electorate, the cities would provide the basis for political progress. And if blacks in the black belt could be enfranchised, the electorate would be greatly expanded through inclusion of this deeply impoverished group of people whose participation would change the nature of the politicians' appeals.

There were other forces for progress at work. In keeping with his generation of social scientists, Key placed hope in industrial growth, a factor distinct from the low black percentage and the rise of cities but related to them. For it was in the cities of the rim South that industry was most expansive. Its primary political effect would be the growth of labor unions, which played an important role in advancing the views of the working class and whose leaders even in the South saw the need to cross racial lines to build an effective workers' alliance. "In all the recent movements for the abolition of the poll tax and for the mitigation of other suffrage restrictions labor unions have played a prominent role. In the factional struggles of particular states organized labor has come to play a controlling role at times."[27]

The growing strength of organized labor would bring about major changes even in the short term, Key predicted, and it would also create a greater propensity among the southern upper class to look northward toward the Republicans as allies. The GOP, in turn, might attempt to recruit adherents in the South. If that happened, the two-party system would finally come to the region, the "politics of disorganization" would disappear, and issues at the state level would be integrated with those of the national parties. The institutionalization of a modified, democratized class conflict would be complete. Although Key did not say so, he implied that with the southern race question no longer on the national agenda, concern with class issues would predominate among the national parties as well.

These results were not fated: "It is not to be supposed that these fundamental trends automatically bring political change. They only create conditions favorable to change that must be wrought by men and women disposed to take advantage of the opportunity to accelerate the inevitable." But, he added, "in every state of the South there are many such persons and their efforts are bringing results to an extent not commonly appreciated outside the South."[28]

Texas: "A Modified Class Politics"

Key depicted Texas as the vanguard of the newly developing South—the state in which the tendencies that he described were furthest developed. Texas had a low black proportion—the lowest, indeed, of the eleven states. In 1940, 69.9 percent of Mississippi's whites lived in counties that were 30 percent or more black. In Texas, the figure was 7.8 percent.

"Texans, unlike white Mississippians, have little cause to be obsessed about the Negro."[29]

There was also rapid industrialization and urbanization resulting from the continuing oil boom and the flocking of workers and their families to the "oil patch." Even in rural East Texas, where the black belt counties were located, Key wrote—in a memorable and often-quoted burst of enthusiasm—"the odor from oil refineries settles over the cotton fields and makes scarcely perceptible the magnolia scent of the Old South."[30] Key's imagery, which captured the raw, untrammeled spirit of the state's industrial capitalism, evoked the portrait sketched by labor historian Ruth Allen earlier in the decade. "Texas is still a frontier state," she observed, and "the coming of the factory creates another frontier. . . . In the midst of the furrows lie the lumber camps and the oil fields and, within reach of all, the smoke of the factory drifts to the horizon and the time clock marks the working day."[31]

Key's theory of southern politics seemed to predict accurately the impact of these accelerating changes in his home state. Conflict was not between sectional interests or between factions battling for control of a personal machine. Least of all was Texas politics in the late 1940s an example of the chaos of multifactionalism, even though Texas was still a one-party state. Instead, he argued,

> Texans are coming to be concerned broadly about what government ought and ought not to do. In our times the grand issues of politics almost invariably turn on the economic policies of government. To what extent shall wealth and power, corporate or personal, be restrained for the protection of the defenseless? What services shall the government perform? Who shall pay for them?
>
> In Texas the vague outlines of a politics are emerging in which irrelevancies are pushed into the background and people divide broadly along liberal and conservative lines. *A modified class politics seems to be evolving. . . .*
>
> The confluence of the anxieties of the newly rich and the repercussions of the New Deal in Texas pushed politics into a battle of conservatives versus liberals, terms of common usage in political discourse in the state. By no means has the pattern appeared consistently, yet after 1940 this alignment emerged in about as sharp a form as is possible under a one-party system. In the process the ties that bind the state to the Democratic party were strained, possibly in portent of the rise of a bipartisan system.[32]

The emergence in Texas of a liberal-conservative split primarily along class lines was a test case for Key's theory of southern politics. There were all the factors that he had enumerated as necessary, first for the rim South and then for the predominantly white counties in the Deep South to overthrow the ancient hegemony of the black belt oligarchs. It is understandable that Key was excited about the prospects for "modified class conflict" in that state. If things did not progress in the direction he predicted within a reasonable time, it would not only prove disappointing to him as a liberal but it would cast serious doubt on his theory.

Texas and Florida, with low black percentages, growing cities, and rapid industrialization, were the states on which Key's theory of southern politics would initially stand or fall. Of the two, Texas clearly seemed to offer the best prospects for a bifactional polarization sufficiently deep to split the Democratic party asunder and to give birth to a genuine two-party system. "All in all Texas has developed the most bitter intra-Democratic fight along New Deal and anti–New Deal lines in the South." And although there were similarities with Florida, "Texans detect a strident tone of irreconciliability in their politics that seems to be missing in the bland politics of Florida."[33] Texas politics, then, prefigured the new southern realignment.

Class Conflict and the Two-Party System

By the term "modified class politics" Key presumably meant that the conflict over economic issues was not likely to result in the extreme forms of agitation and violence predicted by orthodox Marxian analysis. But clearly he meant what sociologists have traditionally intended by class conflict—a political and ideological struggle between broadly based social groupings occupying quite different positions in the economic structure. Classes are not pressure groups in the usual sense. They are not voluntary organizations, but large aggregates into which people are born and from which it is not easy to break free. In this respect they share a greater similarity with racial groups than with organizations like the Lion's Club or Common Cause.

As Key saw it, the struggle between classes by and large overshadowed the religious, racial, sectional, and personal issues that also fomented conflict. These issues may have been present and potentially quite divisive. But they were secondary to issues involving the government's role in distributing benefits and opportunities among classes.

Key's theory about Texas was only roughly sketched out, for he was not interested in painting a detailed canvas of the state's politics. But even from his sketch it is possible to derive several propositions that in the late 1940s Key believed were true and at some point could be tested. Above all, there were at least two major social classes in Texas. One was made up of the very rich who, true to the stereotype, were also the new rich. Another consisted of the "have-nots." The rise of class conflict in the state was occurring "not primarily because of an upthrust of the masses that compels men of substance to unite in self-defense, but because of the personal insecurity of men suddenly made rich who are fearful lest they lose their wealth."[34]

Classes, by implication, were broad-based economic categories that cut across other kinds of economic groupings, such as individual business firms, industrial sectors, and economic pressure groups. In the context of Texas politics, they were statewide, at least. The more politically active members had some notion of their class interests, which were pursued by class leaders and their representatives in the political sphere, who typically focused on the role government should play in managing class conflict, the way in which tax burdens and public goods should be distributed, and the nature of the "rules of the game"—especially those regulating electoral participation—that determined how easy or hard it was for members of the various classes to play.

Key thought that class interests were expressed in Texas by two broadly based coalitions espousing conflicting ideologies that since the early 1940s had borne the labels of liberalism and conservatism. Two facts were implied by this view. First, the competing ideologies were class-based. Liberals came disproportionately from the working classes irrespective of racial groupings and other affiliations, and conservatives came more from the upper classes. This ran counter to the idea that liberalism in Texas was primarily the vehicle of middle-class intellectuals and professionals in combination with minority groups. Second, the liberal-conservative split was a conflict between large numbers of adversaries who, if not evenly matched, at least could not easily prevail over the other. This contradicted the view, often expressed in the decades after *Southern Politics* was published, that the liberal movement in Texas was comprised of a small minority in an overwhelmingly conservative state, unable to muster popular support.

Key's theory also held that over the long term, class issues were more important than were other sorts in the political process. Whether to levy progressive taxes, to tax corporations, to change election rules to encourage the poor to engage in politics; whether to pass laws that protect industrial workers from the hazards of the workplace, to break down barriers to unionization of the work force, to pass laws that provide legal services for low-income people, to create a public utilities commission to regulate private utilities, to make it easier for consumers to protect themselves against harmful products and dishonest merchants; whether to increase the power of the ordinary voters to influence elections: these were the types of issues that, if the theory of class politics were correct, played a larger role in Texas election campaigns and legislative behavior than did other controversies.

Of course, issues would wax and wane in the public mind. A theory of class politics like Key's, which asserts the long-term importance of class issues in the public arena, need not deny the existence of other kinds of controversies or even their temporary dominance. But it does imply that over time, class issues are the most important and durable ones, encouraging class-based coalitions that are stable and well-defined in the public consciousness.

Because of the advantages for the most disorganized groups—the have-nots—that a "modified class politics" offered by clarifying the issues and by identifying the actors associated with conflicting positions, the wealthy would try to depoliticize class conflict and to emphasize instead the issues Key disparaged as "irrelevant appeals, sectional loyalties, local patriotism, personal candidacies, and, above all . . . the specter of the black man."[35] If Key's theory were correct, leading members of the upper class or their political representatives would, for example, oppose racial equality. By the same token, working-class leaders would seize on economic issues to build an interethnic alliance among whites, blacks, and Mexican Americans. Furthermore, because of the benefits to the disadvantaged of a bifactional polarization along class lines within the Democratic party, the upper class would try to discourage this polarization by injecting "irrelevant" appeals that blurred class issues.

Inasmuch as a strong two-party system would sweep away the chaos of one-party politics that so disadvantaged the less affluent, Key's theory implied that the wealthy would try to prevent the formation of a two-party system, preferring even the bifactional polarization of the Democratic party as it was developing in Texas to a system in which Democrats and Republicans were competitive. Pushing this argument a step further, one might also speculate that if the upper classes could not prevent the development of a two-party system, they would desert the Democratic party, join the Republicans, and—hoping to put a damper on the class politics that were likely to develop—continue to emphasize "social" issues, particularly those concerning race. Alternatively, the upper classes might attempt to collude with both the Democrats and the Republicans, creating a two-party system that offered no genuine alternatives.[36]

In any case, the conservative upper class and its political leaders would attempt to insulate state from national politics by breaking the links either between national and state issues, national and state parties, or national and state candidates. Liberal leaders, on the contrary, would try to forge such links.

In developing a Democratic party more responsive to the disadvantaged, liberal leaders would be under constant pressure from the rich, who would make use of their formidable resources to intimidate, to buy off, and otherwise to reduce the leaders' effectiveness. Key wrote of "an impressive solidarity of the upper economic classes that disciplines without mercy, where it can, those who would arouse and rise to power with

Miyers?

the votes of the lower third. Those who cannot be disciplined are bought without hesitation and without remorse." He also alluded to "the siphoning off into the governing classes of men of ability by a social system still remarkably fluid."[37]

Finally, in the ongoing battle between the rich and the disadvantaged, the rich would make ample use of their most important resources—money and the influence it bought in Austin and Washington—and they would try to limit the resources that were most important to the disadvantaged— numbers. "The bulk of the costs of a major campaign must come from a handful of contributors," Key wrote. And elsewhere: "The situation in which the businessman is moved to contribute, not for particular advantage but, as he sees it, to save the capitalist system from the communists, is most apt to occur in those states with a dual factionalism or with a political system that occasionally permits fairly clear class alignments."[38]

Key's theory, spelled out in this manner, depicted politics as a system of rational endeavor—one with competing long-term goals and strategies for achieving them. It challenged a venerable tradition, which portrayed southern politics as resulting largely from random forces, or as merely farcical.

Farcical it often was, Key would have been the first to acknowledge. As his sketches of some of the Texas demagogues implied, more than a few clowns stumbled across the political stage, although the cleverest may only have pretended to stumble. Admitting that, Key would surely have gone on to argue that the drama was complex, fascinating, demanding, rational, and well understood by the leading actors, both liberal and conservative. It was played out in dead earnest for large stakes. If his theory was in the main correct, observers who saw chaos instead of pattern and mere buffoonery instead of the serious underlying drama simply missed the action.

A Test of Key's Theory

Key's theory was dynamic rather than static, premised on the periodic rise of class-oriented crises that every thirty or forty years reshaped the political landscape of the South and, by implication, the nation. Much of the theory's force rested on Key's analysis of the past, as far back as the Civil War. But the present and future, he argued, were also part of the larger ebb and flow of class conflict embroiled with racial struggle. His hopeful view of the future, based partly on his examination of Texas's "modified class conflict," was a projection of past trends at work in the long run.

To test the theory as applied to Texas, therefore, one must take the long view. This book, written in the 1980s, rests on the assumption that enough time has now passed for Key's predictions to have had some chance of realization. Did the politics of class that he believed were coming to the fore in the 1940s continue to develop along the lines he thought probable? Did they overshadow the politics of race? Has the factional division within the Democratic party given way to a two-party system, one liberal and the other conservative? If a realignment has occurred, how has this affected the political interests of the social classes and the races? Who has won? Who has lost?

In chapter 2 we examine the view that, at the grass roots, Texas from the New Deal on has remained an overwhelmingly conservative state. If this is true, it undercuts Key's depiction of a competitive conflict between liberals and conservatives. Chapter 3 is an inquiry into the class structure of Texas. The stage is then set for a detailed inquiry into those groupings that are most important for understanding the liberal-conservative conflict: the business class and the blue-collar stratum. Chapter 4 is a portrait of the former, and chapter 5 describes the institutional networks in modern times that have bound its members together. In chapter 6 we present a portrait of Texas manual workers, among whom the have-nots are concentrated.

Political money is the focus of chapter 7, which examines how money is put to use in elections and lobbying and how it has affected the liberal-conservative struggle. Chapters 8 through 11 concern political parties in Texas as they relate to Key's theory of modified class conflict. Chapter 8 introduces the practical premises on which liberals and conservatives operated between the 1940s and the 1970s in their struggle for control of the Democratic party and tries to make sense out of the liberal coalition's strategy for achieving party control. Chapter 9 is an account of a critical liberal-moderate victory in that struggle.

Chapter 10 is concerned with the rise of the modern Republican party in Texas during the John Tower era and its capture by the right wing. In chapter 11 the factor of race in the growth of two-party politics is examined, and the origins of the current Republican party are traced to decisions made by the right wing in the early 1960s. In chapter 12 we judge the overall success of Key's theory. Perforce, then, this book is an inquiry into the larger significance of the liberal-conservative struggle from the 1940s to the mid-1980s.

2

The Myth of Overwhelming Conservatism

TEXAS is an overwhelmingly conservative state—so it is said. "Democrats vote mostly conservative, and they outvote Republicans five- and six-to-one," wrote a *New York Times* reporter in 1976. Texans favor "the political status quo," the "first axiom" of which is, "the less government . . . the better." According to James Conaway, another journalist writing after a brief stay in Texas during the 1970s, "the liberal cause became synonymous with political obsolescence after the Second World War." These sentiments find ready endorsement by the state's conservative political elite, which purports to speak for what U.S. Senator Lloyd Bentsen calls "the Texas point of view." The conservative caucus on the State Democratic Executive Committee announced in 1977—without any supporting evidence—that 70 percent of Texas voters shared its philosophy. Texas House Speaker Gib Lewis, a conservative, echoed that assertion in 1984. "Most Texans are conservative. They look for a helping hand at the end of their arm," he said.[1]

At first glance this is plausible, even though it is obviously in the interest of conservatives to depict themselves as spokesmen for the vast majority. No Texas liberal has been elected governor or lieutenant governor since 1939, and only one has been elected to the U.S. Senate. From the end of the New Deal period until the 1970s, even moderates had difficulty winning statewide office, and the legislature still today often splits on key votes two-to-one for the conservative position. While liberals in 1982 and 1986 won four second-tier statewide offices, these were quite exceptional in a state where conservatives usually have occupied the most prominent seats of political power.

But election results and policy decisions are insufficient indicators of political tendencies in the populace at large. For example, would anyone seriously argue that the all-white Alabama legislature, in the days before the Voting Rights Act of 1965 enfranchised blacks in that state, accurately reflected the demographic makeup or the views of all Alabamians, a quarter of whom were black?

In making generalizations about popular attitudes, three populations should be distinguished. The largest consists of voting-age adults, the raw material of democratic systems. A much smaller sample is the electorate, the people who go to the polls. The smallest sample consists of elected officials. Is the ratio of conservatives to nonconservatives among top officeholders equal to that among the voters and, more important still, the voting age population? It is this latter aggregate—all adult Texans—that the theory of overwhelming conservatism appears to refer to when it claims that the officeholders are representative of people at the grass roots.

But this is debatable. Central to V. O. Key's argument in *Southern Politics* was the proposition that election rules and one-partyism in southern states severely diminished the political influence—including the ability to elect like-minded officials—of the working classes and minorities, groups that were disproportionately liberal. These rules and the one-party system, he argued, were often intentionally established or maintained by the wealthy and their representatives to exclude the have-nots, to create a governing elite far more conservative than the general population. Was he right?

One way to find out is to analyze the expressed attitudes and voting behavior of grass-roots Texans. Another is to examine the history of racial and class conflict in the state. When issues of great moment were at stake—issues having to do with the role of government in the distribution of income and wealth or with the status of racial minorities—how have Texans acted? Were they basically of one mind on these issues? Or were they deeply divided, with large numbers on both sides? Let us turn to these latter questions first.

A History of Conflict

From the beginnings of Texas as a republic in 1836, Anglo settlers were pitted in violent ethnic struggles over property and basic values against Indians and Mexicans, from whom they wrested the land, and against blacks, whom they held as chattel slaves. Equally important, whites were set against whites. When a referendum on secession from the union occurred in February 1861, almost a quarter of the electorate, following Governor Sam Houston, voted to remain in the Union. "Two German counties . . . cast over 95 percent of their vote against secession."[2]

That referendum, of course, was not open to slaves, who comprised 30 percent of the state's population. Assuming that most blacks would have voted to remain in the Union had they been able to express their opinions, close to half of all Texans were opposed to splitting from the Union on the eve of the Civil War.

The years of agrarian radicalism in the latter third of the nineteenth century also bear witness to deep schisms among Texans. The groundswell of farmer and labor protest, spanning an entire generation after Reconstruction, confronted the wealth holders of that era with a mass-based challenge to their rule, culminating in the Populist revolt, which was "in a very real sense an example of class-consciousness in politics," according to Rupert N. Richardson and his colleagues.[3] The era was marked by bitter industrial conflict nationally, and Texas was the site of vast upheavals. In 1885 Texas ranked ninth among the states in the number of workers involved in strikes, and it was one of the major strongholds of the Knights of Labor. The Populist party in Texas was especially robust.

Agrarian populism was a response to economic forces that developed after the Civil War.[4] A long-term decline in cotton prices, severe economic depressions, and widespread farm foreclosures led to the crop-lien system and virtual peonage for many thousands of farm families. Over time, these developments resulted in the Farmers Alliance, a national movement that began in Texas. In its subsequent political form as the Populist party, the movement proposed numerous solutions to the problem of agrarian poverty, some of which boldly exceeded anything the major parties would then seriously consider.

Opposing the Populists at every turn were the Democrats, the party of white supremacy. Although the Democratic party had adherents on many rungs of the socioeconomic ladder and contained various political tendencies, including a reformist one, it was usually dominated by businessmen and landowners. The latter saw the Populists, a biracial coalition of the poor, as challengers to their rule.[5]

Common economic problems brought the poor together in various organizational arrangements in spite of Democratic efforts to split the coalition asunder with appeals to racial hatred and attempts to co-opt the less radical parts of its programs. Roscoe Martin has shown that Texas farmers on smaller and less productive farms tended to vote for the Populists, while large landowners preferred the Democrats.[6]

Blacks, who were mostly poor, shifted between Republican and third-party candidates in gubernatorial elections between 1880 and 1896. Historian J. Morgan Kousser points to substantial black support for several radical gubernatorial candidates. Almost two-thirds of all adult black males cast their ballots for the Greenback candidate in 1882, 58 percent for the Farmers Alliance candidate in 1888, and 49.9 percent— a plurality—for the Populist candidate in 1896. Only once during the sixteen-year period did blacks give the regular Democrat more than 28 percent of their votes when a third-party candidate was in the governor's race. That was in 1896, when by one estimate 47 percent of the adult black males' votes were counted for the Democrat. However, actual black support that year was probably lower, as Democratic fraud and violence swelled the party's totals.[7] In at least half the cases of radical third-party gubernatorial candidacies between 1880 and 1896, blacks gave a higher percentage of their votes to the radicals than did whites, although whites, because of their greater numbers, constituted the majority of radical voters.[8]

Texas Populists made a genuine effort to breach the color line in politics. Their state executive committee at one point included two blacks. Several of their chief organizers and spokesmen were black, as were many of the rank and file.[9] According to C. Vann Woodward:

> There was in the Populist approach to the Negro a limited type of equalitarianism quite different from that preached by the radical Republicans and wholly absent from the conservative approach. This was an equalitarianism of want and poverty, the kinship of a common grievance and a common oppressor. As a Texas Populist expressed the new equalitarianism, "They are in the ditch just like we are."[10]

Populism, largely a southern movement, was by no means unstained by racism, but the party's record on this score was better in Texas than in any other southern state. Texas Populists "never abandon[ed] their goal of a political coalition of the poor and exploited, black and white, farmer and laborer," according to Bruce Palmer. In their 1896 platform, besides advocating black and white control of their own schools and the allocation of equal per capita funds to schools of both races, the Texas Populists demanded "equal justice and protection under the law to all citizens, without reference to race, color, or nationality."[11]

At the peak of the Populists' influence in 1896, their gubernatorial candidate officially received 44 percent of the vote, although in the absence of voter fraud that year the figure probably would have exceeded the 50 percent mark. Several Populist legislators and local officials were elected. Turnout in the gubernatorial contest rose to 88 percent of the adult male population (and possibly higher among blacks, according to Kousser), the highest rates in Texas before or since. The Democrats barely escaped defeat.

Key, writing of the South as a whole, described the Democrats' reaction. "The story is not well documented," he wrote, "yet it is apparent from scattered evidence that the Bourbon Democrats, to liquidate the opposition, must have applied with savagery all the social and economic sanctions available. The 'better,' the 'respectable' classes were threatened, and no fastidious regard for legality or morality checked the use of any measure that would contribute to their defense." The Texas story is better documented today than it was when Key wrote about it. Murder, fraud, and terror were the order of the day. Armed night riders in East Texas violently destroyed the results of years of organizational effort by black and white Populist leaders. In some communities civil war erupted.[12]

After populism was crushed, the legislature submitted a constitutional amendment to the voters that made payment of the poll tax a prerequisite to voting. The amendment, ratified in a 1902 referendum, passed by a hefty margin in time for the 1904 elections. In 1903 and 1905 the legislature also passed comprehensive election statutes that were hailed as "progressive"; these included the codification of the poll-tax measure and the establishment of a statewide primary system. The statutes, collectively known as the Terrell Election Law, encouraged the use of the all-white primary at the county level, increased the difficulty of third-party competition, and established a poll-tax payment period that ended six months before the primaries and nine months before the general elections.

In some southern states, the disfranchising measures were enacted by the Bourbon Democrats, and in some they were a vehicle by which the defeated white Populists took out their frustrations on their erstwhile black allies. In Texas, disfranchisement was primarily the work of the better-off whites.

The poll tax as a voting prerequisite had been the aim of a faction of the Democratic party ever since the state's Constitutional Convention of 1875. The leaders tried without success for the next twenty-five years to accomplish this goal. They were not poor whites. Some were prominent conservatives whose stated aim was to disfranchise the poor of both races. The tax's most outspoken proponent was Alexander Watkins Terrell, a Virginia-born lawyer and former slaveholder who was married to the daughter of a Texas plantation owner. He served sporadically in the legislature between 1876 and 1906.

Terrell once characterized the Fifteenth Amendment prohibiting the denial of black voting rights as "the political blunder of the century," but he defended the poll tax not only on racial grounds but also as a means to eliminate "the thriftless, idle and semi-vagrant element of *both races*." He was also opposed to a public elementary school system, although he was a booster of public appropriations for the fledgling University of Texas, which in that era was a preserve of the affluent. After the poll-tax law was passed, Terrell, recently returned to the legislature, was the force behind the racially restrictive Terrell Election Law, which was named after him.[13]

Terrell was not a member of the 1901 session that had voted to submit the poll-tax question to a referendum, but conservatives of his ilk dominated it. The legislature's decision to get a poll-tax law passed, writes Kousser, "was the quiet climax of a long drive by a few men, a drive which succeeded when the opposition became dormant."[14]

The effects of the tax were well known at the time the law was passed. An editorial in the *New Orleans Times-Democrat* made the point clearly. "Take the case of Mississippi," the column read. "The poll tax gets rid of most of the negro votes there, *but it gets rid of a great many whites at the same time—in fact a majority of them.*" The Texas Populists had understood this point quite well. As Bruce Palmer notes, it was one of the reasons they had stressed so insistently the need to maintain a biracial coalition. Unlike most Populists in other southern states, the Texans knew that without a sizeable contingency of blacks in the party to keep it strong and competitive, the Democrats would disfranchise both groups—"poor 'white trash and niggers,' " as one Populist editor in 1896 referred, with apparent irony, to the members of his own party.[15]

Undoubtedly many of the amendment's opponents saw it for what it was: a double-edged sword with which to disfranchise both blacks and poor whites. Before the 1902 referendum, outspoken opposition came from several camps: blacks, white Republicans, labor leaders, Populists. Milton Park, the state chairman of the Allied People's party, wrote that "every laboring man who loves liberty, who believes in freedom of suffrage, who prizes his rights of citizenship should vote against the poll tax amendment."[16] The State Federation of Labor and the Populists' main newspaper, the *Southern Mercury*, also opposed it. Opponents saw it as a means for disfranchising the poor, the same view opponents had taken of proposed poll-tax measures in the last quarter of the nineteenth century.

The preponderance of the evidence suggests that the wealthier whites voted most heavily for imposition of the tax. Thirty-five percent of the electorate voted against it. These voters were largely white, since by 1902 most blacks had already been forcibly disfranchised. Among voters opposed to the tax were South Texas machine politicians such as Jim Wells, who controlled some Mexican American votes, and the State Brewer's Association members, who were also known to manipulate ballots. But much of the opposition evidently came from those who resented the tax's discrimination against the poor, including, one must suppose, the poor themselves. Kousser has discovered a positive correlation between the wealth of whites per county and support for the tax. A postelection analysis by the *San Antonio Express* surmised that the "union labor element" voted pretty solidly against it throughout Texas. The Mexican American counties along the Rio Grande River and the strong Populist and labor union counties concentrated in west central and northeast Texas cast the only majorities against the tax.[17]

How unanimous, then, were Texans in supporting the poll tax? Sixty-five percent of the *voters* approved it. But the great majority of blacks were no longer in the electorate by then, and the same was true of many erstwhile white Populists. So, as in the case of the secession referendum, voting returns probably overstate the actual support for the measure.

One Texan in five was black, and the overwhelming majority must have opposed the tax. Nonvoting whites were more likely to be poor and probably opposed it in greater numbers than voting whites because of its regressive nature. If all economic and racial groups had been able to vote in the poll-tax referendum and had done so at equal rates—and had their votes been counted fairly—perhaps 45 percent would have opposed it, and possibly more.

The tax undoubtedly discouraged the majority of Texans from voting after the terror aimed at Populists and blacks had subsided. The tax began with a $1.50 minimum, with surcharges added in some cities and counties. During the first decade of the century the average monthly wage of southerners in manufacturing industries was less than $40.00. Many poorer farmers never saw any cash at all. The effects of the tax on the poor are evident in the following excerpt from a letter written by one Texas brewery official to another in December 1910, during the 1911 poll-tax payment period, when the brewers' concern was to register as many anti-prohibitionist voters as possible: "The time, two weeks before Christmas, is to some extent against us, as the poorer classes need all the money they have for the purchase of Christmas presents and can ill afford to spend the sum of $1.75 State and county, $1 for city tax, total $2.75."[18]

The conservative triumph fundamentally altered the structure of political participation. The groups most likely to raise their voices in economic protest were purged from the electorate, which shrank as a result to about one-third its former size (see fig. 2.1). The range of acceptable political issues was sharply constricted. No longer was the question of black civil rights a fit topic for public discourse, nor were major economic and political changes. The voices of the disadvantaged had been muted, if not silenced.

Such was the achievement of the Bourbon reaction. It was not apathy, but repression followed by bitter despair, and only afterward—with the passage of time—disinterest that caused voter decline in succeeding decades. On this point recent historiography corroborates Key's explanation of twentieth-century nonvoting in Texas.

Liberals against Conservatives

Disfranchisement did not completely throttle the spirit of dissent and reform. Thomas Campbell, who was elected governor in 1906 with support from farmers and labor, led a successful fight for stiffer antitrust laws, tax reform, insurance regulation, and statutes benefiting organized labor. In the decades that followed, Governor James "Farmer Jim" Ferguson and

FIGURE 2.1
Texas Voting-Age Population Voting for Governor,
Democratic Primary and General Election, 1880–1986

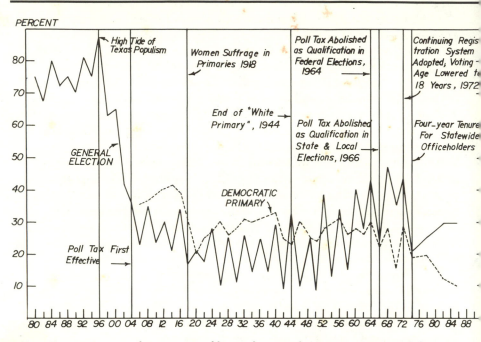

Note: Turnout in twentieth-century Republican gubernatorial primaries never exceeded 2.2 percent the voting-age population until 1982, when it reached 2.4 percent. In 1986 it was 4.6 percent.
    Sources: Data through 1946 are contained in V. O. Key, Jr., *Southern Politics in State and Nation* (New York: Alfred A. Knopf, 1949), 534. Subsequent data were calculated by the author.

then his wife Miriam—who was elected to succeed him after he was removed from office on charges of corruption—sometimes backed progressive legislation, although there was more than a trace of demagoguery in their politics. In the 1920s they opposed the Ku Klux Klan. In the 1930s they were New Dealers.[19]

For the most part, however, between disfranchisement and the New Deal, Texas politics was often chaotic and confused. Nothing like stable factions existed within the Democratic party. This situation gradually changed with the election of Franklin Delano Roosevelt, whose mandate was to move the nation out of the greatest depression it had ever known. This depression was especially devastating in the South, including Texas, where "farmers found themselves in straits of a sort that were beyond memory and even beyond history," writes Monroe Lee Billington. "By the year 1932, which was the depression's worst year, the South was in an almost unimaginable crisis of poverty, accompanied by something approaching social and political despair."[20]

In Texas a split gradually developed along liberal-conservative lines focusing on the New Deal and early civil rights measures, especially the U.S. Supreme Court's 1944 decision declaring the Texas all-white primary unconstitutional. By the early 1940s, this split was clearly visible within the Democratic party, and it manifested itself in a spectacular 1946 gubernatorial primary when New Dealer Homer Rainey, who had recently been fired as the president of the University of Texas by anti–New Deal regents, ran against conservative Beauford Jester and lost.[21]

Thus by the mid-1940s, two broad philosophic coalitions had taken shape, developing leaders and institutions to give them cohesion. These coalitions were loosely structured and allowed for a good deal of dispute and deviation among their members on specific issues. Within each coalition there was a smaller ideological spectrum. Indeed, the conservative camp included several fringe groups that often worked with mainstream conservatives and at times had close ties with major conservative figures such as Governor Allan Shivers. This kind of diversity is in the nature of all mass-based political coalitions that do not impose a rigid set of beliefs on their members, and a simplified liberal-conservative classification seems appropriate in the Texas case, as elsewhere.

The ideological conflict, which took place until quite recently primarily within the Democratic party, has continued from the 1940s to the present, although many of the issues have changed. There have been few statewide election years during these decades in which liberals have not challenged conservatives for at least one major and many lesser posts.[22]

Thus it makes sense to think of the three or four decades beginning with the New Deal as yet a third period of ferment in which progressive forces in Texas rose up to do battle with the conservative status quo. The liberal movement, as it came to be called, drew its strength from the economically and ethnically dispossessed and their allies in the middle classes. After a rather slow beginning in the depression years, it gradually swelled to a climax in the 1960s, when Lyndon B. Johnson as president and Ralph Yarborough as U.S. senator embodied two different strains of a movement that harked back to the Union cause of the 1860s and to the Populist movement of the 1890s.

As with the two previous periods of great political conflict, it is worth asking how well the liberals fared in the postwar years. One approach is to examine the results of statewide contests in which clearly identified liberal and conservative candidates opposed one another. Most such battles were fought in the Democratic primaries between 1946 and 1974, when there were no Republican primaries or when turnout in them was negligible. In a few cases, liberal Democrats won their party's nomination and

Table 2.1
Support for Liberal Gubernatorial or U.S. Senatorial Candidates,
Texas Primary Elections, 1946–1984[a]

Year	Election	Liberal	Office	% of Vote in Democratic Primary[b]	% of Total Primary Vote (Democratic and Republican)
1946	2d	H. P. Rainey	Gov.	34		—[c]
1952	1st	R. W. Yarborough	Gov.	36		—[c]
1954	2d	R. W. Yarborough	Gov.	47		—[c]
1956	2d	R. W. Yarborough	Gov.	49		—[c]
1958	1st	R. W. Yarborough	Sen.	59	(75)	—[c]
1958	1st	H. B. Gonzalez	Gov.	19		—[c]
1962	2d	D. Yarborough	Gov.	49		—[c]
1964	1st	D. Yarborough	Gov.	29		27
1964	1st	R. W. Yarborough	Sen.	57	(56)	53
1966	1st	S. C. Woods	Gov.	23		22
1968	2d	D. Yarborough	Gov.	45		42
1970	1st	R. W. Yarborough	Sen.	47		44
1972	2d	R. W. Yarborough	Sen.	48		—[c]
1972	2d	F. Farenthold	Gov.	45		43
1974	1st	F. Farenthold	Gov.	29		27
1984	2d	L. Doggett	Sen.	50	(41)	—[c]

[a] Years in which either an available gubernatorial or U.S. senatorial seat was contested by a liberal.

[b] Figures in parentheses are liberal candidate's percentage in the general election.

[c] No statewide Republican primary was held, or (in 1972 and 1984) no Republican runoff primary was held for the office in question, thus precluding the aggregating of both primary electorates.

went on to oppose conservative Republicans in general elections, so these contests, too, can be used to measure the size of the opposing forces in the electorate.

Table 2.1 indicates the strength of the liberal voting bloc in this period. The table is limited to those contests in which a clearly identified liberal and conservative opposed each other (usually in a runoff election) or, when head-to-head contests did not occur, to those in which a single liberal opposed more than one conservative. The analysis begins two years after the U.S. Supreme Court in *Smith v. Allwright* held that blacks had a constitutional right to vote in primary elections. At least in theory, therefore, all ethnic groups were able to participate during this period, although apparently few blacks or Mexican Americans voted in the latter half of the 1940s and early 1950s.

The figures in the Democratic nominating primaries are especially good indicators of liberal sentiment in the electorate, for unlike the figures in the November elections enclosed in parentheses in the table, they pertain to elections that are in a sense nonpartisan: that is, there are no party labels after a candidate's name on the primary ballot, and so voters' attachment to the party as opposed to the candidate has no influence on their choice. In the general election, a conservative, for example, might vote for a liberal Democratic candidate simply because of the voter's attachment to the Democratic party.

Table 2.1 shows that after Homer Rainey's race in 1946, the liberal-conservative electoral battles got seriously under way with Yarborough's challenge of Shivers in 1952. Thereafter there was a liberal-conservative contest for major statewide office almost every two years for the next twenty-two years, following which the conservative countermovement began to take its toll on liberals. During the period from 1952 to 1974, the liberal candidates in the Democratic primary received anywhere from 19 to 59 percent of the votes cast in their contests, for a mean of 42.

These figures probably understate the extent of liberalism at the grass-roots level for three reasons. First, as will be seen in chapter 7, in election campaigns, conservative candidates in Texas typically outspent liberals significantly. Conservative Lloyd Bentsen, for example, reported expenses in his 1970 Democratic primary race to be twice as great as those of Yarborough, whom Bentsen defeated. Second, this period was one in which the mass media were usually a conservative monolith, and statewide liberal candidates faced a hostile press. In 1956, when television was not yet a pervasive political medium, no metropolitan daily endorsed Ralph Yarborough's gubernatorial candidacy. In 1962 Don Yarborough, in his extremely close race with John Connally, was endorsed by 1 daily out of 114 in the state.[23] Third, the electorate in these primaries was much smaller than was the state's voting-age population. Between 1952 and 1970 the average primary turnout for Democrats and Republicans combined was only about 27 percent of the voting-age population. Nonvoters were more likely to be liberal than were voters.

Given these considerations, table 2.1 may substantially underestimate the actual extent of grass-roots liberalism. If so, then the losing liberal candidate in several elections—for example, those in 1954, 1956, 1962, 1970, and 1972—probably would have won with adequate resources and equal turnout rates among all social classes.

What were the issues that separated liberals from conservatives during this period, and what are those issues today? Broadly speaking, there is an economic dimension that concerns the distribution of goods and services and avenues for advancement among the social classes; an ethnic dimension, having to do primarily with the rights of blacks and Mexican Americans; and a general social dimension, a residual category that includes other issues especially important to the public.

On economic issues, Texas liberals, like their national counterparts, have favored government intervention in the market to help victims of unrestrained private enterprise. The great causes of the New Deal in Texas included rural electrification, which brought electricity to farm families; banking regulation; Social Security, a major bulwark against penury of the aged and their families; unemployment insurance; public works projects, like the Works Progress Administration and the Civilian Conservation Corps, which put the unemployed to work building bridges, creating amenities in public parks, and the like; home mortgage guarantees; limits on the length of the working day; and welfare measures to cushion the impact of poverty and the uncertainties of the economy.

Throughout the last half century, Texas liberals have also fought to regulate certain industries, to create a public utilities commission to protect consumers, to establish a minimum wage, to prevent the passage of a regressive sales tax, to impose heavier taxes on the oil and gas industry at its time of greatest affluence (especially through elimination of the infamous depletion allowance), to equalize Texas's vastly unequal public school funding program, to impose a statewide corporate and personal income tax in hopes of shifting the state's sharply regressive tax burden toward affluent taxpayers, to make it easier to unionize, to increase public access to higher education, to reform registration and election laws to increase political participation, to establish occupational safety measures, to bring farm laborers under workers' compensation insurance coverage, to increase welfare payments to the very poor, and to limit the influence of the rich in both elections and the lobbying process.

Regarding ethnic issues, liberals have worked to get a federal antilynching law passed, to abolish the exclusively white Democratic primary, to destroy Jim Crow laws in public accommodations, to desegregate schools and neighborhoods, to force the criminal justice system to treat blacks and Mexican Americans equally with white Anglos, to challenge voting laws and practices that hamper minority participation, to prevent discrimination in housing and employment, and, following the major civil rights legislation of the 1960s, to institute affirmative action plans in employment.

The "social liberals" have fought to defend free speech during the McCarthy period and afterward, to establish equal rights for women (including abortion rights), to secure the separation of church and state, to bring to a halt the U.S. war in Vietnam and U.S. military intervention in Latin American countries, to guarantee equal citizenship rights for homosexuals, to secure legal aid for the poor, to abolish capital punishment, and to obtain more humane treatment of prisoners in Texas's overcrowded jails and prisons. Conservatives have taken the opposite position on these questions, although once liberals prevail, the liberal position is frequently accepted and becomes, over time, part of the wisdom of the status quo.

Most people are liberal on some issues and conservative on others. As an East Texas legislator once put it, "I'm a mix of Jerry Falwell and Jim Hightower," referring to the right-wing founder of the Moral Majority and the liberal Texas agriculture commissioner, respectively.[24] But when confronted with a choice between two candidates, one liberal and the other conservative, voters make a choice. In so doing, one predisposition wins out over the other. Too, a sizable number of voters organize their preferences into a more or less consistent pattern and come to think of themselves as predominantly liberal or conservative. These people tend to make up the ideological core of the two opposing political camps, which become clearly distinguished over time in the mass media.

This list of issues demonstrates that the liberal-conservative conflict in Texas is quite similar to its national counterpart. Indeed, there are very few issues that have created controversy nationally that have not filtered down to Texas, where the intensity of the conflict is sometimes even greater than that generated nationally. This may result from the fact that a handful of colorful politicos have captured the imagination of the two ideological factions and have personified their values over an entire generation.

Among the postwar conservatives, Shivers and Connally, both forceful governors who went on to exercise influence nationally—Shivers as president of the U.S. Chamber of Commerce, Connally as cabinet member and adviser in Republican administrations—stand out as the embodiment of Texas conservatism. Both intelligent and charismatic, they were born poor and got rich quickly, gaining acceptance as peers among the upper class. Both were active in the conservative wing of the Democratic party and later in Republican circles.

Republican Senator John Tower was certainly a conservative too. Once asked if "he could think of a single domestic legislative program of . . . John F. Kennedy's to which he could give support," Tower could not.[25] But he lacked the charisma and personal followings of Shivers and Connally. The same might be said for other postwar conservative governors— Beauford Jester, Price Daniel, Preston Smith, Dolph Briscoe, and Bill Clements. Mark White, perhaps best described as a moderate conservative while governor, also fits this description.

The single most influential and popular liberal in the history of Texas *Allred ?* politics is undoubtedly Ralph Yarborough, who was a major force on the political scene from the time he lost his first governor's race against Shivers in 1952 to his failed bid to regain a U.S. Senate seat in 1972.[26] Between 1952 and 1972 Yarborough mounted eight statewide campaigns—three unsuccessful ones for governor and five for the U.S. Senate, three of which he won. He rallied liberals and their moderate allies across the state in grueling, underfinanced, acrimonious campaigns that spanned a period of great political upheaval—a time in which the civil rights movement shook the racist foundations of the South; Joe McCarthy and his allies, many of them Texas-based, fueled a widespread anti-Communist hysteria; the Kennedy and Johnson administrations aggressively restructured government spending; and the Vietnam War and its concurrent issues of black militancy, student unrest, and the "lifestyle revolution" split the liberal coalition in its period of triumph and finally led to Yarborough's defeat.

A list of Yarborough's major accomplishments during his thirteen years in the U.S. Senate elucidates the nature of the Texas liberal agenda and underscores Yarborough's effectiveness once in office. An article in the *Dallas Morning News*, a base for some of his bitterest critics, opined shortly after his defeat in 1970 that "his name is probably attached to more legislation than that of any other senator in Texas history."[27] Sitting on several important committees, including Labor and Public Welfare, of which he eventually became chairman, Yarborough was the guiding force behind numerous major bills.[28] He played a primary role in enacting the Cancer Act of 1971 that launched the federally financed "war on cancer." He was a major sponsor of the Occupational Safety and Health Act, which passed over President Nixon's veto; the Community Mental Health Centers Act; laws to aid the education of handicapped children and to increase hospital and health care; and others benefiting veterans, disadvantaged children (such as that which created the Head Start program), the elderly, and the poor.[29] Shortly before his defeat in 1970, he introduced his comprehensive health insurance bill, modeled on Sweden's health insurance plan. Edward Kennedy, who succeeded him as chairman of the Health Subcommittee, picked it up.[30]

Yarborough was one of the most aggressive and effective champions of environmental legislation in the U.S. Senate. Between 1957 and 1971 he was the author, coauthor, or active sponsor of all the major environmental bills to pass that body.[31] He was given primary credit for passage of the Endangered Species Act. Of the eleven national parks, historical sites, or recreation areas existing in Texas in 1978, six were the result of first efforts by Yarborough.[32] He was the prime mover behind the creation of the 78,000-acre Guadalupe Mountains National Park, the 85,000-acre Big Thicket National Preserve—acquired in spite of intense opposition from East Texas lumber interests and their political retainers—and the 74-mile-long Padre Island National Seashore.[33]

Within months of his election to the Senate, Yarborough became one of only five southern senators—including LBJ—to vote for passage of the momentous Civil Rights Act of 1957. Three years later, he was one of four

Ralph W. Yarborough. The outstanding Texas liberal leader of the postwar period, Yarbor-
ugh was a U.S. senator from 1957 to 1971. Here he speaks at a campaign rally in Paris, Texas,
one of his campaigns for governor in the 1950s. Courtesy of the Barker Texas History Center.

southern senators—again voting with LBJ—to support the Civil Rights
Act of 1960. In 1964, by supporting passage of the most far-reaching civil
rights bill since Reconstruction, he stood alone among the senators of the
eleven states of the old Confederacy. His fellow Texas senator, John
Tower, opposed it. Yarborough was one of only three southern senators—
and the only one from Texas—who voted for the Voting Rights Act of
1965, and one of four supporting the 1968 open housing bill.[34]

He was a vocal opponent of the Vietnam War by 1968 and criticized the
Chicago police force's rampage against antiwar demonstrators at the 1968
Democratic convention. The same year, he backed Eugene McCarthy's
antiwar presidential campaign by introducing him to audiences in Texas.[35]
And in 1969, when President Nixon attempted to place on the Supreme
Court Clement F. Haynsworth, Jr., a southern judge opposed by the civil
rights community, Yarborough was one of two southern senators opposing
his nomination. When Nixon then nominated yet a second judge opposed
by civil rights forces—G. Harrold Carswell—Yarborough was one of four
southern senators who opposed him—an act that would haunt him later
that year when Lloyd Bentsen made the Carswell vote a central issue of
his successful campaign to defeat Yarborough.[36]

It was in the field of educational reform, however, that Yarborough acquired an enduring reputation. On the Education Subcommittee of the Senate's Committee on Labor and Public Welfare, he was a force behind nine major bills, including the National Defense Education Act of 1958, which laid the groundwork for federal aid to education; and the Elementary and Secondary Education Act, which extended federal support to public schools below the college level.[37] The Cold War GI Bill, which subsidized the training and college education of millions of veterans serving after January 31, 1955—and who were thus not eligible under the Korean War benefits program—was first introduced by Yarborough in 1958 and was passed through Yarborough's tenacity in spite of opposition from Presidents Eisenhower, Kennedy, and Johnson.[38] Yarborough's Bilingual Education Bill, passed by Congress, provided federal funds for schools with numerous students from non-English-speaking backgrounds. He was author, coauthor, or active sponsor of every major education bill passed by Congress during his Senate days.[39]

Yarborough, in short, was the embodiment of the post–New Deal liberal spirit in Texas. About the only area in which he parted company with a good many liberals was oil policy.[40] Both his supporters and his opponents in the electorate at large had a fairly good idea of where he stood on the major issues of the day, and he was anathema to the conservative business establishment, which spent great sums to ensure his defeat in 1970.[41]

The period of liberal resurgence following World War II, then, can be seen as another era in which major issues involving the distribution of goods and opportunities came to the fore in Texas politics. At critical moments over the past 150 years, Texans have squared off over fundamentally important issues dealing with race and economic justice. When this has happened, the progressive faction has been able to mobilize a considerable proportion of the state's voters. Were it not for the underrepresentation of the progressives' natural constituency in the electorate, they would have won more victories than history records. And as has been shown regarding both the pre–Civil War and the post-Populist eras, the lower voter turnout in the progressive camp was closely tied to election laws and practices that discriminated against the poor and ethnic minorities.

A Culture of "Folk Conservatism"?

Given the facts so far, why is the perception widespread that Texas is an overwhelmingly conservative state? Conservatives self-servingly portray themselves as spokesmen for a homogeneous conservative population.

Out-of-state journalists all too often come to Texas holding a stereotype of the state that is impervious to the facts. There are other reasons as well.

The perception that political events are reflections of a conservative Texas culture is implicit in many of the explanations for political events as adduced by T. R. Fehrenbach, whose widely read history of the state, *Lone Star*, has popularized the use of the term "folk conservatism" to refer to such a culture.[42] Initially this explanation appears to make sense, all the more so because there are many obvious conservative aspects of Texas culture. But that is the case with any culture, and Fehrenbach never establishes that Texas is more steeped in a conservative culture than are other states or areas.

Nor has any other scholar done so. True, Daniel J. Elazar's work on the political cultures of states and regions, *American Federalism*, classifies Texas as among states in which a culture of traditionalism and individualism prevails. Elazar defines *political culture* as "the particular pattern of orientation to political action in which each political system is imbedded," implying that the culture is the underlying explanation for political behavior.[43]

However, if culture is used to explain politics, one must define it narrowly enough to distinguish it from the phenomena it purports to explain. Otherwise its link to these phenomena is true by definition. Elazar's notion of culture is problematic for this reason. The data from which he developed measures of political culture were drawn from such things as "public pronouncements of state officials . . . newspapers in leading cities . . . voting data . . . and field work or disciplined observation."[44] By lumping together both "political" and "cultural" data, thus muddying the distinction between politics and culture, he deprived his work of testable statements about the influence of culture on politics.

Another line of argument on behalf of a unique Texas conservative culture conjures up a Texas mind-set that developed from the "frontier ethic." This approach also has an initial ring of plausibility. The frontier disappeared quite late in Texas—hardly more than a century ago—and the violence of the Indian wars was frightful. The usual idea of that frontier, shaped not only by the historian Frederick Jackson Turner but by nearly a century of western novels and movies, is of anarchy, violence, rampant individualism, and fear of one's fellow man. Is there not an obvious link between the "go-it-alone" ethic of the frontier and a twentieth-century Texas conservative culture that exalts the virtues of laissez-faire?

This raises two further questions. First, how long-lived are frontier values, assuming that they did in fact predominate? Second, is this depiction of the frontier, surely the ascendant one today, really accurate? With regard to the first question, it is not clear whether Texas's frontier life has had direct political effects on the present, at least outside the realm of imagination and art. The history of the city of Abilene, in West Texas, illustrates this point.

Founded in 1881, about the time that many of the West Texas frontier towns sprung up, Abilene was at first a "wide open" town where "plenty of tough characters hung [out] in the city's nine saloons," according to a history of the town's early days. "Shootings were not infrequent and brawls of every description, as well as all forms of gambling, took place daily and nightly on the streets. . . . The city marshal . . . , a giant of a man . . . and his successor . . . ruled with an iron hand, frequently mixing in fights and hauling the combatants off to the city jail." But a mere twenty-five years later, the city had changed radically. Churches proliferated, saloons had been banned, and "many who returned to the city at this time were absolutely amazed at the great transition, not only in the physical part, but the law and order that prevailed everywhere." A 1900 promotional brochure published by a local newspaper wrote of this famous frontier town: "Law and order and a sure-enough Christian spirit permeate and pervade the community to an exceptionally marked degree. . . . In fact there has been no murder committed here in nearly a decade." Even allowing for booster hyperbole, it is obvious that a rather sudden shift in temper occurred in the town, and there were few traces of the earlier, relatively brief violence. The memory of that short-lived anarchy may live on in the city's periodic celebrations of its frontier heritage, but not much of the frontier ethos seems to have survived in ways that can be directly traced to politics today.[45]

What *was* the frontier ethos? Violence, anarchy, and distrust of government and other efforts at group collaboration? Mody C. Boatright challenged this thesis several decades ago in a provocative article that has yet to be successfully refuted. Frederick Jackson Turner's picture, according to Boatright, exaggerated certain aspects of the frontier at the expense of others. It focused on individualism and violence while downplaying the social solidarity the settlers depended on for their survival in a threatening environment. "Whole church congregations, sometimes virtually whole communities where shifting economic conditions brought hard times, came to the plains of Nebraska and Kansas and other western states," wrote Boatright, "not infrequently under the protection of some organization like the New England Emigrant Aid Society. They came to found communities where they could enjoy a corporate life, typically not with the aim of establishing communistic societies but of recreating on the frontier the simple agrarian and handicraft economy that industrialism was soon to destroy."[46]

Boatright pointed to the characteristic frontier institutions of cooperation: house-raisings, school and church building, logrolling, community plowing and harvesting, and the cooperative "cattle round-up." The latter "began as a cooperative cowhunt in the mountains of the South," wrote

Boatright; "it maintained its cooperative character . . . among all but the largest ranchers. The reminiscences of the trail drivers of Texas stress mutual help, not individualism."[47]

In short, the question is not only whether the Texas frontier spirit survived in the twentieth century but whether it was as anarchistic as some interpretations would suggest. If it was not, then it is worth asking whether the influence it perhaps exerts through the intergenerational transmission of values is wholly or predominantly conservative.

Yet another approach to the question of Texas's culture is to invoke the "conservative" manners and mores of its inhabitants today—the predilection for pickup trucks and cowboy boots, Texas brags, love of chicken fried steak and country and western music, the phenomenon of the "good old boy." The problem is that there is no proven link between, say, a preference for country music and anti-union attitudes or support for a regressive sales tax. No knowledgeable liberal candidate campaigning for office in Texas writes off the working-class voters in industrial suburbs because they belong to the Baptist church or like to dance the Texas two-step or to attend the local livestock show. One of the most popular liberal officials in the state in recent years, Agriculture Commissioner Jim Hightower, typically campaigns in cowboy attire and speaks in the colorful idiom of rural Texas. More to the point, some of these so-called Texas customs are not unique to Texas or even to the South. A poll by Louis Harris in 1986 revealed that the American public's favorite music genre was country and western.

Still another argument on behalf of a peculiarly conservative Texas culture links the rank and file's allegedly conservative views to the predominance of the oil and gas industry in the socioeconomic life of the state and concludes that because oilmen, as a rule, are extremely conservative, Texans as a whole are. It is true that this industry has been the mainstay of the twentieth-century Texas economy. However, by 1974, only two out of seven nonfarm jobs were directly related to petroleum resources. Royalty owners constituted, by one estimate, around 650,000 people—less than 5 percent of the population. Many received very little royalty income because of the practice of distributing an oil well's income to many landowners above the oil pool rather than just to the person on whose land the well was drilled. And while perhaps as much as one-fifth of the state's revenues was derived from the petroleum industry at that time, it is not at all clear how much the political views of the industry's leaders—men of vast wealth and influence—were shared by the general population, or, for that matter, how closely the average Texan identified his or her own interests with those of "big oil."

During the oil crisis of the mid-1970s, scientific samples of Texans' attitudes revealed strong suspicions of oil company complicity in events that led to the crisis. According to sociologist David Gottlieb, 50 percent of one such sample in 1977 believed that "scheming oil companies" were a factor in the energy crisis. By contrast, only 25 percent believed it could be traced to activities by "environmentalists," a favorite whipping boy of oilmen at the time. Another poll the previous year by a nationally respected polling firm revealed that 60 percent of probable Texas voters would be more likely to oppose a candidate if he were supported by the oil industry, as compared to 17 percent who said they would be more likely to support him.[48]

Is Texas culture conservative? To be sure—in some ways and under some conditions. But information about attitudes relating to musical genres or clothing styles, about the history of the frontier, or about the importance of oil in the state's economy tells us little about the political proclivities of Texans. With regard to the actual voting population, voting returns may be more informative than cultural attitudes. When considering the entire adult population—including both voters and nonvoters—the problem is much more difficult.

How Texans Describe Themselves

Having identified several commonsense arguments in support of a general conservative culture in Texas and found them wanting, we turn briefly to a different source of material, one that might be expected to nail down the claim of monolithic conservatism. In 1968, shortly after the post–World War II liberal movement had peaked, a group of political scientists conducted an important study of attitudes based on a sample survey of the entire Texas voting-age population. It is essential to stress that the population sampled was not voters or those who intended to vote—the populations on which most studies of the state's political attitudes have focused. The survey sampled the entire adult population—both voters and nonvoters. It therefore provided information about the political views of the state as a whole, not just the electorate.

The 1968 Texas study was part of a larger analysis of political views and behavior in twelve other states as well and in the United States as a whole. Because the study used the same general methodology in drawing samples and in asking questions in all thirteen states and the nation, it provided an especially useful picture of Texas's ideological makeup at that time. The Comparative State Elections Project's (CSEP) data on ideology are shown in table 2.2.[49]

The figures indicate that only 15 percent of the sample called themselves liberal. Only 34 percent called themselves conservative. Another 11 percent did not label themselves. The largest number—40 percent—called themselves "middle-of-the-roaders." Unless these labels mean

Table 2.2
Ideology of Texas Voting-Age Adults, 1968

Self-Described Ideology	Percent
Liberal	15
Middle of the road	40
Conservative	34
Not sure, etc.	11
Total (N = 681)	100

Source: Data supplied by Comparative State Elections Project, Institute for Research in Social Science, University of North Carolina at Chapel Hill.

something quite different to Texans, the theory of overwhelming conservatism, in the sense of a predominant or majoritarian allegiance to conservative values at the grass roots, is not supported by the CSEP data.

But what did these labels mean to the people who applied them to themselves? In order to find out, interviewers asked the respondents to name their preferred 1968 presidential candidate. The researchers found that 85 percent of the self-described liberals intended to vote for liberal Democrat Hubert Humphrey, 69 percent of the conservatives said they would vote for the two conservatives, Nixon or American party candidate George Wallace, and the middle-of-the-roaders split 51 percent for Humphrey and 49 percent for either Nixon or Wallace. The self labels, then, seemed to measure Texans' attachment to liberal or conservative candidates. It should be added, however, that because 31 percent of the self-labeled conservatives preferred Humphrey to the two conservatives (as opposed to only 15 percent of the liberals who preferred Nixon or Wallace to the liberal), there is reason to believe that self-labeling data may understate somewhat the actual proportion of liberals. Further, it is usually true that most of the people who are unable to label themselves (10 percent of the sample in this case) or who "mislabel" themselves are the poorly educated voters who traditionally rally to the more liberal candidates or party if the candidates are able to gain their attention and to make their case. This is most strikingly borne out among blacks and Hispanics, few of whom call themselves liberal in surveys of this sort but who vote overwhelmingly for liberal candidates.[50]

The distribution of ideological labels in the Texas population appears to be fairly constant. A *New York Times*/CBS poll of "probable voters" in 1980, taken shortly before the presidential election, revealed that 18 percent called themselves liberal, 42 percent moderate, and 34 percent conservative.[51]

FIGURE 2.2

Self-Described Ideology of Adults, Selected States and Nation, 1968
(of those choosing a label)

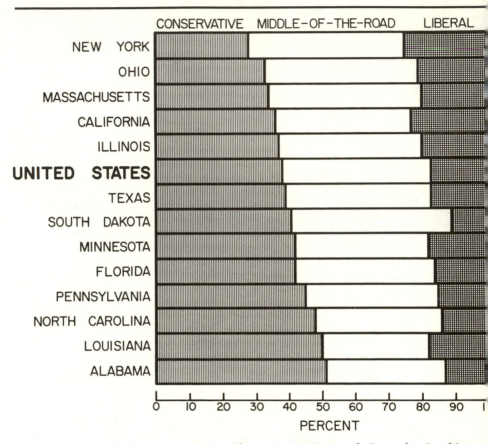

Source: Data supplied by Comparative State Elections Project, Institute for Research in Social Science
University of North Carolina at Chapel Hill.

These figures suggest, then, that in Texas, as in America as a whole,
there is a spectrum of beliefs running from right to left and that the largest
proportion of Texans consists of moderates to whom both liberals and conservatives must appeal to build a winning coalition. As the actual voting
data from table 2.1 above indicate, when the voters were forced to choose
between a liberal and a conservative, they split on average about 55 to 45
for the conservative. That is something very different from an electorate—
or, more to the point, an adult population—that is overwhelmingly conservative.

Indeed, when the distribution of self-labeled liberals, moderates, and conservatives in Texas is compared to that in the twelve other states and in the U.S. as a whole (see figure 2.2), it can be seen that Texas is very close in this regard to the nation. In 1980, the same *New York Times*/CBS poll mentioned earlier provided new evidence of striking ideological similarities between Texas and the nation. Liberals in Texas and the U.S. comprised 17 and 18 percent, respectively, of the probable voters; moderates, 42 and 45 percent; and conservatives, 34 and 32 percent.[52]

Texas had an ideological makeup very similar to that of some states with a reputation for electing liberals and moderates to statewide office. Texas in this regard was hardly distinguishable from Minnesota and Illinois, states with typically more liberal elected officials. How shall we explain this discrepancy between the ideological makeup of grass-roots Texans and that of Texas's elected officials? Key's theory was that the electoral process and other aspects of "class politics" constricted the influence of people at the grass-roots level, who were more likely to be liberal. This hypothesis is explored in the next chapter.

3

The Basis of the Liberal Coalition

TEXAS liberalism broadly defined, as the previous chapter makes clear, has endured for a long time. Like a gnarled cedar tree in a Hill Country gulch, it has survived the vicissitudes of a punishing environment and at times has flourished. Its impact today is especially felt in the state's universities and mass media. Whereas few liberals wrote newspaper columns or editorials in the years following World War II, in the 1980s it was unusual for progressive opinions not to be well represented in the metropolitan media. And despite occasional attempts by conservative university trustees to enforce ideological conformity on some Texas campuses, the professoriat was freer than ever before to express heterodox views.

Liberal Texans in the 1980s were bound together in a coalition of overlapping networks covering the entire state. Thousands of political activists were busy in local and national causes. Like their conservative counterparts, they were linked by precinct networks, get-out-the-vote drives, and pressure groups. Prominent liberal officials such as Attorney General Jim Mattox, Agriculture Commissioner Jim Hightower, State Senator Craig Washington, State Treasurer Ann Richards, and Congressman Henry B. Gonzalez spoke forcefully for progressive ideas.

Liberal writers' views appeared regularly in the *Texas AFL-CIO News*, the *Texas Civil Liberties Reporter*, the *Texas Observer*, and newspapers for black and Hispanic audiences. Others attracted a broader readership writing for the big metropolitan dailies. Among them were Molly Ivins with the *Dallas Times Herald*, Robert Newberry—a black writer—with the *Houston Post*, Kaye Northcott with the *Fort Worth Star-Telegram*, and Maury Maverick, Jr., with the *San Antonio Express-News*. Ben Sargent, the political cartoonist with the *Austin American-Statesman*, was a one-man institution on the order of the *Washington Post*'s Herblock. Harry Hurt III and Tom Curtis were known for their investigative reporting on the staff of the widely read *Texas Monthly*.

Ivins, Northcott, and Hightower are former editors of the *Texas Observer*, a magazine first edited by newspaperman Ronnie Dugger, who later became its publisher. Founded in 1954 as a journal of news, criticism, and opinion, the *Observer*'s paid circulation has seldom exceeded twelve thousand, a number that belies its influence in statewide progressive circles.

5. Progressive activists swap stories. (Left to right) former legislator and gubernatorial candidate Frances ("Sissy") Farenthold, Travis County commissioner then
state treasurer Ann Richards, and writer and humorist John Henry Faulk at a
get-together in the 1970s. Courtesy of the *Texas Observer*.

The very prominence of middle-class liberal journalists, professors,
lawyers, schoolteachers, party activists, and politicians encourages a common misconception that the state's liberal movement is little more than a
small coterie of professionals and intellectuals lacking a mass base. This
misconception gains credibility if liberalism is defined as a consistent,
complex ideology of the sort that an intellectual who has thought hard
about political issues might develop through years of reading and writing.
By this definition there are few liberals in Texas or in the United States,
just as there are few "ideological" conservatives. But if liberalism is defined more broadly, as it was in the previous chapter, and if it is measured
in part by a person's willingness to vote for a major candidate who bears
the liberal label, then it should be obvious that a movement mobilizing
between 40 and 60 percent of the electorate must consist of more than the
intelligentsia.

Who Votes for the Liberals?

In the South as a whole, V. O. Key argued, blacks were obviously attracted to candidates who were progressive on both economic and civil
rights issues. Working-class whites supported economic liberals, at least.
And those whites in areas with few blacks who had earlier backed the
cause of the Union and of populism were more sympathetic to liberal can-

Table 3.1
Average Percentage of the Vote for Liberal Candidates
by Geographic Area of Texas, 1946–1980

Area	Presidential Elections (N=8)	Gubernatorial Primaries (N=10)	Senatorial Primaries (N=4)	Average of Averages
Gulf Coast	47.9	40.7	54.9	47.8
Central	54.9	35.3	52.7	47.6
South	53.6	31.7	57.1	47.5
East	50.3	39.6	51.6	47.2
West	49.9	34.4	49.0	44.4
North	43.7	34.8	49.2	42.6
Southwest	49.9	28.7	46.6	41.7
Panhandle	39.9	31.6	46.3	39.3
Hill Country	33.7	23.2	40.7	32.5
RANGE	21.2	17.5	16.4	15.3

didates. Key noted, however, that Texas liberalism was peculiar among the southern states in lacking a regional concentration. When liberals ran for statewide office, their strongest support was not concentrated in certain geographic areas, suggesting "the hypothesis that voters divide along class lines."[1]

The continuing absence of regional distinctiveness is noteworthy. Table 3.1 indicates the mean liberal voting percentages in the state's major regions between 1946 and 1980. (In presidential elections the Democrat is counted as the liberal.)[2] There was only modest variation, and the differences were roughly the same in the presidential elections as in the Democratic primaries, which at the time drew almost all of the primary vote.

These figures corroborate politicians' views. Legislators told political scientists in the 1950s that when they conferred with like-minded colleagues on controversial issues, the colleagues were chosen on the basis of whether they were liberals or conservatives rather than on whether they represented the same region.[3]

Among voters, social class rather than region has been a crucial influence on their preferences, a fact demonstrated by precinct returns since the 1930s.[4] The figures in table 3.2 leave no doubt that the same coalition operating nationally in support of Democratic presidential candidates operates in Texas. (Tables 3.2 and 3.3 contain all of the previously collected precinct returns, classified by ethnicity and social class, that I could find in Texas cities.)

In all eighteen cases in which the votes of at least two classes of Anglos are compared, lower-income precincts gave significantly greater support

Table 3.2
Presidential Vote in Selected Texas Cities, 1936–1984 (percent Democratic)

	Roosevelt 1936	Roosevelt 1940		Roosevelt 1944			Truman 1948					Stevenson 1952			Stevenson 1956	Kennedy 1960		Johnson 1964		Humphrey 1968	McGovern 1972	Carter 1976	Carter 1980	Mondale 1984
	H	D	FW	H	D	FW	H	D	D	W	FW	D	FW	CC	D	H	D	H	D	H	H	H	H	H
Ethnic Minority																								
Black	—	—	—	—	—	84	—	—	—	—	—	88	71	97	62	85	—	99	—	94	94	98	95	93
Mexican American	—	—	—	—	—	—	—	—	—	—	—	—	—	88	—	—	—	—	—	70	69	81	72	73
Anglo																								
Labor	—	—	—	83	83	85	66	53	—	—	—	58	—	—	—	—	—	—	—	—	—	—	—	—
Lower class	91[a]	—	—	—	—	—	—	—	—	—	58	—	—	—	52	51	45	57	67	30	28	61	53[c]	37
Lower middle	—	—	—	—	—	—	—	—	—	—	—	50	—	—	35	48	37	56	53	25	23	57	—	22
Middle	—	—	—	—	—	—	—	—	—	—	—	—	—	—	—	—	26	—	42	—	—	31	28	22
Upper middle	—	—	—	44[b]	44[b]	—	24[b]	15[b]	—	—	—	41	—	—	39	34	22	48	39	26	20	23	12[b]	15
Upper class	57	50	58	—	—	39	7	—	—	—	—	37	22	—	28	17	23	32	36	17	16	12	—	11

Note: CC = Corpus Christi; D = Dallas; FW = Fort Worth; H = Houston; W = Waco.

Sources: Numan V. Bartley and Hugh D. Graham, *Southern Politics and the Second Reconstruction* (Baltimore and London: Johns Hopkins Press, 1975), 89, 92; Bernard Cosman, *Five States for Goldwater: Continuity and Change in Southern Presidential Voting Patterns* (University, Ala.: University of Alabama Press, 1966), 106; Chandler Davidson, *Biracial Politics: Conflict and Coalition in the Metropolitan South* (Baton Rouge: Louisiana State University Press, 1972), 201; George Norris Green, *The Establishment in Texas Politics: The Primitive Years, 1938–1957* (Westport, Conn. and London: Greenwood Press, 1979), 213–30; Samuel Lubell, *Revolt of the Moderates* (New York: Harper & Brothers, 1956), 186; Donald S. Strong, *Urban Republicanism in the South* (University, Ala.: University of Alabama Press, 1960), 24; Richard Murray, unpublished data (Department of Political Science, University of Houston, 1966–1984); *Houston Chronicle*, 8 November 1984; unpublished data collected by the author.

[a] Lubell does not indicate if these are white precincts only, but the relatively small black vote at the time makes this likely.

[b] Combined percentage of upper-middle and upper class.

[c] Combined percentage of lower and lower-middle class.

to the Democrat.[5] Where voting preferences of several classes are compared, there was a consistent stair-step pattern. In 1960, for example, the least affluent Anglos in Houston gave John F. Kennedy 51 percent, compared with 48 percent from the lower-middle class, 34 percent from the upper-middle class, and 17 percent from the upper class. The least affluent precincts usually gave majorities to the Democrat, while the wealthiest precincts went strongly for the Republican. Never did the least affluent whites give anywhere near as many votes to the Republican candidate as did the richest ones, and generally the poorest precincts gave the Democrat about twice as much support.

In other words, as the Democratic presidential candidates throughout this period have been more liberal than those of the Republicans, working-class whites have voted far more readily for the liberal candidate than have middle-class ones. This fact bears emphasizing, given the propensity of commentators to portray the typical white liberal as a middle-class intellectual.

As table 3.2 indicates, the other major source of liberal support in presidential elections has been the ethnic minorities. At least since 1944, Texas blacks have been strong supporters of the Democratic national ticket. From 1964 on, they have consistently given that ticket more than 90 percent of their vote. Mexican Americans have not been as united, but they have never fallen below two-thirds support for the ticket—a formidable bloc by any standard. Table 3.2 therefore points to the existence of a tri-ethnic liberal coalition in presidential politics that goes back some decades, consisting disproportionately of working-class Anglos, blacks, and Mexican Americans.

This coalition now seems to be under great strain, however. While the ethnic minorities' Democratic allegiances remain strong, Anglo support has shrunk drastically since 1968. The lowest-income whites typically gave more than half their votes to the Democrats in the 1950s. This percentage fell sharply in 1968 to 30 percent and has remained low since, except for Jimmy Carter's 1976 and 1980 campaigns.

Nineteen sixty-four was a watershed year for the South. Barry Goldwater, pursuing his famous southern strategy, carried the five Deep South states. In some of them, class cleavages among whites virtually disappeared.[6] In Birmingham, for example, political scientist Donald S. Strong found that low-income whites voted almost as heavily for the Republican ticket as did those in silk-stocking districts.[7] This did not happen in Texas, probably because of the stronger tradition of class voting there and aggressive trade union support for LBJ. About two-thirds of the white voters in Houston's poorest precincts went Democratic, compared to one-third in the wealthiest ones.

6. Minority senators huddle. (Left to right) liberal state senators Juan Hinojosa, Hector Uribe, Craig Washington, and Carlos Truan talk strategy on the senate floor. Courtesy of Alan Pogue and the *Texas Observer*.

But in 1968, George Wallace's American party, capitalizing on racial tensions and deep conflicts over the Vietnam War, attracted many blue-collar voters in Texas. In 1972, George McGovern's relative unpopularity, combined with Nixon's broad appeal, cut even more deeply into the traditional Democratic vote and, as in 1968, less than one-third of the whites backed the Democrats. Even in these two years, however, the poorest white precincts voted about twice as Democratic as the richest ones. In 1976 and 1980, with Carter's candidacy, the pattern of the 1950s and 1960s reappeared: half or more of the lower-income Anglos supported the Democrats.

The 1984 presidential election was similar in one respect to the normal pattern of previous years and, in another, to the pattern of 1968 and 1972. Its "normality" is evident in the fact that far more lower-income than upper-income voters (37 percent compared with 11 percent) chose the Democratic ticket. But the fact that the Democrats could attract only one-third of the vote in the most Democratic white precincts indicates an alienation of whites from the party reminiscent of the "abnormal" years. Indeed, if the two Carter campaigns are ignored, the so-called abnormal pattern has become the normal one.

There was an extraordinary solidarity among the white elite. By 1944 a majority of the silk-stocking precincts were voting Republican, and by 1968 their bloc vote of almost 90 percent rivaled the cohesion of blacks.

At this point a skeptic might wonder if lower-income white support for the Democrats really indicates support for liberalism. After all, many people vote for a party out of traditional allegiance. And one could argue that less-educated voters are more likely to be swayed by such fealty than better-educated ones, so blue-collar votes for liberal presidential candidates simply reflect an unthinking identification with the party, not with liberalism.

Analysis of the Democratic primaries between 1946 and 1984 clarifies this issue. For much of the period they were the only primaries that mattered, and both Democrats and Republicans voted in them. Liberal candidates opposed conservatives for statewide office; and since primary ballots are in a sense nonpartisan—there are no party labels on them—one of the most distinctive features of the leading candidates during the campaigns analyzed was their political ideology.

The first major statewide primary race in the modern era between a liberal and a conservative, where both social class and race were prominent issues, was the 1946 Rainey-Jester gubernatorial contest. Right-wing businessmen—predominantly Republicans—on the University of Texas board of regents had fired Homer Rainey as president because, among other things, of his refusal to dismiss a small band of pro–New Deal professors. The Democratic primary, two years after the U.S. Supreme Court had enabled blacks to vote in it, was the first in the century in which blacks could participate unhindered with full knowledge from the beginning of the campaign that they could vote. Rainey, while not outspoken in his appeal to blacks, sought their support, and some of his opponents tried to provoke a white backlash. He was a harbinger of the racial-economic liberalism that was to become a fixture in Texas politics.

Table 3.3 indicates a voting pattern quite similar to the one in presidential elections. The Rainey vote in Anglo labor precincts ranged from 59 percent in Houston to 31 percent in Fort Worth, but in all three cities the

7. Homer P. Rainey. Inaugurated as president of the University of Texas in 1939, Rainey (second from left) is flanked on his right by Governor W. Lee ("Pappy") O'Daniel, who would later appoint anti–New Deal university regents instrumental in firing Rainey for refusing to dismiss pro–New Deal economics professors. Liberal oilman Jubal R. Parten (looking toward camera), a holdover regent from the administration of New Deal governor James V. Allred, was a defender of Rainey and later backed him in his unsuccessful gubernatorial bid in 1946. Courtesy of the Barker Texas History Center.

voters in these precincts gave far more backing to Rainey than did the upper and upper-middle classes.

Ralph Yarborough was a model of the progressive Texas candidate. In the 1956 gubernatorial runoff, the poorest white precincts in Waco and Fort Worth gave him 60 percent of the vote, while the wealthiest ones gave him 29 and 20 percent, respectively. Class voting was also pronounced in the races of Don Yarborough, Frances Farenthold, and Lloyd Doggett. Unlike class voting in the presidential contests, it has not seemed to diminish in state ones.

Blacks strongly supported the liberals, as did Mexican Americans. The same tri-ethnic coalition that rallied behind Democratic presidential tickets also supported liberals in the Texas primaries, where reflexive party allegiance obviously cannot explain voting differences along class lines. Perhaps one-third or more of upper-middle-class whites—the locus of what political observers call "independent liberals"—joined this coali-

Table 3.3

Democratic Primary Vote in Selected Texas Cities, 1946–1984 (percent liberal)

	H. Rainey Gubernatorial Race 1946			R. Yarborough Gubernatorial Runoff 1954				R. Yarborough Gubernatorial Runoff 1956			D. Yarborough 1st Gubernatorial Race 1962	R. Yarborough Senatorial Race 1964		D. Yarborough Gubernatorial Race 1964	R. Yarborough Senatorial Race 1970				Farenthold Gubernatorial Runoff 1972		Farenthold Gubernatorial Race 1974	Doggett U.S. Senatorial Runoff 1984
	H[a]	D[b]	FW[c]	D	W	FW	JC	W	H	FW	FW[f]	H	SA	H	SA	H	W	FW	H	W	H	H
Ethnic Minority																						
Black	90	—	66	—	87	94 (84)[e]	94	85	93	97	47	90	91	66	71	97	86	97	90	78	60	92
Mexican American	—	—	—	—	—	—	—	—	—	—	—	—	87	—	76	—	—	—	75	—	45	75
Anglo																						
Organized labor	59	41	31	60	—	68	72	—	61	—	27	—	—	—	—	—	—	—	—	—	—	—
Lower class	—	—	—	—	61	60	—	60	—	60	—	57	—	62	—	55	61	62	54	43	—	65
Lower middle	—	—	—	—	49	52	—	49	—	55	—	57	—	61	—	52	54	52	58	39	—	59
Upper middle	—	—	—	—	34	29	—	41	—	28	—	46	—	46	—	38	37	28	48	33	—	46
Upper class	22[d]	18[d]	18[d]	31	19	21 (16)[e]	12[d]	29	13	20	11	29	—	23	—	23	24	24	46	27	29	32
"Blue collar"	—	—	—	—	—	—	—	—	—	—	—	—	63	—	38	—	—	—	59	—	33	—
"High income"	—	—	—	—	—	—	—	—	—	—	—	—	40	—	20	—	—	—	—	—	—	—

Note: CC = Corpus Christi; D = Dallas; FW = Fort Worth; H = Houston; JC = Jefferson County (urban boxes); SA = San Antonio; W = Waco.

Sources: Numan V. Bartley and Hugh D. Graham, *Southern Politics and the Second Reconstruction* (Baltimore and London: Johns Hopkins University Press, 1975), 43, 161, 169; Chandler Davidson, *Biracial Politics: Conflict and Coalition in the Metropolitan South* (Baton Rouge: Louisiana State University Press, 1972), 196, 201; George Norris Green, *The Establishment in Texas Politics: The Primitive Years, 1938–1957* (Westport, Conn. and London: Greenwood Press, 1979), 211–30; Penn Kimball, *The Disconnected* (New York: Columbia University Press, 1972), 241.

[a] First primary, percentage of Jester-Rainey vote only. In Houston, black votes were calculated using precincts 24, 25, 30, and 47. See Green, *The Establishment in Texas Politics*, 214.

[b] Second primary.

[c] First primary, percentage of total vote in 14-candidate field.

[d] Combined percentage of upper-middle and upper class.

[e] Estimate in parentheses is by a different author.

[f] Percent of Connally, Daniel, and Yarborough votes only, in a six-candidate field.

tion. But the Anglo working class was numerically and proportionately more important.

Taken together, the three foregoing tables bear out the continuing validity of Key's theory of Texas politics on this point. He saw that whites divide over economic issues, especially when the electoral environment gives them a choice at the ballot box. Key thought that a two-party system would provide precisely that choice.

The Impact of Low Turnout on Liberal Voting Strength

Observing the liberal coalition develop in the Democratic primaries, Key envisaged a two-party system that would subordinate racial issues to class ones. From this it can be inferred that the economic-racial conservatives on the upper rungs of the class ladder who had made up the Democratic establishment would be eased out of the party as newly enfranchised minorities and poor whites became voters and swelled the liberal ranks. The Republican party, taking advantage of the affluent voters' disenchantment with the Democrats, would gradually become competitive. The two Texas parties would roughly approximate the national ones and would aggressively contest elections.

Implicit in this model of realignment were two assumptions: first, that racial issues would gradually disappear, thus allowing class issues to assume their "natural" importance; second, that nonvoters, more liberal than conservative, would join the electorate once the two-party system gave them a chance to have their views and policy preferences articulated by the reformed Democratic party. The migration of nonvoters into such a party would strengthen it relative to the growing Republican party, while the latter would embrace voters who had developed a habit of voting for Republican presidential candidates in November. Let us first examine the second assumption, leaving the first one to be taken up in chapter 11. Were Key's hopes for an expanded and more liberal electorate realized?

It has long been known that less-affluent Americans vote at lower rates than those above them on the class ladder. This is true whatever the race of the individuals and whatever the region of the country they reside in. Low income and, more important, lack of education, are correlates of nonvoting.[8]

Raymond E. Wolfinger and Steven J. Rosenstone attribute the strong relation between education and voter turnout to three factors. First, education increases cognitive skills, which aid in learning about politics. Second, better-educated people usually have a stronger sense of citizen duty, feel a moral pressure to participate in elections, and receive personal gratification from voting. Third, education "imparts experience with a variety of bureaucratic relationships." One learns about requirements, how to fill out forms, and how to meet deadlines. "This experience," they write, "helps one overcome the procedural hurdles required first to register and then to vote."[9]

There are more obvious barriers to voting as well. Registration laws are still a problem. The U.S. census bureau found that in 1976, one-third of those adults who did not register to vote said they were unable to. Of those, about two in ten lacked transportation, found the hours or place of registration inconvenient, or did not know how or where to register. An additional one in ten was prevented from registering by a permanent illness or disability. These barriers are still a problem today.[10]

Once registered, people face other difficulties. Many employers will not allow workers time off to vote during the working day. One national survey found that over one-third of business firms did not allow workers time off.[11] A census bureau study of those who in 1980 registered but did not vote found that almost one in eight reported either having no transportation to the polls or being unable to take time off from work.[12] Many of the factors that impede registration and voting—lack of transportation, permanent illness, inability to get away during working hours—are most prevalent among the disadvantaged.

In short, for many reasons the working class, which on economic issues is more liberal than the upper class, has been underrepresented among voters, especially in the South, where poverty is greater than in other regions of the country.

The conventional view, therefore, is that an increase in the working-class vote, among whites and minorities combined, would make the electorate more liberal. While the change would not be great, so it is argued, a few percentage points of difference could be enough to change election results in some cases. Table 2.1 in chapter 2 indicates that five times between 1952 and 1972, when almost all the primary voters were voting in the Democratic primaries, a liberal candidate lost a major race for a gubernatorial or senatorial nomination by six points or less.

The hypothesis that turnout differences among classes result in a more conservative electorate is widely accepted by Texas politicians, who tend to equate low overall turnout with a more conservative electorate. Thus conservative candidates take a low turnout as a good augury. Anticipating the 1972 Democratic gubernatorial primary runoff, for example, conservative Democrat Dolph Briscoe, who faced a strong opponent in liberal state representative Frances ("Sissy") Farenthold, hoped for a low turnout and sizable Republican crossover voting.[13] And although Republican gubernatorial candidate Bill Clements publicly denied that he had banked on a low turnout in November 1978, Tom Reed, a Clements campaign director, attributed Clements's victory to it.[14] As shall be shown, this assumption may not be uniformly correct, particularly not since the 1960s. Nonetheless it has been widely accepted, and for a long time it may have been true.

Texas politicians also grasp the basic rule that election laws are never neutral in their effects. Conservatives have attempted to enact laws that would disproportionately discourage poor people from voting, although the ostensible reasons given are usually benign. Liberals have tried to block the conservatives on this.

As demonstrated in the previous chapter, the poll tax as a voting requirement, which was adopted in 1902, was a tremendous economic burden for the poor, as was the early registration requirement. The white primary, encouraged by the Terrell Election Law passed soon thereafter, placed an even greater specific burden on blacks. None of the three—the poll tax, the early registration system, and the white primary—was voluntarily repealed by the Texas legislature or the electorate. The U.S. Supreme Court pronounced the white primary unconstitutional in 1944.[15] Conservatives successfully fought until 1966 to maintain the poll tax and until 1971 to maintain the early registration law in spite of liberal efforts from the 1940s on to abolish them.

When President Kennedy's Commission on Registration and Voting Participation issued its report in 1963, only three of the eighteen measures it recommended to encourage voter participation were part of Texas law. In 1964 Texas ranked forty-fourth among the states in presidential voter turnout rate.[16] Twenty years later it ranked forty-fifth, although because its voting-age population contained an appreciable number of noncitizens, Texas undoubtedly ranked somewhat higher in turnout measured as the percentage of voting-age citizens.[17]

Passage of the 24th Amendment led to the abolition of the poll tax in federal elections in 1964. When a federal court ruled in 1966 that the tax was unconstitutional in state and local elections as well, Governor John Connally called a special session of the legislature. In spite of concrete proposals by liberals, organized labor, and the League of Women Voters for permanent registration, Connally charged Texas lawmakers to draw up an annual registration system described by one reporter as "patterned on the old poll tax system, but minus the tax."[18] Annual registration was incorporated into a proposed state constitutional amendment, ostensibly abolishing the already illegal poll tax, to be submitted to the voters in November. Connally justified his bill as "the most logical means of preventing fraud and guaranteeing purity of the ballot box"—the old canard of turn-of-the-century disfranchisers.[19] The measure, worded in a way that failed to mention the annual registration system, was passed in November. Thus the new Texas law not only reinstituted annual registra-

8. Henry B. Gonzalez. A liberal Democrat from San Antonio, Gonzalez held various elective offices, including that of state senator, before becoming the first Mexican American congressman from Texas. Courtesy of Alan Pogue and the *Texas
Observer*.

tion—at a time when only five other states required it—but retained the
four-month registration period that began October 1 in the year preceding
elections.[20]

By 1970 no other state had a comparable limitation. And with the exception of North Dakota, which had no registration system, and South
Carolina, with a decennial registration period, all other states had some
form of permanent or quasi-permanent registration.[21] Political scientist
Allen Shinn's analysis of the Texas registration period at this time revealed
its restrictive impact on voting.[22]

In a suit brought by liberal Democrats, civil rights groups, and Republicans, a federal court declared the law unconstitutional in 1971. (The one
area in which Texas's Republicans have usually cooperated with ethnic
minorities is in challenges to election laws that have discriminated against
both groups.) The conservative Democratic establishment was finally
forced to capitulate. Today voters can register up to thirty days before an
election, and then they are permanently registered so long as they vote at
least once every three years and do not move from their voting precinct—
two requirements that still keep many potential voters off the rolls.

The long struggle to abolish the poll tax was largely concerned with
whether to deter minorities and disadvantaged whites from voting, just as

the struggle to establish it had been, more than half a century earlier. In a speech at the height of the controversy in 1963, San Antonio congressman Henry B. Gonzalez said:

> The poll tax is an economic deterrent against voting to the poorer classes. . . . It has discouraged the poor white man's vote just as it has minimized the Negro vote and the Mexican vote. The law dictionaries define poll tax as a capitation tax, that is, a head tax. It would be more accurate to call it a decapitation tax, because it has served to behead large bodies of voters, to snuff out their political lives.[23]

The abolition of the poll tax and the creation of a fairer registration law did not end efforts to shape the ideological makeup of the electorate, however. The 1960s were threatening years for the conservative Democratic establishment, which still controlled the legislature. They watched in dismay as federal courts, the Voting Rights Act of 1965, and a federal constitutional amendment gradually destroyed key provisions in the carefully crafted Texas election code that had made the mere act of voting burdensome for minorities and poor whites.

In gubernatorial elections, moreover, turnout rose dramatically in this period, suggesting to many that a surge of have-nots into the electorate might actually be occurring. Turnout in gubernatorial general elections in the 1950s averaged 21 percent of the voting-age population. In the 1960s, as black and Mexican American voters came into their own, and organized labor and liberals worked to increase participation, gubernatorial turnout increased, averaging 36 percent of the voting-age population—a 70 percent jump over the 1950s. By 1968 almost 50 percent of the potential electorate was voting in the November gubernatorial race, indicating a level of interest that had not been reached since 1900, before the poll tax went into effect.

It is an elementary fact of voting behavior that turnout is lower in off years than in presidential election years. Between 1944 and 1964, for example, turnout in the general gubernatorial election in presidential years averaged 35 percent of the voting-age population; turnout in off years averaged 14 percent.

Thus, if increased turnout liberalized the electorate at that time, presidential-year gubernatorial elections would appear to have hurt conservative candidates in state contests. But it was not only a matter of turnout that was of concern to conservatives. The introduction of presidential campaign issues into state and local politics was also seen as helping liberals. V. O. Key's earlier observation that liberals benefited from linking presidential with state-level politics when a popular national Democratic party was ascendant expressed a common perception among political professionals. Ralph Yarborough, after all, had won a smashing senatorial victory in 1964 on the same ticket with Lyndon Johnson. His reelection seemed to augur a progressive breakthrough.

Connally persuaded the legislature in 1965 to submit a constitutional referendum to the voters that would change the tenure of statewide offices—including that of governor—from two to four years and that would require elections in off years. This was remarkable because Connally had campaigned in 1962 for retention of a two-year governor's term. His ostensible reason for the about-face was that two-year terms diminished the governor's administrative capacity by forcing him to spend too much time campaigning. Why a governor's administrative power would be enhanced by off-year elections was not clear. The measure would have become effective in 1966, thus permanently divorcing statewide elections from national ones.

Connally's most outspoken legislative opponents on the issue included representatives Bob Eckhardt, a Houston liberal; Bill Hollowell, an East Texas populist; and liberal Galveston state senator A. R. ("Babe") Schwartz. U.S. Senator Yarborough sharply attacked the proposal before the vote, and state leaders of the AFL-CIO worked against it as well, although some liberals and labor leaders had supported it during the special session.[24] Throughout the debate, the proposal's opponents hardly mentioned the fact that off-year gubernatorial elections would sharply reduce turnout. The proposal was rejected at the polls in November.[25]

But still the issue was not settled. In 1972, with a bank scandal at the center of public attention, essentially the same constitutional amendment slipped quietly through the legislature, this time guided by Lieutenant Governor Ben Barnes, a protégé of Connally. Oscar Mauzy, a liberal Senate leader, later remembered having gone along with the four-year term but not with the off-year elections.[26] Curiously, the liberal *Texas Observer* actually endorsed the proposed amendment for reasons similar to those Connally had given seven years earlier: introducing "statesmanship" into the executive branch. The endorsement made no mention of the effects of divorcing gubernatorial elections from presidential ones, which included the likelihood of a sharp decline in voter turnout.[27] The proposed amendment, one of fourteen on the ballot, was approved later in the year without much serious discussion.

The results were predictable. As figure 3.1 indicates, voter turnout in presidential-year gubernatorial elections was typically much higher than in off years from 1944 through 1972, differing hardly at all from turnout in the presidential contests. After 1972 gubernatorial turnout was much lower. Between 1960 and 1972, the average (presidential and off years combined) was 37 percent; between 1974 and 1986, for off years alone, it was 26 percent. Turnout in races for the most important offices in state government had been effectively slashed by one-third as a result of a change in election law.[28]

FIGURE 3.1
Voter Turnout in Texas General Elections,
Contests for President and Governor, 1944–1986

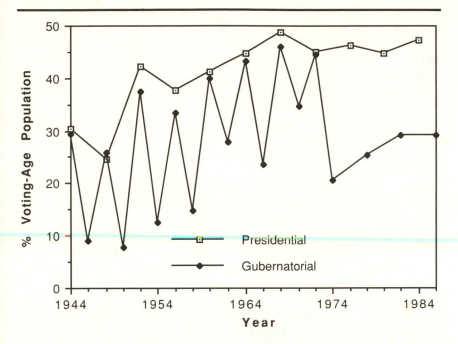

The Failure of the Have-nots to Mobilize

To return to the question posed earlier: Have Key's hopes for increased turnout been realized in Texas? In presidential elections there has been a long-term rise in voting since 1944, when voter turnout was 31 percent. From 1960, turnout ranged from 41 to 49 percent. It was 47 percent in 1984.

In general gubernatorial elections, as shown, a gradual rise occurred from the 1940s through the 1960s. Turnout in 1944 was 29 percent, and it peaked at 47 percent in 1968. When the Texas constitutional provision eliminated presidential-year elections for state office, turnout dropped sharply. In 1986 as in 1944, 29 percent of adults cast a ballot for governor.

Primaries present yet a different pattern, as seen in figure 2.1 in chapter 2. In 1944, turnout was 22 percent in the Democratic gubernatorial primary. Republicans did not hold one. Turnout over the next twenty years did not increase sharply, but by the mid-1960s it was around 30 percent. A typical year was 1968, when 28 percent of adults voted in the Democratic primary and an additional 2 percent voted in that of the Republicans.

Following the 1972 abolition of gubernatorial elections in presidential years, primary participation plummeted. In 1974, for example, the first year the new law was in effect, participation in both primaries totaled 20 percent, and by 1986 it had dropped to 14 percent (9 in the Democratic primary, 5 in the Republican one), the lowest on record. To the degree that primary turnout for statewide office is a gauge of party vitality, the two-party system in Texas was seriously weakened even while realignment was under way.

To summarize, turnout trends between 1944 and the 1980s were different in each type of election. Voting increased in presidential elections from 31 to 47 percent in 1984. There was no consistent long-term gain in general gubernatorial elections, thanks to the 1972 constitutional amendment. In both 1944 and 1986, turnout was 29 percent. In statewide primaries there was serious erosion in voter participation, which also might partly have been caused by the switch to off-year elections. In 1944, turnout in the Democratic primary, the only one held, was 22 percent; in 1986 it was 14 in both parties' primaries combined.

Only in presidential elections, therefore, did turnout increase as Key had thought it might; and it was a fairly modest gain. Even on this score, it is not certain that the increase in presidential voting is evidence for a rise in turnout among the have-nots relative to the haves, turnout that is replenishing Democratic ranks as conservatives migrate to the Republican party. On the contrary, voting among the Texas working class—Anglos and minority persons combined—actually may have declined in some areas since the 1960s.

Nonvoting among minorities alone illustrates the problem of lower turnout among the disadvantaged. At first glance, the sizable and growing minority population in the state would seem to provide the liberal coalition with a significant advantage, especially given their bloc-voting propensities. In 1980, 12 percent of the population was black and 21 percent was Hispanic. The black proportion has gradually dropped since 1870, and then leveled off in recent decades. The Hispanic percentage has increased sharply since 1960.

But blacks and Hispanics are on average younger than Anglos, and in addition, as many as one in six Hispanics were estimated to be noncitizens in 1980. Thus the *voting-age* population of minority *citizens* is lower than the original figures indicate, even before other factors take their toll.

The figures for the 1978 and 1982 gubernatorial general elections, shown in table 3.4, underscore the extent of this toll. Texas Hispanics have one of the lowest turnout rates in the country for their group.[29] The state's blacks also vote at a lower rate than do Anglos.

Table 3.4 shows that unequal turnout rates alone, among eligible voters, reduced the black proportion of the actual electorate by as much as

Table 3.4

Relative Voter Turnout among Texas Minorities,
General Gubernatorial Elections, 1978 and 1982 (percentages)

	1980			1978	1982
	Total Population	Voting-Age Population	Voting-Age Citizens	Gubernatorial Voters	Gubernatorial Voters
Anglo[a]	67	71	73	86	81
Black	12	11	12	8	9
Hispanic	21	18	15	6	10
Total	100	100	100	100	100

Sources: U.S. Bureau of the Census, General Population Characteristics: Texas (PC80-1-B45 Tex) (Washington, D.C.: U.S. Government Printing Office, 1982), tables 15, 16, and 19; Texas Almanac and Industrial Guide (Dallas: A. H. Belo, 1982), 499. Estimates of Hispanic citizens were provided by Robert Brischetto, Southwest Voter Research Institute, San Antonio. Estimates of minority turnout appeared in Dan Weiser and Kay deWit, "The 1982 Texas Election Analysis," The Forum: A Journal of Political and Social Issues (Dallas Democratic Forum) 1 (spring and summer 1983): 3–5.

[a] All nonblack, non-Hispanic persons.

one-third and the Hispanic proportion by more than one-half in 1978 and by one-third in 1982. (In the 1984 presidential election, Texas Hispanics cast 7 percent of the state's votes.)[30] The difference minority turnout can make is suggested by the fact that in 1978 Republican Bill Clements won the governor's race, while in 1982, thanks in part to a relatively larger minority turnout, Democrat Mark White eked out a narrow victory over him.

A similar attrition process is at work simultaneously within the Anglo population, diminishing the proportion of lower-income voters there, too. The most affluent one-third of Anglos in Texas, who make up only about one-fourth of the state's voting-age citizens, may constitute 40 percent or more of the actual voters.

The discussion so far has assumed, as Key did, that an increase in relative turnout among people of low socioeconomic status would usually benefit liberal candidates and exert pressure for liberal programs. This supposition has recently been questioned by political scientist James DeNardo, who doubts whether an increase in the relative turnout of lower-income voters would ordinarily benefit Democrats (and by extension, liberals) in an age when party loyalty is particularly weak, as it has been for over two decades. DeNardo presents limited evidence that even when the less affluent, who usually do not vote and who tend to call themselves Democrats, surge to the polls at higher rates than normal, they are more likely than stable voters to cross party lines in numbers that actually give a net benefit to the Republicans.[31] This hypothesis has not yet been proven; but

9. Willie Velasquez. A militant who came out of the Chicano politics of San Antonio and South Texas in the
1960s, Velasquez later was instrumental in establishing
the Southwest Voter Research Institute, the role of
which has been to increase Mexican American registration and turnout. Velasquez died of cancer in 1988 at age
44. Courtesy of the *Texas Observer*.

the argument underlying it, as well as the evidence to date, at least raise
questions about Key's opposite assumption as it applies to recent times.
Key's thesis probably is most valid today when a surge of typical nonvoters
to the polls consists disproportionately of blacks and Hispanics, as was
apparently the case in the gubernatorial election of 1982 (see table 3.4
above). But if the surge consists mostly of whites—even working-class
whites who could once be counted on to pull the Democratic lever—
DeNardo may be closer to the mark.

Southern Strategies Old and New

We now can answer more fully the question posed in chapter 2. If Texas historically has not been as conservative at the grass roots as conventional thinking contends, why is it that its elected officialdom has been so heavily conservative? The answer is that for much of the nineteenth and twentieth centuries, election laws and threats of violence have discouraged or prevented great numbers of the most liberal Texans from voting, thus maintaining an unnaturally conservative electorate. Before commentators on Texas political history invest too much energy speculating about the relation between "folk conservatism" and politics in the Lone Star State, therefore, they should acknowledge the measurable impact of election laws on the makeup of the electorate—that highly skewed sample of the voting-age population that actually votes candidates into office.

Trends beginning in the 1960s, however, suggest that other forces are at work that account for Texas's low turnout rate today, making the relation between nonvoting and conservative advantage more complex. The decline in Democratic presidential voting among the white working class after 1964, demonstrated in table 3.2, indicates that something was happening at the grass roots independent of conservatives' manipulation of voting laws. And it stands to reason that the cause of this working-class disenchantment with Democrats among voters was also affecting people's decisions on whether to vote at all.

A possible cause is suggested by the fact that in 1968 the lowest-income white precincts in Houston gave Democrat Hubert Humphrey a mere 30 percent of their vote, compared to the 57 percent LBJ had gotten in 1964 and to the similarly high percentages the Democratic ticket had received earlier. But George Wallace, running on the American party ticket in 1968, got most of the rest of the votes in these precincts, not Richard Nixon.

What marked that fateful year was a split in the New Deal coalition brought about by the continuing racial crisis and the allegiance of the national Democratic party to civil rights. Early on, Wallace's Georgia state campaign chairman, Roy V. Harris, had predicted that "there's really only going to be one issue [in 1968], and you spell it n-i-g-g-e-r."[32] Wallace used code words such as "law and order" to mask his blatant appeals to prejudice, but his campaign was aimed at the racial resentments of whites. To a lesser degree, so was that of Nixon, but Wallace's pitch won over thousands of working-class whites who found it difficult to vote Republican. A sample that year of white Texans belonging to the households of "operatives and laborers" revealed that 23 percent favored Nixon; 47 percent, Humphrey; and 30 percent, Wallace.[33] The working-class

Wallace voters (in addition to the sizable number of middle-class ones) were aggressively pursued by Texas Republicans in the 1970s and by the Reagan campaign in 1976. Only in 1976 and 1980, the years in which Jimmy Carter, a southern Evangelical, ran for the presidency, did the lowest-income white precincts in Texas give the Democratic ticket anything like the support they had consistently given Democratic contenders prior to 1968.

Obviously those whose hopes were raised by Key's theory of mobilizing the dispossessed have been disappointed in the years following the southern civil rights movement. As he envisioned, the old turn-of-the-century election restrictions were finally abolished, as was the edifice of Jim Crow. Both developments gave rise to a new wave of minority politics and increasing minority demands for government to overcome the remaining barriers to equal opportunity.

But these demands were resisted by many whites and led the Republican party to take advantage of the racial conflict. Racial issues, far from disappearing after the collapse of Jim Crow, have assumed a new importance in comparison with issues of economic class. And they have led conservatives to develop the mirror-opposite of Key's "southern strategy," which was posited on the increasing importance of economic struggles between the haves and the have-nots in the postwar era.

Part Two

CLASS STRUCTURES

4

The Upper Class

The fabulously rich, as well as the mere millionaires, are still very much among us; moreover,
since the organization of the United States for
World War II, new types of "rich men" with
new types of power and prerogative have joined
their ranks. Together they form the corporate
rich of America, whose wealth and power is
today comparable with those of any stratum,
anywhere or anytime in world history.
  (C. Wright Mills, *The Power Elite*)

Just leave us alone, and let the free enterprise
system work.
  (Corbin Robertson, in *The Texans*)

IN THE twentieth century, the idea of outrageous wealth came to be associated with Texas oil millionaires. Legends developed around them that
they embroidered upon. A stereotype was born in the national imagination, and John Bainbridge called it "the super-American":

> a canny, adventurous millionaire whose approach to business is strictly free-
> style. In what appears to be an unquenchably lighthearted and casual mood, he
> is constantly in the process of extending his enterprises by buying, selling, bor-
> rowing, merging, and trading. His transactions, always called deals, usually
> involve sums of at least seven digits; to save time in calculating, he customarily
> drops the last five. He keeps no regular hours. He may spend the morning at his
> office and by late afternoon be fishing in the Gulf or watching the races at Aque-
> duct or Santa Anita. He shuns conferences, paperwork, consultations with law-
> yers, and other time-consuming activities that pass for accomplishment in the
> life of the ordinary businessman.[1]

A throwback to an earlier age of enterprise, in this stereotype the Texas
millionaire is a man on the make and a man on his own. At heart he is an
individualist: an enemy of all binding ties, whether governmental re-
straints or the social bonds that complicate life in civil society. His deepest
desire is to be left free to make his fortune, untaxed and unregulated. He
is a loner, a capitalist cowboy.

This stereotype no doubt fits some cases, even though the loudest champions of laissez-faire are usually the first to take advantage of government bounties that come their way—often as a result of their own maneuvering. Eddie Chiles, Fort Worth oil millionaire and husband of Fran Chiles, Republican national committeewoman, launched a series of "anti-Big Government" commercials that by 1980 were playing twice daily on 465 radio stations in fourteen states and costing $1 million annually. Chiles, the recipient of $108 million in federal loan guarantees to build drilling rigs, included a plug for his oil company in his commercials, which were tax-deductible as a business expense.[2] But for all their talk about the sanctity of the individual and the benefits of competition in a free market, the Texas rich are bound together in complex ways. Instead of a band of pecuniary cowboys seeking their individual fortunes, they are an upper class in the precise meaning of the term: a social group whose common background and effective control of wealth bring them together politically.

This does not mean that they are always, or ever entirely, in agreement. They can compete fiercely. But like members of an athletic team riven by individual competition, they join forces against common enemies. On the "broad, philosophical questions" this "hard core of Texas conservatism" stands together, as James Soukup and his colleagues argued in the 1960s.[3]

An upper class is not necessarily a ruling class. It is "upper" in that it consists of the wealthiest families in the state and the top managers of the large corporations. Together they control much of the state's private capital. But wealth does not always prevail against opposing forces, even though it is a formidable weapon when it is used by a small, cohesive group of astute men and women who own the mass media, contribute the lion's share of winning candidates' campaign funds, and work with lawyer-lobbyists—often part of the upper class themselves—to engineer government policies that benefit the rich. Whether a particular upper class in a specific era is also a ruling class is an empirical question.

Furthermore, an upper class—even a ruling one—may not always act as though its interests oppose those of other classes. The interests of different classes sometimes overlap. And a wise upper class may forego the pursuit of certain interests to prevent battles it might lose and to achieve more substantial goals later on.

An upper class may well exist without its being called such either by political commentators or by members of the class itself. R. H. Tawney observed long ago that "the word 'class' is fraught with unpleasing associations, so that to linger upon it is apt to be interpreted as the symptom of a perverted mind and a jaundiced spirit." It is nonetheless an indispensable term for making sense out of Texas politics.

The Super Rich

The Texas upper class, let us say tentatively, consists of those people who control the state's private assets. They are either personally rich or, as corporate chieftains, they are in control of great sums of finance capital. Often they are both. There is a continuing debate over whether the personally rich and the corporate executives in the nation as a whole are part of a single class or whether, on the contrary, with the increasing separation of corporate ownership and control, they have split into two new classes with different interests.[4] Do they, in Texas, turn out to be distinct classes or do they meld together into an upper class that, at the national level, C. Wright Mills called "the corporate rich"?

A decision about whom to include in a study of the personally rich must be rather arbitrary.[5] For our purposes, we shall define them as the approximately 2 percent of Texas families who in the early 1980s had a net worth of at least $500,000 and together owned perhaps two-fifths of the state's private wealth.[6] At the apex of this stratum are the super rich, whom we shall define as those Texans whose individual or nuclear family fortunes in 1980 were reliably estimated to be at least $50 million net.[7] Two studies by financial reporters around that time led to the creation of a list of ninety-nine such people, who will be referred to hereafter simply as "the ninety-nine" or the super rich. They are probably different from the merely rich in ways that go beyond the possession of wealth. They may be thought of as the leadership stratum of the personally rich. Let us examine them first and begin by asking whether they are an aristocracy.

If, as Adam Smith put it, superiority of birth supposes an ancient superiority of fortune, the answer is no. Of the ninety-two whose origins could be traced, only seven were inheritors of fortunes that originated as far back as the nineteenth century. From this perspective, Texas wealth is indeed new, even by Eastern Seaboard standards. On the other hand, of the ninety-five whose backgrounds could be determined, at least 62 percent were either inheritors or, in a few cases, they had married those who were already rich.

Even among the first-generation big rich there were several who did not start near the bottom of the social ladder. Some were financed by affluent kin. Developer Harold Farb, worth $200 million in the early 1980s, went into business after World War II with his father, who had assets in movie theaters and other ventures.[8] Developer Trammell Crow came from humble origins, but early on used his wife's inheritance to create an empire now valued at more than $500 million.[9]

Most of the first-generation ninety-nine were college graduates. By comparison, in the period between the two world wars when they came to maturity, only 11 percent of the U.S. college-age population was enrolled in college in any given year, and a far smaller proportion ever graduated.[10] In a state where race is a fundamental determinant of opportunity, all of the ninety-nine were Anglos, the overwhelming majority from Protestant stock. Eighteen were women, of whom fourteen inherited their wealth. (Widows of first-generation men count as first generation if they married before they and their husbands became wealthy.)

The super rich are often closely integrated into family networks that enable them to pool their wealth for entrepreneurial and political purposes. At least thirty-seven were close kin to one or more other members. Two major clans were represented—ten heirs of Dallas oilman H. L. Hunt and five of Houston oilman Hugh Roy Cullen. Sometimes such kin groups behave as a unit and sometimes they do not. At one extreme was the tightly knit Cullen clan, whose destiny was linked to Quintana Petroleum. The combined fortunes of the Cullens among the ninety-nine came to around $500 million in 1983.[11] As the 1980s began, they were guided by Corbin J. Robertson, a son-in-law of the founding father.[12] Members of the Cullen group sometimes pooled their money to support political candidates.

In contrast, the Hunts consisted of two branches in Dallas whose respective members were not on good terms. Hunt had long kept the two families secret from each other. After his first wife, Lyda, died, he married his secretary Ruth Ray, by whom he had already fathered four children. Ruth inherited Hunt Oil Company and other properties in 1974, and these became the substance of H. L.'s "second" Dallas family's empire.[13]

Ruth Ray and her children formed one fairly close unit in which her son, Ray Lee Hunt, emerged as the leader, cutting a figure in Dallas politics and civic affairs. (One member of this family, who was living at the time in Denver, was not included among the ninety-nine.) The other family, probably less cohesive, consisted of the six children of H. L.'s first wife, Lyda.[14] *Forbes* magazine in 1985 estimated the six-member first family's wealth at $4.9 billion.[15]

Other members of the ninety-nine acted as a unit in some contexts. For example, Perry Richardson Bass and Sid Richardson Bass, a father-and-son team and the inheritors of a portion of the fortune of Perry's uncle, Sid Richardson, together held assets "in excess of $2 billion" in 1982.[16] By the mid-1980s, *Forbes* estimated each of Perry Bass's four Yale-educated sons, including Sid, to have at least $500 million, and their combined assets exceeded $3 billion.[17]

These examples suggest that by using individual rather than family wealth as the criterion for the super rich, one almost certainly understates the actual assets available to many of them. The individual approach also overlooks those who personally do not have fortunes of $50 million but who belong to one of the noted Texas extended families that sometimes act as a unit—the Moodys and Kempners of Galveston, the O'Connors of Victoria, the "King Ranch family," and the Bentsens—some of whose members and financial retainers together control fortunes of several hundred millions.

The stereotype of the Texas rich as oilmen is not without foundation. For at least two-thirds of the ninety-nine, the original money source was oil, although several first became rich in construction, banking, or ranching and then acquired oil leases, interests in drilling rigs, or major shares in an oil/gas pipeline company. Owners of large ranches often became "oilmen" when leases on their land, held by oil firms, produced royalties. Such was the good fortune of the King Ranch family and of Dolph Briscoe, Jr.

But the facts are more complicated. Take the case of the Hunts in Dallas—oil wealth personified. Among their assets in 1980 was the undeniable petroleum base: Placid Oil Company, one of the largest independents in the country; Penrod, "the largest privately held drilling contractor"; oil and gas wells in eight states; a refinery; and two pipelines. But this was only the core. The Hunts also held what was probably the largest share of individually controlled silver; one of the largest U.S. sugar beet refining operations; perhaps more land owned by a single family—several million acres in the U.S., not counting at least four million in Australia; "2.5 million tons of coal reserves; and the largest string of thoroughbred race horses [one thousand] owned by an American." The Hunts were also behind numerous ventures in Dallas—office buildings, hotels, shopping centers, and housing developments. Brothers Bunker and William had also purchased "more than 3 percent of Bache Group Inc." This was in addition to investments in several other oil companies. In commercial sports, Lamar Hunt owned the Kansas City Chiefs, the Dallas Tornado (a soccer team), and World Championship Tennis. At the bottom of the list of major holdings were four hundred Shakey's Pizza Parlors.[18]

Calling the Hunts oil people grossly misdescribes the nature of this $5 billion family circa 1980—some fifty years after their father swapped "Dad" Joiner out of his oil leases once the aging Joiner had miraculously discovered the giant East Texas field. And they are by no means unique in the extent of their diverse holdings.

Writing about "the Texas tycoon" in the early 1960s, a *Time* magazine reporter observed that "though his poke may have started in oil (and gained by the 27 1/2% depletion allowance), much of it now comes from electronics, real estate, insurance or shipping." And for the "new Texan," he added, "Texas is no longer big enough. Ranging across the nation like eager bird dogs, Texas businessmen are supplying capital, entrepreneurial vigor and acumen in nearly every area of the U.S. economy."[19]

The holdings of the Murchison brothers at that time underscore the point. "Oilmen" John (Hotchkiss, Yale) and Clint, Jr. (Lawrenceville, an M.A. in mathematics from MIT) claimed to have lived by their father's guiding principle: "Money is like manure. If you spread it around, it does a lot of good. But if you pile it up in one place, it stinks like hell." They spread it around. At the time of their famous takeover of the Allegheny Corporation, they had interests in at least one hundred companies, in-including insurance firms, banks, country clubs, hotels, oil and gas companies, chemical manufacturing plants, the publishing house of Holt, Rinehart and Winston, the Dallas Cowboys, one of the nation's largest construction firms, railway lines (including the New York Central), and an investment firm that handled the world's largest mutual fund.[20]

Another example of diversification was the late George Rufus Brown, a Houston member of the ninety-nine, whose meteoric success in construction and petroleum was symbiotic with the political career of his friend Lyndon Johnson. An oil and gas millionaire Brown certainly was. After World War II, he helped found Texas Eastern Gas Transmission, one of the nation's largest gas-gathering companies; and by 1975 he was the largest individual stockholder, with 350,489 shares of common stock.[21] But Texas Eastern was more than a gas company. It was also a major real estate developer. In 1970, with Brown as chairman, the corporation announced it had bought a thirty-two-block area in downtown Houston on which to build a central-city complex of futuristic design that would require an investment in the billions. It was at the time the largest realty acquisition in the city's history.[22]

Brown's involvement in Texas Eastern and his numerous other oil and gas ventures was made possible by his earlier success in the construction firm of Brown and Root, which he and his brother Herman built to gigantic proportions. With his Washington contacts, LBJ foremost among them, Brown the engineer became a major military contractor from World War II on, building everything from destroyer escorts and submarine chasers in the 1940s to much of the American infrastructure in South Vietnam in the 1960s—airfields, headquarters, barracks, and roads.[23] Elsewhere, Brown and Root built dams, international highways, bridges, buildings, and a nuclear power plant. By 1969, with a $1.77 billion volume, it had become the nation's largest construction company, its projects spread from Thailand to Haiti to Australia to the Persian Gulf, and to many points in between.[24]

Brown was also a heavy investor in bank stock. His 66,611 shares in First City Bancorporation, one of the state's largest bank holding companies in the 1970s, were exceeded in number by those of only two other directors in 1973, one of whom was chairman and son of the bank's founder.[25]

The myth of the big rich as "just oilmen" is as far off the mark as is the idea that Texas corporations are just oil companies. By the 1970s, only eleven of the twenty largest Texas-based public corporations were primarily affiliated with oil, gas, or related industries. Even the nature of some of the eleven oil companies defied simple classification. Tenneco, for example, usually thought of as a gas pipeline firm, was in 1974 also a chemical producer in America and overseas, a major real estate and agribusiness firm in various states, a shipbuilder for the U.S. Navy, an automotive components manufacturer, and a producer of farm equipment through its subsidiary, J. I. Case Company.[26]

The super rich invest in a spectrum of industries that requires them to consider the interests of many sectors and of capital in general. However seductive the idea of being self-made or self-sustaining may be to them, it is no more than an illusion. As we shall see, entrepreneurship at this level means working through large corporations, family networks, and overarching political organizations to pressure the government for special favors—sometimes for one of their own companies, sometimes for an entire industry, sometimes for big business as a whole. It is this larger notion of their interests that transforms the very rich from a mere stratum of rich people into a genuine class.

The Corporate Elite

Like the big rich, the small number of men and women who occupy the command posts in the major Texas financial institutions exercise control over great wealth. Let us call them the corporate elite. What kind of people are they? What are their backgrounds? What are their economic interests, their political views? Would a collective portrait of this select group reveal a new breed of organization men (and women) who differ sharply from the big rich in outlook? Or do the similarities outweigh the differences? If the latter is true, is it correct to speak of the corporate elite as part of an upper class?

In the mid-1970s, using standard biographical sources, a study was conducted to answer these questions. The elite was operationally defined as the 610 directors of the following institutions headquartered in the state: the largest 29 general business corporations, the top 3 power companies, the largest independent insurance company, the largest 7 multibank holding companies, and the top 10 foundations—50 major economic institutions in all.[27] Privately held corporations were excluded because they are not required by law to make public the financial data necessary for ranking.

The top 50 economic institutions were quite large. Several were on the "*Fortune* 500" list of largest American industrials, and three—Shell Oil, LTV, and Tenneco—were among its top 30. All of the 29 Texas general business corporations had sales of over $300 million in 1973; the bank holding companies had deposits exceeding $1 billion, and the power companies also had assets in excess of that amount. The insurance company had $11 billion of insurance in force. Four of the foundations were among the nation's 38 largest in assets.

Significantly, 27 of the 99 richest Texans—more than one-fourth—were among the corporate elite, and in several cases they sat on more than one board that would have qualified them for elite membership. Often, several were clustered on the same board. To take a more recent example, in 1985, 6 members of the 99 were directors of MCorp, the multibank holding company. Given our narrow definition of the Texas elite, the figures say nothing about the corporate connections the super rich had with major companies based elsewhere but active in Texas or with Texas subsidiaries of companies headquartered elsewhere—such as Houston-based Exxon, U.S.A. Too, the elite list was derived from publicly held corporations only; had it included privately held firms of comparable size, the number of super rich who belonged would have been larger. (Some of these privately held, family-dominated firms, such as Scurlock Oil, had sales of over $300 million in 1973.) Even so, it is obvious that the big rich are often involved in top corporate management.

To obtain detailed information about this management, questionnaires were sent to a random sample of 200 of the 610 directors, 60 of whom responded. Though unintended, the sample of 60 was biased in favor of top managers: 70 percent were chairmen, CEOs, or presidents. All but 2 of the 60 were men. (The women were foundation trustees.) Only 48 percent had been born in Texas. Few were from humble origins. Of the 43 whose fathers' occupation was given, 53 percent had businessmen or managers for fathers, including 9 percent who were founders or CEOs of a company; another 26 percent were descended from "professionals." In other words, 79 percent came from the most privileged occupational strata, which, in 1940 or before, when most of the elite was growing up, constituted less than 15 percent of the male work force.[28] Only 2 percent had fathers who were urban manual workers.

In religious affiliation, 85 percent were Protestant, compared to roughly 69 percent of religious adherents in Texas. Twenty-four percent were Episcopalian and 19 percent Presbyterian—the 2 preferred denominations of the American upper class. (Among Texas religious adherents as a whole, 2 percent and 3 percent were Episcopalian and Presbyterian, respectively.) Only 10 percent of the sample were Baptist, compared to 34 percent of all Texas adherents who were Southern Baptists.[29]

The extent of the elite's unusual backgrounds is also suggested by their educational achievements. Seventy-six percent had graduated from college, and 30 percent had an advanced degree. Almost one-third had attended an Ivy League university, about the same percentage as the national business elite. A few, sons or sons-in-law of businessmen, had gone directly from school into the family firm, where they moved up the corporate chain of command to top executive posts. Charles and Robert Cullum, sons of the founder of the Cullum Company, attended Southern Methodist University in the 1930s and by 1976 were board chairman and executive committee chairman, respectively, of the family firm. Charles C. Butt, whose father was founder and chairman of a grocery store chain, attended the Wharton School of Finance, graduated in 1959, and went to work for his family firm. After a decade of executive duties, he was elected president in 1971, at age thirty-three.

Most of the managers were linked to other corporations as outside directors. Only eleven of the sixty belonged to no board of a for-profit firm beyond that of the company they were primarily affiliated with or one of its subsidiaries. The median number of outside directorships was two. (The respondents were asked to list all their directorships, and several listed both present and past affiliations, among which it was impossible to differentiate.) Twenty-eight members of the elite sat on at least three other boards, two of whom sat on eight, one on eleven, and another on twenty-six.

The Texas corporate elite was connected to various other elites as well. Approximately one-fifth of the 610 directors were listed in the *Social Directory* of Dallas, Fort Worth, or Houston. Forty-two were university trustees; of these, some sat on more than one university board.

The personal wealth of the top managers deserves special comment in light of the uncertainty over whether they have interests separate from those of the big rich. We have seen already that 27 of the 99 Texans with a net worth of $50 million or more belonged to the corporate elite in 1974. But what of the typical top managers of the 50 largest Texas corporations? What is the extent of their wealth? Are they closer to the big rich or to the ordinary run of salaried employees in corporate management positions—those who might be called the upper middle class?

In 1982 B. John Mackin of the Zapata Corporation received the smallest compensation among the fifty best-paid CEOs of a Texas publicly held company. His salary, bonus, benefits, and stock options brought him a total earned annual income of $500,000. The highest paid was John Dixon of E-Systems in Dallas, with a total compensation package of $2.29 million. Dixon, sixty-three, had been with the company for twenty-one years and had been its CEO for fourteen. Thirteen others among the fifty also had total company compensation of more than $1 million in 1982. This was "earned" income, exclusive of returns on investments.[30]

The top executives' compensation package typically consisted of a salary and a bonus combined with deferred compensation, profit sharing, pensions, and stock options. Only the salary and bonus—averaging less than half of the total after-tax compensation—were taxed at the ordinary rate on marginal income. The other income segments were sheltered in various ways, especially the stock options, the return from which was usually treated as a capital gain.[31] The usefulness of this tax treatment is obvious in cases like that of the president of Texas Instruments, whose salary and bonuses came to less than $164,000 in 1972, a year he exercised his option to pay $2.7 million for Texas Instruments stock valued at $5.9 million.[32]

Receiving this level of income for a few years, top managers can become multimillionaires, and as such would be among the top wealth holders even among the upper class—the richest 2 or 3 percent of all Texans. Suggestive of the extent of their wealth holdings is Wilbur Lewellen's research on the top five executives in each of the fifty largest U.S. industrial corporations, which revealed that by 1963 the average manager owned $2.4 million of his company's stock, to say nothing of his holdings in other companies.[33] As millionaires in their own right, as stockholders in the companies they run and those others run, and as men whose business reputation and compensation appear to be pegged to the profitability of their firm, the top corporate executives are almost as far-removed from the stereotypical salaried bureaucrat as from the blue-collar wage worker at the bottom of the organizational chart.

The Politics of the Ninety-nine

While similarities of backgrounds and extent of wealth suggest similar political views, further evidence is needed to determine whether the rich act as a class. We have already seen in chapter 3 the extraordinary degree of solidarity manifested in candidate preference in urban silk-stocking neighborhoods over the past fifty years when Texas election contests pitted liberals against conservatives. We shall now take another tack by examining the publicly known political activities of the ninety-nine, the very richest of the rich in those same precincts. More than half turned out to be quite active politically. The following profiles, current through 1986, hint at the nature of their involvement, although we can describe only a few persons and give only the merest sketches of their multifarious projects across many years.

PERRY BASS AND SONS: Forth Worth oilmen with a combined net worth of over $3 billion in 1985. The senior Bass was a long-time friend of John Connally. The latter became rich while working for Bass's uncle, Sid Richardson, who helped bankroll his friend Dwight Eisenhower into the White House. The Basses were major backers of Lloyd Bentsen, who tried unsuccessfully to amend federal law in 1983 to allow the sons to split many of their holdings without having to pay taxes. Bass money goes to Democrats and Republicans, liberals and conservatives, though primarily to the latter. They have had two war chests—the Good Government Fund, for Texas races; and the Bass Brothers Political Action Committee, for national ones. Reporters in early 1986 identified the family as the biggest backer of Mark White's gubernatorial reelection campaign to date that year, having contributed $86,000.[34]

HARVEY R. ("BUM") BRIGHT: Dallas oil and trucking magnate worth over $475 million in 1985. He lived next door to Nelson Bunker Hunt and seemed to share many of his political views, describing himself as a "rightwinger." Along with Hunt and another millionaire, he purchased the famous ad in the *Dallas Morning News* the day of JFK's assassination that attacked the president as soft on communism. In the 1980s he still defended it as a "good ad." He was a Goldwater supporter in 1964, then finance chairman of Bill Clements's successful 1978 gubernatorial campaign, and then Clements's appointee to the Texas A&M Board of Regents, of which he became chairman. Bright fell out with Clements in 1985 and supported Kent Hance, a competitor, in the 1986 Republican primary. He was a member of Phil Gramm's finance committee in his 1984 senatorial bid.[35]

DOLPH BRISCOE, JR.: Uvalde rancher and banker worth $200 million or more in 1985. A state legislator from 1949 to 1957 and Democratic governor from 1973 to 1979, he is one of the largest landowners in Texas. He loaned his campaigns millions of dollars, which were repaid by lobbyists and friends through "Briscoe Appreciation Dinners" after his election. The Southern Regional Council in 1977 called him "the most recalcitrant of all Southern governors" in implementing health service planning legislation passed by Congress three years earlier.[36]

GEORGE R. BROWN: Houston construction tycoon worth $100 million in 1982, shortly before his death, although much of his wealth had been given to the Brown Foundation. A master of behind-the-scenes politics, he and his brother Herman were powerful even among their peers. "Every Texas governor for thirty years sought their counsel and support. . . . They actively backed conservative candidates in the South and were strong supporters of Lyndon Johnson." Their political obsession was

10. Bill Clements and George Bush. Clements, the first Republican governor of Texas since Reconstruction (from 1979 to 1983 and from 1987 to the present), listens as presidential candidate George Bush addresses the legislature during the 1980 primary campaign. Courtesy of Alan Pogue and the *Texas Observer*.

union busting, and they played a crucial role in passing Texas anti-union legislation and the Taft-Hartley Act.[37]

WILLIAM P. (BILL) CLEMENTS, JR.: Dallas drilling contractor, estimates of whose worth vary greatly. In the late 1970s, they ranged from $29.4 million to $50–75 million. President Nixon appointed him to a blue-ribbon committee to study Pentagon defense policies in 1969–1970. He was Texas cochairman of the Committee to Re-elect the President in 1972. As deputy secretary of defense from 1973 to 1977, he was "the top Pentagon official responsible for supervising the multi-billion-dollar development and procurement of major weapons." He married Rita Bass, Republican national committeewoman, in 1975. Starting his 1978 campaign with virtually no name recognition, he borrowed $4.5 million from himself, outspent his Democratic opponent $7.1 to $2.8 million, and became Texas's first Republican governor since Reconstruction. He was defeated in 1982 by Mark White, despite outspending him $13.3 to $7.2 million. Clements was on Phil Gramm's finance committee in 1984, along with several others among the ninety-nine. In 1986 he defeated White for the governorship.[38]

TRAMMELL CROW: Dallas builder worth at least $550 million in 1985. He is a contributor and fund-raiser for conservative Democrats and Republicans. With a friend, he financed a 1974 operation to help Dolph Briscoe control the state Democratic party apparatus, then under siege by liberals

11. Oveta Culp Hobby. Along with her husband, former governor William P. Hobby, she owned and directed a sprawling media empire that included the *Houston Post*. The Hobbys were influential members of the Texas conservative establishment. She helped deliver Texas Republican votes for Dwight Eisenhower in his nomination battle against Robert Taft in the spring of 1952, and then she teamed up with Democratic governor Allan Shivers to help Eisenhower carry Texas against Adlai Stevenson in November. Here she is sworn in as the nation's first secretary of Health, Education, and Welfare. Eisenhower looks on. Courtesy of the Houston Metropolitan Archives.

and moderates. He was a major organizer of funds for Gerald Ford in his 1976 primary battle against Ronald Reagan and then for Reagan in the 1980s.[39]

MICHEL T. HALBOUTY: Houston oilman worth between $50–$75 million in the late 1970s. A money raiser for Ford and Reagan, he also contributed to many other conservative candidates. He resigned from the Ford campaign committee in 1975, demanded his money back, and switched to Reagan when Ford opposed Halbouty on an energy bill. One of President Reagan's top energy advisers, he declined to be considered for secretary of energy because he did not want to divest himself of millions in personal holdings, as the law would have required. He headed the steering committee for Republican Rob Mosbacher's 1984 U.S. Senate campaign. The latter is a son of another member of the ninety-nine.[40]

OVETA CULP HOBBY: Houston publisher whose empire of over $400 million in 1985 was in the name of heirs but reputedly was still largely controlled by her. The daughter of a state representative, she studied law and became parliamentarian of the Texas House, an assistant city attorney, and an unsuccessful legislative candidate before marrying former governor William P. Hobby, *Houston Post* president and publisher. Her son William, Jr. (Bill), parliamentarian of the state senate as well as executive editor of the paper, won the powerful lieutenant governorship in November 1972 with substantial backing—monetary and editorial—from his family and the *Post*. George Brown, a close friend of Oveta, was a big contributor, too. Bill, a moderate conservative who gained the respect of many liberals and conservatives, was lieutenant governor and presiding officer of the senate longer than anyone in Texas history.

Oveta was the director of the Women's Army Auxiliary Corps in World War II. In 1952 she backed Eisenhower, who appointed her as the first secretary of the Department of Health, Education, and Welfare, where she served from 1953 to 1955. From 1955, when she succeeded her husband as president of the *Post*, until 1983, when the paper was sold, Hobby was a major presence in local and state politics. In general, she was a moderate conservative, but she backed Allan Shivers for governor against Ralph Yarborough at a time when Shivers was an outspoken supporter of Senator Joe McCarthy.[41]

NELSON BUNKER HUNT: Dallas oilman worth at least $900 million in 1985. A member of the John Birch Society's governing board, he had had many other affiliations with far right organizations, including the Manion Forum, the Southern States Industrial Council—"an organization opposed to unions, civil rights, foreign aid, and the Tennessee Valley Authority"—and the International Committee for the Defense of Christian Culture, founded by an ex-Nazi. In 1968 he set up a secret $1 million trust fund to convince General Curtis LeMay to be George Wallace's American party running mate. A big contributor to Billy Graham's organization, he also helped found Campus Crusade for Christ, to which he pledged $10 million in the late 1970s. In 1980 Hunt sponsored a rally of four thousand people at his ranch for evangelist Pat Robertson, who was then testing the presidential campaign waters. In 1981 Hunt reportedly made a $1 million contribution to Moral Majority, the ultraconservative religious organization. His friends among right-wing notables included Dallas congressman Jim Collins, who challenged Lloyd Bentsen in 1984, labeling him a "liberal"; southern senators Jesse Helms, Strom Thurmond, and James Eastland; and John Connally. In 1982 Hunt and fellow Republicans raised $350,000 for the right-wing National Conservative Political Action Committee (NCPAC), much of which went toward efforts to defeat Bentsen and Congressman Jim Wright. He was the largest financial supporter—as of 1983—of the Institute of American Relations, one of several nonprofit foundations controlled by Jesse Helms that undertook research on a host of social, economic, and foreign policy problems. During the 1984 Republican national convention in Dallas, Hunt hosted a $1,000-a-plate party for NCPAC, attended by 1,650 people, that the *New York Times* described as "certainly the most elaborate of many social extravaganzas related to the Republican National Convention."[42]

RAY LEE HUNT: Leader of Hunt's "second family," worth over $300 million in 1985. In the 1970s, he began to turn up in conservative Texas political circles. He was a member of the Dallas coordinating committee for Dolph Briscoe in 1972, chairman of Young Men for Bush in George Bush's unsuccessful 1970 U.S. Senate race; chairman of Young Men for James Collins in Collins's 1970 congressional race; and a founder of the Aardvark Society, a conservative young people's "economic dinner-discussion group." He was also active in civic-minded Dallas clubs and committees that his father and half-brothers had ignored and by the 1980s was in the leadership group of the influential Dallas Citizens Council. Hunt was the principal backer of *D, the Magazine of Dallas*, one of the more successful city-based magazines founded during the 1970s. He also gained control of *Houston City Magazine*. He was on Phil Gramm's finance committee in his 1984 Senate race.[43]

J. ERIK JONSSON: One of the founders of Texas Instruments, worth $75–100 million in 1979. Mayor of Dallas for several years, Jonsson was described "as one of the half-dozen most important people in the city's history—the man who brought Dallas back from the depths of its post-JFK assassination disgrace and, through his 'Goals for Dallas' program, plotted the city's development into the next century."[44]

S. M. McASHAN, JR.: Retired chairman of and major stockholder in Houston "*Fortune* 500" company, Anderson Clayton, he was worth $75–100 million in 1979. His wife Susan—the daughter of Will Clayton, company founder and under secretary of state for economic affairs under Harry Truman—sometimes gave to liberal causes and politicians. Susan's sister, Ellen St. John Garwood, made headlines in 1985 by donating $115,000 toward the purchase of a helicopter and supplies for anti-Sandinista troops in Nicaragua. McAshan was a longtime member of the Business Council, a national organization of top businessmen who coordinate political strategies of big business.[45]

W. A. ("MONTY") MONCRIEF, SR., AND W. A. ("TEX") MONCRIEF, JR.: Fort Worth oilmen together worth over $400 million in 1985, they were contributors to candidates of both parties, primarily conservatives. Tex gave Governor Clements $17,500 in 1982. Mike Moncrief, another of Monty's sons, was a former state legislator and then county judge of Tarrant County (Fort Worth)—its chief executive officer. House Majority

Leader Jim Wright unsuccessfully went to bat for Monty in 1980 after the old man's grandson had cut Wright in on an oil deal that led to quick profits for him. Wright lobbied Anwar Sadat on behalf of Monty's oil venture off the coast of the Sinai Peninsula. He also appealed to former secretary of state Cyrus Vance and the Carter White House. When Wright's pressure was disclosed, his office described his overtures to Sadat as "illustrative of the effort he customarily extends" for businessmen in his district.[46]

ROBERT MOSBACHER: Houston oilman and a renowned yachtsman worth $150 million in 1984, Mosbacher was a close friend of fellow oilman George Bush. A member of the National Petroleum Council, which advises the interior department on energy matters, he was also a major GOP fund-raiser. As national finance chairman for Gerald Ford in 1976, Mosbacher warned "that the alternative [to Ford] is going to be socialism." He was also national finance chairman of Bush's 1980 presidential bid and cochairman of the Republican National Finance Committee. The *New York Times* mentioned him as a heavyweight in Washington during the Reagan years. Mosbacher was a member of the Eagles—contributors who gave $10,000 or more annually to the GOP. Along with Amarillo corporate raider T. Boone Pickens, Mosbacher hosted a $1,000-a-head luncheon with Reagan and Bush during the 1984 Republican convention in Dallas. His son Robert, Jr., for several years an aide to U.S. senator Howard Baker, ran against Phil Gramm in the 1984 senatorial primary and lost.[47]

H. ROSS PEROT: Founder of the Dallas electronic data management firm, Electronic Data Systems Corp. (EDS), whose net worth of $1.8 billion in 1985 placed him second on the *Forbes* list of the 400 richest Americans. In the 1960s he was a close friend of Richard Nixon and John Mitchell and worked with Mitchell on Nixon's 1968 campaign. Ten to fifteen of Perot's management people worked on it as well while on the company payroll. Perot, in turn, used Nixon's and Mitchell's former law firm in New York for his personal legal matters. In 1974 he reportedly gave $90,000 in political donations, including (with his company's executives) $15,000 to members of the U.S. House Ways and Means Committee and U.S. Senate Finance Committee—both of which oversee Medicaid and Medicare legislation. Perot's firm had major data-processing contracts involving these federal programs. He has often been described as the most influential businessman in Texas politics. When his good friend Governor Clements pushed the legislature to enact "war on drugs" bills, Perot organized and financed a successful lobbying effort resulting in a variety of laws, some of which were strongly opposed by the American Civil Liberties Union. In spite of Perot's $10,000 contribution to Clements in 1982,

Mark White, who defeated Clements, appointed Perot chairman of the state Select Committee on Public Education (SCOPE), which Perot largely financed, reportedly at a cost of $500,000. SCOPE was instrumental in enacting some of the most significant school reforms in decades. Felton West, a reporter, criticized Perot's private financing of SCOPE and said "the money he spent for hired lobbyists pushing his education goals made him the most potent force during the legislative fight over changes." He is a man of great energy, with much time to devote to politics. He is seen as deeply conservative on many issues, but pragmatic. *Texas Business* magazine gave him its first "Texan of the Year" award in 1984.[48]

ARTHUR E. TEMPLE, JR.: Heir to a vast East Texas lumber empire, he was estimated in 1979 to be worth $50–75 million. The Temple family fortune may now exceed $550 million. A liberal on many issues, Temple is a committed environmentalist and was an early supporter of racial integration in the "Deep South" area of Texas where he lives. Temple is called by some "the most powerful man in East Texas." The Temple family became the largest Time, Inc., shareholder in 1973, selling their timber concern to Time in exchange for 15 percent of its stock. Temple became Time's vice-chairman. His son Arthur III ("Buddy") was a moderate-liberal legislator in the 1970s. Heavily financed by his father in 1980, he became the first challenger in forty-two years to beat an incumbent commissioner on the Texas Railroad Commission, the state's energy regulator. He was also the only candidate to outspend an incumbent commissioner on a regulatory board whose incumbents can depend on lavish funding by oil, gas, and transportation interests. Arthur III ran for the Democratic gubernatorial nomination in 1982, got into a runoff with Attorney General Mark White, then bowed out in the name of party unity against Clements. He spent $1.3 million on his primary campaign; his father paid off loans of more than $1 million.[49]

These sketches underscore the intense political involvement of many of the super rich, mainly as conservatives or reactionaries, but with a sprinkling of moderates and an occasional liberal. Significantly, they were involved not simply as outsiders pressuring government in conventional ways; they were often part of that government themselves. One of the ninety-nine sat on a school board; two were governors; another had a son who was a legislator and then chief executive of a major urban county; one had been a cabinet member whose father, husband, and son were legislator, governor, and lieutenant governor, respectively. Many had sat on state and national agencies and commissions. Few indeed had not made considerable political donations. For several, politics was a consuming passion.

Upper-class Cohesion

The ninety-nine and their likes stand at the apex of the very wealthy. What about the rest of the richest 2 percent of Texans as well as the top managers? Are they sufficiently united in their politics to merit being called a class? Because they are a relatively small group, polls of the general population do not include enough of them to provide an answer to this question. Two studies bear on the issue.

The first was a poll of Texas Manufacturers Association (TMA) officials in 1958, when conservatives were still in control of the state Democratic party. James Soukup and his colleagues sent questionnaires to officials in widely scattered areas of the state. They found that whatever the officials' party preference and wherever they lived, they overwhelmingly supported conservatives. Eighty-seven percent had voted for all Republican presidential candidates in the past three elections, including Thomas Dewey, who won only 25 percent of the Texas popular vote in 1948. Eighty-five percent preferred conservative Democrats or Republicans. Six percent indicated other party preferences. Among those whose party preference was Democratic, 74 percent had voted consistently for Republican presidential candidates since 1948.[50]

Another telling illustration of upper-class cohesion is revealed by the candidate preferences of major Texas political donors in 1972. The Citizens' Research Foundation (CRF), whose analyses of campaign financing are among the most authoritative in the nation, published a list of contributors and lenders of $10,000 or more to federal candidates or committees in 1972 as well as to candidates for state offices in twelve states, including Texas.[51] Unfortunately, federal reporting laws contained significant loopholes prior to April 7, 1972, when the Federal Election Campaign Act of 1971 went into effect; the same was true of Texas statutes, which, in addition, were and still are haphazardly enforced. This may account for the fact that the CRF report did not even list Dolph Briscoe as a contributor or lender in 1972, in spite of his having spent over $1 million of his own money on three races he made for governor, including his first successful one in 1972.[52] Nor does the CRF data include the name of Clinton Manges, a millionaire South Texas rancher who gave Briscoe $15,000 in cash for his campaign in 1972. Briscoe did not report the donation because, as he later explained when the fact came to light, he had planned to return it but never could get Manges to come by and pick it up.[53] Nevertheless, the CRF report contains the best systematic information available on Texas spending patterns in an election in which the choice between George McGovern and Richard Nixon was billed by Nixon supporters as "a showdown on the free enterprise system."[54]

The CRF data for 1972 indicate that 183 Texans—including twenty-five of "the ninety-nine"—gave or loaned state or federal candidates at least $10,000 (almost $24,000 in 1985 buying power). More actually did so, some giving very large amounts; chapter 7 will show how some of the very rich were able to disguise much of their giving in that particular election.

In the races for president and governor and for Texas's U.S. Senate seat, the lieutenant governor's office, and various congressional and state legislative seats, almost none of "the ninety-nine" who contributed supported a liberal candidate. The noteworthy exceptions were John and Dominique de Menil, transplanted French natives whose liberal tastes in politics, as in art, set them apart from many in the Texas upper class.

As table 4.1 shows, 20 (15.3 percent) of the 131 presidential backers gave only to liberal/moderate candidates. Ten (8.6 percent) of the 116 contributors to the governor's race gave only to liberals. (The preferences of the twenty-five members of "the ninety-nine" in the table were similar to those of the other big donors.) By contrast, the Democratic runoff primary electorate gave 45 percent of its vote to Frances Farenthold, the liberal Democratic gubernatorial candidate, in spite of her severe underfunding and consequent limited media access.

The import of these figures is clear. If one focuses not on the party of

Table 4.1

Support from Major Texas Donors to Conservative, Moderate, and Liberal Candidates in Presidential and Texas Gubernatorial Races, 1972[a]

		Donors Giving to Presidential Candidates[b]				
		Conservative	Liberal/ Moderate	Split	No Support	Row Total
Donors	Conservative	70	7	1	27	105
Giving to	Liberal	2	6	0	2	10
Texas	Split	0	1	0	0	1
Gubernatorial	No support	37	6	1	23	67
Candidates[c]	Column total	109	20	2	52	183

Source: Calculated from data in Barbara D. Paul et al., *CRF Listing of: Political Contributors and Lenders of $10,000 or More in 1972* (Princeton, N.J.: Citizens' Research Foundation, 1975).

[a] Cell entries show the number of the 183 Texas donors who gave or loaned $10,000 or more in any state or federal election in 1972 who contributed to candidates of various ideological proclivities in either the presidential or the Texas gubernatorial race or, in some cases, to neither. Thus in the conservative–conservative cell, 70 donors gave only to conservatives in both races; in the liberal–liberal cell, 6 donors gave only to liberals in both races; in the no support–no support cell, 23 donors did not contribute either to a presidential candidate or Texas gubernatorial candidate, contributing instead to other federal or state races.

[b] Conservative presidential candidates were Nixon, Mills, and Wallace; liberals or moderates were McGovern, Muskie, Humphrey, Shriver, Sanford, and Jackson.

[c] Of the many gubernatorial candidates in 1972, only Frances Farenthold (Democrat) and Ramsey Muñiz (La Raza Unida party) were liberals.

the candidate to whom donations were made but rather on the candidate's ideology, the rich and the corporate elite give evidence of great solidarity, a fact prefigured in chapter 3, in which voting behavior in the affluent suburbs was examined. About 90 percent of the big donors gave only to conservatives in either presidential or gubernatorial elections. While the 1972 presidential elections may have been unusual in that McGovern was perceived as outside the Democratic mainstream, a casual survey of the spending patterns of the Texas big rich reveals no significant differences in other years, except 1964, when much money went to LBJ, long a powerful defender of oil interests and a potent ally, in Texas-level matters, of the state's business establishment.

The Political Strength of the Upper Class

In his work on southern politics, V. O. Key wrote of "an impressive solidarity of the upper economic classes that disciplines without mercy, where it can, those who would arouse and rise to power with the votes of the lower third."[55] The purpose of the present chapter has been to see whether upper-class solidarity is a fact in Texas. Examining the big rich—those Texans worth $50 million or more—we learned that about two-thirds inherited their money or married into it. Of white Anglo-Saxon stock, they were highly educated. They were closely linked through blood and friendship to other members of their class and affiliated with the old-line, upper-class religious denominations.

Much the same pattern emerged when we examined the corporate elite—directors of the largest Texas-based corporations and foundations. They, too, largely inherited their status, 79 percent coming from managerial and professional families, only 2 percent from the urban working class. Their ethnic backgrounds were almost identical to those of the big rich. Moreover, membership in the corporate elite appeared to overlap significantly with that of the personal wealth-holding class. Twenty-seven of the ninety-nine big rich, indeed, belonged to the corporate elite in the late 1970s. And because of the princely compensation received by many in that elite, a good number themselves amassed enough wealth to become millionaires.

Thus, in terms of their economic and social position, both the personally rich and the top managers appear to have more in common with each other than with those below them. An examination of the politics of the upper class is consistent with this. Solidarity, measured in three ways—by voting returns from silk-stocking precincts, by questionnaire responses from officials of the preeminent Texas manufacturing trade group, and by political spending patterns of $10,000-plus Texas donors—turned out to be quite high among the top managers and big rich who together made up what Mills called the "corporate rich." Approximately 90 percent consistently favored conservatives, whether Democrats or Republicans, in elections that pitted conservatives against moderates or liberals. Blacks were the only other demographic group in Texas politics that typically voted with such near-unanimity, although in the opposite direction.

The top members of the Texas upper class, while likely to be connected in some way with oil, are men and women whose interests often extend beyond the boundaries of a particular firm or industry. They move easily from boardroom to boardroom and in the process develop a classwide perspective that takes in the big picture. They are the antithesis of the economic cowboy, the rugged individualist, or the loner. They are well aware of the need to work together to elect and then to keep in line candidates who understand the business point of view.

The corporate rich are the busy rich and also the political rich. They run the influential Texas Research League, a business-oriented research and pressure group. They make up the influential Dallas Citizens Council and the board of the Houston Chamber of Commerce. They host the frequent fund-raisers for conservative politicos and fly to Washington to meet with top officials of both parties and chairmen of the major congressional committees. Many are on a first-name basis with the U.S. House or Senate majority leader and important committee chairmen, and in any given administration, they may be friends with the president or the vice president as well.

It would be a mistake to assume that the Texas upper class is a ruling class, however much it might wish to be one. These profiles of the big rich reveal significant instances of their failure to achieve their goals, to elect their candidates, and to defeat their enemies. And indeed, because they are so small a part of the overall electorate, they must depend at election time on the help of the classes below them—especially the members of the upper-middle class who, as tables 3.2 and 3.3 in the previous chapter demonstrate, provide this assistance.

Yet an honest appraisal cannot ignore the inordinate power of the upper class. "The larger problem for a political democracy is not that of a few self-seeking individuals," wrote Robert Engler in his classic work, *The Politics of Oil*, "but rather the voice and representation far out of proportion to numbers accorded the economically powerful in the processes of public policy making."[56] When they have dug in and decided to stand their ground—by opposing a corporate profits tax, industrial safety regulation, laws encouraging union organizing, or more humane welfare payments—the upper class and their political retainers have usually prevailed against their liberal enemies concentrated in the working class. If the Texas corporate rich are not a ruling class, they are not just another class.

Nor are they just first among equals. In state politics, they are a formidable force that wins more often than it loses in confrontations with what Key called "the lower third," the largely depoliticized masses that party realignment has not succeeded in mobilizing.

5

Upper-Class Institutions

EXCERPTS from the 1969 diary of Dallas entrepreneur Jim Ling, founder of Ling-Temco-Vought (LTV) Corporation:

March 22

Even before I picked up the phone this afternoon, I knew something big had happened. I was at Brook Hollow Country Club. . . . [LTV's general counsel] had just got a call from Washington. . . . We were about to have an antitrust suit filed against us.

March 24

We were wheels up out of Grand Prairie, where we keep our jet at the LTV Aerospace plant, at six this morning. . . . When we landed at Dulles International, Ted Mann of our Washington office was waiting to brief us and drive us into the city. . . .

There were a lot of reporters hanging around when we arrived at the Justice Department, so we were taken up in the private elevator of the Attorney General.

April 9

I have a meeting this afternoon in New York with our investment bankers . . . to consider some of the options we have for getting out from under. . . . The plane we were taking, the one I usually fly, the jet Falcon 570L, was parked against the fence. . . .

In the last three years, I've been spending at least 600 hours a year in the air. That means I am airborne roughly fifteen forty-hour weeks a year.

April 10

This morning I got a call from Gus Levy to tell me that Charlie Bluhdorn [head of Gulf & Western, another major conglomerate] had placed an order for 10,000 shares of LTV "to help old Jimmy." Gus also told me that one of his partners had met a former law partner of President Nixon who had said that one of the reasons Justice filed the suit was because of some documents they had found in J&L's files, a master list of suppliers as well as customers.

April 16

We flew up to Chicago this afternoon. I have to make a speech here tomorrow at a luncheon meeting of the National Industrial Conference Board.

April 17

My speech at the Conference Board went over well. A lot of people came over afterward to express their support. But we were supposed to be in Oklahoma City at 4:30 P.M. for a big reception. They had declared it LTV-Wilson Week in Oklahoma. So I rushed like hell to get to the airport. . . . There was no way to make up the lost time, so the Governor couldn't wait to meet us, but the Mayor and a lot of other dignitaries were there.

Tomorrow, Clyde [Skeen, LTV president] and I, who were both born in Oklahoma, are going to get honorary Doctor of Law degrees at Oklahoma Christian College. . . . On Saturday, we go over to Arkansas to meet with Governor Winthrop Rockefeller and then I'll get another degree at the College of the Ozarks.

May 1

Off to Boston this morning. . . .

We stopped at John Hancock Life to talk to Bob Slater, the president, about being on the board of LTV Development Corporation, a company we are thinking about setting up with a broader representation of directors than we have had before, including a West Coast banker and John Murchison, who is from Dallas but is regarded as a national figure in the investment community. . . .

I rehearsed the Harvard speech at the Ritz-Carlton, and I cut it some more. Good turnout, and the audience seemed very sympathetic to our situation. . . .

Next we had a meeting with the economics department of Harvard. . . . Then came the Boston University events, some cocktail parties and the dinner with me speaking. . . .

May 2

We flew down to Washington, where I had a lunch date with Ted Mann and Admirals Tom Walker and Tom Connally, who are among our biggest customers at the Pentagon, both great guys, the epitome of what military people ought to be. We met them at Burning Tree [Country Club], talked awhile over lunch, then played golf.

May 3

Today Ted and I played golf with Judge Hamer Budge, new chairman of the SEC. . . .

That evening I was the guest of *Newsweek* at the White House Correspondents' Dinner. . . .

In about twenty minutes, [Jim] Bishop covered the whole Washington scene with me, including Judge Budge, McLaren, and all the rest. The President arrived, pretty much on time. LBJ would never get any place on time.

May 8

Since one of our biggest long-term creditors is Troy Post [of Dallas], who owns roughly $80 million worth of our 5-percent of 1988 debentures, which he got when we bought Greatamerica Corporation from him, I stopped by to visit with him for a few minutes this evening. . . .

June 27–28

I was invited to a two-day golf outing at Arnold Palmer's home course, Laurel Valley, in Latrobe, Pennsylvania, as the guest of the Mellon Bank. They had invited maybe forty or fifty top executives of American industry to play in a golf tournament. . . .

Friday night, after dinner, Johnny Mayer, the president of the Mellon Bank, introduced Charlie Walker, the Under-secretary of the Treasury. He gave us a briefing on some of the current policies of the Nixon Administration . . . [that] did not sit well with most people present, and they said so. They seemed to think most of Nixon's moves were anti-business. . . .

On one of the days I played with George Love [chairman of Consolidated Coal]. . . . [He] said that I ought to become a member of the [Laurel Valley Country] club. . . . I saw a lot of American industry there that I don't get involved with too often. This seems to be their place, so I might very well join the club.

July 8–12

Off to Alexandria, Minnesota, with Dorothy and the Wilson Schoellkopfs. For the last several years, we have been houseguests here of either the Jim Chambers or the Joe Cowdreys. Jim is my friend, a director of LTV and publisher of the Dallas *Times Herald*, and Joe is the senior man in Dallas with Merrill Lynch. They usually take off for the better part of the summer in this little area. It's a beautiful part of the country, and it's an old watering hole for the old Dallas families that probably dates from the early part of the century, from the days before air conditioning.

July 19

I was supposed to fly to Lubbock this morning for a meeting of the Board of Regents of Texas Tech, of which I am proud to say I am a member. But I had to cancel my appearance because we had too much work to do.

August 19

Up at 5:25, so I read awhile. I have an advance paper from the Hudson Institute, Herman Kahn's think tank, on which I'm privileged to serve as a public trustee.

August 23

I went out to the Cotton Bowl tonight and saw the Dallas Cowboys—I'm on their board—break the Green Bay jinx for the first time.

September 5

Tonight I attended a cocktail party and dinner at the Lancer Club on top of the LTV Tower in honor of Senator John Tower. Some of the Republican hierarchy were there besides John. Erik Jonsson of Texas Instruments, who is Mayor of Dallas, Peter O'Donnell, the young fellow who is head of the Republican organization here, and some others. . . .[1]

In 1969, when his financial empire was under siege by government antitrust lawyers, Jim Ling was no ordinary Texas multimillionaire. His conglomerate, LTV, was ranked by *Fortune* magazine as the fourteenth largest industrial enterprise in the nation, and the decision by the Nixon administration to press antitrust charges put Ling in the national limelight and ultimately led to his downfall.[2] His diary sheds light on a life-style that is common to both the Texas big rich and the corporate elite. More important, it illuminates the institutional arrangements that bring men like Ling together as members of a regional and national upper class and thus is a suggestive introduction to the present chapter, which demonstrates how the Texas upper class is structured through institutional networks.

The World of Status

At the core of the upper class is a status group, a community of people who consider each other as equals or near-equals and everybody else as outsiders. This group gives structure to the business class primarily by reconciling old money with new. Its boundaries in Texas are not so rigid as those delimiting "proper Bostonians" or old family New Orleanians, but they are nonetheless real, and they are maintained in much the same way as elsewhere: by educating the children of the affluent to think and to behave in certain ways; by various rites of passage; and through clubs, summer camps, and fraternities organized to admit only "the best people."

While there are differences from city to city, big money usually wins acceptance by the Texas elite fairly quickly throughout the state—in spectacular cases in one generation, almost always in two. "Texas money used to have different odors," John Leeper, a San Antonio museum curator, once observed. "Cattle money had the most cachet, merchandising was acceptable and oil money was *nouveau*. But the oil money usually came from land that had been owned for a long while, so oil money, too, became okay."[3]

Acceptance of new money never comes automatically. John Bainbridge could still write in 1961 that no officer of Houston's Allegro Club was "in oil."[4] On the other hand, there is a pragmatism among the inheritors of Texas old money, who understand the need to replenish their ranks with newly created wealth, "sucking upwards the ablest elements of the lower classes," as Paul M. Sweezy once put it.[5] The old rich thus open their doors to the more seemly of the new moguls and corporate executives.

Within a year of his arrival in Houston, John Bookout, the president of Shell Oil, became a member of the Ramada, one of the choice Houston clubs, thus leapfrogging a line of aspirants who had been on the waiting list for years.[6]

The Texas upper class, like their counterparts everywhere, reside in a few exclusive enclaves. "Down in Houston," Congressman Wright Patman used to say, "there are some neighborhoods so rich that every flea has his own dog." Patman probably had in mind River Oaks, a subdivision of Houston with its own police force, or the Memorial Drive area. In San Antonio, the rich live in Olmos Park, Terrell Hills, and Alamo Heights. In Dallas it is Highland Park. In the suburbs of Fort Worth, it is Westover Hills.

These enclaves are typically walled off by physical barriers—heavy foliage, high brick walls, perhaps a bayou. The socioeconomic barriers are even more formidable. Speaking to a reporter at the nadir of the 1974–1975 recession, Highland Park businessman Al Cooter said, "I can't recall any bad period. Even back in the 1950s when there was supposed to be a bad recession, I never felt it. . . . My wife went out and bought a new three-quarter-length mink the other day."[7]

Blacks, except as servants, are unwelcome. In 1983 a former police officer in Highland Park revealed that the city demanded that its policemen "make illegal searches, seizures, and arrests" of minority persons who did not live there. He decided to cooperate with a federal investigation, he said, "after repeatedly seeing 'people incarcerated who were completely innocent, just because of the color of their skin.' " He had been harassed by city officials and finally fired for refusing to cover up the city's policy.[8]

Houston, Dallas, and Fort Worth have "blue books" that are put together by local social arbiters. The Houston version was first published in 1950. In 1978 it listed the names of about three thousand families, or approximately 3 percent of the city's total. About two-thirds of those listed lived in either River Oaks or the Memorial area.[9]

Elite socialization begins in the intimacy of the family, where children are taught early that they are different from common people and have special entitlements. In more enlightened homes, they are taught that they have special obligations as well.[10] A sense of uniqueness is ingrained by the private schools to which elite children are sent—the "status seminaries," as Peter Cookson and Caroline Persell call them in their study of prep schools.[11] In Texas these have existed for some time, although entry became more competitive after racial desegregation occurred in public schools. In 1975 the headmaster of Houston's St. John's said that the growth in applications was "unbelievable."[12] This upsurge followed court-mandated desegregation in Houston, which impelled residents of a white, high-income area close by St. John's to try to de-annex the portion of Houston Independent School District in which they lived.[13]

Strong bonds develop in the elite schools, most of which are as rigorous as the better-known day schools on the East Coast. St. Stephen's in Austin, Hockaday and St. Mark's in Dallas, Trinity Valley in Fort Worth, Kinkaid and St. John's in Houston are the more exclusive ones.[14] During children's school years, summer camps along the Guadalupe River in the Texas hill country provide further socialization for society children. In the tradition of the Eastern rural boarding school, the camps get the children out of the big cities and into the manicured loveliness of the countryside. Among the more famous ones are Camp Kickapoo, Waldemar, Mystic, Stewart, and Heart o' the Hills. The waiting lists are long.[15]

Unlike the Eastern elites, those in Texas, as a rule, send their children not to Ivy League schools but to the University of Texas at Austin, where they join the more selective fraternities and sororities. Twenty-eight percent of the male heads of family in a sample drawn from the Houston Blue Book in the late 1970s held a degree from Texas, and another 11 percent attended Rice University. (In Dallas, Southern Methodist University would probably have ranked second behind the University of Texas.) Next in order were Texas A&M (8 percent), Yale (4 percent), and Princeton (3 percent). G. William Domhoff's analysis of the graduates of St. John's in Houston who went to college between 1951 and 1973 revealed that, while more went to the University of Texas (124) and Rice (68) than to any other, 128 went to Harvard, Stanford, Yale, Princeton, or Williams.[16]

Society daughters make their debut while at the university. The first debut in Texas was held in San Antonio in 1880 and Dallas followed eight years later.[17] The young ladies are presented to society between the ages of nineteen and twenty-two by a small number of clubs—Allegro in Houston or the German Club in San Antonio, for example. In Dallas the Idlewild, dominated by bankers, ranchers, developers, and oilmen, using secret criteria, typically presents about seven debutantes each year. As one observer describes the essence of coming out in Dallas, it requires not only money but endurance:

> From the time the young woman makes her first bow in her white gown at the Idlewild Ball at the end of October, until she makes her final bow in her pastel gown at the Terpsichorean Ball three months later, she will have attended two to three parties each day in her honor, six days each week; purchased an inestimable number of ball gowns, cocktail dresses, luncheon dresses, suits and casual wear; written approximately 1,600 thank-you notes, and learned how to make a full court bow without toppling as well as how to remain cordial in the face of battle fatigue.[18]

DeWitt Ray 3d, a past president of Idlewild, summed up the philosophy behind what might superficially appear to be nothing but a series of parties for the benefit of the debutantes themselves: "Our main question always is: 'How can we involve the best people, the ones who have made the strongest impact, more directly into the community?' . . . So we don't seek out the debs just for the frivolity of having a party. . . . Everything is tied in. Civic, business and social affairs. This is a community where people work with folks they know, and surround themselves with the best of everything." The best of everything, in the case of the parents of a Dallas debutante, is likely to cost between $50,000 and $500,000 for the season's festivities.[19] The same point made by the Idlewild president was stressed in the chairman's fiftieth anniversary message to the members of Houston's Allegro: "The whole affair tends to pull the Society together on several age levels."[20]

After university and professional school, when the men have settled into a career, there are the men's clubs—"the glue, the binding agent of the downtown business community," according to Ray Watts, manager of the Houston Club, one of the city's larger and less exclusive ones that had almost four thousand members in 1980.[21] In the 1970s it was in the three smaller, more exclusive of the five downtown Houston clubs—the Ramada, Coronado, and Tejas—where the corporate elite mixed most intimately with the city's old families. None admitted women, although some let in a few of the members' wives as "associates." The women, excluded as they were from the male clubs, were exclusive as well. A study of the Dallas Junior League by Prudence Mackintosh found that it had "made some concessions—a handful of Jews here, a Spanish surname there, and perhaps a few black transfers—but it remains almost exclusively a WASP enclave."[22] In the Houston clubs, there was a small sprinkling of Jews, although Tejas, most heavily "old family," had none as late as 1979, and others had earlier kept them out. None of the really elite clubs had at that time opened its doors to blacks—or to Mexican Americans, in spite of the clubs' Hispanic names—except as employees.[23]

"On any given workday," Harry Hurt wrote of the Ramada in the mid-1970s, "the main dining room will be crowded with the state's most prestigious Big Corporate figures: John Connally may be lunching with James Elkins or Marvin Collie. Allan Shivers, Robert Stewart, or James Aston may be in town for a meeting of the board of one of their banks. . . . George Brown will usually be there, seated at his favorite right corner table. . . . On the occasions when he lunches with Oveta Hobby, friends can be seen passing by their table, imparting a respectful greeting and bowing noticeably. . . . There is no other place in Texas where so many people nominated as the most powerful in Texas meet so often and for such extended periods."[24]

Texas society, in summary, is the meeting ground where old money meets new and the interests of the two groups are accommodated. From early schooling through adulthood, a network of social institutions develops the class consciousness of the rich. No doubt these institutions have other functions, including the ostensible ones: formal education, entertainment, charity, sport. But their role in maintaining class solidarity, primarily by bringing together the rich as friends, business partners, political co-workers or potential spouses—in other words, their role as a status group—belies the curious notion that in Texas, unlike almost everywhere else, social class does not really matter.

The Corporation in Politics

In 1900 nothing in the state's economy prefigured the scope and influence of the modern business corporation. There were, to be sure, gentlemen of property and standing—the local banker, leading merchants, a scattering of capitalists with big ideas and entrepreneurial know-how. A few, like East Texas lumberman John Henry Kirby or Houston banker Jesse Jones, would become quite wealthy. But the economic base of turn-of-the-century Texas more closely resembled the proto-capitalism described by Adam Smith in 1776 than the business system in 1950.

By 1985 twenty-eight of the *"Fortune* 500"—the nation's largest industrial firms, ranked by sales—were headquartered in the state.[25] Hundreds of other large corporations had mushroomed, many with global sales and production territories, and with employees numbering in the tens of thousands. Huge enterprises based elsewhere in the country were a major presence in Texas as well. The economic position of these institutions today translates into appreciable political power that stems from two sources.

First, as organizations that hierarchically regiment armies of employees, the corporations are bureaucracies as potentially threatening to individual freedom and to the public interest as the governmental bureaucracies that businessmen inveigh against. Second, these corporations control huge financial resources. The largest have funds far greater than the treasuries of all but the world's major nations. In 1973 the combined sales of the four biggest oil companies in the nation—Exxon, Texaco, Mobil, and Gulf—came to $57 billion compared to $8 billion in revenues taken in by the state of Texas. None was headquartered in the state, but all had major political and economic ties to it. The largest three publicly held firms based in Texas that year—Shell, LTV, and Tenneco—had combined revenues of $13 billion.[26]

As a bureaucracy, a corporation has considerable influence on its employees and the public; this influence is often used for political ends. Writing in the *Texas Business Review*, Duane Windsor observed that in 1980, "at least 80 percent of the Fortune 500 firms had a formally organized public affairs function," the purposes of which included "forecasting social and political trends," publishing employee newsletters, "running speak-ers bureaus and economic education programs, and supervising PACs and direct lobbying."[27] Windsor urged Texas businessmen to emulate those firms, but many were already doing so. For example, in-house efforts to propagandize employees appeared to be fairly common. Excerpts from an interview with a Houston employee with Coastal States Gas Corpora-tion in the late 1970s give the flavor of this effort in one major Texas enterprise.

A memo was sent around one day announcing the second phase of "Coastal Action Program," and all of us were requested to attend. Although it was "vol-untary," you knew you'd better go. Times were scheduled for all employees. I put it off till the last session, and then my supervisor insisted that I go.

We went to a special "classroom" with a number of people in the audience. There was coffee, snacks. A three-hour presentation. It began with a film featur-ing the president and other corporation officials. Then an executive—with man-nerisms like a car salesman—got up and explained the nature of the program. Tenneco and others were involved in this program to educate employees about the facts of oil and gas.

Then a very young emotional-seeming man got up. He went over the answers to the quiz, expounding on each answer: "When your neighbor says such and such, you can say, by way of rebuttal, etc., etc."

Then came the really obnoxious part, to me. A slide show that was brilliantly done, not like the juvenile film at first. Very professionally-made. No reference to Coastal States in particular.

I later asked the fellow who it was that produced it, but he was very evasive. It seems like it was produced locally, for the Chamber of Commerce. He said a lot of the companies around town are doing this.

It addressed political issues as they relate to the oil and gas industry. Deregu-lation of natural gas, etc. The slides were connected with materials in a packet, called "Coastal Action Program." Very much anti-federal control.

Then followed a discussion group. People began to ask, "What can I do indi-vidually to help keep government regulation off our back? How can we help the company?" These were questions, I think, from the less sophisticated employ-ees. The executives answered, "Write your congressman." One drew a diagram on the board. Told you who to write.

They announced that an "objective congressman"—[Republican] Bill Archer —would be there for a round-table discussion, to which all employees would be invited in small groups, probably over a week's time.[28]

Employees with liberal values usually learn to keep quiet about them while on the job if they are not protected by unions. There is no statutory or constitutional protection for workers whose private employers fire them for their political views—expressed on or off the job.[29]

At higher command levels, executives may be expected to make political contributions. If they are required to do so, or if they are reimbursed from corporate funds, it is illegal. A report by the Texas Senate Subcommittee on Consumer Affairs, which investigated political activities of Southwestern Bell in 1975, at least suggested that such behavior occurred. The senators discovered that several upper-echelon managers were "routinely 'requested' to make regular contributions to the [company's] political fund." Frequently the executives had no knowledge of where their money was going—that was a matter decided by the company lobbyists who ultimately dispensed it. According to the committee report, "Bell pays its corporate employees to deliver political gifts and to campaign for candidates on company time. This expense is accounted as operating cost and ultimately paid by telephone rate payers."[30]

Corporations sometimes pressure employees to influence lawmakers on issues affecting the firm or the industry. When a legislator proposed a limitation on the growth of bank holding companies at the 1974 constitutional convention, Ben Love, chairman of Texas Commerce Bancshares, one of the state's largest holding companies, sent a memorandum to all division managers urging them to meet with subordinates, explain the "danger" of the proposal to their jobs, and ask them to write letters to their representatives and make personal contacts with them.[31]

Houston Lighting and Power, a major utility, was revealed in 1986 to have organized a program in which it paid its executives bonuses totaling between $20,000 and $100,000 a year regularly to "contact more than two hundred designated public officials ranging from fire marshals to members of Congress."[32]

Texas corporations have long gotten their employees involved at campaign time as well. James Soukup and his colleagues noted that in the 1960 Democratic primary in Houston, "at least twelve of the conservative candidates for precinct chair[persons] were management employees of Sheffield Steel, another nine [worked for] Humble Oil, and several others [were management employees with] Gulf Oil, . . . A. O. Smith Corporation, Tennessee Gas, Sohio Petroleum, and Brown and Root." Many won.[33]

Texas corporations also use their money unabashedly to propagandize nonemployees. In the 1970s, businesses throughout the state decided that the principles of free enterprise were not being sufficiently inculcated in the schools and universities. Businessmen donated endowed "free enterprise chairs" to universities, and in 1981 the legislature passed a law requiring students to take a high school course in economics "with emphasis on the free enterprise system and its benefits."[34] College professors received handsome brochures from oil companies offering from their speakers' bureau "a number of specialists who can discuss energy- and business-related issues—free of charge—before your group or organization."[35] Corporations got school systems to introduce packaged probusiness programs on free enterprise in the classroom. Houston Natural Gas, for example, persuaded twenty-three school districts in the Houston area, including the Houston district itself, to participate in a yearlong program called "Economics for Young Americans." The program provided "more than 200 secondary schools with special audiovisual material." Industry representatives were made available to classroom teachers. Students were urged to enter a theme-writing contest based on the meaning of free enterprise. The material was developed by the politically conservative U.S. Chamber of Commerce.[36]

The schools themselves sometimes took up the cause of business propaganda on their own. The superintendent for instruction of the Houston Independent School District (HISD) in 1977 refused to remove anti-union pamphlets used in classes on the free enterprise system, ignoring objections by local labor leaders. One pamphlet, entitled *Unions Are Obsolete*, referred to union members as "goons" and contained other such derogatory terms. It was printed by the United States Industrial Council, a so-called "right-to-work group." Another was entitled *The Absurdity of OSHA* (the federal Occupational Safety and Health Administration). The superintendent of schools prevented the pamphlets' further distribution when three prolabor state senators said they would not vote for a school bill he favored unless HISD backed down.[37]

The political power of large individual Texas corporations is vast, but it is vaster still when they join together with others to pursue common political interests. Such coalitions do not result from a grand conspiracy. Partly they result from the constant intermingling of leaders of the business class and the development of cooperative attitudes.

But more than random mingling is involved. If there is not a single, gigantic conspiracy, there are continual "mini-conspiracies"—planned meetings of like-minded members of the upper class to develop strategies for projects large and small, and often with political overtones. "It is not by chance if [corporate executives] Boone Pickens of Amarillo, Ben Love of Houston and Bill Clements of Dallas all meet at [former U.S. Ambassador to Britain] Anne Armstrong's ranch in South Texas," says Dallas public relations man Andy Stern, a corporate image maker. "People like this get together because they are concerned with a variety of issues that affect all Texans."[38]

It is useful, then, to examine some of the organizations that bring the corporate rich and the politicians together on a regular basis.

The Corporate Law Firms

One of these organizations is the metropolitan corporate law office, as epitomized by those Houston firms known as the Big Three: Vinson &

12. Anne Armstrong. A South Texas rancher and influential Republican, Armstrong was named U.S. ambassador to England by President Reagan, with whom she here shares the stage. Courtesy of the *Texas Observer*.

Elkins, Fulbright & Jaworski, and Baker & Botts. They are Texas versions of the blue-chip Wall Street law factory.

Vinson & Elkins and Fulbright & Jaworski are among the largest law firms in the nation, and Baker & Botts is not far behind. Vinson & Elkins, the state's largest in 1983, ranked seventh nationally in terms of the number of lawyers on the payroll. In 1986, the Big Three employed 1,063 lawyers. The five other largest Houston firms employed another 640.[39] The city of Houston's legal department that year employed 63 lawyers, at least one of whom—the city attorney—had been recruited from one of the big firms. (Recruitment, when it occurs between the city and the big firms, is likely to be in the other direction; starting salaries in the firms hovered at mid-decade around $50,000, compared to $30,000 for city lawyers.)[40]

The law factory is a big business in its own right. Vinson & Elkins and Fulbright & Jaworski were among the twenty-one law firms in the nation with 1986 gross revenues of over $100 million.[41] Partners are the senior members who own the firm. Associates are usually young lawyers who generate most of the fees through an arduous work schedule, spurred on by the hope of becoming partners themselves. In 1983, the Big Three's new partners, typically in their early or mid-thirties, earned around $100,000, and partners who had been in their firms longer may have earned as much as half a million dollars.[42] Many of the top partners are millionaires.

As with the other pillars of the upper class, the elite law firms have traditionally been comprised overwhelmingly of white, Anglo-Saxon Protestant males. A 1980 survey of the 1,045 lawyers in Houston's largest firms turned up only ten blacks, and none had become partners at that time.[43] Women and, to a lesser extent, minorities were recruited more assiduously in the 1980s, however. Women now make up a sizable number of the younger lawyers.

As their name implies, corporate lawyers sell their labor primarily to corporations and to other select clients who can afford them. Corporations, even those with their own in-house counsel, usually depend on those large law firms whose size has allowed them to develop a range of specialties. For their money, clients get lawyers who pursue the kind of law practice "in which no stone is left unturned, no matter how seemingly insignificant, and with virtually no regard for time or money," according to James Stewart, a former big-firm lawyer himself.[44]

The firms' income and political influence derive largely from the corporate clients for whom they work, and until quite recently this has led the firms to discourage employees from offering free services to public interest causes—*pro bono publica* work, as it is called—except in very unusual cases. A spectacular example of such cases was conservative Democrat Leon Jaworski's service as the special Watergate prosecutor who drove Richard Nixon from office. But while he was willing to bend the rules for himself, he left no doubt in employees' minds how he felt about their using their talents for *pro bono* work.

"How would a client who pays us a retainer react if he found that one of our boys was sitting on the other side helping to agitate a lawsuit against him?" he responded in 1973 to reporter Griffin Smith's question about *pro bono* work for an environmental group "like the Sierra Club or the League of Conservation Voters," which might ask a lawyer in his firm to contribute time in a class action suit on behalf of citizens seeking to stop industrial pollution or freeway construction. "We can't trample on our clients' interests by turning one of our boys loose to foment litigation."[45]

Ironically, the need for *pro bono* work is probably greater in Texas than in the Northeast, where such work is an established tradition among corporate firms. Trying to persuade big-firm lawyers to give free legal services to the needy, state Supreme Court Justice John Hill estimated in 1985 that more than five hundred thousand of the poor in Texas could not afford a lawyer to handle civil problems. Only one poor person in ten had access to free legal services, he said.[46]

By the mid-1980s, a younger generation of lawyers appeared to be responding to such appeals. Barbara Rodnofsky with Vinson & Elkins was honored by the Texas Young Lawyers Association for her *pro bono* work on AIDS-related issues as well as on immigration and criminal law. Scott Atlas, also with Vinson & Elkins, gained public attention for his work on behalf of poor criminal defendants and for organizing lawyers around the state to represent indigent clients on appeal. Lawyers from Baker & Botts, Fulbright & Jaworski, and other Texas corporate firms were also involved in such efforts.[47] For most of the postwar period, however, the attitudes of the Big Three were markedly different, and it is unclear still today how representative the new *pro bono* lawyers are.

Each of the Big Three was traditionally connected to one of the state's leading banks, which have since become integrated into large multibank holding companies. "Judge" James Elkins, a longtime power broker in Texas, founded what became the flagship of First City Bancorporation. The firm and the bank grew together. Both banker and lawyer, Elkins brought many of the new rich oilmen to his bank, and his firm handled their legal problems. Bankers know what businesses are new, what their problems are, and the kind of legal work that is needed. Having inside connections to a bank is therefore quite useful. In the old days, Elkins's firm would hire "the sons of clients and judges"— "young men," reporter Smith gently put it, "whose legal abilities were not always readily apparent."[48] These appointments seemed to pay off in other ways, however.

Baker & Botts has long had close ties with the late Jesse Jones's banking empire, now embodied in Texas Commerce Bancshares. Fulbright & Jaworski was linked closely to Bank of the Southwest, which in the 1970s became the flagship of Southwest Bancshares, another of the big holding companies. So tight were the connections that when Southwest Bancshares merged with Mercantile of Dallas, Fulbright & Jaworski tried for a while to negotiate a merger with Mercantile's Dallas firm, Hughes & Hill.[49]

Another interlock occurs through "outside counsel," whereby senior law partners become directors of corporations, sometimes exercising real managerial power. Nationally the job of outside counsel has been around

13. The Texas establishment at its zenith. (Left to right) former governor Allan Shivers, U.S. Supreme Court Justice Tom Clark, corporate lawyer "Judge" James Elkins, and Houston insurance mogul Gus Wortham at a reception at the University of Texas. Courtesy of the Barker Texas History Center.

at least since the 1880s. "The lawyer now boldly enters into the business end of his client's transactions," legal scholar John R. Dos Passos wrote in 1907, "[and] he sells him prudence and experience, sometimes even usurping the client's discretion and judgment."[50] From its inception, the role of outside counsel was criticized by those who asserted that business considerations tend to skew professional objectivity. It continues to be, both by the bar and federal regulators.[51]

Each of the Big Three is interlocked through outside counsel with several corporations. A study of the phenomenon revealed that Baker & Botts lawyers sat on the boards of twelve companies in 1974–1975.[52] In 1974 it ranked among the top five law firms in the nation "in terms of total fees collected from corporations on whose boards their partners sat." Altogether fifteen corporate law firms in Houston and another fifteen in Dallas were linked with business corporations through such interlocks. In some cases, two or more major Houston law firms were linked through common membership on the board of large banks or industrial companies. In all, forty-six Texas law firms were interlocked with seventy-five different corporations, twenty-four of which were the largest Texas-based corporations at that time. Most of the links were to oil companies or banks.[53]

The major corporate law firms exert political influence in several ways. Many of the leading figures in conservative Texas politics have been ensconced in the state's better-known firms: James Elkins (father and son),

John Connally, Leon Jaworski, James Baker III, and lobbyist Searcy Bracewell in Houston; Democratic national party chairman and presidential adviser Robert Strauss in Dallas; lobbyist Ed Clark and former congressman Joe Kilgore in Austin; and power broker Tom Sealy in Midland.

John Connally went to Vinson & Elkins after his stint as governor, and his presence and contacts brought the firm much business. In return, he found the prestige of the firm useful in launching his various business and political efforts in the 1970s and 1980s. When he was under indictment for alleged Watergate era crimes, his situation at Vinson & Elkins paid off well. Richard Keeton, one of the firm's rising stars and son of the emeritus dean of the University of Texas Law School, went on semidetached status for a year while working on the Connally case. Indeed, the entire firm was more or less at Connally's disposal during those tense days. "You might say it's an all-hands-on-deck situation," one of the lawyers said. "If you get a call to help out, by God you drop everything and *help*!"[54] Connally was later acquitted.

Because they are partnerships, not corporations, the big firms are exempt from the state law that prevents corporations from contributing directly to political candidates. Such firms are typically big spenders. With the rise of political action committees (PACs) in the 1970s, their activity in this realm appears to have increased. In 1982, Fulbright & Jaworski's two state PACs gave $100,000; Baker & Botts's, $148,000; and Vinson & Elkins's, $185,900. The latter gave more to candidates for federal office in 1981–1982 than did any other law firm in the nation.[55]

Their influence in the area of campaign finance, however, was not unchallenged in the 1980s, as trial lawyers raised considerable sums and helped elect a far more liberal Supreme Court—the state's highest civil appeals court—than the Big Three had been used to. Their clout, nonetheless, was still acknowledged. "They are able to raise big bucks—not necessarily from the law firm itself, but [from] the clients they represent," state Supreme Court Justice C. L. Ray told reporter Lee Jones. "I have tried real hard not to make any enemies out of that group, knowing I might run again."[56] According to one Texas senator, "All the state officials go down and see them, hat in hand. . . . You have to go through the firm before you get to the client. You have to run the gauntlet first."[57] A partner at Vinson & Elkins ruminated: "If you are going into Texas politics, you can assume that VE will be there throughout your career . . . for good or ill, of course."[58]

Judge Elkins's political power in Texas derived in large measure from his fund-raising abilities. Elkins's son, James, Jr., followed in his father's footsteps both as a banker and a power broker, although not a lawyer. He took the helm of his father's bank, which was still connected to the law firm through board interlocks in the 1980s (Connally sat on the bank's board as Vinson & Elkins's representative for some years). Elkins, Jr., is married to the former Margaret Wiess, daughter of a founder of Humble Oil, which later became part of Exxon.

The other big firms are also thought to make use of their corporate connections in raising political money. Fulbright & Jaworski has long been connected with Anderson Clayton, a *Fortune* 500 multinational controlled until 1986 by one of "the ninety-nine" and his family. Two of the three trustees of the M. D. Anderson Foundation, with 1983 assets valued at $66 million, formed from Anderson Clayton profits, were Fulbright & Jaworski lawyers. The foundation owned a major share of Southwest Bancshares, since merged with MCorp, and two Fulbright & Jaworski partners sat on the bank's board at the time of Lee Jones's study.[59] Big-firm political influence is also exerted through the state and local bar associations.[60] Members of the Big Three claimed in the 1970s that they held "a virtual veto over Harris County judicial appointments."[61] A senior partner in another Houston law firm obviously had these kinds of connections in mind when he said that the Big Three are "kind of the glue between the political system and the business community." [62]

The big firms supply some of the ablest members of the federal, state, and local political elite—attorneys general and state supreme court judges; leaders of conservative coalitions, such as the chairman of the George Wallace-for-President forces in Texas; assistants to the top state-wide officeholders; county chairpersons of both parties and national chairperson of one; major lobbyists; federal judges; campaign directors for prominent conservative candidates, including presidential ones, at the state and national level; strategists in legislative redistricting battles; advisers to every president since Eisenhower. When the Business Roundtable, consisting of 180 chief executives of the leading U.S. corporations, took a hard line in opposing the 1977 consumer protection bill then before Congress, it hired Leon Jaworski, still at the pinnacle of influence after the Watergate scandals, to contact members of the House Government Operations Committee.[63] When the Houston Chamber of Commerce began looking for someone to replace former mayor Louie Welch as president, William Harvin, a top Baker & Botts attorney, led the search committee.[64]

The boundaries separating public office from the big firms are highly permeable, as an oilman might say. When Ronald Reagan tapped two Vinson & Elkins lawyers for subcabinet posts (one in Treasury, one in Justice), nothing seemed less surprising to those who understood the nature of power in Texas. When state supreme court chief justice Joe Greenhill resigned shortly before the 1982 elections, thus making it possible for Republican governor Bill Clements to appoint the judge's successor to the elective post, it appeared entirely normal when Greenhill became a partner with Baker & Botts. When Governor Mark White, who defeated Clements, took office a few months later, it was not remarkable that Pike Powers went on leave from Fulbright & Jaworski to work as White's top assistant.

As these events suggest, the big firms are active participants in revolving-door politics. Taking leaves of absence, their lawyers sit on important regulatory agencies and return to their firms with newly acquired insights and contacts. Most of the big Texas firms have close ties to Austin and Washington. In 1983, Robert Strauss's firm of Akin, Gump, Strauss, Hauer, and Feld had more lawyers in its Washington office—ninety-seven—than it had in Dallas.[65] At one point, Fulbright & Jaworski's Washington staff included Everett Hutchinson, former chairman of the Interstate Commerce Commission and an under secretary of Transportation, and former employees of the Treasury Department, the Securities and Exchange Commission, the Department of Transportation, and the Federal Power Commission (FPC). Washington staff with the other Big Three firms at that time included former general counsels for the FPC and the California Public Utilities Commission.[66]

Many members of the big firms' Washington staffs also have had extensive experience in electoral politics, for obvious reasons. After Republican majority leader Howard Baker retired from the U.S. Senate in 1985 and before he became President Reagan's chief of staff, he was a senior partner in the Washington office of Vinson & Elkins, earning a salary in excess of $700,000. He was known as a "rainmaker": "Corporate clients would look at him and think he could give them access in the highest places," another lawyer explained.[67]

Most of the regulatory posts held by Texas big-firm lawyers have been related to oil and gas. The nomination of Vinson & Elkins's Lynn Coleman as general counsel for the newly created U.S. Department of Energy in 1977 focused national attention on the Big Three's revolving-door practices in this industry. "For several years," the New York Times wrote, "there has been steady traffic between Washington energy agencies and Houston law firms."[68] Two Federal Energy Administration (FEA) assistant administrators, as well as the two highest officials in the FEA's general counsel's office, had recently come from Houston corporate law offices.

The big firms are a diamond-hard fact of politics in Texas. Without them, corporate enterprise and state politics would come to a standstill, at least as they now operate. Has their power as a conservative force been diminished by the deaths of the likes of Judge Elkins and Leon Jaworski or with the retirement of John Connally? Perhaps. But there are new leaders always in the making, new opportunities to be seized, and always a demand for the diverse and specialized talents that are big-firm hallmarks. In 1985 the *National Law Journal* published a list of 100 lawyers it considered to be the most powerful in the country. Seven were from Texas. Four worked for Houston's Big Three. Another, Robert Strauss, was a Dallas corporate lawyer.[69]

The Inner Lobby

"Texas political life has been directed by a single moneyed establishment," assert Neal R. Peirce and Jerry Hagstrom, whose study of the fifty American states allows them to speak with authority. "In no other state has the control been so direct and unambiguous."[70] The most visible means of Texas's business-class influence is the lobby. In the 1977 legislative session, there were "over 3,000" registered lobbyists, compared to about four hundred in the state with the next highest number.[71] Over 75 percent of the registered Texas lobbyists in 1981 represented "big business interests."[72] In 1982, the lobby spent an average of "$5,500 per legislator" during the session. At that time the lawmakers' annual salary was $7,200.[73]

Some lobbyists represent a single organization with narrow legislative concerns. Others represent entire industries—the utilities, oil and gas, railroads—or they handle several influential corporations and interests. Then there are those whose clientele are, without exaggeration, a cross section of the entire Texas business class. Lobbyists representing industrial trade groups and class-wide networks constitute what former legislator Frances Farenthold has called "the lobby within the lobby." When a member of this elite corps enters a lawmaker's office, it is an important event. Bob Eckhardt, a legislator and later a congressman, once observed that the Texas lobby operates "like a kind of foreign service, with its ambassadors in Austin representing the business interests in Houston and Dallas and elsewhere. It's become less a purveyor of beef and bourbon than an ambassador for the local chambers of commerce." He was obviously referring to the inner lobby.[74]

Who are these unelected representatives who wield such power? Some are top executives of the major corporations and banks. Some are partners of the big law firms whose primary duty is to lobby. Others are well-heeled public relations operatives or executives of business umbrella groups—the Association of Manufacturers and the Texas Research League, for example, or the metropolitan chambers of commerce.[75] Many are former legislators.

Whatever their background, the members of the inner lobby generally line up together on key class-based issues. "I don't know anywhere else where the people of substance have this type of working political relationship to each other," lawyer Ed Clark said in 1960. "You know, not like it's schemed out, but everybody just gets the idea and they go the same way."[76] Clark, a premier lobbyist himself, was overly modest. He knew quite well how carefully "schemed out" key legislative strategies are.

In any decade over the past fifty years, a few men, usually corporate lawyers representing oil companies or trade groups, stand out as maestros of legislative influence—brilliant practitioners of horse trading, guile, the jovial but serious threat, the offer that can't be refused. It is they who decide when the time is ripe to introduce a regressive tax, to savage organized labor, to gerrymander enemies out of a seat. They help decide on whom to place the big money at election time. They set up private parleys of their peers to discuss election strategy—as happened in the 1972 governor's and lieutenant governor's race.[77] They keep an eye out for comers among the younger representatives, and when they see a winner, as the powerful Texas Chemical Council's Harry Whitworth saw in Ben Barnes back in 1963, they provide him with the "entrees, money, and information" necessary to elevate him to higher office.[78] In the 1980s, Whitworth, still lobbying for the council, had a conservative son-in-law who was chairman of the house calendars committee that determined which bills got to the floor.[79] The son-in-law has since become a lobbyist himself.

These men write bills for friendly lawmakers to introduce. They work year-round every year, during the brief 140-day span every other year when the legislature is in session, and during the much longer period when it is not. And the most proficient of them manage their job with a style that is much appreciated by the capitol crowd. Like "Boss" Jimmy Day, they bring "a sense of taste, an instinct for what's appropriate to the Austin government," in the words of Lee Clark, a state representative's wife, in 1968. (Day was later convicted on several counts of fraud.)[80]

The acknowledged master in the 1930s was Roy Miller, lobbyist for Texas Gulf Sulphur, onetime mayor of Corpus Christi, and linked by marriage to the King Ranch fortune.[81] Operating both in Texas and Washington, Miller was a political ally of Vice President John Nance Garner, another wealthy South Texan. Lyndon Johnson, through Miller's intervention, was hired in 1931 as private secretary to King Ranch heir Dick Kleberg, a conservative congressman.[82] A man who in private vehemently attacked FDR for his "socialism," Miller apparently had huge funds at his disposal. The *Austin American-Statesman* opined that he was "perhaps the most effective single lobbyist Washington has ever known"; the *Saturday Evening Post* said that "perhaps no one outside official life has a wider acquaintance among congressmen. . . . For twenty years he has had the status of a quasi-public figure."[83]

Alvin Wirtz was a contemporary of Miller. A former state senator, he was the senior partner in an Austin firm. "Alvin Wirtz was my dearest friend, my most trusted counselor," Lyndon Johnson once said—with how much hyperbole it is difficult to know.[84] A quiet man with a preference for the telephone over written communication ("Senator didn't want anything on paper that didn't have to be," a junior partner once remarked), he represented two of the largest competing oil companies in the state, Humble Oil & Refining and Magnolia Petroleum Company. Robert Caro's cameo of Wirtz captures the essential Texas style of a leading member of the inner lobby:

> As a lobbyist—for the same reactionary oil interests he had been representing unofficially as a legislator—his technique was as soft as his drawl. A threat or an offer was never direct. The most he might say to a legislator was, "I just want you to know that I have been employed by a group to help pass this bill. There is a great deal of interest in seeing that it is passed. I hope you'll vote the courage of your convictions." But a legislator who didn't take the hint would find arrayed against him the power [of the two most powerful oil companies in Texas].[85]

In the post–World War II era, Austin's premier lobbyist was Ed Clark. Like Wirtz, he had close political and business ties to LBJ and the Brown brothers, Herman and George. He was a godfather to one of Johnson's daughters. A lobbyist, he once averred, should want to be a Christian gentleman and true to his trust, just like everybody else.[86] New Deal governor James Allred made Clark his personal secretary, then appointed him secretary of state. Clark later grew rich from banking, timber, ranching, and his corporate law practice. After Clark's lobbying days were over, LBJ appointed him ambassador to Australia, and then he became a University of Texas regent. But his reputation was clinched in 1947 when he and Wirtz were instrumental in getting the legislature to enact nine bills crafted to undercut the power of organized labor in the state. The bills were backed by the Browns, much of whose wealth and power derived from government cost-plus contracts before and during World War II. Wirtz and Clark, as lobbyists for the Browns, worked in tandem with right-wing lieutenant governor Ben Ramsey to put the show together in the legislature. The anti-union laws, including a so-called "right to work" provision that denied unions the right to negotiate a union shop with their employers, made Texas one of the most anti-union states in the country and the only major industrial state that prohibited the closed shop.[87] "Mr. [Herman] Brown personally attended every labor committee hearing in both House and Senate," charged the executive secretary of the state labor organization at its annual convention that year, "and was usually ably supported by such counsel as . . . ex-Senator Wirtz, and had for his principal lobbyist, Ed Clark."[88]

This "boss of the legislature," as *Reader's Digest* once called Clark, was an ally of conservatives, a friend of LBJ throughout the latter's career, a fund-raiser for John Tower, and, curiously, a friend and sometime fund-raiser for Ralph Yarborough. The latter relationship was said to have resulted from the two men's origins in East Texas and their early days together as assistant attorneys general under Allred.[89] "Purely from a 'technical standpoint,'—for want of a better phrase to describe a lobbyist at work," wrote newsman Larry Goodwyn with grudging awe in the 1960s, "Ed Clark is a master craftsman."[90]

As Clark's power waned, the focus of lobby influence began to shift from the Austin law firms to those in Houston. Searcy Bracewell, a partner in the Houston firm of Bracewell & Patterson, emerged as a leader. Bracewell had served in both the Texas house and senate in the 1940s and 1950s and ran an unsuccessful U.S. senatorial campaign in 1956–1957, attacking a liberal opponent's support of the U.S. Supreme Court's school desegregation decision.[91] Shortly after retiring from the legislature, Bracewell helped establish "Citizens for a Sales Tax," an alliance of businessmen whose efforts resulted in the state's first broad-based sales tax in 1961.[92]

His job as a super lobbyist made Bracewell something of a "one-man political machine," according to reporter Molly Ivins. He personally recruited candidates, lined up money for them, drew legislative redistricting maps designed to dilute liberal and black votes, advised local newspaper editors, and, on top of all that, performed his regular tasks in Austin as a lobbyist for major utilities and other corporate interests. "Searcy is like the Indians," said another veteran lobbyist. "When you see him coming, you'd better worry. When you don't see him coming, you really better worry."[93]

Bracewell's 1975 lobbyist's disclosure statement revealed the scope of his representation. As the lobbyist for the Texas Association of Taxpayers, a fifteen-thousand-member businessmen's group whose main purpose was to oppose a corporate income tax bill in the legislature, he represented dozens of the largest corporations both in Texas and the United States, including firms in banking, groceries, oil, accounting, life insurance, and chemicals. Bracewell also represented four major Texas-based utility companies (with Joe Foy, another utilities lobbyist, he wrote a bill to establish a weaker public utilities commission than the one actually created in 1975), the Texas Society of Certified Public Accountants, Friends of the Arts and Humanities, and the Texas Good Roads/Transportation Association, an extremely influential pressure group comprised of numerous industries—including oil and gas firms—involved directly or indirectly in highway construction.[94]

In the 1980s, two of the top business lobbyists were George Christian, head of a public relations firm in Austin and a former press secretary to both LBJ and John Connally; and Marion ("Sandy") Sanford, a partner at the time in Vinson & Elkins in Houston. Both men represented a wide spectrum of institutions. Christian, an ardent conservative who helped John Connally coordinate Texas Democrats for Nixon in 1972, preferred clients who were conservatives and, for the most part, big businessmen.[95] Also influential was Billy Clayton, a West Texas agribusiness millionaire and a former Speaker of the House, whose connections gave him added clout. "There are a lot of people in the Legislature who owe Clayton," an observer told a reporter. A conservative Democrat turned Republican, Clayton represented some extremely right-wing organizations, although he claimed to have some clients who were not "true-blue conservative."[96]

The inner lobby is a coterie of men of experience, connections, and know-how, with vast reserves of money at their disposal. They are proud of their ability to cut a sharp deal. Above all, they are a business lobby. Standing in the long political shadows of the great corporations and law firms in Dallas and Houston, the inner lobby often speaks for an entire social class.

The Limits of Upper-Class Institutions

We have focused on institutions that contribute to upper-class solidarity in Texas. There are limits, however, to their ability to create unity and thus enhance the political power of the rich. Anyone familiar with Texas culture knows that tendencies toward exclusion, snobbism, and elitism are at war with a native egalitarianism. No spokesman for the rich, no lobbyist on their behalf, would get very far without cultivating a populist style and adopting a rhetoric of equal opportunity and fairness to all. Sometimes, under some conditions, style and rhetoric actually mesh with genuine commitments to these values. To the extent that this occurs, class solidarity is weakened.

Furthermore, even in the most privileged families, one often finds a sense of concern for the have-nots, the manifestations of which can range from small acts of charity to magnanimous donations of time and money to social causes or larger public enterprises.[97] To the extent that such generosity enlarges one's sympathies, the pursuit of narrow class interest is made more difficult.

It is also true that the institutions that socialize members of the affluent to think and act as a class never fully succeed in their mission. This means simply that in any generation, a number of individuals who go to private schools, attend the right summer camps, belong to the right college fraternities and sororities, and get jobs with the right firms do not end up identifying with the interests of the upper class. Indeed, there are well-known Texas liberals with social pedigrees, even a few who have worked

for the big corporate law firms or held command posts in business enterprises.

Furthermore, the profit motive itself can militate against the development of upper-class solidarity. In today's mixed economy, its capitalist
component is still driven to a considerable extent by the spirit of competition. This means that when political necessity requires the business class
to rechannel its competitive instincts "for the good of the team," the players may find it difficult to do so. This is especially true when there are
debates over what is really good for the team or, in other words, over what
the interests of the class really are in a particular situation.

Thus there are several sources of class division. In addition, even when
the upper class is fairly unified, it cannot always succeed in its goals. This
is another way of reiterating an earlier point: An upper class is not necessarily a ruling class. Any upper class is small in numbers; and while this
facilitates intraclass communication and political involvement, it places
the class at risk when popular opinion runs strongly against its interests or
when forces beyond its control intervene, particularly those emanating
from the federal government.

In spite of these qualifications, the institutional arrangements so far described have worked in the modern era to produce a Texas upper class that
is unusually united in its politics, and, thanks to the extraordinary resources at its disposal, it has been able to prevail in most of the major
battles it has chosen to fight.

6

Blue-Collar Texans

LYNDA Faye Spradling was five months pregnant. Her one-year-old son, Robert Avery, was with her in the car the sultry afternoon of June 18, 1965, as she waited outside the Upjohn chemical plant in a Houston industrial suburb for her husband to finish his shift. Suddenly Robert "started coughing and turned real red and started sweating." She picked him up, "thinking he had something stuck in his throat." Then she began coughing and choking too. While trying to get out of the car she lost consciousness. When she came to, she was being given oxygen in the plant office. A blowdown scrubber at the plant had malfunctioned, releasing phosgene, a chemical that accounted for most of the poison gas casualties in World War I. It damages lungs even in minute amounts and can kill before its victim smells it.[1]

In a series of articles on the Upjohn plant, Harold Scarlett, an environmental reporter for the *Houston Post*, told the stories of several people who had encountered phosgene.

The Spradlings filed suit, and court records later showed that Robert and his younger brother Kenneth Wayne, with whom Mrs. Spradling had been pregnant, "suffered bone and brain abnormalities." Mrs. Spradling told Scarlett in 1983 that ever since the accident, she and both sons had been troubled with respiratory problems—"colds, asthma, pneumonia." Before a third child was born she had suffered "several miscarriages." In their suit against Upjohn, which was owned by the pharmaceutical company, the Spradlings and their physicians were unable to establish a definite link between the boys' problems and phosgene exposure. Their suit eventually resulted in a $127,500 agreed settlement.[2]

Phosgene is an essential component of polyurethane, which in foam or hardened form is used for insulation, stuffing for upholstered products, molded automobile grills and panels, and as a component of many other commodities "from home appliances to bowling balls." In 1957 only five million pounds of phosgene were produced in the U.S. Upjohn alone produced about three hundred million pounds in 1982.[3]

There were other incidents at Upjohn. Danny Allen Dubose, a chemical operator, "mistakenly opened a wrong valve" in 1981 and was sprayed with phosgene. He "insisted the incident was not serious and said he smelled no phosgene. . . . Dubose collapsed while refusing to go to the first-aid station and died in a hospital a week later." Shelby Stephen Jackson, working for a service company at the Upjohn plant the same year, was "cleaning out tubing . . . with a waterblasting lance when carbon bits containing phosgene blew back out of the tube and peppered his body like birdshot." His physician, a biochemist, blamed the exposure for "skin sores" and "cellular changes" that were potentially lethal. In his suit against Upjohn, Jackson claimed that he had not been trained to use the lance and "was told nothing about the presence or hazards of phosgene."[4]

A scrubber failure on July 17, 1981, caused the release of a cloud of gas that drifted onto the property of the US Industrial Chemicals plant, where eighteen Brown & Root employees were doing maintenance work. All eighteen were hospitalized. Brown & Root was later fined $800 by the federal Occupational Safety and Health Administration (OSHA) for not giving its workers adequate training or warning them about the hazards of phosgene.[5] On March 11, 1982, about 220 pounds of phosgene accidentally escaped into the air within forty minutes. A few months later, two gallons of liquid phosgene escaped when a flange was unbolted, and as it vaporized, the cloud drifted across the plant, contaminating thirteen workers. Eight were hospitalized for observation and five received first aid. OSHA did not cite Upjohn for any violations in that incident even though company standards had been broken.[6]

Most of the phosgene-related lawsuits claimed that gas inhalation damaged respiration. Kris Wayne Dean, a boilermaker and pipefitter, alleged that "a flange broke and gassed him" while he was working at Upjohn for a service company. He was hospitalized for the next month, the medical bills for which came to approximately $30,000. Dean said that after the accident he was not able to work, "except for a few months as a sweeper." At the time of Scarlett's investigation, Dean was "relying on Social Security disability payments of $570 a month to support his wife and 11-year-old daughter. . . . 'Just breathing is hard,' he said. 'To exert myself in any way is painful to my breathing.' "[7]

Scarlett's investigation revealed that court dockets since the Spradling incident in 1965 had seldom been free of suits against Upjohn claiming personal injuries from phosgene exposure. At the time his articles appeared, "eight phosgene suits [were] pending and at least half a dozen older suits" had been closed out.[8] Moreover, "since workers injured on the job cannot [ordinarily] sue their own employer for damages under the Texas workmen's compensation system," most of the actions "were filed by contract or maintenance workers or even truck drivers visiting the plant."[9]

For their part, plant officials admitted to Scarlett only one recorded fatality—Dubose—"and only three instances in which workers [had been] in critical condition for a time from phosgene exposure" in the previous twenty-one years. "We think we have a safe plant," a company official told Scarlett. "We think we have a well-trained plant. We don't think we are any worse—and unfortunately we are not much better—than the industry as a whole." The company admitted to seventeen accidental phosgene releases between 1974 and May 1983.[10]

The Manual Workers

Manual workers are those people who perform labor with their hands and bodies. Society attaches less esteem to their work even though it often requires classic human virtues—skill, judgment, perseverance, strength, and courage, not to speak of self-sacrifice. Another characteristic of most manual workers is their lack of authority in the workplace.

Also, as events at Upjohn suggest, these workers are far more likely than others to encounter danger to life and limb. "Imagine for a moment," writes Andrew Levison, "the universal outcry that would occur if every year several corporate headquarters routinely collapsed like mines, crushing sixty or seventy executives. Or suppose that all the banks were filled with an invisible noxious dust that constantly produced cancer in the managers, clerks, and tellers. Finally, try to imagine the horror that would be expressed in every newspaper in the country if thousands of university professors were deafened every year or lost fingers, hands, sometimes eyes, while on their jobs."[11] The fact that manual workers suffer these disasters routinely and that this is accepted with equanimity by the rest of society illuminates a fundamental difference between the working class and the middle and upper classes.

The U.S. Census Bureau distinguishes broadly between nonmanual "white-collar" jobs and manual "blue-collar" ones; this distinction shall be used throughout this chapter when we refer to manual occupations, except that we will include under the manual category not only production jobs involved in the creation of physical products but also what the Census Bureau calls service jobs—such as waiter, repairman, mail carrier, and the like—but not clerical and sales positions.[12]

The jobs held by people in manual occupations are varied.[13] They work as servants in affluent homes, pick up garbage as part of the municipal work force, build skyscrapers, tend crops in the Rio Grande Valley and the Panhandle, patrol apartment complexes as security guards or handymen, wrestle drill pipe out of the ground on oil derrick floors.

They are assemblers. They put together ready-to-wear clothing in sweatshops along the Mexican border, computers on assembly lines, helicopters and hydrogen bomb warheads in the factories of Fort Worth and Amarillo, and fast foods in the great nationwide fast-food chains.

They drive eighteen-wheelers, work at metal lathes, lay pipelines, and unload cargo at Gulf Coast ports. They repair cars and telephone lines. They work in canneries in the South Texas "Winter Garden," serve food in restaurants, paint houses. A few still ride the range as cowboys. A somewhat larger number ply the coastal waters for seafood. Others follow the railroad trades. Many work in the smelly refineries in La Porte, Texas City, and Port Arthur.

They are the people who labor during most of their adult lives in hundreds of physically demanding jobs that often require long hours and shift work. Sometimes their jobs pay well, but more often they do not. By and large they are jobs that do not reward a creative bent or an innovative spirit. They leave people exhausted if not physically damaged and, over the years, diminished in their hopes and aspirations. But the work is necessary. Without it industrial society would immediately collapse.

In 1940 the Texas urban manual work force was 40 percent of the total, a group larger than either the nonmanual or the farm work force, and it was growing rapidly as the decline of marginal farming operations led to a major migration to the cities. At the time V. O. Key wrote *Southern Politics*, it appeared that urban manual workers would soon constitute a significant majority of the labor force. This did not occur, however. The zenith of manual-worker strength, in percentage terms, was reached in 1960, when it comprised 48.5 percent. The rise of white-collar workers was even more rapid, and by 1980 they were a majority of the work force (see table 6.1).

In spite of the vast reaches of the state, its working class is concentrated and urbanized. Eighty percent of manual workers in 1980 lived in one of the state's twenty-six standard metropolitan statistical areas (SMSAs). Almost one-fourth of these metropolitan workers lived in a single conurbation along the upper Gulf Coast, the Houston-Galveston Standard Consolidated Statistical Area (SCSA), a rapidly growing complex abutting on the Beaumont-Port Arthur-Orange SMSA, itself a heavily industrialized area with a strong labor union tradition. If urban concentration alone were sufficient to bring about a politically organized working class, Texas would certainly have one. In fact, it does not.

The Disorganized

The small Texas upper class acts as a group on important classwide issues. In contrast, manual workers are quite disorganized. This is partly the result of historic barriers to political participation described in chapter 3. It is also the result of Texas's long tradition of one-partyism.

Table 6.1
Occupational Groups in the Employed
Work Force, Texas, 1940–1980 (percent)

	1940	1950	1960	1970	1980
Nonmanual	30.0	36.8	43.3	48.5	53.1
Manual	40.2	47.5	48.5	47.5	44.0
Farm	29.8	15.7	8.2	4.0	2.9
Total	100.0	100.0	100.0	100.0	100.0

Sources: Calculated from data contained in U.S. Bureau of the Census, Census of the Population, *Texas: General Social and Economic Characteristics* (PC(1)45C, 1960), 340; (PC(1)C45, 1970), 445; (PC80-1-C45, 1980), 115.

There are other reasons as well. While the upper class live in a few cloistered neighborhoods and intermingle in exclusive clubs, the working class reside in hundreds of inner-city enclaves and industrial suburbs. Geographical sprawl, in theory, can be overcome by institutional networks linked by telephones, freeways, or the mail service. But in reality, members of the working class have remained politically disorganized.

It is true that many manual workers are "joiners." But per capita, they belong to far fewer organizations than middle-class people. And the organizations they join are more likely to be church-related or lodges like the Benevolent and Protective Order of the Elks than ones with political goals.[14] Their social world is made up largely of nonpolitical matters— whether the fish are biting on Lake Texarkana or how much the price of the new Ford pickup will increase next year. When their concerns have political implications, often they do not grasp them. In the memorable phrase of C. Wright Mills, they cannot translate their personal troubles into public issues.

Not once in the twentieth century has a majority of the total voting-age population of Texas gone to the polls in a single election. It is unlikely that as many as a third of manual workers have voted at one time, even in presidential elections. In off-year general elections and important state-wide primaries, blue-collar turnout probably averages in the neighborhood of 5 to 15 percent. In municipal races, where *total* turnout as a proportion of the voting-age population may vary from 5 to 20 percent, the working-class vote is even lower.

But low participation extends beyond the realm of voting. There is a virtual absence of manual workers from governmental elites. Among the 181-member legislature, for example, only two persons could be identified as blue-collar workers in 1983.[15] And aside from the union movement and a scattering of local protest organizations, there are few institutional means to develop leadership. When blue-collarites occasionally emerge as leaders, the business community attempts to co-opt them. Factory workers get promoted to supervisory status and thus suddenly become part of "management." Or a city councilman who owns the Buick dealership brings them in as partners on business deals.

Even leaders who come up through the ranks of organized labor may be persuaded to throw in their lot with the "better" classes. "The lure of associating with executives is too much for them," longtime political activist Margaret Carter once observed of younger labor leaders in her home town of Fort Worth, "especially as they get into positions where they have to maneuver so as to satisfy conservative people or go back into the plant."[16]

The problem is even more acute at the poverty level, where resources are desperately few. The poor—welfare recipients and ethnic minorities in particular—are separated from the rest of the working class by the stigma of poverty. While in 1979, minorities in the nation as a whole came nowhere near comprising as much as half the government-defined poor, Texas blacks and Hispanics made up 63 percent of the state's two million poor. In Massachusetts in 1979, by comparison, the poor were 82 percent white, 10.3 percent black, and 9.3 percent Hispanic.[17] Taken together, Texas's large poverty population—almost 15 percent in 1979—and its huge minority component pose special problems for worker unity.

Both factors are partly the result of immigration from Mexico. Texas's 889-mile international boundary provides Mexicans the chance to escape an even more wretched existence than is the lot of the Texas poor. They settle in semirural *colonias* along the border or in urban *barrios* already inhabited by Mexican American citizens, many of whom are the children of earlier migrant waves. Conditions in the *colonias* are so desperate that they have been likened to Third World settlements.[18]

Probably fewer than 300,000 illegal aliens—most of them from Mexico—were living in the state in 1980, but their number increased by between 10,000 and 25,000 annually over the next few years.[19] Mexico's phenomenal population growth—from 20 million in 1945 to 60 million thirty years later and projected to be 120 million by the year 2000—and its lack of effective social security or unemployment insurance make it likely that the illegal population in Texas will continue to grow even in the face of more restrictive legislation to keep it down.

Students of immigration disagree both over whether immigrants take jobs from U.S. citizens or simply fill jobs that the latter are unwilling to take and over whether immigrants add more to the U.S. economy through taxes and other inputs than they extract from it in social services. These are not recent controversies. Carey McWilliams, writing sympathetically a generation ago about Mexican immigrants, spoke of the "fable," as he put it, "that Mexican workers are only imported because resident workers will not accept certain types of employment at the 'prevailing rate.' But the truth of the matter has always been that the availability of 'cheap Mexican labor' is what has determined the prevailing rate."[20] This view was consonant with the work of a *Wall Street Journal* writer in 1985 who described illegal workers, whose "willingness . . . to work for the minimum wage or less has helped preserve the Sun Belt as a largely nonunion, cheap-labor zone for businesses moving from the North." Employers of cheap illegal labor argue that closing the border would destroy numerous industries. "They're what make this impoverished economy tick," according to David Eymard, president of the Texas Shrimp Association.[21]

From a purely political point of view, Mexican immigration divides the manual stratum, especially during periods of high unemployment. To the extent that trade unionists believe their organizing efforts are stymied by the influx of low-wage workers and to the degree that American blue-collar workers of whatever ethnicity, including Chicanos, attribute unemployment in their ranks to immigration, large-scale migration fractures the unity of manual workers. The importance of the issue is suggested by a 1983 poll of national samples of blacks and Hispanics, 82 percent and 58 percent of whom, respectively, said they believed that illegal aliens "take jobs from Americans."[22] Symbolic of this division was the conflict over immigration policy between two liberal Texans in the Carter administration—Leonel Castillo, the first Hispanic director of the Immigration and Naturalization Service in the nation's history, and F. Ray Marshall, the secretary of labor—both outspoken opponents of discrimination against blacks and Mexican Americans.[23]

As a southern state, Texas has also inherited the traditional black-white caste system. V. O. Key believed that system was collapsing in Texas even as he wrote, and blacks have indeed made important gains since then. But there is still great tension between blacks and Anglos and somewhat less between Anglos and Hispanics. There is also some black-Hispanic hostility, although usually it is not as great as that between the two minority groups and the dominant Anglos.

These tensions are more obvious among manual workers because they are much more ethnically diverse than the upper and upper-middle classes.[24] Only 61 percent of manual workers were Anglo in 1980. Fifteen percent were black and almost 24 percent were Hispanic, with the latter figure expected to grow rapidly. The political fissures among the working class in statewide liberal-conservative contests or partisan presidential races are clearly demonstrated in tables 3.2 and 3.3 in chapter 3, most especially when Anglos are compared to the two ethnic minorities.

In summary, the weakness of the Texas manual stratum stems from several factors. In addition to the historic political barriers to full partici-

pation, neighborhood dispersion and ethnic division combine with economic differences among blue-collar workers to decrease unity. Another
cause is the relative weakness of Texas labor unions, which in other industrial states traditionally have been a source of political strength. A further
examination of a central problem of manual labor—danger on the job—
will point to the implications of that weakness for enacting policies to protect workers' health and well-being.

Danger on the Job

Consider the issues raised by events at the Upjohn plant. Society now
believes it must have polyurethane. As with many "indispensable" products, the manufacture of this product entails dangers. Production work
often involves hazardous machinery and procedures, or contact with
harmful chemicals. This is especially true for unskilled laborers, to be
sure, but it is common in the skilled trades as well. Danny Dubose at
Upjohn, a family man with a college welding course behind him, was making $25,000 a year when he died at age twenty-four. In America one man-
ual (nonservice) or farm worker in five is injured on the job each year.
Among white-collar workers, only one in twenty is. Service workers fall in
between, at about one in eleven. Injury rates are higher among low-paid
workers. These rates do not pertain to occupational diseases, which are
also much more prevalent among manual workers.[25]

Workplace danger is a fact the middle class would rather not think
about, even though they consume products whose manufacture entails
worker death and injury. There is an iron link between worker sacrifice
and consumer enjoyment. George Orwell once drew the connection between society as a consumer of coal and the almost unbelievable sacrifices
of British coal miners of his day. "In the metabolism of the Western world
the coal-miner is second in importance only to the man who ploughs the
soil," he wrote. "He is a sort of grimy caryatid upon whose shoulders
nearly everything that is *not* grimy is supported."[26]

The caryatid metaphor applies just as well to many manual workers
today. It applies with particular aptness to agricultural workers, the products of whose labor even many principled vegetarians, repulsed by the
violence and cruelty involved in raising and slaughtering animals, think
nothing about eating.

The hardships under which agricultural laborers toil exemplify the dangers of work at the bottom of the manual hierarchy. The workers are primarily Hispanic migratory laborers, and along with blacks in East Texas
they have remained one of the most exploited sectors of the work force.

They and their families have constituted a small but significant part of the labor force for decades. An estimated two hundred thousand migrant farm workers were in Texas in the early 1980s, living at home and on small farms half the year and then traveling elsewhere in Texas and the nation in large family units to earn money to survive.

In the early 1980s, the median income of U.S. migrant families of six members was $3,900, less than one-third of the federal poverty threshold of $12,499. "Only 14 of every 100 [migrant] children graduate from high school, compared to 75 out of . . . 100" for children generally. "Malnutrition and inadequate medical treatment are as routine as the next day's trip to the fields. Diarrhea and parasites are expected; tuberculosis is common," according to a recent study. "Life expectancy is 49 years, roughly two-thirds the national average."[27]

Farm workers' problems have remained depressingly similar from one decade to the next: extremely inadequate housing on the job, exploitation by crew leaders, lack of protective legislation available to other workers, including child labor protection. Writing in 1976, Ruth Graves concluded: "Over thirty states have enacted legislation designed to meet one or more of these needs. Texas has enacted only one law specifically aimed at the migrant problem: a requirement that persons seeking migratory work have a health certificate showing results of a recent tuberculosis examination."[28] Only in 1981—after the United Farm Workers' first statewide convention in 1979—did the Texas legislature finally outlaw the use of the torturous short-handled hoe and require that toilets and drinking water be made available in the fields.

Even that triumph was illusory. Farmers evaded the short-handled hoe prohibition by requiring workers to use knives instead of hoes, which still forced them to stoop or work on hands and knees, a form of labor that over time is permanently disabling. When Texas Senator Hector Uribe sponsored a bill plugging the loophole and managed to get it through the legislature in 1987, Governor Clements vetoed it. The laws passed to require toilets and drinking water still were not being properly enforced as late as 1988, leading to lawsuits and demonstrations by the United Farm Workers.[29]

Only in 1984, after lengthy court battles waged by the Texas Civil Liberties Union had put pressure on the legislature to act, were agricultural employees in Texas brought under the Workers' Compensation Act, from which they had been excluded since workers' compensation was established in the state in 1913, despite the fact that agricultural labor has one of the highest accidental death rates of any major industry in Texas.[30] In 1985, again under pressure as a result of court victories by the Texas Civil Liberties Union, the legislature granted unemployment benefits to farm and ranch workers who had been denied them for almost half a century, thanks largely to the opposition of the Farm Bureau, the trade group of agribusiness interests.[31]

The difficulties of the agricultural worker's job are often severe. Workers are subject to extremes of heat and cold. They use tools and machines that cause serious injury—tractors, spray rigs, movable bins, ladders, knives, and conveyor belts, among others. Sonia Jasso and Maria Mazorra have described the special difficulties women farm workers face, difficulties that stem not only from sex discrimination in the fields (they are more likely to be paid for their grueling labor at piecework rates instead of hourly wages) but also from the additional burden of child raising and household chores in the makeshift communities of migrant camps.[32]

A continuing problem is pesticides. Often the poisons are transferred from sprayed plants that are still wet. Workers sometimes spray with hand-held machines that leak the poison fluids onto them. Sometimes workers are directly sprayed by crop dusters. In 1984 a comprehensive study of pesticide regulation in Texas concluded that pesticides are widely used in Texas. "The present state program," it said, "includes few inspectors and imposes few requirements beyond those of the federal program."[33] A study jointly funded by the National Academy of Sciences and the Environmental Protection Agency found that "56 percent of . . . agricultural workers surveyed had abnormal liver and kidney functions, 78 percent reported chronic skin rash and 54 percent had chest cavity abnormalities."[34]

Tough new regulations on pesticide use in the state promulgated by agriculture commissioner Jim Hightower caused an angry backlash in the 1985 session of the legislature, a backlash led by the Farm Bureau, the Texas chemical lobby, and conservative lawmakers. However, liberals and moderates were successful in beating back the conservatives' efforts to strip Hightower of his regulatory power and to bleed the agriculture department's budget.[35] The regulations stayed in place.

Conditions of Upjohn employees and Texas farm workers illustrate some of the dangers in high- and low-paying manual jobs. One could have focused on numerous other occupations—for example, manual jobs in the much ballyhooed high-tech industries Texas began luring in the 1970s.

In the popular mind, high-tech jobs symbolize the new shape of work in "postindustrial" society. Most of the production workers are women, and their jobs are often described as clean, in contrast to those in smokestack industries. But the basic "tools" of electronics manufacturing "are a wide variety of chemicals," write Robin Baker and Sharon Woodrow. These chemicals are used "for cleaning, stripping, and degreasing operations," and "are known to cause . . . dermatitis, nausea, liver and kidney damage, cancer."[36]

14. Jim Hightower and Henry Cisneros. Former editor of the liberal *Texas Observer* and, since 1983, Texas commissioner of agriculture, Hightower (left) confers with moderate San Antonio mayor Cisneros. Courtesy of Alan Pogue and the *Texas Observer*.

In Texas, judging from anecdotal information, employers' pursuit of profit at the expense of worker safety appears to be widespread. One of the most callous instances of willful neglect of workers' rights in recent American history came to national attention in the early 1970s, shortly after the Pittsburgh Corning asbestos plant closed down in Tyler, a small city in the East Texas piney woods. The plant's owners apparently had decided to shut down in anticipation of a storm of protest and lawsuits resulting from medical horrors at the plant that would soon be made public. As a result of management's deliberate failure to meet safety and health standards for accumulation of asbestos dust in the plant, for years hundreds of workers had been needlessly exposed without knowing it to dangerous levels of asbestos.

What made the case particularly outrageous was that federal inspectors, although fully aware of the effects of workers' contact with asbestos, had known as early as 1963 that the plant was violating recommended standards. The inspectors had informed management, but not the workers, of the fact. When many of the workers developed fatal cancers and asbestosis, a chronic lung disease, they filed a class action suit against both Pittsburgh Corning and the federal government.[37] At that point, conservative legislator Billy Williamson, a Democrat from Tyler, opined that it was "much better to have a little bit of crud in our lungs [than to allow citizens to file lawsuits every time they think someone is violating antipollution laws.] I don't need some bunch of dogooder nuts telling me what's good to breathe," Williamson allowed. "And I don't want a bunch of environmentalists and communists telling me what's good for my life and family."[38] The workers won a multimillion-dollar settlement.

A year after Pittsburgh Corning shut down, four thousand Shell Oil Company workers in the Oil, Chemical, and Atomic Workers Union (OCAW) went on strike, many in Texas refineries, primarily over the workplace environment. Unlike most of the major oil companies, Shell had refused to allow noncompany scientists to examine conditions on the job, nor would it pay doctors to give workers appropriate medical examinations. It even refused to give the union each year available data on employee sickness and death rates. The company only gave in on the latter issue when the strike ended four and a half months later.[39] The problems of chemicals in the workplace and Texas employers' refusal to let the workers know about them continue to crop up in the state's press.[40]

The Struggle for Job Safety Programs

Reliable statistics on work-related accidents and disease in Texas are difficult to obtain, for reasons to be explained shortly, but experts believe that Texas has a very high accidental injury and fatality rate. Between 1980 and 1984, according to the National Institute for Occupational Safety and Health, the state's average annual number of traumatic occupational fatalities—792—was the nation's largest. The state's fatality rate per 100,000 workers ranked thirteenth among the fifty states. By another measure—years of potential life lost as a result of those 792 deaths per year—it ranked ninth.[41] In 1980 Texas was second in the nation in the number of job-related injuries. Yet only three states ranked lower than Texas in the amount of the maximum weekly workers' compensation allowed injured workers.[42]

These figures do not include thousands of workers who suffered and sometimes died from diseases resulting from routine contact with chemicals. According to one widely used estimate, each year as many as 100,000 workers in the United States die from occupational disease, and 390,000 new cases appear. Only a small proportion of disease-related traumas are covered under workers' compensation laws.[43]

Publicity about the physical and chemical dangers of the workplace led Congress—under pressure from organized labor—to pass the Occupational Safety and Health Act of 1970, requiring a workplace free from health hazards that were known to have caused or were likely to cause death or serious physical harm.[44] While the Occupational Safety and Health Administration (OSHA) has never been effective in achieving this goal, the Reagan administration weakened the agency considerably by siding with businessmen and economists who argued that OSHA rules were needlessly complex and depressed productivity.[45] In 1984, Reagan put Texas lawyer and Republican fund-raiser Robert Rowland in charge of OSHA, which drew criticism because Rowland owned stock in companies subject to OSHA's regulatory decisions. Rowland's conception of the agency, like Reagan's, was that it should be "non-adversarial," imposing small fines, conducting few inspections, and confining its work primarily to urging employers to improve job safety. Between 1980 and 1987, the number of OSHA inspectors nationally decreased from 1,328 to 1,044.[46]

The ineffectiveness of OSHA cannot be blamed solely on Reagan. Shortly before Rowland resigned in May 1985, a study by the Congressional Office of Technology Assessment concluded that in the first thirteen years of its existence, OSHA had little measurable effect in protecting workers from accidents or exposure to health hazards.[47] The magnitude of the problem from the beginning was pointed out by a U.S. labor department report in 1980. While data from the National Occupational Hazard Survey indicated that about "25 million [U.S.] workers" were "potentially exposed to an OSHA-regulated health hazard," only 2 percent of that number were at work sites that were visited by OSHA investigators annually. In Texas in 1987, there were fewer than one hundred OSHA inspectors for a work force of 6.7 million. Moreover, the maximum penalty of "$1,000 for a serious violation" of an OSHA standard was, in the jargon of the report, "a minor cost factor for a firm faced with major expenditures for environmental and engineering controls."[48]

If OSHA is so ineffective, what can be said about state-level work-site regulation in Texas? In 1967, almost eighty years after the state embarked on its path toward industrialization, the legislature passed a job safety law known as the Texas Occupational Safety Act. It represented a compromise between organized labor and the Texas Manufacturers' Association. By one account, a major reason for employers' support of the bill was a hope that a job safety law at the state level would delay federal legislation, such as that which created OSHA. The Texas measure fell short of providing "a comprehensive assault on the long-neglected problem of industrial safety," according to Clifton McCleskey and his colleagues, but it was "an important first step."[49] In 1969, U.S. secretary of labor Willard W. Wirtz testified that Texas and Oklahoma ranked lower than any other state in the union on safety department expenditures—$0.02 per worker annually as compared with $0.33 nationwide and $2.11 in Oregon.[50]

In spite of the Texas job safety program's uncertain beginnings, by 1974 its annual appropriation had grown from $100,000 to $1.1 million, and thirty-eight field safety engineers were conducting more than eight thousand job-site inspections annually. These concentrated on employers in the workers' compensation system whose losses were above average in their industry—"debit-rated employers," they are called, indicating that their work sites were the most dangerous. But in 1975, the legislature cut off all funding for the state program, bowing to the argument that the federal OSHA was adequate for regulating job safety. Texas and Pennsylvania were the only states in the nation to discontinue their entire state programs. In Texas the number of safety engineers was cut from thirty-eight to seven, and funding was slashed from $1.1 million to the $250,000 made available for Texas that year by OSHA.[51]

The legislature even abolished funding for the state program to cooperate with the U.S. Bureau of Labor Statistics in collecting reliable job injury and illness data at the state level. Through 1974, Texas had cooperated with the bureau, and the federal government had paid half the cost. Several groups and individuals have urged the legislature to renew this cooperative venture, including the state Department of Health, the Texas Industrial Accident Board, and two separate task forces—one appointed by a Republican governor, the other by a Democrat. The legislature has repeatedly turned a deaf ear. (The cost in 1985 of tying in with the federal statistical programs—one an employer survey, the other a study of workers' compensation claims—was estimated at $350,000.)[52]

Thus Texas, unlike a majority of states, lacks reliable data on job injuries and diseases, cannot determine with accuracy the distribution of job injuries among industries, lacks a strong scientific data base for studying the major causes of injuries and diseases, and cannot compare the data it does have with those from the states that participate in the Bureau of Labor Statistics' uniform data collection program. Table 6.2 indicates that Texas's 1981 funding, compared to that of four other heavily industrialized states, was less than one-tenth of Michigan's, the next lowest state, whose work force was only three-fourths the size.

Job safety expenditures alone, of course, cannot abolish job accidents. Yet the 1982 job injury task force report to Governor Clements claimed that experience with accident-prevention programs indicated that half of all occupational injuries and diseases "could be eliminated with the institution of proper safety standards and enforcement in the workplace."[53]

In 1961 Charles Hughes, a young legislator from Sherman, Texas, led a group of liberals in support of an expanded state safety program. Approximately one thousand workers died each year in Texas occupational accidents, he told the House labor committee, and more than four hundred thousand were injured. Fred Schmidt, secretary-treasurer of the state AFL-CIO, added: "This is the twelfth year this bill has been before you. What new can be said, except to update figures? Why is there a complete

Table 6.2
Funding for Job Safety Programs, Selected States, 1981

	State	Federal	Total
California	$10,025,707	$9,796,568	$19,822,275
New Jersey	3,094,498	3,238,945	6,333,443
New York	4,215,722	1,871,292	6,087,014
Michigan	2,000,000	3,700,000	5,700,000
Texas	0	500,000	500,000

Source: Texas Department of Health, "Occupational Safety in Texas" (Austin, n.d.), attachment 2 (mimeo).

absence of safety laws in Texas dealing with the technology our workers face?" Employer groups defeated the bill.[54]

A quarter of a century later, Harry Hubbard, president of the Texas AFL-CIO, called for sweeping changes in the law to protect workers on the job. Nearly four thousand workers had died at work in the first half of the 1980s, he said. "Job safety and health conditions in Texas have become intolerable," he stated in letters to Governor-elect Clements and the legislature. He added that workers who refused to risk their lives or who reported unsafe conditions could be fired without legal recourse, unless covered by a labor contract.[55] His pleas were ignored.

The Unions

Key's vision of the future of Texas was partly premised on the growth of organized labor, which he thought could help strengthen the have-nots, presumably by accomplishing what American unions at their best are justly famous for—tackling low wages, long hours, autocratic employers, exploitation of children, and degrading treatment by supervisors.

Key had reason to be hopeful. The unions were growing rapidly. Historically they had secured not only wage gains but insurance, old-age pensions, unemployment insurance, workers' compensation, paid vacations, and fair grievance procedures—not only for their members, but for other workers as well.[56] Both during and after the New Deal, the more progressive unions were in the vanguard of political efforts to achieve goals that benefited the larger society.

There is another side to unions. Sometimes they are corrupt, practice racial discrimination, drive up labor costs unreasonably, and diminish productivity. Yet recent studies by economists indicate that the deleterious effects of unions are exaggerated by their enemies.[57] Most unions, in contrast to the stereotype, are neither corrupt nor undemocratic. Indeed, they are more democratic by far than most other economic organizations, particularly business corporations.

Since Key's work, the Texas labor movement has remained far ahead of the business class on most of the social issues of the day. This is true even concerning racial justice, in spite of the well-documented resistance of many unionists to integration.[58] By 1974 two of the most militant civil rights advocates in the legislature at the time, Mickey Leland and Ben Reyes—a black and a Mexican American, respectively—claimed in a joint statement that industrial unions "have been among the staunchest fighters for civil rights, and blacks and browns in the plants and shops of Texas got their first crack at good wages and decent working conditions when organized labor first signed collective bargaining contracts with management."[59] A decade later, the AFL-CIO's Hubbard estimated, with some pride, that a majority of organized labor's rank and file in Texas was made up of blacks, Mexican Americans, and women. This development was undoubtedly facilitated by the Civil Rights Act of 1964, which several state and local union leaders in Texas supported strongly.[60]

As an indispensible component of the state's liberal coalition, labor has worked hard in election campaigns, contributing money and manpower to liberal candidates and churning out political propaganda for its membership. In spite of this, it has fallen far short of providing a counterbalance to the power of interconnected business institutions, as reflected in its failure to achieve the abolition of the state's so-called right-to-work law. In the 1980s, *Labor News*, the official publication of the Texas AFL-CIO, no longer published ratings of lawmakers at the end of the biennial sessions because enemies of pro-labor legislators turned them to better advantage in campaigns than did organized labor itself.[61]

A standard explanation for labor's weakness is that "southern culture" is less receptive to unions than is that of the rest of the country. Before examining that claim, it is worth noting another possibility, namely, that in Texas the upper class, whose cohesion has been demonstrated, has played an important role in limiting the power of labor. There is much to be said for this proposition.

The American Federation of Labor (AFL) made important strides in Texas during the early twentieth century, helped especially by the economic expansion during World War I.[62] But these gains led to a reaction by employers in the 1920s that was spearheaded by the open-shop movement. Chambers of commerce ran free employment agencies placing nonunion workers. Thousands of Mexican nationals were brought in. Special training schools were established to create a nonunion work force, and large numbers of strikebreakers were hired. In 1920 Governor William P. Hobby was persuaded by the Southwest Open Shop Association in Dallas to send the militia to Galveston to break the famous longshoremen's

15. Mickey Leland. A liberal legislator and then U.S. congressman who succeeded Barbara Jordan in Houston's inner-city eighteenth district, Leland became preoccupied with the problem of world hunger. In 1989 he died in an airplane crash in Ethiopia. Courtesy of Alan Pogue and the *Texas Observer*.

strike. Only in Fort Worth and Houston, two of the state's larger cities, were unions able to survive the onslaught of the open-shop movement.[63]

A decade later, however, the Great Depression and the New Deal gave rise to a wave of union activism. The most conspicuous development was the birth in 1938 and the rapid growth of the Congress of Industrial Organizations (CIO), led by AFL dissidents such as John L. Lewis. Unions in Texas made headway during the 1940s, thanks to wartime industrialization, especially in metropolitan Houston and in the so-called Golden Triangle of the upper Gulf Coast, which contains vast refinery complexes. "Houston was bringing in basic industry, and when basic industry came into Texas, it brought in organization in the industry which had already been established elsewhere," recalls Bob Eckhardt, a labor lawyer and CIO lobbyist in the 1940s. "It is not correct that these were imported workers. . . . They were local people. Of course, the conservatives, the reactionaries in Texas were trying to depict them as outlanders coming into the area."[64]

The antilabor propaganda, in the viciousness of its attacks, the hysterical tone of its rhetoric, and the frequency of its allusions to "outside agitators," bore a striking resemblance to race-hate literature. This similarity is not surprising, for both were often run by the same right-wing millionaires and religious-patriotic cranks—people such as Vance Muse, a founder of Christian Americans. Bankrolled by wealthy reactionaries, Christian Americans' propaganda inveighed against communism, atheism, blacks, Jews, and labor unions.[65]

For several decades, both "respectable" and "radical" conservatives in Texas tried to link desegregation and unionism in the public mind. Muse set the tone for this strategy early on. "I like the nigger—in his place," he said. And he averred that the open-shop amendment "helps the nigger. Good niggers, not these communist niggers."

The CIO, to its credit, was particularly vulnerable to race-baiting. In Texas and the South it had "organized black workers, supported the Fair Employment Practices Committee, and sought to abolish the poll tax" at a time when blacks had just won the right to vote in the Democratic primary. At the 1948 Democratic state convention, CIO leaders opposed the party hierarchy by insisting that blacks be given equal rights as delegates.[66]

Another weapon of union foes was a paranoid brand of anticommunism. Numerous extremist groups and demagogues employed it and were abetted by the major daily newspapers. Even the AFL leadership itself was not above alleging that the CIO was Communist-led. From 1938 to 1944, East Texas congressman Martin Dies used his chairmanship of the House Un-American Activities Committee to publicize his false allegation that the CIO was Communist-dominated.[67]

Unlike that of many European labor movements, the leadership of the AFL and the CIO never questioned the premise of capitalism, "the basic management mandate independent of government or labor." There was, however, significant Communist influence in the CIO nationally from its inception, though nothing that approached control.[68] Yet antilabor propaganda in Texas often sounded as though the unions were directly run from Moscow. In fact, according to historian Don Carleton, during the period of Communist influence in the CIO, there were never more than half a dozen Communist professionals in the entire state at any one time nor more than one thousand dues-paying members of the party, many of whom did not belong to unions. In the Houston CIO locals, there were probably no more than a dozen actual Communists, although they held some important posts in the local chapters of the National Maritime Union.[69]

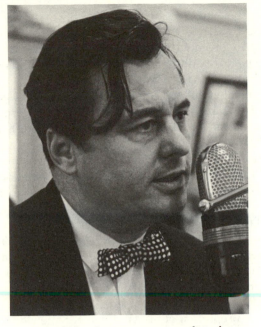

16. Bob Eckhardt. His career in politics began at the University of Texas in the 1930s. He lost his reelection bid as a congressman in the Reagan landslide of 1980. A labor lawyer, political cartoonist, lobbyist for the CIO, and legislator, Eckhardt was also a U.S. representative from 1966 to 1981. Courtesy of the Barker Texas History Center (Russell Lee Collection).

The Texas press was hardly kinder to labor than were the demagogues and conservative politicos. A study of editorial content in 1945 examined ten of the dominant metropolitan dailies. Of 381 editorials dealing with labor, 77 percent were "hostile" to labor's position, 22 percent "took no position," and four editorials—1 percent—were "prolabor."[70]

The 1930s and 1940s were crucial decades for the union movement. Employers hired spies and "enforcer" squads to ferret out union sympathizers and bring them into line—through intimidation, threats, tarring and feathering, and beatings. According to a Texas government textbook, "it was a period of class warfare."[71] The CIO was at the center of controversy. In contrast to the AFL's policy of political quiescence at the time, the decision of the CIO to push for electoral reforms, in hopes of building an alliance with blacks, dismayed the business class. The CIO Political Action Committee's support for FDR in 1944 and for liberal Homer Rainey in the 1946 gubernatorial election signaled to the establishment the incipient development of a broadly based movement with class overtones that went beyond the narrow confines of "bread and butter union-ism" advocated by the AFL's guiding spirit, Samuel Gompers. Revelations of instances of union corruption, often exaggerated by a hostile press, and the unions' widespread strike activity, sometimes accompanied by violence, dismayed many Texans.

Prominent members of the business class took the lead in curtailing union power. Herman Brown of the Brown and Root corporation coordinated business efforts. Based in Houston, he and his brother George were fiercely anti-union, often supplying their firm's workers as scabs to break strikes at other locations around the state.[72] The Brown brothers and their attorneys and lobbyists are credited with personally steering through the state legislature nine antilabor laws that, in combination with the national Taft-Hartley Act in 1947 and the Landrum-Griffin Act in 1959, slowed the momentum of the union movement by making organizing activities more difficult.[73] However, according to Houston labor lawyer Chris Dixie, the Texas statutes were less important than the Taft-Hartley measure, which preempted state law. Most significant, in his view, was Taft-Hartley's prohibition of various kinds of secondary boycotts.[74]

After the Taft-Hartley Act was passed, Texas unions for a while continued to grow as a proportion of the labor force. Statewide membership in 1939 had been 111,000, or 10.3 percent of nonagricultural workers.[75] In the years following the war, membership increased more rapidly than in the United States as a whole, reaching about 375,000 by the mid-1950s—approximately 17 percent of the nonagricultural labor force.[76] Even at its peak, however, Texas union membership remained among the lowest, proportionally, of any state in the union. Decline set in during the 1960s, and by 1982 only 13 percent of the industrial work force was unionized. In this respect Texas, very nearly back to its 1939 percentage, ranked forty-second among the states.[77]

Sources of Hostility to Unions

One commonly given reason for union weakness in Texas is grass-roots individualism stemming from the state's traditionally southern, Anglo-Protestant agricultural background. "The archetypical story of the union organizer being run out of town by the local sheriff is not a myth," observe economists Richard B. Freeman and James L. Medoff.[78] There may be some truth in this cultural explanation, but it bears further inquiry. In the first place, sheriffs and other law enforcement officials are not likely to be representative of the employee population. The people most actively involved in running union organizers out of town or making their tasks difficult may well be officers acting in the interests of a city's most powerful

17. George and Herman Brown. Houston industrialists, philanthropists, and op-
ponents of organized labor, the Brown brothers were friends and advisers of
Lyndon Johnson. In the postwar years they were the personification of the
Democratic conservative establishment. Courtesy of the Houston Metropolitan
Archives.

elites. Robert Coles's anecdotal account (as told in the words of a South
Texas grower's son) of the close cooperation between the sheriff and a
town's leading citizens in intimidating union organizers raises the possibility that there is more to the story than grass-roots anti-union sentiment.[79]

It is impossible to know precisely how pervasive anti-unionism is
among ordinary Texans, as distinct from law enforcement officials, newspaper editorialists, or businessmen. However, Freeman and Medoff present data that show how widespread union membership is among certain
demographic categories and regions in the United States. They also show
how many nonunion people would like to join a union. Table 6.3 is constructed from their data.

These figures point to a tremendous unmet demand for unions in the
South, particularly among the manual workers—among whom almost half
of unorganized workers would join a union if given the chance—but also
among white-collar workers, among whom one-fourth would join. Among
southern blue-collar and white-collar workers combined, 35 percent of all
unorganized employees in the South would vote for a union by secret
ballot.

Freeman and Medoff's data on union membership are combined in
table 6.4 with their data on unrepresented workers' desire to join a
union.[80] One can then estimate in each of the four regions the combined

Table 6.3

National and Southern Union Data, 1977

	United States		South	
	Blue-Collar[a] (%)	White-Collar[b] (%)	Blue-Collar (%)	White-Collar (%)
Who belongs to unions?[c] (of all workers)	30	9	18	5
Who wants unions?[d] (of all nonrepresented employees)	39	28	46	25

Source: Richard B. Freeman and James L. Medoff, *What Do Unions Do?* (New York: Basic Books, 1984), 27 and 29. Data are based on surveys conducted in 1977.

[a] Blue-collar workers include those in the following occupations: craftsmen and kindred workers, operatives, nonfarm laborers, private household workers, all other service workers, and farm laborers and foremen.

[b] White-collar workers include those in the following occupations: professional, technical and kindred workers, managers and administrators (except farm), sales workers, clerical and kindred workers, and farmers and farm managers.

[c] Percentage of private-sector wage and salary employees who belong to a labor union or association similar to a labor union.

[d] Percentage of private-sector wage and salary nonrepresented employees who answered "For" to the question: "If an election were held with secret ballots, would you vote for or against having a union or employees' association represent you?"

percentage of blue-collar employees who were either union members or who would like to be.

The South, a large proportion of whose people are comprised of Texans, is the area of the country with the smallest blue-collar unionized work force by far. But it has the largest demand for unions among the unorganized. If union members are combined with workers who would like to join, there is apparently little difference among blue-collar workers in the four regions, regarding their "propensity to unionize."

But if the desire for unions among workers in the South is no different from that elsewhere in the country, what explains the South's low rate of unionization? The figures in table 6.4 suggest that explanations invoking a peculiar culture—in this case, a southern one—are no more helpful than they were in chapter 2.

A more likely explanation is that industries that are traditionally unionized in the United States are underrepresented in Texas's industrial structure.[81] Another not incompatible explanation –as has already been argued—is the existence of a powerful, well-orchestrated anti-union effort over many years by the business community, the Radical Right, and the mass media. This anti-union force undoubtedly owes part of its success to

Table 6.4
Blue-Collar Employees Who Are Union
Members or Who Would Like to Be,
1977

	Members (%)	Want to Be (%)	Total (%)
Northeast	38	23	61
Central	38	17	55
South	18	38	56
West	30	27	57

Source: Data calculated from sources cited
in table 6.3.

the permeable Mexican border. "The ease with which workers can be
replaced in an economy that has a large reservoir of unskilled labor on
which to draw has been an important influence shaping labor relations in
industries along the Texas border," according to economists Robert W.
Glover and Allan G. King.[82]

They cite the example of the protracted and bitter strike at the Farah
Manufacturing Company in the border city of El Paso during the 1970s.
The plant, which manufactures clothing, remained in operation continu-
ously by replacing striking workers with domestic and foreign ones, while
numerous unfair labor practice charges were processed by the National
Labor Relations Board, and lawsuits wended their way through the
courts. "The nature of the labor markets along the Texas border have virtually eliminated the strike as a viable union weapon," argue Glover and
King.[83]

An understanding of Texas manual workers as a political phenomenon
must therefore take note of two important facts, which in turn must be
dealt with in assessing Key's theory of Texas politics. First, it is true today
as it was when he wrote that manual workers are so disorganized that they
hardly merit being called a class, as that term has been used to describe
the stratum of the very rich. Second, unionism has not succeeded in the
organizing role that Key and many liberals of his generation anticipated
for it.

This is not to say that labor unions have failed in all that they have
attempted. On the contrary. They have gotten many job and health benefits for union members and for nonunion workers whose employers have
tried to stay abreast of labor-negotiated standards to keep their own work
force from unionizing. The union leadership, and some of the rank and
file, have played a significant role in the struggle for racial justice from the
1940s on. They have also taken progressive stands for women's rights,

especially as more women have joined unions. The continuing role of organized labor in election campaigns, in funding labor and liberal candidates, and in lobbying the legislature must be acknowledged. But it is still true that unions in Texas have not come anywhere near to fulfilling their potential. And their continuing numerical decline makes it doubtful whether they will be able to maintain even the limited influence they have had since World War II.

7

Money and Politics

THIS CHAPTER will address the claim that conservative money, coming disproportionately from the Texas business class, makes a difference in closely matched races where economic liberals face conservatives. If true, this would help to explain the puzzle in chapter 2: Assuming that Texas's grass-roots conservatism is less widespread than is commonly believed, why have so few liberals gained statewide office in the past fifty years?

Part of the answer, as has been shown, lies in the voting rates of blue-collar Texans. This in turn is the result of many things, among which are a high poverty rate, the presence of recent Hispanic immigrants, and the failure of labor unions to increase voter turnout. Business-class cohesion is also a factor.

Another is the superior finances of the conservatives. Texas elections have long been expensive, especially at the statewide level, but they are extraordinarily so today. By the middle of the 1980s it was not uncommon for winning candidates to spend $10 million in pursuit of the governorship or a U.S. Senate seat. What does such campaign money buy? Does it purchase elections outright? Are campaign costs so great that competent people of ordinary means have great difficulty winning office? Are certain interests, or even entire social classes, able to burn their exclusive brand on public policy? Are important viewpoints denied a hearing because their advocates lack financial resources? These are questions of moment.

The Relation of Money and Votes

Certainly money does not buy elections in every case. The biggest spenders do not always win. Even when they do, this is not sufficient evidence that money is decisive, because other factors are often correlated with expenditures—the candidates' incumbency, for example, or their ethnicity, personal attractiveness, gender, political ideology, experience, party ties, and the like. Too, factors besides the candidates' traits also impinge on the outcome—the voters' inclinations at a campaign's start, the weather on election day, and political events beyond the candidates' control, to name but three. Many of these factors are difficult, if not impossible, to measure.

Yet it is still possible to get a rough idea of the relation between money spent and votes obtained and to control for the effects of some measurable variables. To do this, a study was made of all statewide election contests, excluding judgeships, in 1972 and 1974, in which at least two major-party candidates vied for office. These were election years in which grass-roots liberal sentiment was substantial and well-known liberal Democrats waged campaigns for the U.S. Senate and the governorship. Uncontested races were excluded as were those in general elections in which a single Democrat or Republican opposed only a La Raza Unida or other splinter-party candidate. Primary contests were treated as separate, and the money candidates reported spending in the primary period was treated separately from that spent in the general election.[1]

Figure 7.1 indicates a high linear relation between the percentage of candidates' total expenditures and the share of votes they received in thirty-four contests. The winner was the highest spender 76 percent of the time. Yet in twenty-one of those races, the highest spender was also the incumbent. To separate the effects of money from incumbency, the thirteen races without an incumbent were analyzed. In those, the highest spenders were winners in all but two. Further, twelve of the thirteen contests without incumbents were between persons of the same party opposing each other in a first or second primary, suggesting that money had an impact independent of the candidates' party affiliation.

Another study that attempted to measure money's influence in Texas campaigns was conducted by political scientist David Prindle, who analyzed all Texas Railroad Commission races in the Democratic primary contests, in which party label is obviously not a factor, every two years between 1962 and 1978. The commission is the state regulator of the oil and gas industry. In these typically low-profile races, Prindle found, winners were without exception the candidates with the largest receipts—all pro-industry candidates. This was true even in those rare cases when the industry candidate was not an incumbent.[2] In short, money seems to have independent influence on election outcomes in Texas.

Raising political money can be a full-time job. One reason is that Texas is so big. And for some time now, its population has been one of the nation's largest and most rapidly growing. The distance between El Paso on the state's far western edge and Beaumont on its eastern one is 837 miles, roughly the distance between New York City and Atlanta or Chicago. As the crow flies, it is 798 miles from Brownsville at the state's southern tip to Amarillo in the Panhandle, a greater distance than separates Kansas City from Birmingham or Atlanta from Detroit.

Moreover, the state's 1980 population, exceeding 14 million, was greater than the population of 12.3 million persons then inhabiting New England, which elects ten U.S. senators, or the 11.4 million persons in

FIGURE 7.1

Statewide Candidates' Share of Expenditures and Share of Votes, 1972–1974

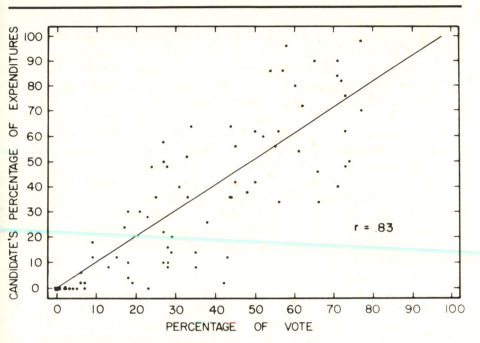

Source: Calculated from data supplied by the Texas secretary of state.

the eight-state Rocky Mountain region, which elects sixteen. None of the other ten states of the old Confederacy, including Virginia, Georgia, or North Carolina, had half as many people as Texas. And while most Texans are clustered in about two dozen major metropolitan areas, these areas are themselves widely scattered.

From the perspective of a candidate for statewide office who cannot easily overcome these distances with television advertising, the only bright spot in this demographic prospect is the fact that the three major population centers—Houston, Dallas–Fort Worth, and San Antonio—are at the apexes of a triangle roughly 200 miles from each other in the eastern central part of the state, and Austin, the state capital, is enclosed in that triangle. The 1980 population of these three centers—6.9 million—comprised almost half the state's residents. But the remaining half, which no serious politician can afford to write off, are scattered far and wide across the state.

Thus serious money is necessary at the beginning of a statewide campaign if a candidate is to have any hope of paying for the air transportation needed to reach the main population centers frequently during the long months from January to November in election years, which often encompass two primaries and a general election, and to pay for the media advertising that substitutes for personal contact with the electorate.

Experienced candidates budget most of their expenses for television and radio spots. In 1982, Mark White was said to have allocated 60 percent of his total budget to television and other mass media appeals, in his challenge to Governor Bill Clements, who spent about half of his much larger budget on the media. Long before that tremendously expensive campaign was over, Clements reported paying $2.2 million to a single Boston company for production and placement of television ads.[3]

Candidates also budget for get-out-the-vote operations. Specialized consultants handle this aspect of the campaign, just as they plot advertising strategies. For example, Market Opinion Research of Detroit handled Clements's telephone bank operations in 1982, a several-hundred-thousand-dollar enterprise aimed at reaching two million homes. The Republican party was paid $126,398 to distribute more than a million copies of a right-wing tabloid describing White's drunken driving arrest as a college student nineteen years earlier.[4]

Candidates' quests for money are not impeded significantly by legal restrictions on gifts. To be sure, the post-Watergate era reforms, which apply only to federal elections, have modified the practice of individuals' giving hundreds of thousands of dollars to a single candidate. According to current statutes, individuals are limited to a donation of no more than $2,000 directly to a federal candidate for a primary and general election combined and to no more than $5,000 to a committee. But a loophole still gives enterprising donors a chance to dispense huge sums. If donors spend money on a candidate's behalf without provably coordinating it with the candidate's organization, they are still free to spend as much as they like.

Thus Cecil R. Haden, owner of a Houston tugboat company, spent more than five times as much as anyone else in the country in 1980 on federal candidates—$599,333—most of which went to Ronald Reagan and John Connally in their presidential bids. Two other Houstonians were among the eight top spenders in the United States that year: Theodore N. Law and former state senator Henry Grover, both right-wing Republicans.[5]

Even without this loophole, the impact of money in federal elections would still be felt. Thanks to another feature of the same reform laws, business corporation political action committees (PACs) are now allowed to collect huge sums through voluntary donations from employees and stockholders and to dispense them to an unlimited number of targets. While each PAC is limited to a contribution of $5,000 per federal candidate, PAC proliferation appears to have compensated amply for the decrease in the donations given directly to candidates by rich individuals.

In state races, according to James E. Anderson and his colleagues, political money "is controlled only in the sense that contributions and expenditures must be reported."[6] State Senator John Montford, who had failed in two previous attempts to pass comprehensive campaign reform laws, called the lack of regulation "the Wild West syndrome. Anything goes."[7] For example, Clinton Manges, a South Texas rancher, spent about $2 million on candidates, including a few liberals, in 1982. Robert J. Perry, a Houston real estate developer, spent $320,000 in the first half of 1982 alone on Texas candidates and two PACs. His gifts went mostly to Republicans, including $15,000 to Clements, who had earlier appointed him to the state banking board. Perry gave several other candidates sums ranging from $9,000 to $30,000.[8]

The Monetary Resources of Liberals and Conservatives

Several hard-fought liberal-conservative battles occurred during the 1960s, the decade of civil rights upheavals, Lyndon Johnson's Great Society programs, and America's war in Vietnam. These tumultuous events pitted Right against Left in emotional confrontations. An analysis of liberal-conservative expenditures in Texas during that decade was conducted using information compiled by Clifton McCleskey, a political scientist, on important races between 1962 and 1970.

The data in table 7.1 cover all contests for governor and U.S. senator featuring a liberal-conservative fight. Eight such contests occurred—five Democratic primaries, two primary runoffs, and a general election. Liberals were outspent in every one, usually by a factor of two. In some cases, the reported figures probably understate the liberal disadvantage. The small differences in the 1962 Democratic runoff between John Connally and Don Yarborough, a popular liberal and a hard campaigner, are particularly suspect. Neither was an incumbent. Connally, who had recently resigned as secretary of the navy, was said to have run an extremely well-funded campaign. Yarborough (no kin to Ralph) complained of funding troubles throughout the race.

The table reveals that, except for Ralph Yarborough in 1964, the liberals lost. Yarborough overcame the financial advantage of Gordon McClendon, owner of a mass media empire and one of the ninety-nine richest Texans, and went on to defeat Republican challenger George Bush. Two factors probably offset Yarborough's monetary disadvantage. He was an incumbent, having originally won by a plurality in a 1957 special election

Table 7.1

Campaign Expenditures of Leading Candidates in
Selected Liberal-Conservative Races, 1962–1970[a]

Election and Candidate	Ideology	1st Demo. Primary (Amount)	(%)	2d Demo. Primary (Amount)	(%)	General Election (Amount)	(%
Governor (1962)							
John Connally[b]	Cons.	$278,339	72	$134,540	52	—	—
Don Yarborough	Lib.	109,577	28	122,287	48	—	—
Governor (1964)							
John Connally[b]	Cons.	220,786	62	—	—	—	—
Don Yarborough	Lib.	135,895	38	—	—	—	—
U.S. Senate (1964)							
Gordon McClendon	Cons.	311,191	72	—	—	—	—
Ralph Yarborough[b]	Lib.	123,880	28	—	—	$87,786	2:
George Bush	Cons.	—	—	—	—	288,284	7"
Governor (1968)							
Preston Smith[b]	Cons.	415,163	13	430,485	65	—	—
John Hill	Cons.	413,632	13	—	—	—	—
Edward Whittenburg	Cons.	560,232	18	—	—	—	—
Waggoner Carr	Cons.	193,840	6	—	—	—	—
Dolph Briscoe	Cons.	696,180	22	—	—	—	—
Eugene Locke	Cons.	654,170	21	—	—	—	—
Don Yarborough	Lib.	162,865	5	227,757	35	—	—
U.S. Senate (1970)							
Lloyd Bentsen[b]	Cons.	572,582	65	—	—	—	—
Ralph Yarborough	Lib.	311,125[c]	35	—	—	—	—

Source: Clifton McCleskey, *The Government and Politics of Texas*, 2d ed. (Boston: Little, Brown and Company, 1966), 72; 4th ed. (1972), 63.

[a] Only the leading candidates, in terms of votes obtained, are included in the table. The contests depicted are those in which a clearly identified liberal was in contention with one or more clearly identified conservatives. Percentages are shares of top two vote getters' expenditures.

[b] Eventual winner of general election.

[c] Includes entries under "debts incurred."

that did not require a majority vote to win, and he ran on a ticket with incumbent Lyndon Johnson, the native son who carried the state by an even greater landslide against Barry Goldwater than the one by which he carried the nation. Johnson, it was rumored, had given instructions to his conservative Democratic allies not to oppose Yarborough for fear that liberals would withdraw their support of LBJ in the November election if Yarborough were defeated in the primary. McClendon, a maverick operating outside the Democratic establishment, ran anyway.

Why are liberals unable to raise as much money as conservatives? One answer is that liberals in the state are typically outnumbered. But it is also possible that a larger percentage of conservatives give campaign donations than do liberals, because they are on average wealthier. Furthermore, conservatives who contribute probably give larger donations per capita than do liberals, for the same reason. These two tendencies may expand conservative candidates' monetary advantage.

Let us make the reasonable assumption that most donors of $500, or more recently, $1,000, are affluent.[9] On this assumption, we can explore the political spending habits of the well-off by focusing on the big donors. What we find is that at least by World War II in Texas, these big donors gave overwhelmingly to Republicans in presidential elections and to conservatives of either party from the top of the ballot to the bottom.

A privately compiled list of the 212 major Texas contributors to national party campaign committees in 1944—those who gave $500 or more, or roughly the equivalent of $3,000 or more in 1985 dollars—contained the names of the most prominent members of the Texas upper class of the day, many of whose heirs were still big contributors in the 1980s. It included oil moguls like H. L. Hunt, Harry Bass, Jake Hamon, Harry Wiess, various Cullens, Jim and Wesley West, and Glenn McCarthy. There were also members of the King Ranch clan; Stanley Marcus, the Dallas merchant; various family members and executives connected with Anderson-Clayton, the Houston cotton factors; brothers Herman and George Brown of Brown & Root, the construction firm; and Oveta and William P. Hobby, Sr., publishers of the *Houston Post*. Most of them were people of secure and even gargantuan fortunes whose individual campaign contributions over decades probably amounted to hundreds of thousands—perhaps millions—of dollars.[10]

In a year when FDR received 71 percent of the Texas vote, 66 percent of the big contributors in 1944 gave their money to Republican committees and only 34 percent to Democratic ones. Seventy-one percent of the aggregate $410,410 went to the Republicans.[11] In other words, this preference for the GOP existed before the Dixiecrat party of 1948 and the Eisenhower campaigns of the 1950s. In two-party contests where Republicans have had a chance of winning, the Texas big donors have long favored them. They voted for conservative Democrats at the state and local level, apparently, because Republican candidates had no chance of winning. Big-donor preference for Republicans further down the ballot has increased as Republican chances have grown.

Candidate ideology rather than party label, then, is the predictor of upper-class preferences. Table 4.1 in chapter 4 indicates that of the 131 Texas donors or lenders of $10,000 or more—roughly $26,000 in 1985 dollars—to presidential candidates in 1972, 83 percent gave to conservatives, 15 percent gave to liberals or moderates, and 2 percent split their contributions. One hundred sixteen Texans gave or loaned at least $10,000 that year to gubernatorial candidates, and 91 percent gave to conservatives, 9 percent gave to liberals, and 1 percent split their contributions.

The 1972 gubernatorial elections deserve special comment. In the Democratic primary, Frances Farenthold, a liberal, opposed three important conservatives: Dolph Briscoe, Lieutenant Governor Ben Barnes, and Governor Preston Smith. In the Republican primary the same day, six conservatives contended. The distribution of receipts from individual contributors of $500 or more is shown in table 7.2, which contains figures for the runoffs and general elections as well.

Distinguishing candidates by ideology rather than by party is essential for understanding Texas politics. If recipients of large donations had been classified only on the basis of party, a puzzling pattern would have emerged—big donors giving almost ten times as much money to Democrats as to Republicans in the two primaries combined, and then, in a dramatic about-face, giving the Republican candidate about twice as much as his opponents in November.

When the focus is on candidates' ideology, however, a perfectly rational strategy of the wealthy is evident. In the two primaries, they gave almost 90 percent of their aggregate donations to conservatives, putting most of that into the races of conservative Democrats, in order to prevent the nomination of a liberal. They paid little attention to the Republican primaries in which the two serious candidates, Fay and Grover, were right wing and reactionary, respectively.

But the rich spent their money very differently in the general election. Far Right Republican Grover there confronted conservative Democrat Briscoe. (Ramsey Muñiz, La Raza Unida party's candidate, was also in the race but had no chance.) Given the choice between a Far Right Republican and a conservative Democrat, large donors pumped considerably more money into the Republican's campaign.

These figures apply only to individual donors' direct contributions to candidates. What about the ideological preference of PACs? According to reporter Jon Ford, who made a systematic assessment of Texas PACs in 1974, most supported winning candidates who tended to be "conservative Democrats with known voting records." The PACs sometimes hedged their bets by supporting multiple candidates in a race. Liberals were not entirely ignored, Ford observed, "but their cut was certainly smaller than that of the conservatives." Labor committees were a major source of liberal PAC money.[12]

There has been a small group of wealthy Texas liberals who carry a heavy burden at election time, and their names are well known to supplicants. During the past forty years or so, they have included Walter Hall, small-town banker; Bernard Rapoport, Waco insurance company owner;

Table 7.2
Individual Contributions of $500 or More, Gubernatorial Contests, 1972[a]

FIRST PRIMARY

Democrats

Farenthold	(liberal)	$133,635 ($N = 48$)[b]
Briscoe	(conservative)	
Smith	(conservative)	$983,426 ($N = 717$)
Barnes	(conservative)	

Republicans   (all conservatives)

Fay		
Grover		
Reagan		$119,551 ($N = 59$)
McElroy		
Jenkins		
Hall		

Summary, Both Parties Combined

Contributions to liberals	$ 133,635 (11%)
Contributions to conservatives	$1,102,977 (89%)
Total contributions	$1,236,612 (100%)

RUNOFF PRIMARY

Democrats

Farenthold	(liberal)	$ 83,500 ($N = 43$)
Briscoe	(conservative)	$487,609 ($N = 338$)

Republicans

Grover	(conservative)	
Fay	(conservative)	$ 66,886 ($N = 43$)

Summary, Both Parties Combined

Contributions to liberals	$ 83,500 (13%)
Contributions to conservatives	$ 554,495 (87%)
Total contributions	$ 637,995 (100%)

GENERAL ELECTIONS

Muñiz (RUP)	$ 10,665 ($N = 6$)
Briscoe (D)	$297,775 ($N = 221$)
Grover (R)	$562,523 ($N = 113$)

Summary

Contributions to liberals	$ 10,665 (1%)
Contributions to conservatives	$860,298 (99%)
Total contributions	$870,963 (100%)

Source: Calculated from data in Herbert E. Alexander and Katharine C. Fischer, eds., *CRF Listing of: Political Contributors of $500 or More in 1972 to Candidates and Committees in Twelve States* (Princeton, N.J.: Citizens' Research Foundation, 1974).

[a] Husband-wife contributors are counted as a single unit if their contributions went to the same candidate. As the Alexander-Fischer data do not distinguish between first- and second-primary donations, primary donations listed after May 6, the day of the first primary, are counted as second-primary donations. Primary donations not dated are apportioned equally between the first and second primaries. Alexander and Fischer distinguish between primary and general-election contributions.

[b] N = number of contributions to candidates in amounts of $500 or more.

18. Don Yarborough. A popular liberal lawyer, Yarborough (no kin to Ralph) came close to defeating John
Connally in the 1962 Democratic primary race for the
gubernatorial nomination, in spite of Connally's strong
establishment backing. Yarborough ran again in 1964 and
1968. Courtesy of Russell Lee and the *Texas Observer*.

Jubal Parten, a rare liberal oilman; Frankie Randolph, scion of banking
and lumber fortunes; Nina Cullinan, daughter of Texaco founder Joseph
"Buckskin Joe" Cullinan; John and Dominique de Menil, heirs of the
Schlumberger oil well service fortune; Billy Goldberg, Houston banker;
oilman Jim Calaway, and a few others.[13] This handful of liberals were exceptions to the conservative tendencies of most big Texas donors. In the
1980s, the liberals were joined by trial lawyers and by some big donors
from other states. But large contributions are still today much easier for
conservative candidates to obtain than they are for liberal ones.

This is not necessarily a calamity for liberals. If there were other money
sources besides the Texas wealthy—the Democratic party's coffers or out-
of-state liberal donors, for example—then they would not with certainty
be outspent. But in fact they usually are outspent, and as the big spenders

19. On the rubber-chicken circuit. Banker Walter Hall
(left) of Dickinson congratulates Ralph Yarborough after
a fund-raiser in Yarborough's honor. Hall, a small-town
banker, supporter of organized labor, and liberal Democrat, was one of the few people of wealth in Texas to give
Yarborough (and other liberal candidates) appreciable
financial backing. Courtesy of the *Texas Observer*.

tend to win, the liberals lose. The huge amounts required to run a serious
race may also have scared off a good many potential liberal candidates.

The Big Donors

Big donations are aggregated into even bigger funding pools by those
whom George Thayer once called "key men with access."[14] They are men
of the upper class who represent themselves to politicians as spokesmen

for that class and who have managed to convince others that they have the politicians' ear. They are influential in their own right, and so it is something of a misnomer to call them "power brokers" as though they were mere go-betweens.

The way key men with access gather money in Texas was strikingly revealed by events in 1972, when the Watergate scandal triggered the most painstaking investigations of campaign financing in the nation's history—investigations that shed light on the methods the rich employed to hide the extent of their giving.

Congressional and FBI investigations revealed that large sums of Republican money from Texas and surrounding areas were being collected in the Pennzoil Company's offices in Houston. Robert H. Allen, president of a Houston conglomerate, Gulf Resources & Chemical Company, and William Liedtke, Jr., Pennzoil president, were the chief fund-raisers. Together they managed an operation that accumulated $700,000, including $100,000 that came originally from the corporate bank account of Allen's company, a subsidiary of which the Environmental Protection Agency was then pressuring to correct air and water pollution problems. (The $700,000 would have had a purchasing power of $1.8 million in 1985.)

To obscure the source of the $100,000—Allen's personal contribution— he "laundered" it by sending it to a Gulf Resources subsidiary in Mexico, where an attorney negotiated bank drafts for $89,000 that were then given, along with $11,000 in cash, to Diaz de Leon, the subsidiary's president, who delivered the total amount to the Pennzoil offices in Houston. Later the same day, the laundered money was stuffed into a suitcase along with the remaining $600,000, and a Pennzoil vice president flew it to Washington on a Pennzoil plane, where it was given to Hugh W. Sloan, Jr., treasurer of the Finance Committee to Re-Elect the President (FCRP).

The gift arrived in time to beat by two days the April 7 disclosure deadline, mandated by the new Federal Election Campaign Act, after which date far more detailed information on contributors and their donations would be required. Sloan later testified to a U.S. Senate committee that the four Mexican bank drafts brought to Houston by de Leon, totaling $89,000, were passed on to G. Gordon Liddy, an FCRP lawyer who was later convicted for his role in the Watergate conspiracy. After Bernard L. Barker was caught with four accomplices in the break-in at the Watergate Hotel, the bank drafts were found in his Miami bank account.[15]

The sensational laundering of the $100,000, however, deflected attention from the entirely legal and quite common practice by which a few key fund-raisers pool the resources of the business class and deliver huge sums of cash either to a PAC or to a candidate, who is made aware of its sources.

In the case just mentioned, part of the $700,000, it was later disclosed, "had been contributed by executives of three firms that had won a billion dollar contract to bring natural gas from the Soviet Union to the United States." The three companies, all located in Houston, were Brown & Root, Texas Eastern Transmission, and Tenneco.[16] At the time, George Brown, who was chairman of Brown & Root, was also chairman of Texas Eastern's executive committee.

Another contributor to the "Pennzoil fund," in the amount of $26,013, was Texas Instruments' Erik Jonsson, whose employees also donated $21,025 to Nixon. Like Brown, Jonsson was one of the ninety-nine richest Texans described in chapter 4. He was also chairman of the Nixon reelection campaign in Texas. As early as the summer of 1971, the White House had developed a plan to use the federal government as a tool to drum up campaign support for Nixon. Several major grants were dispensed for this purpose, including one by the U.S. Department of Transportation for $7.6 million to the Dallas–Ft. Worth Regional Airport to help build a shuttle transportation system. The chairman of the Texas Airport Authority, which benefited from the grant, was Erik Jonsson.[17]

Rather than give directly to candidates, of course, donors may give to committees, thus making it more difficult for outsiders to trace the source. Seventeen of the ninety-nine—or close family members—gave at least $1,000 to the Committee to Re-elect the President. Many of these contributions were in excess of $25,000. During the 1972 campaign, Clint Murchison and his brother John D. Murchison, for example, gave $50,000 in cash.[18]

In some cases, big donors may give small amounts while the corporations they control give large ones, either through PACs or individual executives' donations. While these donations, if legal, must be given voluntarily, the corporation heads often get the credit from the candidate. H. Ross Perot, one of the ninety-nine, was not among those listed by the Citizens Research Foundation as having donated $500 or more in 1972. Yet investigations by the Watergate Committee revealed that the two largest donations to the presidential campaign of Arkansas congressman Wilbur Mills—at the time the powerful chairman of the House Ways and Means Committee, highly relevant to the fortunes of Perot's company, Electronic Data Systems (EDS)—were from Milledge A. Hart III, president of EDS, and Mervin L. Stauffer, Perot's personal assistant. Hart's donation of $51,000, when added to Stauffer's $49,000, came to exactly $100,000, which represented almost one-seventh of the $730,000 spent on behalf of Mills's campaign.[19] Information collected by Common Cause at the time of the Watergate revelations also revealed that the president and vice president of Perot's company gave $109,342 and $114,549, respectively, to Nixon's 1972 campaign. Five current or former executives of Texas Instruments contributed $127,774.[20]

Twelve years later, in 1984, Jim Francis, a well-known political operative, was a key fund-raiser for the 1984 GOP convention in Dallas. Francis did not belong to the big rich, but Harvey ("Bum") Bright, the owner of Bright Industries, where Francis was an executive, was a member of the ninety-nine.[21] Francis exemplifies the continuing role that executives for the big rich play as key men with access.

PACs and Super-PACs

The big corporate PACs, as noted, have become major players in Texas and national politics, proliferating explosively since the 1970s. Some of the large Texas-based conglomerates give huge sums. The Federal Election Commission found as early as 1976—just as PACs were beginning to multiply as a result of congressional reforms five years earlier—that only 9 corporate PACs among the 450 contributing money to federal campaigns that year accounted for nearly 20 percent of the total donations by those 450 PACs. LTV Corporation of Dallas was one of the 9.[22]

Individual enterprises and industrial trade groups formed PACs in the late 1970s to fund state political campaigns as well. In 1976, 491 PACs were registered with the secretary of state, and most were citizen groups and labor union committees. Two years later, the number had increased to 1,209, and nearly all of the new PACs were corporate or trade-group committees. Among the larger individual business firm PACs were those connected with Braniff Airlines ($28,550), ALCOA ($29,600), Brown & Root ($37,500), Perry Bass enterprises ($74,559), Dow Chemical ($55,150), Texas Power & Light ($58,025), First City Bancorporation ($67,723), LTV ($209,216), and Empire Drilling ($48,470).[23]

Industry-wide PACs were among the largest contributors. These committees combined funds from a number of separate enterprises and presumably represented a point of view common to all contributors. Among them were Life Underwriters PAC (insurance, $139,250), PACT (oil and gas, $236,574), TREPAC (realtors, $459,740), BALLOT (bankers, $137,281), and Big 50 PAC (builders, $133,275).[24]

Another kind of committee, the super-PAC, which represents not so much a particular company or industry but entire class-wide interests, is even more important as a source of funding. Playing somewhat the same role as the big banks and the huge corporate law firms described in chapter 5, super-PACs pool vast resources and bring key men with access together to decide major questions—in this case, who will get corporate money and who will be targeted for defeat.

When the super-PACs link up with major individual donors and with corporate PACs connected to a powerful industry, they can be formidable.

Numerous industries whose interests sometimes clash nonetheless crowd together with the oil industry under the ideological umbrellas of class-wide PACs. One such group is HOUPAC, the Houston business community's biggest funding organization in the early 1980s. The organization took part in 132 election contests in 1982, although in that year—a recessionary one that was bad for Republicans—slightly more than half of its candidates lost.[25]

Founded in the mid-1970s, HOUPAC began as an independent oilmen's group, but it has since opened its doors to all interested members of the city's business community. According to its executive director, the majority of its contributors come from non-oil interests. While HOUPAC is concerned with the candidates' "philosophy" rather than with their party membership, it gives primarily to Republicans. It generates money through an annual giving plan, by which method 180 members gave $1,000 and "several hundred others" gave lesser amounts in 1982. Most of HOUPAC's donations go out of state.[26] In 1984, one such donation went to North Carolina's Jesse Helms in his successful bid for reelection to the U.S. Senate. That was a year in which many of the big Republican donors in Texas—including ex-governor Clements—were also contributing to the campaign of the reactionary Helms.[27]

In addition to super-PACs, some of the more diversified corporate PACs also have an unusually broad scope of targets and resources. Houston-based Tenneco, for example, has evolved from a gas transmission firm to become a major "diversified energy company." In 1982 the Tenneco Employees Good Government Fund—"the largest corporate PAC in the nation" that year—spent $425,000 in 225 U.S. House and Senate races. Supported by voluntary employee contributions, its goal was to "back candidates who support free enterprise," according to PAC chairman Macon Freeman.[28]

While some Texas-based PACs spend most of their money outside the state, the same is not true of a coalition of lobbyists such as the Associated Research Group (ARG), which in the early 1980s collected and spent large sums of money, intensively screened candidates at election time, and then, once the election was over, went on to lobby the winners.

According to reporter Virginia Ellis, in 1982 this super lobby included among its members the Texas Medical Association, the Texas Association of Realtors, and the Texas Automobile Dealers Association, whose individual PACs were the largest contributors to the 1982 Texas campaigns. Other members were statewide lobbyists for the restaurateurs, truckers, chemical industry, dairy producers, savings-and-loan companies, and retailers, a diversity that underscores its class-wide function. By the end of the spring primaries, members of ARG had donated more than $1 million to 150 political campaigns.[29]

The "research" of the Associated Research Group involved finding out whether candidates were conservative enough to suit the super lobby's tastes. For this purpose, in 1982 ARG fielded a panel of ten influential and experienced lobbyists who convened in Austin and invited some—but not all—of the legislative candidates to travel to the capital at their own expense to be interviewed.

The session was harrowing for some candidates, who came away with the impression that the wrong answer to a single lobbyist's question had hurt their chances of getting contributions from others. If correct, that fact too suggests a coherence that transcends industries' and individual trade groups' interests. One candidate said he was asked his position on Sunday blue laws, product liability, the issue of shifting more power to county government, and "interest rates." He said that when he told the group that he did not favor increasing interest rates, "one lobbyist slammed his notebook shut and stalked out of the room." There was a thoroughness to the procedure that did not go unnoticed by the candidates. One said that the public relations man representing all members of ARG "produced extensive research" on each contest and legislative district, including computerized data on "voting trends, racial mix, and voter turnout. 'They knew more about my district than I did,' " he said.[30]

Even this kind of power is not invincible. ARG's candidates that year, during the deep recession popularly associated with the Reagan administration, did not fare nearly as well as the group had hoped. However, the specter of a class-wide centralized group with extensive information on candidates and more than $1 million to spend is a strong incentive for politicians to tailor their views to fit those of the lobby.

The extent to which reported expenditures by business PACs are supplemented by illegal money is impossible to know, although occasional scandals involving slush funds suggest that it is considerable. Information brought to light by the Watergate investigations indicated that under-the-table cash transactions were routinely made by several major corporations, some of which had extensive Texas ties.

Claude Wild, Jr., Gulf Oil's former top lobbyist, admitted in 1978 that he dispensed more than $5 million in corporate funds illegally to political candidates between 1960 and 1973. (Gulf gave politicos both in the U.S. and overseas between $10 and $12 million from its slush fund over the thirteen-year period.) Between $30,000 and $85,000 was paid solely to Texas political candidates and officials each year from 1962 through 1972, although the candidates did not know the contributions were illegal, said Wild. Other companies whose illegal slush funds operated in Texas were Phillips Petroleum, which admitted to contributing to numerous candidates for the Texas house and senate and for statewide office, and Occidental Petroleum. None of these oil giants was headquartered in the state.

However, a number of Texas-based companies also were guilty of illegal political payments in the 1960s and early 1970s.[31]

The focus of this discussion of PACs has been on business-connected committees, particularly those with a classwide aim or basis of support. In the ongoing conflict between the business class and the working class, the money spent by business PACs in Texas dwarfs that spent by committees directly representing workers. Research by journalists indicates that business-related state and local PACs in 1978 and 1980 spent at least twenty times as much as did the Texas AFL-CIO and perhaps even more.[32]

Returns on Investments

What do big donors expect from their candidates once they are in office? Nothing of any import, according to one point of view. "Do you know what most of those big political contributors want for their money?" Lieutenant Governor Ben Barnes once asked a writer. "Nothing to do with taxes or politics or legislation. They just want me to spend an hour or two with them in public. They want me to sit next to them at a football game or be an honored guest at a big dinner."[33] Another answer is: everything, at least with regard to "taxes or politics or legislation," as Barnes put it. In this view, campaign donations are little more than bribes to enact laws for the donor's benefit.

Searching for the answer to this question, in the early 1970s reporter Jon Ford interviewed several politicians and officeholders in a project designed by Herbert E. Alexander of the Citizens Research Foundation. One was Houston attorney Searcy Bracewell, a former senator and then a key Austin lobbyist for business interests. The year Ford interviewed him, Bracewell had given $9,000 to candidates in amounts of $500 or greater. "Most politicians," Bracewell allowed, were "pretty idealistic and sincere." But he hastened to add that "politics is no different than anything else. People do business with their friends. Politicians can't help rationalizing a controversial matter in favor of their friends. They do it unwittingly." Or perhaps not so unwittingly. Allan Shivers, in discussing appointees with Ford, said, "I took the position while I was in office that I would rather appoint my friends than my enemies."[34]

Some officeholders denied vigorously that it was normal for big donors to ask favors after the election. Yet one official—a veteran of many state and local campaigns and a former legislative lobbyist—was more cynical. Lawmakers who defend the innocence of contributors are simply not truthful, he insisted. "It is almost a daily occurrence in statewide campaigns for people to give a candidate money for a specific purpose," he said. "After he gets elected, a man finds out too often that the reason he got the $500 contribution was that the donor has a problem with the regulatory agency the candidate now heads. A large portion of money given to a statewide campaign has this kind of invisible string attached."

Not that the chips are often called in by a particular donor. That would be too crude. But according to this source—who wished to remain anonymous because of the high post he held—"I know of no official who hasn't had major contributors come to him and say, 'I've never asked you for anything before, but I must have this favor.' Legislators are faced with that same problem on many of their crucial votes." And while "money doesn't buy politicians," liberal state senator A. R. ("Babe") Schwartz told Ford, "I'll tell you what it does: It hardens the lines of loyalties."[35]

One source of information on this subject that has usually been ignored by research is the large donors themselves. Larry Berg and his colleagues asked a sample of such donors in California whether they thought that large contributors expected something in return from the candidates. Only one respondent in seven said that the expectation of a quid pro quo was not very important as a motive. Exactly half opined that "large campaign donations from a few wealthy individuals" affect the politician's decisions a great deal once they are elected, and another 23 percent said it affects their decisions somewhat.[36]

Many big contributors undoubtedly evaluate their investment in very concrete terms after a legislative session has ended. In an internal memorandum that fell into the hands of the press in 1986, the PAC of Gulf States Utilities in Beaumont congratulated itself and other utilities that, it said, "came through the 69th Legislature with virtually no harm done, thanks to the efforts of the lawmakers we have supported with our time and our dollars. . . . With very few exceptions, these senators and representatives listened carefully when we had problems with certain proposals and either helped keep them from passing or worked out amendments that made the bills satisfactory to the industry." The memorandum, sent to members of its PAC, explained that forty bills had been identified as potentially harmful to electric utilities. Only one made it to the governor's desk, it said, and "before the measure was passed, compromises had been struck, making the bill at least acceptable to us."[37]

Large contributions influence policy most crucially, it appears, by helping elect people whom the donors consider like-minded. Also, the money buys the donor access once his candidate is elected: a chance to sit down with the official, perhaps in very comfortable surroundings—say, the donor's ranch or club—and to get a respectful hearing. If it is a matter on which the officeholder has some room to maneuver, he will probably come through, both to pay off a debt and to lay the groundwork for a future contribution. This is all the more likely if the donor is well known and has a reputation for generating campaign revenues among his contacts—people like Trammell Crow or Ray Hunt in Dallas, Walter Mischer or George Strake in Houston, Eddie Chiles in Fort Worth, T. Boone Pickens in Amarillo, men who can invite a few dozen friends over to the club and raise hundreds of thousands of dollars in an evening.[38] Big donations also buy appointments to prestigious boards and commissions. As Shivers's interview made clear, he was more likely to appoint "friends" than "enemies," and friends are easy to identify on any list of campaign contributors. A 1985 analysis of Mark White's appointees revealed that over two-thirds of the choice appointments on seventeen top-ranked boards were White's financial supporters, almost all of whom had "donated at least $1,000," and some many times that much. Positions on the boards of regents of Texas's two premier state universities tended to go to White's very big contributors or loan guarantors.[39]

The big donors and the big fund-raisers are not all-powerful. There are some politicians who cannot be bought. And even the great majority— those subject to big money's influence—must also weigh the interests of other actors who will play a role in their next campaigns. But once this is granted, the question still remains: What is the overarching impact of money in Texas?

Over the long term, money has tipped the scales in favor of the conservatives. Campaign money is thus one more aspect of the state's political structure that militates against grass-roots liberal success. Given the huge amounts of money available to conservative candidates in Texas and the have-nots' weakness in mobilizing other resources, money is more important there than in most American states.

According to democratic theory, however, there is another powerful political resource in the continuing conflict between the rich and the have-nots, and this is party organization. As V. O. Key argued, a two-party system will be most advantageous to the politically disorganized because in its structuring function it puts them on equal political footing with the organized.

Part Three

PARTY POLITICS

8

The Struggle for Control of the Democratic Party

"THE ONLY effective continuing organization in the fight for political power is the political party," a liberal Texas activist told a researcher in the 1960s at a time when conservative Democrats, who were often presidential Republicans, still controlled the state Democratic party. "So we have no effective continuing organization in the fight for power because, essentially, we have no party." A third-party effort was not feasible. "It's just too hard to build a homogeneous party outside the regular party. You can't develop any party discipline and you can't develop a cadre of workers."[1]

Following this reasoning, Texas liberals attached great importance to capturing the party with the help of moderates and "brass-collar Democrats," thereby encouraging conservatives to join the Republicans. Indeed, the liberals were as eager as the new generation of Republicans to see a realignment occur.

Parties have had many functions. They mobilize voters to nominate candidates in primaries and then to elect them in November. They have the potential to organize legislative struggles. They often perform an educational role, not only on voting procedures and candidates' views but on major issues of the day. In Texas, parties have traditionally performed variations of these functions through the convention, or caucus, system.

To most modern-day Americans whose only contact with a party caucus is viewing presidential nominating conventions on television, the term *caucus* may suggest a cross between a circus and a pep rally—a view that is not far off the mark in an era when presidential conventions do little more than rubber-stamp a nomination decided in the primaries weeks or months in advance.

In Texas, however, conventions have sometimes exemplified a fundamental type of grass-roots democracy. In recent times, voters in the party primaries meet in a precinct convention after the polls close and elect delegates to a county or state-senatorial district convention held several days later. The precinct conventions, write Clifton McCleskey and his colleagues, "provide the rank-and-file member with his only direct opportunity to voice his sentiments and to be an active participant in formal party deliberations."[2] In presidential election years, the county and district conventions then elect delegates to a summer state convention at which delegates to the national convention are selected. (Since the 1970s, one or both of the parties have sometimes experimented with choosing at least some presidential delegates through a primary, although to date neither party has dispensed with the convention system.) In both presidential and off years, there is a fall convention at which the party governing body is chosen, the party's nominees are certified, and a platform is adopted.

When factional conflict is anticipated, leaders of the factions begin recruiting their troops to attend precinct conventions months in advance, and part of the recruitment process involves educating voters on the issues and leaders involved. As chapter 9 will show, the legislature's passage in February 1975 of the highly controversial "Bentsen bill"—designed to curtail liberal clout in the nominating sweepstakes and to boost conservative Lloyd Bentsen's presidential bid the following year—set off explosions of activity among Democratic party leaders more than a year in advance of the first round of conventions. Liberal precinct organizer Billie Carr's peregrinations around the state for the seventeen months preceding the 1976 fall convention were accompanied by similar activities on the part of activists representing other subfactions of the liberals as well as of moderate and conservative Democrats.

The extent of this grass-roots activity is significant. Participants typically number between fifty and seventy-five thousand and consist of people from many walks of life. The convention process is a kind of participatory democracy, and because of reforms made in the late 1960s and early 1970s, it has finally become open to anyone wanting to get involved.

It was not always so among Democrats. Indeed, the takeover of state party machinery by liberals and moderates in 1976 described below, a maneuver made possible by national party reforms a few years earlier, resulted in a fully open process for the first time in the twentieth century. It was a victory that liberal strategists had pursued for a generation.

Chapters 8 and 9 will focus on the Democratic party, which until the 1960s was really the only party that existed at the state level, regularly holding primaries and supplying almost all officeholders. This changed rapidly in the 1970s. In chapter 10 the story of emerging Republicanism will be told; in chapter 11 we will investigate the nature of the realignment that has occurred.

The liberal Democrats had a grand vision of party control, one born in the 1940s when they and other Roosevelt Democrats were pretty evenly matched against conservatives in convention battles. This vision was challenged when the conservative establishment excluded liberals from state party influence throughout most of the 1950s and 1960s. When national Democratic reforms in 1968 and 1972 gave liberals a chance to exert influence in proportion to their numbers, Texas progressives' long-sought goal seemed within their grasp.

Why did liberals put so much stock in reforming the convention system? The answer, in a word, is organization. In keeping with V. O. Key's notion of the Democratic party in a two-party system as the vehicle for organizing the have-nots and ethnic minorities, liberals saw conventions ideally as the party activity best suited to teach ordinary people how to play politics. Convention participation was far superior to simply voting, for it presented an opportunity to meet like-minded people and to hear them debate issues and strategy in preconvention caucuses held by their faction. There was a chance to meet and work with grass-roots leaders and party officials then and afterward in the fall campaign. As a delegate, one had a chance to attend the national nominating convention and to win a seat on important party committees. And one could establish contact with people and talk politics with them between conventions.

In many areas of Texas life, "talking politics" outside the home can be risky. On the job, voicing the wrong political views can get you fired. In the neighborhood, it can sometimes lead to derision or harassment. In a small town where an establishment of notables sets the limits of tolerated opinion, people's heterodox politics can make their lives miserable. A subscriber to the liberal weekly, the *Texas Observer*, who lived in a small West Texas hamlet wrote the editor in 1976 expressing a common view: "You can't imagine how good it is to be reassured by you that we aren't the only ones with 'strange notions.' Without the *Observer*, we might become paranoid."[3]

Even when political talk is not risky, it is often just talk—like talk about the weather, it leads nowhere. Since a party convention encourages delegates to take sides on policy issues and make common cause with others, it may provide participants with their only opportunity to get encouragement and sustenance from political friends. Pendleton Herring noted long ago that the value of conventions "lies in . . . permitting the rank and file of the party to participate physically and emotionally in a common enterprise. . . . Here they have their chance to meet, to act together, to feel together."[4]

This is especially true for ordinary people without access to the Lion's Club, the Rotary Club, or other such organizations, conservative in spirit, to which the affluent belong. Active lifelong political involvement has often begun when voters tentatively showed up at a precinct convention and learned—sometimes to their great surprise—that they had political allies in the same neighborhood.

One can develop a feeling for a shared cause by participating in a campaign, of course. But the convention instructs about the internal affairs of the party in ways that an election campaign usually does not. Moreover, the convention delegate, in an important sense, is an equal with everyone else, whereas a campaign volunteer, especially the neophyte, may be little more than a stamp-licker.

The stakes at a convention can be considerable. The Texas delegation to the national convention is one of the largest, and the faction that dominates it may have important leverage. In addition, the State Democratic Executive Committee (SDEC) is the state party's permanent organization; depending on the dominant faction's philosophy, it can sit on its hands or it can help candidates raise money and get out the vote at election time. It can also act as a link between the rank and file and the state legislature. Finally, the SDEC has important functions during the convention itself. The committee canvasses the votes in the primaries and can sometimes make the difference in who the party's nominees are in contested elections.

Liberals have long perceived conventions to be an important means for recruiting the apolitical masses. And one of the principal liberal goals from the 1940s on has been to make the convention system open and easy to participate in, hoping that when this happened the party would become more like the national Democrats. It is perhaps not too much to say that the convention system was seen by many liberals as the most important kind of party activity—not only because of its recruiting function but because when their faction was able to participate fully in conventions, their organizing skills would outweigh money's influence in internal party politics and fall election campaigns. The history of liberal-conservative conflict in Texas politics, therefore, is at least as much a story of the battle for control of the Democratic party through the convention process as it is the much better-known account of electoral struggle between liberal and conservative candidates for public office.

The Rise of Factions in the Democratic Party

The convention battles of the modern era followed a period of calm during the Great Depression. The description of an Austin precinct convention in 1936 by Stuart Long, a newspaperman and New Deal liberal, captures the contemporary mood. "Nobody was there but one lady and me as a reporter," Long said.

> We waited quite a while for somebody else to show up, and finally she said, "Well, I guess we're the only ones who are coming, young man. Suppose you make a motion that I be elected chairman of this convention, in absence of the precinct chairman."

So I made the motion, and she declared it carried. Then she said, "Suppose you move that I be elected delegate to the county convention and be instructed to vote for Franklin D. Roosevelt." So I made the motion. She carried it.

"Now you make the motion to adjourn," she said, "and we'll be through."

Long obeyed, and they went their separate ways into the summer evening.[5]

But in 1944, the growing feud between supporters of President Roosevelt and conservatives broke into the open. The conservative faction, calling itself the Texas Regulars, was part of a South-wide movement among the upper classes to reassert its strength within the party. The faction's strategy was to elect unpledged Democratic electors in the May convention who, in combination with other unpledged slates throughout the South, would withhold a majority of votes from FDR in the electoral college and throw the election into the House of Representatives.

Using the state party machinery, the Democratic chairman contacted leaders in every precinct in the state informing them of the Regulars' strategy, and conservatives dominated the May convention, electing an unpledged slate of electors in spite of a walkout by liberal delegates. The Regulars' momentum had been given a boost shortly before the convention when the U.S. Supreme Court announced its landmark decision in *Smith v. Allwright*, striking down the Texas "white primary" that had excluded blacks from party membership. *Smith* was sharply criticized by the predominantly conservative Texas delegation at the national convention.[6]

The pro-Roosevelt faction undid the Regulars' mischief by organizing at the precinct level after the national convention and electing a different set of delegates to the September state convention. Once in control, the liberals and loyalists purged the electors on the Regulars' slate who refused to support FDR. The president went on to win 71 percent of the Texas vote in November. The liberal-loyalist triumph also gave them control of the SDEC for the next two years, enabling them to prevent some federal patronage appointments of Regulars.[7]

The fight over FDR's fourth term brought together liberals and loyalists from across the state on an organized basis. "It was the first time that we even got to know who the other liberals were," later recalled Walter Hall, a banker in Dickinson who had taken a lead in the convention battles. "That was the beginning of the modern Texas liberal movement."[8]

Once in control of the SDEC, the liberal-loyalist faction began organizing a campaign network to recruit party activists and to raise money at the grass roots to counteract the huge funds that always seemed to be at the conservatives' disposal. Hall, one of the few persons of means among the liberals, sized up the situation in the fall of 1944 in a letter to fellow members of the executive committee: "Most of the wealthy people are lined up against Roosevelt and accordingly we cannot expect much in the way of large contributions. The money will have to come from people who will contribute from one dollar to one hundred dollars."[9]

By the end of 1945, the SDEC had begun to put the state party on a firm organizational basis, perhaps for the first time in its history. Under liberal control, its goals fit remarkably the definition of "strong local parties" given by political scientist James Gibson and his colleagues forty years later: "bureaucratized organizations characterized by professionalized and formalized structure, with adequate resources and sustained year-round activity."[10]

"Starting without any records and with an empty treasury," wrote chairman Harry L. Seay proudly, "we were able to conduct a vigorous and successful campaign for Roosevelt and Truman, and since that time we have kept in operation a full time office."[11] In the meantime, banker Hall compiled lists of party officials and active workers who were then contacted by the chairman's office. Plans were made to establish systematic funding of the party with rebates from Texans' donations to the Democratic National Committee. And the SDEC was preparing a manual for the guidance of party officials and workers to prevent "the unfaithful elements" from taking control of the party machinery "with a small but arrogant minority, well supplied with funds and well schooled in parliamentary tactics," in the words of Seay.[12] The money for the manual was being raised through small donations.

These efforts in the 1940s to establish a continuing party organization with a full-time office staff in order to identify and activate grass-roots supporters of the national party were derived from the liberals' philosophy that the party should serve as an organizing weapon for the less affluent. But the liberals were ousted from control following the defeat of Homer Rainey, the liberal gubernatorial candidate in 1946. Their early attempts to build an open, ongoing party organization, made as members of the SDEC, would not bear fruit until reforms had resulted in the return of liberals to power thirty years later.

In the meantime, the conservatives' strategy was the opposite of that of the liberals. The conservatives' concern was to prevent the Democratic party from developing a mass base. This meant freezing liberals out of the party's governing body, discouraging grass-roots participation in party affairs by the less affluent and ethnic minorities, and urging presidential Republicans and ticket-splitters to participate in all aspects of party activities—from voting in the Democratic primaries to attending the national Democratic conventions.

The conservatives' strategy was dependent on the unit rule then governing Texas conventions, a winner-take-all device that operated from the precinct conventions up. Its effectiveness rested in part on the lower turnout of liberals that often occurred in the Democratic primaries, participation in which was a prerequisite for attending the precinct conventions, and in part on the liberals' lower turnout in the conventions themselves. Because of the unit rule, narrow margins of victory by conservatives at the lowest stages could be transformed into a comfortable majority at the state convention. Decisive conservative domination there could result in a delegation to the national convention that was firmly in the pocket of the conservative governor, to bargain with as he pleased during the nomination fight.

Because a few delegates could make the difference between a faction's getting to elect no delegates, or all of them, to the next stage, there were intense fights between factions over such elementary issues as whom to seat. Parliamentary legerdemain was common, and disputes over rules and credentials could easily dissolve into fistfights. Those in control tried to keep the unwritten and often-changed rules secret until the convention began. Wilbourn E. Benton, writing when the unit rule was in effect, observed that "many people attending precinct conventions do not fully understand the procedures, issues, and conflicts. This is especially true if they did not attend the [preconvention] caucus or were not briefed. . . . The convention may be over before they realize it has begun. . . . The name-calling and discourtesy common to many precinct conventions fall far short of the basic rules of democratic procedure."[13]

In 1948 the liberals briefly regained control of the SDEC, working with "brass-collar" Democrats to take over the September convention once Harry Truman had the presidential nomination safely in hand and many of the Regulars had deserted. Once more the SDEC set to work to build a broad organizational base for the party. In 1949, however, moderate conservative Governor Beauford Jester died of a heart attack, and right-wing lieutenant governor Allan Shivers succeeded him. Shivers moved quickly to remove liberals and loyalists from the SDEC. Dominating the 1950 September state convention, he became the first Texas governor—but not the last—to purge state committee nominees who had been selected by their own senatorial district caucuses, thus keeping several loyalists off the committee, which he stacked with his own appointees.[14] This exercise of personal gubernatorial power continued for years.

Shivers, titular leader of the Democrats, soon set in motion a train of events that would enable him to hand the party over to the Republicans. In 1951 he signed a bill permitting candidates to cross-file in both parties. The following year, he led a pledged delegation bound by the unit rule to the national convention. The "Shivercrats" were seated instead of a liberal-loyal challenge delegation but only after Shivers privately promised House Speaker Sam Rayburn (so Rayburn claimed and Shivers later denied) that Shivers would support the Democratic ticket.[15] After the convention had nominated Adlai Stevenson, the Shivers machine in Texas began actively supporting Eisenhower.

The challenging delegation had been selected at a rump convention of liberal-loyalists led by Maury Maverick, Sr., who had walked out of the May convention in San Antonio. The social class and racial makeup of the rump faction is reflected in the following description by an observer:

> In going about one could easily size up the crowd. While most of the leaders were evidently of the professional and middle classes—lawyers, some business-men, a few members of the academic profession, some Negroes, and a few Latin-Americans—without doubt, the majority of the rank-and-file were obvi-ously working class people, many of them Negroes, and some Latin-Americans. Indeed, the general atmosphere was a unique mixture of a western religious camp meeting (considering the fervor of most of the speakers), a labor union picnic, and a Tammany Hall clambake without the clams.[16]

At the September convention that year in Amarillo, the airport was "choked with oil company planes" that had flown in from all over the state.[17] Their passengers and others like them were backing Eisenhower and were "in control of the moneybags," as Sam Rayburn would describe them a few days later. According to O. Douglas Weeks, a political scientist covering the convention, "the latter statement was one of the most impor-tant statements Rayburn made, for it was quite evident that the large contributors were mainly subsidizing the Texas Democrats for Eisen-hower and the Republicans. The national Democrats were in no such for-tunate financial position. To raise funds, Rayburn's headquarters an-nounced a 'five dollars for Stevenson' system."[18]

After the 1952 elections, liberals faced up to the fact that the state party had been taken over by the right wing. McCarthyism was ascendant. Shivers, a McCarthy admirer, was attracting national press coverage by advocating the death penalty for "convicted Communists" and serving on the board of oilman H. L. Hunt's paranoid propaganda organization, Facts Forum. The liberal-loyalist leaders, many of whom had been active in Ralph Yarborough's primary campaign against Shivers the previous sum-mer, decided that statewide organizing should be undertaken on a contin-uing basis to prepare for the party battles of the 1950s. They established precinct organizations in major cities that were coordinated by an um-brella group, known in one incarnation after another in the 1950s as the Democratic Organizing Committee, the Texas Advisory Council (of the Democratic Organizing Committee, appointed by National Chairman Stephen Mitchell), and the Democrats of Texas.

A central figure in these insurgent groups was Frankie Randolph of Houston, an heir to a lumber and banking fortune who was often labeled by her enemies as a traitor to her class. Not only did she establish a superb county precinct organization that still functioned in the 1980s both locally and as a nucleus of the statewide liberal network, but Mrs. Randolph helped found and then became publisher of the *Texas Observer*, a crusading statewide weekly newspaper that first appeared late in 1954.[19] Under editor Ronnie Dugger, the *Observer* quickly became an intellectual focus and a source of political information for the state's liberals.

In spite of the impressive support that developed for Yarborough in his second challenge to Shivers in 1954, the liberals were unable to take control of the party at the conventions. Their treatment at the state convention at Mineral Wells that year is indicative of the manner in which conservatives maintained dominance over party affairs. State officials did not allocate hotel rooms for liberal delegates in the city, and blacks were not allowed in hotels anyway. Liberals thus were forced to stay as far as one hundred miles from the convention hall. When they tried to hold a pre-convention caucus in a city park, the county's mounted posse arrived with billy clubs and threatened to arrest them for meeting without a permit.

Once inside the convention hall, the liberals were seated at the back, and their chairs were tied together with chains bolted to the floor. "We had one chair for every two delegates," liberal organizer Billie Carr recalled, "and no one was allowed to stand inside the convention hall, so we rotated and took turns sitting outside on the steps in the hot sun every hour." Their microphones were cut off, and they were not allowed to speak or to make motions from the floor. The keynote speaker referred to the liberals as Communists.

Outside the convention hall, restaurants refused to serve those delegates wearing "liberal" badges, and blacks were not served at all. For a price, a women's church auxiliary served liberal delegates sandwiches and lemonade. The final indignity came at the end of the convention. "Many of our cars were missing," Carr remembers, "and we found them in the city pound where we all had to pay $13 to get them out. We drove back home disillusioned, bitter, and determined to fight for better representation."[20]

Two years later, the political scene looked more auspicious to liberal-loyalists. Several members of the Shivers crowd were implicated in a series of fraud and bribery scandals, and the governor decided not to run again. Lyndon Johnson, whose presidential ambitions required a Texas delegation to the national convention that could be trusted to support the party's nominee, plotted with Rayburn to dislodge the Shivers faction from state party control. The strategy involved a marriage of convenience with the liberals, who by early 1956 had the only precinct organization capable of effecting a coup. Rayburn announced in March that Johnson was mounting a favorite-son candidacy for the presidential nomination and that Johnson planned to lead the Texas delegation, thereby usurping

Shivers's self-arrogated prerogative. The governor was furious, as he had planned to deliver the Democratic machinery once again to Eisenhower.[21] The liberals, leery of Johnson, nonetheless went along, expecting to share in party control.[22]

Shivers was indeed ousted in the spring convention. But Johnson squelched the liberals' attempt to ban party officials who refused to pledge support to the party's nominees. The liberals, in turn, prevented Johnson's forces from electing Beryl Bentsen, wife of former congressman Lloyd Bentsen, as Texas's national committeewoman. (Texas at the time had one national committeeman and one national committeewoman.) Mrs. Bentsen had not been active in party affairs and was seen as a mere stand-in for her husband, a conservative businessman.[23] Frankie Randolph was elected instead. Her victory was potent with symbolism, for her commitment to a programmatic, disciplined party with a broad base among the less affluent and minorities was well known. Putting aside their quarrels with LBJ, however, the liberals stood behind his candidacy at the national convention as they had pledged to do, in spite of Adlai Stevenson's popularity.[24]

For their pains, the liberals soon got special treatment in Fort Worth, where the September state convention was held. But it was not the treatment they had expected. Behind their backs, Shivers's forces and Johnson made a deal. Yarborough, the liberals' standard-bearer, had narrowly lost his third bid for the governor's nomination to conservative Price Daniel, and evidence in several counties pointed to ballot fraud that might have changed the outcome. Shivers, among others, spread the rumor that a liberal SDEC might oust Daniel as the nominee when it canvassed the primary vote and install Yarborough in his stead. Johnson feared a Yarborough victory as a challenge to his own power. When the liberals arrived in Fort Worth, they found their two largest delegations—those from El Paso and Houston—facing a credentials challenge. Despite strong evidence that both delegations had been fairly selected, Johnson forces got them barred from the convention and conservatives seated in their place. Mrs. Randolph, the leader of the Houston delegation and Texas's sole national Democratic committeewoman, was never allowed to set foot on the convention floor.[25] Liberals were completely shut out of the new SDEC.

The treachery of LBJ stung the liberals deeply. They met in December to revive their statewide organizing effort. Now calling themselves the Democrats of Texas (DOT), they rallied behind Mrs. Randolph—liberal intellectuals such as longtime Austin activist lawyer Creekmore Fath, minority group leaders, loyalist party workers, and labor leaders such as Jerry Holleman, president of the Texas AFL-CIO. Their program would include efforts to take over the 1958 convention and work to increase

20. Creekmore Fath and Mrs. R. D. ("Frankie") Randolph. Influential leaders in Texas liberal political circles, Fath of Austin and Randolph of Houston prepare to speak to a gathering of "Democrats of Texas," a grass-roots organization they helped found in the 1950s. Courtesy of United Press International and the *Texas Observer*.

party registration, to abolish the poll tax, and to reform the state party rules. Professor Byron R. Abernethy of Lubbock, who delivered the keynote address to the DOT, was fired for his efforts a few months later by the board of trustees of Texas Technological College.[26]

In 1958, the state party was tightly controlled by LBJ, Rayburn, and Governor Price Daniel, easily beating back the DOT challenge at the convention. So hostile was the governor to the liberals that his Committee on Nominations rejected the only two DOT nominees selected in senatorial district caucuses for membership on the sixty-two-member SDEC, thus keeping the party's governing body completely free of liberal contamination.[27] This shut-out occurred at a time, ironically, when Yarborough had just won the nomination for a full term in the U.S. Senate with 59 percent of the Democratic primary vote in a race against arch-conservative William Blakley.

In 1960 Johnson again decided to lead the Texas delegation to the national convention as favorite son. He picked an overwhelmingly conservative delegation made up mostly of lawyers, elected officials, and businessmen. Yarborough was excluded. According to O. Douglas Weeks, "very few delegates could be classified as representing labor, agriculture and the professions other than law."[28] Only 20 of the more than 180 delegates or alternates were women. There were 2 blacks and 1 Mexican American.[29] At least 40 in the contingent had publicly supported Republican candidates in the past, which suggests why Mrs. Randolph's forces were unsuccessful in attempting to require a party loyalty pledge at the state convention.[30] Mrs. Randolph, ousted by the Johnson forces as Texas's national committeewoman, was not a delegate.

The exclusion of liberals from the SDEC and the presidential nominating process seemed complete. In the early 1950s, they had been subjected to this indignity by the "Shivercrats." In the latter years, Johnson was responsible. In the summer of 1960, it looked to the liberals as though the new decade offered no more hope than had the 1950s.

Reform of the Party Rules

Events at the 1960 national convention, however, held out to them exciting new prospects. With LBJ suddenly John Kennedy's running mate, the Texas liberals saw all sorts of possibilities arising. So did the Johnson machine in Texas, which included Connally. The two factions entered into a rather delicate modus vivendi, one result of which was that the bloodletting that had marred state conventions for so long ended abruptly after 1960 and did not occur again until 1968.

John Tower's unexpected victory in a special 1961 election to fill LBJ's vacant Senate seat underscored the need for Democrats to close ranks. The next year, a right-wing Republican oilman, Jack Cox, made a serious run for the governorship. Liberal and moderate-conservative Democrats had good reasons to lay down their arms at the 1962 convention once John Connally had defeated incumbent Price Daniel and liberal Don Yarborough for the Democratic nomination. The September convention in El Paso was the most harmonious in some time.[31]

In 1964, Johnson was president, and he was especially concerned that conservatives not antagonize liberals. Ralph Yarborough and his supporters were also eager for harmony, for he was in a reelection campaign against George Bush, who was running as a Goldwaterite. At the June

21. The high tide of Texas liberalism. (Left to right) President Lyndon B. Johnson, Vice President Hubert Humphrey, and U.S. Senator Ralph Yarborough at a 1964 campaign rally in Austin. H. S. ("Hank") Brown, president of the Texas AFL-CIO, is on Yarborough's left. Courtesy of the Barker Texas History Center (Russell Lee Collection).

convention that year, the Connally-Johnson conservatives were in firm control and selected a largely conservative delegation to Miami Beach that, in spite of displeasure with the national party's liberal platform, did what an equally liberal delegation would have done—supported the Johnson-Humphrey ticket.[32] And in 1966, except for a dispute over eight seats on the SDEC that the liberals claimed to have won (they were accorded four and rejected them), there were "no annoying rattles, no discordant pings," in the words of journalist Greg Olds. "The 'governor's . . . convention,' so-called never more aptly, was a mechanic's dream."[33]

It was a different story in 1968, a year of great national turmoil. LBJ had announced in the spring that he would not run for reelection. The outcome of the liberal-conservative battle in the Texas Democratic party, fought with renewed ferocity, spelled the beginning of the end of conservative control. What should have been, under two successive liberal presidents, a thriving, well-staffed national party organization working to channel the energies of the newly politicized protest groups into significant party activities was in actuality a rusty old hulk of a machine. Kennedy and Johnson, both jealous of presidential prerogatives and deeply suspicious of an independent power base represented by an efficient party organization, had encouraged this state of affairs.

LBJ had all but dismantled the Democratic National Committee (DNC), thus completing a process begun by Kennedy. Johnson's chief lieutenant, Marvin Watson, Jr., a canny conservative political operative from East Texas, was given the task of allocating "funds for voter registration programs, patronage, and other matters" that the DNC, in cooperation with the executive department, had routinely handled.[34]

David Broder of the *Washington Post* described the party's disarray in 1966:

> The decimation of the Democratic Party structure—the abolition of the centralized voter-registration effort that was the keystone of the Kennedy campaign, the 50 percent cutback in manpower at the Democratic National Committee, and the collapse of communications between Washington and state party chairmen—all these things have been described by critics as an expression of the antagonism to party organization that has been growing for eighteen years in Mr. Johnson, ever since he ended the first phase of his political career as a loyal Roosevelt agent within the Democratic Party.[35]

The president, in other words, was at loggerheads with Texas liberals so far as the importance of party organization was concerned.

Reformers nationwide criticized this state of affairs, lambasting Democrats and Republicans alike as "effectively closed political organizations whose operations frustrate broad citizen participation in politics." The target of their reform was "a handful of party notables, key officeholders and party professionals [who] actually control the party organizations within the states and at the federal level."[36] If the reformers who wrote these words had added "conservative" to their description of the notables, it would have fit the Texas case perfectly.

In addition to unabashed racial and factional discrimination, the class prerogatives built into the party structure served to diminish grass-roots participation. Delegations to the national convention had long been filled with rich people. Regarding the 1952 convention, political scientist Paul T. David and his colleagues wrote, "When $100-a-plate fund-raising dinners are held in a state during the preconvention campaign, it is assumed that delegates will attend." They pointed out that some states still required large contributions to party treasuries from all delegates. In addition, personal travel and living expenses incurred at the convention were the delegates' responsibility, as were contributions to maintaining the state delegation's convention headquarters. David observed that "delegations of both parties from Texas, Oklahoma, and Louisiana were studded with the names of wealthy individuals."[37] Their observations were just as applicable in 1968 as they had been in 1952.

In Texas as elsewhere, a serious split was developing among liberals. Many middle-class, college-educated whites and sizable numbers of minorities opposed Johnson's Vietnam policy. Most of organized labor supported the president. This schism was manifested in a conflict between backers of Senators Eugene McCarthy and Robert Kennedy on one hand and supporters of Vice President Hubert Humphrey on the other.

Governor Connally intended to lead the Texas delegation, bound by the unit rule, to Chicago. He planned on forcing compromises from Humphrey, whom he loathed, that would please Texas conservatives. The Texas McCarthy forces initially tried to forge an anti-Connally alliance with Kennedy backers and pro-Humphrey labor elements. H. S. ("Hank") Brown, president of the Texas AFL-CIO and a longtime liberal activist, was receptive to such a strategy so long as it was agreed that if the liberal forces prevailed in controlling the state convention, the Texas delegation would be split proportionately so that Humphrey would get his fair share of delegates. The McCarthy leaders unwisely refused and then attacked Brown publicly for his refusal to go along with the anti-Connally plan.[38]

Before the summer convention was held, Robert Kennedy was assassinated, and the possibility of a McCarthy-Kennedy coalition became moot. By the time the convention met in Dallas, the conservatives had a five-to-one edge in delegate strength. Connally, using the favorite-son gambit, was able to lead a bound delegation to the national convention. The dispirited liberals rumped and decided to challenge the seating of Connally's delegation, along with the unit rule, in Chicago.[39]

Some liberals saw both challenges as hopeless. But Greg Olds, then editor of the *Texas Observer*, opined "that there would be some propaganda value in raising some nationally-televised hell [in Chicago] this August; the example of the Mississippi Freedom Democratic Party at the 1964 convention is evidence that there is some worth in boat rocking."[40] Connally, trying to take as much wind out of the liberals' sails as possible, included in the delegation a number of them elected from senatorial-district caucuses—including labor leader Hank Brown. They too were bound to Connally by the unit rule, however. Billie Carr was among the liberals who were offered the opportunity to go but declined. State senator Barbara Jordan accepted, as did banker Hall, a fervent Humphrey man who supported Johnson's Vietnam War effort.

As the summer progressed, hope began to mount among the insurgents that both the Connally and Humphrey forces could be stopped. Allard Lowenstein, the liberal New York party activist, called the "Chicago Conference for an Open Convention" on June 29 and 30, and some Texas McCarthy supporters attended.[41]

Efforts were made in Texas to strengthen the rump delegation's credentials claims by documenting unfair procedures in precinct and county conventions and by formulating arguments against the unit rule. In Chicago the liberal challengers argued that they were entitled to fifty seats in the

22. John Connally. An active and charismatic participant
in conservative Democratic and then Republican politics, and an adviser to the rich and powerful—including
at least three presidents—Connally was governor from
1963 to 1969. He was seriously injured during the assassination of John F. Kennedy in Dallas. Courtesy of Alan
Pogue and the *Texas Observer*.

Texas delegation. They focused on the unit rule's effect in excluding minority delegates. According to the challengers' brief, Mexican Americans
constituted over 14.8 percent of Texas's population in 1960 and blacks,
12.4 percent, yet in the Connally delegation they amounted to 5 and 4.1
percents, respectively.[42] Even this small number may have resulted from
a requirement mandated at the 1964 national convention that any delegation in 1968 that excluded racial minorities would be barred.

The irony of this underrepresentation, the liberal speakers noted, was
that the two ethnic minorities traditionally provided far greater propor-

tional support for the Democratic ticket in Texas than did the Anglos—especially the kind of Anglos who typically were chosen by the conservative governors to make the trip to the convention. (In 1968, Shivers was in the Democratic delegation, although LBJ was the only Democratic presidential nominee he had publicly supported since 1948. Another delegate was alleged to have been a local "campaign manager for Goldwater in 1964.")[43] Among the challenging delegation, at least thirty-six of the one hundred members were either blacks or Mexican Americans.[44]

The liberals' challenge ultimately failed. And like most of the other events inside the convention hall, it would soon be upstaged by a bloody conflict between antiwar protestors and the Chicago police. On another front, however, the liberals succeeded. Reformers, led by followers of Eugene McCarthy and the late Robert Kennedy, were intent on abolishing the unit rule. Texas was a prime target. Its delegation was bound to Connally as its favorite son on every ballot until he released them. It was also the largest delegation among the five states still employing the rule.[45] Connally and his outspoken lieutenant, national committeeman Frank C. Erwin, Jr., were its most ardent defenders. The rule was "the very essence of pure democracy," said Connally.[46]

Addressing the rules committee, Erwin explained that while the Connally faction did not have to put "loyalists" (i.e., liberals and national Democrats) on the delegation, it had nonetheless done so. Then, provoking laughter from the committee by his very effrontery, he added: "We put them on there because we knew we could control them under the unit rule."[47]

At one point Connally and Erwin threatened to deliver Texas's entire 104 votes to Lyndon Johnson—who was not a candidate—if the full convention voted to abolish the rule.[48] Erwin said that abolition might lead the state's Democratic presidential electors to cast their votes for George Wallace.

Speaking against the rule was former legislator Maury Maverick, Jr., whose father had spearheaded the liberals' challenge to the Shivers delegation at the national convention in 1952. Along with him were Yarborough, black state representative Curtis Graves, San Antonio county commissioner Albert Peña, and state representative Don Gladden of Fort Worth.

A subcommittee of the rules committee found for the liberal challengers, substituting a "freedom of conscience" proposal for the unit rule. The Connally delegation then submitted a minority report, bringing the issue to the full convention, which abolished the rule's use that year by a voice vote.[49] More important, the convention voted to eliminate the unit rule from all stages of the delegate selection process in 1972 stipulating that "all feasible efforts be made to assure that delegates are selected through party primary, convention, or committee procedures open to public participation within the calendar year of the national convention."[50] Connally's people saw the handwriting on the wall. "This crumbles the whole foundation of our control," a state party official, who asked not to be identified, remarked to a reporter.[51]

In combination with successful minority reports from two other committees, that of the rules committee became the mandate that between 1968 and 1972 blew open the clogged access routes to Democratic party power both nationally and in Texas. The Commission on Party Structure and Delegate Selection (later called the McGovern-Fraser Commission after its first two chairmen, Senator George McGovern of South Dakota and Minnesota representative Donald Fraser) became the focus of an intense struggle between "regulars" and "reformers."

The commission's members were appointed by Senator Fred Harris of Oklahoma, then the national party chairman. It took its job seriously, holding numerous meetings in major cities, at which over five hundred witnesses testified. Texas liberals and moderates were active in mobilizing support for reforms. A fundamental revision of the delegate selection process was finally worked out late in 1969. By the following February, McGovern had written letters to all state chairmen spelling out the criteria for compliance and analyzing each state's current delegate selection process. States that did not conform to the new rules were notified of it via detailed descriptions.[52]

Among the major changes were the requirement of written party rules (Texas had had none), the inclusion of a number of procedural safeguards designed to make participation easier and fairer (such as removal of all fees over $10), and the requirement "that racial minorities, women, and youth be represented 'in reasonable relationship to their presence in the population of the state.' " The latter measure met with immediate and heated opposition from Will D. Davis, who had recently stepped down as Connally's state party chairman.[53]

While the writing of Texas party rules provoked a sharp conflict between liberals and conservatives, the national reform commissions set fairly narrow limits on the conservatives' response. When the 1972 convention opened in Miami Beach, the reform mandate had been faithfully translated into practice. According to historian Herbert Parmet, the results of this four-year reform effort were "the most significant changes since the elimination of the two-thirds rule in 1936,"[54] a rule that had given the South veto power over the party's choice of a presidential nominee. In Texas, the "flexible quota" provision provided a battering ram for the rank-and-file participants—women, minorities, and Anglo liberals—who for so long had been knocking futilely on the door of the party's inner sanctum.

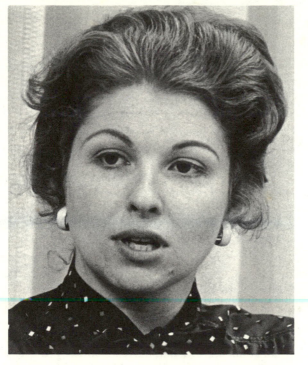

23. Sarah Weddington. A liberal legislator and lawyer, she successfully argued *Roe v. Wade*, the 1973 U.S. Supreme Court abortion rights decision, not long after graduating from law school. Courtesy of the *Texas Observer*.

The Results of Proportional Representation

"Even in Texas," wrote the *Texas Observer*'s Ronnie Dugger in the summer of 1972, "the McGovernized . . . system is better than the old boss-run, winner-take-all system. Without the reforms, the Texas conservatives, who gave [George] Wallace 35 percent of the Democratic delegates [at the state convention] this year, would have been shaping up deals with the Humphrey people to deny McGovern all of his 28 percent of the delegates."[55]

In Miami Beach, 41.5 percent of the Texas delegation's vote went to McGovern, 36.9 percent went to Wallace, and the remainder was split among minor candidates.[56] Unlike conservative delegation heads of years past, Democratic gubernatorial nominee Dolph Briscoe, although conservative, had very little power. His designation as head was largely ceremonial, and his ineptitude angered every faction in his delegation. He had first voted for Wallace and then, in the hullaballoo that followed, he switched to McGovern.

Things were different at the September state convention as well. Conservatives maintained tenuous control of the SDEC, although the number of "hard core" liberals increased from none a few years earlier to twenty-five out of sixty-two. Also elected were several moderates who would align themselves with the liberals on some issues.[57] The three new Texas seats on the DNC created by the McGovern-Fraser reforms were all filled by liberals, two of whom were minority group members. The gains made by minorities and women under the new rules were most apparent in the complexion of the Texas delegation to Miami Beach. In 1972, blacks constituted 10 percent, compared with 5 percent in 1968; Mexican Americans increased from 5 to 14 percent.[58] And unlike earlier years, their vote was not determined by the unit rule.

A closer look at the minority delegates revealed even sharper departures from the 1968 pattern. Those in Connally's last delegation had typically been older, "establishment" people representing the premilitant style of ethnic politics, while the 1972 delegation bristled with younger and more outspoken activists. Women, too, increased their proportion: from 13 percent in 1968 to about 33 percent four years later—compared to 40 percent for women in the national convention as a whole.[59] And the delegates' social class changed appreciably. As table 8.1 indicates, the Texas Democrats with incomes under $20,000 increased sharply, from 20 to 41 percent, while it actually decreased among Republican delegates, whose party underwent no reform.

In spite of the crushing defeat in 1972 of the Democratic ticket—a ticket many of the reformers had helped nominate—Texas liberals faced the 1970s with hope. For the first time in a quarter of a century, they anticipated having clout in party affairs in proportion to their numbers. Some even dared to hope for eventual party control.

The achievement of this goal, however, was still beset with difficulties. Following the McGovern-Shriver defeat in 1972, Jean Westwood, the national party chairperson, stepped down and, to the consternation of reformers, she was succeeded by Robert Strauss of Dallas, a close friend of Connally and a prominent fixture in the Texas conservative establishment. Strauss had helped Connally fend off the Texas insurgents' credentials challenge at the 1968 Chicago convention.[60]

Strauss's ascendancy represented a push by "regulars"—including southern conservatives and some northern union leaders—to roll back or significantly to modify the reforms. While Strauss lent his influence to their efforts, his reputation as a fixer, or, more grandly, as a statesman, demanded that he bring some semblance of unity to the party after the 1972 debacle.

Table 8.1

Income of Texas Delegates to National
Conventions, 1968 and 1972

	(1976 Dollars)[a]			
	Under $10,000 (%)	$10,000– 20,000 (%)	Over $20,000 (%)	N
1968				
Republicans	0	22	78	(18)
Democrats	0	20	80	(30)
1972				
Republicans	0	17	83	(18)
Democrats	6	35	58	(31)

Source: A retrospective survey carried out by John M. Perkins, a Rice University student, under the author's supervision. Questionnaires were sent to 340 delegates, and 97 usable ones (28.5 percent) were returned.

[a] Respondents' income in 1976, at the time of the survey.

The forces of reform seemed so thoroughly entrenched that any sudden attempt to gut the new rules would have torn the party apart. Moreover, Billie Carr, Strauss's old foe in Texas Democratic politics, had managed to capture a seat on the Democratic National Committee; and as the able and experienced leader of the committee's Progressive Caucus, she fought to a draw several of Strauss's attempts at diluting the reforms.

Early in 1973, a new Commission on Delegate Selection, created by the 1972 convention, set about reviewing the McGovern-Fraser guidelines. Named the Mikulski Commission for its chairperson, Baltimore city councilwoman Barbara Mikulski, it abolished the winner-take-all presidential preference primaries of the sort that had enabled McGovern to capture the entire California delegation in 1972. The Mikulski Commission still allowed one type of winner-take-all primary, however. Under rule 11-4, a state's convention delegates could be elected without proportional representation according to delegates' presidential preferences, in districts the size of congressional districts or smaller.

Insiders thought they saw the hand of Strauss in maintaining the "loophole primary" rule for use in seven of the ten largest states in 1976—including Texas.[61] Taking advantage of rule 11-4, in 1975 the Texas legislature passed a bill drafted by Bentsen's staff, which drastically revised the state's presidential nomination process and set up what seemed to be a sure-fire method for enabling Bentsen to win a "favorite son" nomination in Texas and lead a virtually bound delegation to the national convention. The reaction to the so-called Bentsen bill will be described in the following chapter. Suffice it to say that this was the last effort by the conservative wing of the party to make use of a winner-take-all rule in the presidential nomination process. The fact that Jimmy Carter ended up with the lion's share of the votes under the bill's rules was especially galling to the conservatives.

The 1976 national convention finally plugged the last winner-take-all loophole, and proportional representation seemed for the time being to be firmly embedded in the presidential selection process. In Texas, liberals came close to electing a liberal party chairman to replace Governor Briscoe's personally chosen incumbent, Calvin Guest. Indeed, Briscoe and Guest were forced to make compromises with some of the liberals in order to guarantee Guest's victory. And a close analysis of the makeup of the new SDEC revealed that more than half were liberals or moderates. Previously criticized for failing to call SDEC meetings, to give young people and minorities a significant role in party affairs, to disclose publicly how party funds were spent, and to wage a voter registration campaign, Guest gave in to the liberal-moderate forces on each of those counts, although informally he was still Briscoe's "hand-picked" state chairman.[62]

But even that rather weak link between the conservative establishment and the party machinery was soon broken. In 1978 John Hill, the moderate gubernatorial nominee, accommodated the progressive faction following his upset of Briscoe by naming a moderate-to-liberal state chairman, Houston financier Billy Goldberg. Goldberg had been one of the few members of his class to support Yarborough during his statewide campaigns. In the September convention that year, liberals and moderates captured about two-thirds of the SDEC seats (thirty liberals and fourteen "liberal-to-moderate" members, according to one estimate).[63] This independence of the party from the governor's personal organization was strengthened markedly when Hill was defeated by Republican Bill Clements in November, and for the first time in the twentieth century, not the governor but the state chairman was actually the party's head.

The fall elections of 1980 were the culmination of a series of disasters for the Democrats both nationally and in Texas. Senator Edward Kennedy's challenge to President Carter, the faltering incumbent, along with the independent candidacy of John Anderson, threw the party into disarray. At the June state convention, Carter nonetheless captured about two-thirds of the delegates, Kennedy only a fourth. The remainder were uncommitted.[64] The delegation was more liberal than those figures suggest, however, as a number of liberals had been committed to Carter, including Yarborough and black congressman Mickey Leland of Houston. In New York, the Texas delegation split 50-50 on the platform plank calling for national health insurance, which Yarborough felt was a good indicator of the ideological makeup of the Texas group. (The Texas Republican delegation passed a resolution against national health insurance.) And in September, the liberal-moderate coalition captured fully two-thirds of the SDEC seats once more and elected the chairman of their choice. "It's a good representative mix of Democrats," a party officer opined. "[It's] probably the beginning of the new era of the party not being dominated by gubernatorial candidates."[65]

The effects of the decade-long movement for party reform were quite obvious in the makeup of the delegation to New York: 11 percent black, 13 percent Mexican American, and 38 percent women. The average age of delegates was thirty-nine. The old conservative hegemony undergirded by the unit rule was not even a memory in the minds of some of the younger delegates.

As the curtain went up on the 1980s, Texas liberals found themselves better off in some respects than they had been in a long time, which seemed paradoxical in light of Ronald Reagan's ascendancy at the national level. Several liberal candidates for statewide office were able to win the Democratic primary nomination in May 1982. Then, in a general election marked by a relatively strong turnout in minority precincts, the liberals handily defeated their Republican opponents. More important, perhaps, was Mark White's narrow victory over Governor Clements. To the surprise of many observers, White, who was branded a conservative in most press accounts, set out on a far more moderate course than had any recent Democratic governor. He had won with the strong backing of numerous liberal groups, and in his appointments, political rhetoric, and policies during the 1983 legislative session, White established a distinctly centrist record.

His election in November 1982 followed an amazingly harmonious September Democratic convention. According to Billie Carr, the platform was the most liberal in Texas history. She praised the state party chairman for including every element of the party in its preparation, saying it was the first time in her thirty years as a party activist that such an effort at fairness to every group had been made.[66] Ralph Yarborough drew sustained applause from the delegates, whom he entertained with a fiery stump speech.[67]

Liberals maintained a firm grip on the reins of the SDEC. And in the general election that fall, White's support was strikingly similar to that received by Yarborough in his earlier statewide campaigns: 71 percent of lower-income whites, 16 percent of upper-income whites, virtually 100 percent of blacks, and 86 percent of Mexican Americans.[68] Asked to comment on the liberals' efforts that year, Allan Shivers replied, "You have got to give them credit for the organization they have put together. That's the way to win elections."[69] Considering the source, it was praise of the highest order.

The Liberal-Conservative Struggle in Retrospect

After a struggle reaching back to 1944, the liberal-loyalists finally managed to break the conservatives' hammerlock on the Democratic state party machinery. By 1982 a clear-cut realignment in convention politics and party executive committee membership was evident. Much credit for this must go to hardworking liberal visionaries who fought the trench warfare of Texas convention politics.

As the foregoing account of this struggle makes clear, the caricature of Texas liberal activism as carried out primarily by middle-class intellectuals is far off the mark. The organizational core of the Texas liberal movement consists of a good number of both blue-collar and middle-class activists recruited from the three ethnic bases described in chapter 3—activists whose avocation and sometimes vocation as well is dedicated to building a grass-roots party. The convention system during the years under discussion enabled them to join together in common cause and, after the party reforms that began in 1968, to use their most potent resource—"ordinary people" getting together in precinct conventions across the state—to neutralize the effects of the conservatives' money. In this sense, the liberals' struggles for party control have been in the best tradition of participatory democracy.

At the same time they were winning their struggle within the party, however, changes were occurring, the most important of which was a shift in voter preference toward the Republican party. This was what the liberals had long hoped would happen, for it would signal an exodus of conservatives from the Democratic party, which would give liberal candidates a better chance to win the nomination. This train of events indeed occurred, but it soon became obvious that a Democratic nomination was no longer tantamount to election in November.

Ralph Yarborough, the liberals' hero, who in 1968 as Texas's senior senator had led the challenge to the unit rule in Chicago, was in 1970 defeated in his bid for the Democratic nomination by Lloyd Bentsen, the establishment's candidate. In a comeback try two years later, Yarborough was again defeated in the primary. State representative Frances Farenthold, the liberal gubernatorial candidate who also articulated the reform spirit abroad in Texas at the time, was beaten decisively in the 1972 Democratic primary and even more painfully in 1974. Yarborough and Farenthold were the last major liberal statewide candidates to run in the Democratic primary electorate while it was still dominated by conservatives.

The changing nature of the primary electorate became evident when moderate Democrat John Hill challenged the conservative Briscoe in the 1978 primary and defeated him. But for the first time since Reconstruction, obtaining the Democratic nomination was no longer sufficient to win the governorship. Hill was defeated in the general election. In 1982 four liberals won second-level statewide offices, suggesting that a liberal could win at a higher level. State senator Lloyd Doggett tested that hypothesis in 1984, when he narrowly edged out a moderate and a conservative to win the Democratic nomination for the U.S. Senate seat John Tower had announced he was giving up. He was the first authentic liberal to run for governor or U.S. senator since Farenthold ten years before. Doggett lost to right-wing Republican Phil Gramm, fifty-nine to forty-one. In contests for top statewide positions, therefore, the Democratic primary electorate had become more liberal, but the general electorate had not. This was true even though the four liberals elected in 1982 to second-echelon statewide offices were reelected in 1986, and "plaintiff-oriented" candidates had won a majority of seats on the Texas Supreme Court in low-profile races during the decade.

Given the trend generally (but not entirely) favoring conservatives, we may ask how significant was the liberal-moderate capture of the Democratic party machinery. The answer requires us to examine modern Republicanism in Texas. Before doing so, however, it is worth looking back to 1976, the year the liberals and their moderate allies captured the Democratic machinery. The complexity and intensity of the liberal-conservative battle is exemplified in that pivotal year's presidential politics.

9

The Year of the Liberal Breakthrough

BEFORE she was forty, Billie Carr had joined the top ranks of Texas politicos. It is hard to imagine a greater contrast than that between Carr and Frankie Randolph, the grande dame of the state's liberal movement in the 1950s who taught her the ropes. Randolph was descended from an old Texas lumber and banking family. A member of Houston's exclusive Bayou Club, Randolph horrified her own social class by launching the *Texas Observer*, a muckraking liberal newspaper. She is remembered as a hard drinker, a hard fighter, and a courageous tactician who led the liberals not only against the "Shivercrats"—the conservative Democrats who followed Governor Allan Shivers into the Eisenhower camp in 1952—but also against the Johnson-Rayburn forces when they connived with the Texas power structure to exclude liberals from party control.

The most obvious trait Carr shared with her late mentor, aside from her salty language, was the undisputed title as the best Democratic organizer of her day in Texas and, so some people said, in the country. Carr came from a working-class background, and her formal education ended with high school. She married a steelworker who introduced her to precinct politics in the labor union neighborhoods of northeast Houston. During a visit to Austin in the early 1950s, Carr met Shivers face to face, and she told him frankly what she thought of him, which was not complimentary. As she later recounted the story, Shivers smiled and replied that it did not really matter what she thought. "The fact is, young lady, I hold this state in the palm of my hand."[1]

His words had the effect on her of an epiphany. She came back to Houston resolved to pry loose the state's political machinery from the conservatives' grip. Carr learned precinct organizing and Democratic convention tactics from the ground up. She became a sought-after operative as Randolph's health declined. A divorce briefly removed her from politics, but she soon returned to full-time grass-roots organizing for Harris County Democrats, the liberal Houston club Randolph was instrumental in founding.

With the defeat of Ralph Yarborough by Lloyd Bentsen in the 1970 primary, Carr became a leading light in the progressive coalition. After a stint on the State Democratic Executive Committee (SDEC), she managed to win a seat on the Democratic National Committee (DNC) in 1972. There her impressive political skills, her experience as an organizer for Eugene McCarthy in 1968 and George McGovern in 1972, and her grasp

THE
GODMOTHER

24. Billie Carr. A liberal precinct organizer from Houston, Carr has been active on the State Democratic Executive Committee and the Democratic National Committee. Courtesy of Alan Pogue and the *Texas Observer*.

of the modus operandi of national chairman Robert Strauss, fellow Texan
and arch rival, led to her election as whip of the progressive caucus on the
Democratic National Committee.

The most striking feature of Carr's success was that over the years she
achieved something like the position of a boss with a statewide constituency—after the movie *The Godfather* appeared, her lieutenants began
referring to her as The Godmother—but one without money, offices, or
perquisites to dispense. Working out of a small, ramshackle office near
downtown Houston, Carr and a handful of volunteers, mostly women,
coordinated the progressives' guerrilla struggle against the conservatives
who ran the state's government.

On the afternoon of September 16, 1976, Carr and her volunteer staff
occupied a suite in the Fort Worth Sheraton Hotel that they had rented as

a command post for the liberals when the state convention began the next day. It was to be the second such convention of that presidential election year. The first, in June, had met to select delegates to New York. The second, known as the governor's convention, was to decide control of the state party. This was done by electing SDEC members and a party chairman. It was called the governor's convention because traditionally the governor named his choice of chairman, usually a trusted personal friend and ideological comrade, and the convention rubber-stamped the choice. But the liberals sometimes contested the governor's nominee, and the resulting battles were bitter and, on occasion, closely contested.

On that September afternoon, Carr lay barefoot on a king-size bed, cigarette in hand, talking into a telephone. Nearby, Ed Cogburn, a Houston lawyer and state committeeman who worked closely with Carr, nervously paced the room. A volunteer worker sitting on the carpet folded freshly mimeographed pamphlets containing the platform of John Henry Tatum, an East Texas county attorney with populist leanings who was running for the party chairman's post. On another telephone, Esther Williams, a black precinct judge, was trying to locate a hotel room for her friend. Waiting for Carr to hang up was Colin Carl, an intense young state committeeman from Austin who worked in the attorney general's office. Carr and her friends had good reason that afternoon to hope that their forces would be able to unseat the incumbent chairman, Calvin Guest, a savings-and-loan company executive from Bryan who had been appointed by conservative governor Dolph Briscoe, and thereby take over the machinery of the Texas Democratic party.

The "Bentsen Primary"

The events leading up to Carr's presence in the Sheraton had begun to unfold a year and a half earlier, on the day Bentsen had announced that he would run for the presidency in 1976. Soon after his defeat of Yarborough six years before, it became obvious that Bentsen had presidential ambitions. Having run on a platform that sounded many of George Wallace's reactionary 1968 themes, the newly elected Bentsen quickly adopted a stance of moderation. After the 1972 elections, Robert Strauss, first appointed to the DNC by his old friend Connally, gave Bentsen the chairmanship of the Democratic Senatorial Campaign Committee, a plum for an aspiring presidential candidate since it involved traveling widely around the country to meet the party's most influential donors.

Bentsen announced his candidacy on February 17, 1975, and Governor Briscoe and Lieutenant Governor Bill Hobby immediately endorsed him.[2] The same day the Texas House Elections Committee hastily reported out a bill that provided for the first presidential preference primary in the state's history.[3] Among its many ingenious features was a "winner-take-all" provision of the kind that many delegates to the 1972 Democratic convention in Miami Beach thought they had amended the party's rules to prohibit. It actually did not ensure that the winner would get all the delegates, but it was designed to give him vastly disproportionate delegate strength relative to his popular vote. As the senator was expected to be the primary's beneficiary, the press promptly labeled it "the Bentsen bill." The epithet was doubly appropriate for it was soon learned that Bentsen's staff had helped draw it up.[4]

Bentsen's timing was excellent, at least from the conservatives' vantage point. The national Democratic party's abolition of the unit rule in 1968 and its introduction of reforms in 1972, all of which aimed at increased representation of women, minorities, the less affluent, and young people in the convention process, had weakened the Texas establishment's influence within the party. Thus in 1972, the Wallace and McGovern contingents comprised over 70 percent of the Texas Democratic delegates to the national convention in Miami Beach. The conservative regulars were able to control the SDEC that year only through an alliance with the Wallacites. This alliance was shaky, however, because the Wallace people distrusted establishment Democrats and vice versa. Therefore, Chairman Guest held SDEC meetings quite rarely. Most of the committee's work was done either in private get-togethers arranged by Guest to exclude liberals or in carefully stacked subcommittees.[5]

Briscoe and Bentsen mounted a computerized campaign to increase conservative turnout at the 1974 precinct conventions. But despite spending upward of $20,000 in mailing costs alone, the conservative elite was barely able to control the state committee. Moreover, pundits were predicting that California's Ronald Reagan would oppose Gerald Ford for the 1976 Republican nomination, which would draw conservatives from the Democratic primary.

The Bentsen bill capitalized on a loophole in the national party rules that allowed up to three-quarters of a state's presidential delegation to be selected in "winner-take-all" primaries. This would presumably enable a popular favorite-son candidate to capture most of the elected delegates by obtaining a mere plurality of votes. Not only would that strengthen the conservatives' hand at the national convention, but it would also help them retain control of the state party.

The initial bill contained several noteworthy features. For a candidate to run for president in Texas, slates of three or four "delegate candidates" pledged to a given presidential hopeful had to appear on the primary ballot in each of Texas's thirty-one senatorial districts. Uncommitted delegate slates were prohibited, which would work against a liberal counter-strategy of persuading progressive presidential candidates to stay off the Texas ballot in order to pool liberal votes as uncommitted.

The bill in its early version discriminated sharply against out-of-state candidates who would be required, by one estimate, to obtain as many as sixty thousand voters' signatures and field candidates in all thirty-one state senatorial districts. By contrast, a gubernatorial candidate needed only five thousand signatures to get his name on the ballot.[6] It was unclear how the other fourth of the delegates and all the alternates were to be apportioned. Consequently, if the Bentsen forces controlled the convention, there was the possibility that they could appoint more than their share of the remaining delegates.[7]

When questioned about these features, Bentsen spoke solemnly about the bill's providing greater public participation in the presidential selection process. "It would take it out of the smoke-filled rooms," he repeatedly told a skeptical group of reporters. He denied that it was intended as a "winner-take-all" bill. A reporter asked him if it would enable him to get more delegates than he would receive on the basis of proportional representation. "Frankly," the senator replied, "I don't know." He was correct on that point, as later events would demonstrate. But in the spring of 1975, informed opinion was that Bentsen was the bill's main beneficiary.[8]

For one brief moment, it looked as though liberal legislators might defeat the bill. On February 25 they joined with Republicans and Wallacites on a procedural issue and by a narrow vote temporarily halted the measure's progress. But a group of Houston liberals with ties to labor, including black representatives Senfronia Thompson and Anthony Hall, refused to go along with the anti-Bentsen move. Both of them later appeared on the ballot as Bentsen delegate candidates.

Following this temporary setback, Bentsen's forces labored far into the night, working with Speaker Billy Clayton and Representative Tom Schieffer, the bill's sponsor, among others, to get the measure back on track. Legislators who had held the bill up began getting calls from financial backers who were Bentsen people. Mexican American lawmakers from the Rio Grande Valley, Bentsen territory, were pressed especially hard.[9] Several, along with some Republicans and liberals, switched sides the next day on a "compromise" substitute that in many respects turned out to be more prejudicial on behalf of Bentsen than the original had been.[10]

As the spring of 1975 wore on, the best that the bill's opponents could do was water down some of its more extreme features and append a self-destruct clause effective in 1977. In the version finally signed by Briscoe, the bill reaffirmed the existing law, used by Lyndon Johnson in his 1960 presidential effort, to permit Bentsen to run for two offices at once—a law that was to prove helpful to Bentsen once more in 1988 in his vice presidential bid.[11]

To try to work out a counterstrategy in the face of Bentsen's well-financed campaign, Carr issued a call for a statewide liberal meeting that

25. Billy Clayton. A wealthy agribusinessman from West
Texas, Clayton was one of the more powerful Speakers of
the Texas House. While in that capacity he was a conservative Democrat. After leaving elective office he joined
the Republican party and became a lobbyist for big business. Courtesy of Larry Murphy and the *Texas Observer*.

September at Scholz Beer Garten in Austin. Over three hundred activists
heard Carr, Yarborough, and other liberals lambast Bentsen and propose
plans to defeat him.

Carr went over the options. First, she said, "you can sell out to
Bentsen." He would probably not last beyond one ballot at the convention, and then delegates could switch. The catch was that the delegate
nominees for Bentsen would be chosen by his handpicked selection committees. A second option was to join forces with George Wallace on the
assumption that he would run Bentsen a close race in several districts and
could gain a plurality in them with liberal help. The problem was that
Wallace might last through more than one ballot. And again: "Do you
really want to be a Wallace delegate?" A third choice was to work for a
slate of delegates committed to an acceptable candidate. But this raised
the specter of several liberal candidates competing among themselves and
leaving Bentsen or Wallace with the bulk of votes.

There was also talk, Carr said, of liberals' running a favorite son or daughter, such as Yarborough or former gubernatorial candidate Frances Farenthold. But new party rules had virtually eliminated modestly financed "favorite child" candidates. To be nominated as one, a candidate had to have at least two hundred delegates from five states. Besides, Carr asked, "How can we charge that Bentsen is not a serious candidate and then run somebody less serious?"

Carr favored liberal uncommitted delegate slates in districts where such candidates might have a chance to win. This strategy, she admitted, also had its problems. "It's true that uncommitted delegates are tough to sell. It rubs liberals the wrong way to use the word 'uncommitted.' Our whole makeup is to be *for* someone." Even so, she argued, the uncommitted ploy would prevent liberals from splitting their votes, if liberal candidates could be persuaded to stay off the ballot in Texas. It would be a statewide strategy that could be adopted in each "viable" district, providing a liberal focus.

Carr's plan immediately ran into trouble from supporters of former Oklahoma senator Fred Harris. Their self-styled populist candidate had already generated enthusiasm among university students in the progressive coalition, but Harris was having trouble getting publicity and building an organization. It was deemed important to get his name on the primary ballot, which would help build his strength in a state with populist roots. An early start was essential. Moreover, Harris people doubted that Carr could keep other progressive candidates out of the primary. It was rumored that U.S. senator Morris Udall had already made up his mind to enter the race.

The two-day meeting in Austin ended after the liberals broke up into senatorial district caucuses and elected representatives to the statewide anti-Bentsen effort, which Carr named "Operation '76." She persuaded the group not to make any formal strategy decisions at that time but rather to meet twice more in the fall and see how things developed. She knew that the longer the liberals could be kept from making a formal commitment, the less likelihood there was of infighting. Her audience had laughed appreciatively when she joked that if Texas liberals were ever conscripted into a firing squad, they would undoubtedly form a circle.[12]

The Rise of Jimmy Carter

The liberals' next two meetings, one in October 1975 and the last in December of that year, appeared to do little more than publicize their disarray. In October, Carr reported on the thoroughness with which the Strauss faction on the DNC had suppressed the liberal challenge of the Bentsen bill's legality. Moreover, organized labor was rumored to be leaning toward Bentsen because he was so heavily favored to win the Texas delegation. Only three of the thirty-one senatorial district spokespersons, when polled, believed Carr's uncommitted strategy would work in their districts. But Carr was still unwilling to give it up.

The December meeting ended in an apparent fiasco for her. Harris, the only national candidate to attend, made a highly effective speech boosting his "new populism" and announced his intention to run in Texas. His partisans, who had come to the meeting on a chartered bus from Austin, applauded wildly, and a straw poll of those in attendance indicated that he was the favorite with 39 percent of the total vote. In addition, the word was out that Georgia's Jimmy Carter would also ignore Carr's plea to stay out of the primary as a statewide candidate. About the only good news from her vantage point was Yarborough's announcement that he would not run as a favorite son. But she was resolutely cheerful in assessing for reporters the outcome of the final strategy session. "We're not through yet," she said. "I just have a hunch that we can work it out. Who knows who's going to hate Bentsen besides us by May 1."[13]

Carr may have known more than she cared to reveal. She had noticed the explosive growth of the Carter movement before it had captured the attention of the press, and she had begun to weigh the man carefully. John Pouland, a twenty-two-year-old liberal Carter organizer, later credited as the person most responsible for getting Carter's name on the ballot in all thirty-one Texas districts, had begun putting together delegate slates for his man.

Carr and Pouland were friends. Pouland generally relied on liberals for his initial contacts in a district. Before long, Carr was giving Pouland advice on likely candidates in districts where her uncommitted strategy was not employed. At one point, as Carr tells it, Pouland said, "Okay, Billie. We can pick bad people or good people, and I don't want to send any 'Nazis' to the national convention, or 'Baptists,' and that's all I've got, if you don't help me."[14] Carr helped him. In nine districts, all of the Carter delegates on the ballot were allied with Carr's "Texas Democrats" group.[15] Pouland later estimated that only ten to twenty of the ninety-two elected Carter delegates were conservative, while twenty to thirty were moderate and forty to fifty were liberal.[16]

While Carr was building bridges to the Carter campaign, she convinced many of Sargent Shriver's backers—largely Hispanics—to field uncommitted slates simultaneously with Shriver slates in case their candidate withdrew before the primary, as in fact he did.[17]

Yet as the filing deadline approached, liberal chances for success appeared to vanish. The U.S. Justice Department had already approved the legality of the new primary law. Texas AFL-CIO president Harry Hubbard announced his personal support for Bentsen.[18] And while Shriver

had agreed to a nonaggression pact with Carr and her uncommitted liberals—they would not compete in the same districts—Harris's backers
began petition drives in several districts that Carr had targeted for uncommitted slates.

The filing deadline was February 2. When the dust cleared, Bentsen,
Wallace, and, to the surprise of many observers, Carter had qualified delegate slates in every district. Full slates for the uncommitted liberals, as
well as for Harris and Shriver, were qualified in eighteen, fourteen, and
six districts respectively, but there was an extensive overlap among them.
To add to the liberals' woes, some of their own number turned up on
Bentsen slates. The senator had offered to a sprinkling of black, Chicano,
and Anglo liberals what seemed at the time to be safe seats in the Texas
delegation, and, for various reasons, several had accepted.[19]

Among the converts were the state senators, A. R. ("Babe") Schwartz—
who had inserted the self-destruct clause in the Bentsen bill—and Oscar
Mauzy, and black state representatives Senfronia Thompson, Anthony
Hall, and Eddie Bernice Johnson. Opponents of the Bentsen bill were
surprised to discover that one of its most articulate critics, Carrin Patman,
a former national committeewoman, was also a Bentsen delegate candidate. Patman, however, drove an interesting bargain with Bentsen as her
price for running on his slate: the senator's promise that she would be
appointed to the temporary rules committee of the national convention in
New York. The promise was kept, and Patman then led the successful
fight to ban future primaries of the Bentsen variety.[20]

In a period of fifty weeks, the Bentsen strategy had triumphed over
almost every obstacle. The liberals were in more than their usual confusion. All challenges to the new primary system had been beaten back. The
overall Bentsen program had served to unify, at least temporarily, several
conservative factions in the party. The operation was a stunning technical
success.

But eight days after the filing deadline, the senator announced that his
national campaign was finished. He had raised and spent large sums of
money—$2.3 million, according to the Federal Election Commission.[21]
His experienced, hardworking staff had skillfully cultivated the good will
of party professionals around the country. The only thing lacking was popular support. But in calling off his national campaign, Bentsen promised to
stay on the ballot as a favorite son candidate "to see that the Texas viewpoint is expressed at the Democratic convention," he said, "and . . . that
nominees are selected who will represent the Texas viewpoint."[22]

Around the country, other candidates began to founder in Carter's
wake. Shriver and Harris withdrew. By April, it was apparent that developments in the Republican party would also affect the outcome of the
Democratic primary. The unelected president, Gerald Ford, was under

attack from Ronald Reagan, long a hero of the state's right-wing Republicans. Many voters who otherwise favored Bentsen would be drawn to that contest in the Republican primary.

Four days before the Texas primary election, Carter scored a smashing victory in Pennsylvania over Senator Henry Jackson of Washington, who had the backing of labor leaders and many party regulars. Jackson withdrew as an active candidate. Minnesota senator Hubert Humphrey announced that he would not compete for the nomination. By primary election day in Texas, Carter was the strong Democratic frontrunner.

Turnout in the Democratic primary on May 1 was light, only slightly greater than the 1.5 million primary voters in 1974, an off year. But the Republican turnout in the state's first presidential preference primary broke all records, with over 419,000 participating, almost tripling their previous primary turnout record of 143,000 in 1964, when Barry Goldwater had created prairie fire excitement among conservatives.

To the delight of Bentsen's liberal foes, his "winner-take-all" plan succeeded beyond everyone's expectations. The winner, Jimmy Carter, took practically all—ninety-two of ninety-eight delegates—while receiving only 49 percent of the Democratic vote statewide. Bentsen, trailing badly with 21 percent, got six delegates, three from his own district. The payoff in the Republican primary went to Reagan, who with about two-thirds of the vote captured all of the elected Republican delegates and resuscitated for a while longer what until then had been a faltering challenge to Ford.

As the returns came in that night, it was clear that the Bentsen-Briscoe wing of the party was in trouble. Even if they were able at the upcoming state convention to capture all thirty-two of the remaining delegate seats, they would go to New York as a distinct minority unless they could make inroads among Carter delegates. Moreover, Republican primary voters were legally prohibited from participating in the upcoming Democratic convention process. Hence conservatives who were drawn into the Reagan-Ford contest would be unable to join forces with the Democratic establishment at either the June or September state conventions. For the first time in many years, liberals and moderates had a chance to wrest control of the SDEC from the conservatives, an eventuality the Bentsen gambit had been designed to prevent.

After the results of the Bentsen bill became obvious, Speaker Billy Clayton—a key conservative Democratic leader who would later switch to the Republicans—called for a new law altogether. An enthusiastic champion of the Bentsen bill the previous year, Clayton had then defended it as fair and bravely dared the chips to fall where they might. Now he proposed a "unitary primary"—one that would allow voters in the Republican presidential primary to vote in the Democratic state primary and to attend the Democratic convention.[23]

Clayton's thinking was in line with other conservative Democrats on this point. Their caucus at the September convention would endorse a resolution to abolish the second state convention in presidential years and one to lengthen the tenure of the party chairman and the SDEC—to be elected in off years—to a four-year term. The purpose, it was explained, was "to divorce presidential politics from state politics."[24] This had been the strategy of the conservative Democrats for at least a generation and it probably explains their successful attempt earlier in the decade to abolish elections for statewide office in presidential years.

The Delegation to New York

With the primaries over, liberal and conservative Democrats began scheming to influence the composition of the delegation to New York at the June state convention. The liberals triumphed. In a key roll-call vote, the convention barred at-large members of the Dallas delegation whom conservatives—including Governor Briscoe's chief fund-raiser, Jess Hay—had stacked with "uncommitted conservatives" in violation of the party's proportionality rule. Briscoe's prestige was obviously involved in the outcome. The vote went three-to-two against the establishment conservatives.

Liberals, minorities, and labor captured five of the seven Texas seats on the DNC. Carr retained hers, easily defeating the conservatives who had singled her out for defeat. Hay, barred as a delegate to the state convention after losing his group's credentials fight, was nonetheless retained on the DNC at the governor's insistence and was later given an alternate delegate's credentials to New York.

It looked as though about 40 percent of the Carterites at the Houston convention were firm liberals—more than enough, if Carr's forces could swing it, to unseat Guest, Briscoe's personally designated party chairman, in September. Carr and her self-styled "Texas Democrats" were exultant that convention night. After sixteen months in dubious battle against the Bentsen primary strategy, the liberals and moderates were suddenly no longer the underdogs. His face flushed, grinning broadly, Carr's ally Ed Cogburn quoted an apposite if somewhat mangled passage from the Book of Proverbs: "He who diggeth a pit for his neighbor will fall himself therein."

The Texas delegates to New York were described as "definitely the most liberal delegation Texas ever had to a national convention."[25] Many were neophytes of the sort attracted to the party in 1972 by the McGovern campaign. Forty-one percent were women—a higher proportion than in the convention as a whole. Fourteen percent were black and another 17 percent were Chicano. Eleven percent were labor unionists. Cecile Harrison, a black Texas delegate who sat on the credentials committee, said she was impressed with the percentage of black delegates from Texas as compared with those in various other states with a reputation as more racially tolerant.[26]

A preview of things to come occurred when the Texas delegation got together for its first meeting in New York. Land Commissioner Bob Armstrong introduced Briscoe as the group's official chairperson. There was a polite sprinkling of applause. Armstrong then introduced Ralph Yarborough, leader of the uncommitted delegates. The audience responded with a standing ovation. "Everybody in the place clapped and yelled and stood," said Carr. "It startled both the [former] senator and the governor, I think, as well as Armstrong, who wouldn't have done it if he had known."[27]

Walter Mondale, with 40 percent of the vote, was the Texas delegation's favorite candidate for vice president, a poll taken before Carter's announcement of his choice revealed.[28] Edmund Muskie ranked second. John Glenn, Briscoe's choice, was favored by 8 percent. A heavy majority of the delegation supported Carrin Patman's amendment to abolish the loophole allowing winner-take-all primaries, in spite of opposition from Briscoe, Guest, Strauss, and Carter himself.[29]

The Fight for Party Control

Preparations now intensified for the struggle over party control in September. Carr's liberals began to cast about for a likely candidate to depose Guest, and finally settled on John Henry Tatum, a self-described populist who was county attorney in the deep East Texas town of Lufkin. Tatum had good liberal credentials. He had been an early Carter supporter whose wife won her contest as a Carter delegate in the May primary. A long-standing progressive, Tatum had played a major role in previous campaigns of Yarborough and Farenthold. An elected official with a good record on racial matters, an experienced party worker, a good stump speaker with a piney woods twang in his voice, "John Henry," as everyone called him, was a promising challenger.

Briscoe was hard at work trying to persuade Jimmy Carter to announce his support for Guest as state chairman, arguing that a fight over the party chairmanship would hurt Carter in Texas. The liberals had reason to hope that Carter would not buy this, since he had labeled the Bentsen bill "the most disgraceful law in the whole United States" during his primary campaign. And Carter's national political director earlier had stated that the Carter organization would "not involve itself in intrastate party disputes."[30]

Yet Briscoe and Guest quickly mended their fences with Carter. In May, Briscoe fund-raiser Hay, a mortgage investment banker, was named Carter's Texas finance chairman. The Carter camp had also consented to let Briscoe head the delegation to New York. In late June, Carter announced that Guest would cochair his fall campaign with Bob Armstrong, who had managed Carter's Texas primary campaign.

As far as presidential politics was concerned, Carter's proffering an olive branch to the conservatives was sensible. As the September convention approached, however, the liberals were afraid that Briscoe and Guest would take Carter's olive branch and beat them over the head with it. Their growing concern was that Armstrong, despite his good intentions, would concede too much to the conservatives.

Their worries appeared confirmed in August, when delegates to the forthcoming state convention received a letter from Frank Moore, Carter's deputy campaign director for southern states, pleading with them to stop fighting over Guest's reelection bid. Moore concluded: "Bob Armstrong and the entire Carter national campaign organization join me in urging Calvin Guest's re-election this September."[31]

Moore's letter brought Bob Bullock, the state controller, into the battle. Bullock had aided Carr at the June convention when the Briscoe forces had tried to remove her from the DNC. He called a news conference to announce that he was backing Tatum against Guest. The state party chairmanship was "little more than a cabinet post appointed by the governor," he said. "That's why we have the sorriest Democratic Party organization in all the southern and southwestern states. It's pathetic." Then, turning to the matter of the Moore letter, Bullock said, "I don't know whether Gov. Carter knew of this letter being written, but if he did, shame on Gov. Carter. . . . [Tatum] worked for Jimmy Carter at the same time Calvin Guest and Dolph Briscoe were out beating the bushes for Sen. Lloyd Bentsen. . . . What Guest and Briscoe traded to get that type of endorsement, I don't know, but I'd sure like to know."[32]

The Briscoe camp worked hard to pry liberal delegates away from a commitment to Tatum. In a series of private meetings in Austin, Guest and AFL-CIO president Hubbard tried to convince liberal and minority national committeepeople from Texas of the virtues of party unity. The bait consisted mainly of an offer to let them name convention committee appointees at the Fort Worth convention and to share the stage there with Guest.

Tatum meanwhile criticized Guest for not effectively raising money for the party, arguing that this fact was obscured by Guest's faulty bookkeeping at Democratic headquarters. The issue was much larger than one of sound bookkeeping principles, for liberals had long criticized the conservatives in control of the party machinery for not raising money and using it to strengthen the party's mobilizing function. Instead—the argument went—the controlling establishment raised money for individual conservative candidates, both Democratic and Republican, outside the party structure, thus denying the rest of the Democratic candidates the benefits of a strong, revenue-generating organization.

Reporters were rummaging around in the party's financial records. Little in the way of records was found, which was not surprising, because yearly audits were not required either by law or by party rules, and record keeping had always been haphazard at best. The public airing of this fact, however, was rather embarrassing to a party chairman who was a professional auditor and president of a savings-and-loan company.

Guest at first met reporters' queries with vague replies. Then he issued a guarded statement that the party during his administration had always stayed "on the black side of the ledger."[33] But a reporter's check of records in the secretary of state's office revealed, on the contrary, that expenditures had pretty consistently exceeded contributions during 1976.[34]

Attempts by a member of Guest's staff to explain the discrepancy only added to the confusion, and one Harold Figg, an unknown in party circles, was suddenly introduced by Guest as the party's treasurer, personally hired by the chairman. This announcement was met with surprise by party activists, as the Democrats did not have an official treasurer's post, and several members of the SDEC professed never to have heard of either the post or Figg. He was not much help in any case, as he could not unscramble the confusion or produce a statement of the party's assets and liabilities, the only information under the circumstances that would have resolved the problem.

As the controversy expanded, fueled by more charges from Tatum, Guest announced the creation of a "party finance council" that presumably would concern itself with future record keeping. As chairman he named Bernard Rapoport, one of the state's few affluent liberal businessmen of consequence. Guest also managed to get a quick audit of the party's books, giving him a clean bill of health. Or so it seemed, until one read the fine print. The exceedingly cautious language in which the accounting firm announced its results stressed that the party's records were "not intended to present results of operations in conformity with generally accepted accounting principles, nor [were] they intended to present the financial position of the party."[35]

Happily for Guest, a deus ex machina of his own contrivance was waiting in the wings to extract him from his difficulties with party finances. Earlier in the summer, he had quietly struck a deal with Mexican American leader Leonel Castillo, the Houston city controller and Guest's 1974 challenger. To pacify the more dissatisfied Mexican American activists, Guest offered to create an official treasurer's post at the Fort Worth convention. Castillo could have it, he said. Thus one of the highest party posts would be occupied for the first time by a Mexican American. Castillo accepted, although he made it clear that he would remain committed to Tatum. He subsequently stuck to his word, despite strong pressure from Briscoe to switch.[36]

Castillo's acceptance, when it became known at the convention, clearly benefited Guest. It accommodated Chicanos' complaints of exclusion from major party office, and it defused the issue of Guest's financial stewardship, given Castillo's reputation for honesty and efficiency as Houston's city controller. Entering the home stretch, Guest's chances were suddenly much brighter.

He waged a vigorous campaign in the last days before the convention. A paid staff that included a state representative worked the delegates by phone and in person. Guest traveled extensively around the state in a private airplane. Tatum relied on volunteers and a camper truck. He later estimated the cost of his campaign at $2,000 and that of Guest at around $50,000—a figure that Guest denied, although he refused to give one of his own.[37]

When delegates began arriving in Fort Worth, it was obvious that Guest had made deep inroads into Tatum's support. The AFL-CIO leadership had endorsed Guest—a decision that was binding on labor delegates. State Representative Mickey Leland, who Carr had hoped would persuade the black caucus to endorse Tatum, announced shortly before the convention that he had accepted a paid staff position in the Carter campaign and had consequently agreed not to take part in the chairmanship fight. Ann Marek, a Carter organizer in Fort Worth, made a similar announcement. Bernard Rapoport, the liberal businessman, endorsed Guest at a press conference, standing beside the governor.

The extent of the defections was evident in the preconvention caucuses. Labor endorsed Guest. Both the women's caucus and the black caucus abstained. Only three—the "Charter Carter Caucus," the Billie Carr–led liberal caucus, and the Mexican American Democrats (MAD)—supported Tatum. Even the impact of MAD's endorsement was diminished by the formation of a splinter group, "Mexican Americans for Guest," whose caucus drew a number of Chicanos, primarily from South Texas.

The reasons some liberals gave for backing Guest were varied, although there were common themes. Many spoke of the alleged cliquishness of Billie Carr's faction-within-a-faction. Hubbard, president of the AFL-CIO, mentioned the friendly appointments to state boards and commissions that Briscoe had made after labor backed Guest over Castillo in 1974. Guest, it was rumored, had told Hubbard that when the head of the

Texas Employment Commission stepped down, labor could pick his replacement. And indeed, a friendly appointment was later made. Labor was also allegedly promised an acceptable appointment to the Industrial Accident Board. To the independent liberals, Guest vowed that the party would become more accessible to minorities and women.

The long-awaited vote took place on Saturday, September 18. In spite of his impressive gains as it approached, Guest left nothing to chance. His well-publicized "opening to the liberals" incensed some of the party's most conservative members who had not defected to the Republicans that year. Led by John Brunson, a Houston lawyer and former protégé of Connally, they formed a caucus and served notice to Guest that further compromises with the moderates and liberals would lead to a walkout before the vote. Their threat brought Briscoe himself to address the conservatives early Saturday morning, and apparently only his personal intervention blocked the incipient revolt.

In the meantime, Guest's staff had launched a massive telephone campaign to persuade their absent delegates to come to Fort Worth. Then, still fearing conservative defections if the vote were not taken until evening when it was scheduled, the Guest-dominated rules committee voted out a report urging suspension of the agenda to allow early balloting. The convention chairman gaveled the motion through on a voice vote.

The roll call began around noon. As the counties announced their tallies, the trend for Guest was unmistakable. When all the votes were in, Tatum's total came to 41 percent—almost exactly the proportion that the liberal Castillo had garnered in his race with Guest two years before.

The Aftermath

In a surprising twist of events, the Carr faction, while losing the chairmanship battle, helped win the liberals' war for party control. The vice chairperson was a black woman—Eddie Bernice Johnson—and more than Congresswoman Barbara Jordan, whom she succeeded, Johnson was active in state party affairs as distinct from national ones. The treasurer was Castillo, whom President Carter would soon appoint as director of the U.S. Immigration and Naturalization Service. Castillo would be succeeded as treasurer by a feisty Hispanic state representative, Ben Reyes, who was also active in party affairs. Liberals and moderates had earlier that year captured five of Texas's seven seats on the Democratic National Committee, and now at the September convention they captured more than half of the SDEC. Carr managed to keep her positions with both groups.

Something important had happened. It began to look as though the liberals had taken de facto control of the party for the first time since 1948. "Briscoe even spoke to me backstage after the vote," Carr said sardonically. "Before, he usually hasn't acknowledged my existence." Gleefully she told reporters, "Calvin [Guest] has to be good now, because two-thirds of the [state] committee can remove the chairman."[38]

The conservatives hoped that the liberals' successes in 1976 were a fluke—the result of conservatives temporarily deserting the Democrats to vote in the Republican presidential primary. But it would take two years to test that hypothesis, and in the meantime Guest had little recourse but to go along with the SDEC majority.

Liberals later praised Guest for honoring the spirit as well as the letter of his commitments made during the heat of the chairmanship fight. These included a year-round voter registration program to enroll nonvoters and Guest's intercession with his Washington connections on behalf of minority appointments to the Carter administration. "Mickey and I would go through fire for Calvin after his performance the last couple of years," said Reyes in 1978, referring to his black legislative colleague, Mickey Leland, who later took Barbara Jordan's seat in Congress. Also employing a fiery metaphor, Brunson, the conservative Houston lawyer, described the experience of the conservatives on the committee in 1977–1978 as "hell."[39] Hard-line conservatives of Brunson's views numbered only about seven of the sixty-two committeepersons.

Events in 1978 proved that the liberal victory in the struggle for party control two years earlier was no fluke. On the contrary, from the vantage point of the 1980s, the year 1976 was a watershed. John Hill upset Briscoe in the 1978 Democratic primary only to lose narrowly to Bill Clements in November. Before his defeat, Hill's choice of party chairman was moderate-to-liberal Billy Goldberg, who, without an incumbent Democratic governor to answer to, was actual as well as titular head of the party. Goldberg was succeeded in 1980 by Bob Slagle, another moderate. Slagle was the first state chairman in memory who was not selected by the Democratic gubernatorial nominee. Rather, he was chosen by the grass-roots delegates at the 1980 "governor's convention"—surely a misnomer in a year when there was no gubernatorial primary and the incumbent was a Republican.

Slagle remained the state chairman in 1982, when the party's nominee, Mark White, was elected, and he continued as chairman throughout the 1980s. Thus was established a precedent of party independence from the governor that would be difficult to reverse. As long as the liberal-moderate coalition controlled the convention process, there was little likelihood that a conservative governor would have even the diminished power in party affairs that Briscoe exercised in 1976. Indeed, given the changing constituency of the Texas party, the prospects were remote that a conservative Democratic gubernatorial candidate in the old establishment mold could win the nomination or, having done so, would pick a fight with the party rank and file over the chairmanship.

The guerrilla movement sparked by Billie Carr thus succeeded in ways that surprised even its leaders. The party machinery has been controlled since the coup by the liberal-moderate faction. It should come as no surprise that the Texas Republican party grew rapidly thereafter, as both liberals and Republicans had predicted.

10

The Rise of Right-Wing Republicanism

When [Lloyd Bentsen, Sr., father of the U.S. senator] first moved to the Valley, he went to see R. B. Creager of Brownsville, state chairman of the Republican party during its dormant years.

"I told Mr. Creager that I wanted to join the Republican party since my daddy had always been a rock-ribbed Republican in South Dakota. He said, 'Young man, do you want to do what's best for Texas?' I said I did. And he told me, 'You go back to Mission and join the Democratic party, because what's best for Texas is for every state in the union to have a two-party system and for Texas to be a one-party state. When you have a one-party state, your men stay in Congress longer and build up seniority.' I took his advice."[1]

THE MODERN Texas Republican party was born in 1961 with the election of John Tower to the U.S. Senate, although there were adumbrations of it in the 1950s.[2] Tower in 1960 had opposed Lyndon Johnson, the incumbent, who ran simultaneously for the Senate and the vice presidency thanks to a law the legislature had passed the year before at Johnson's behest. Tower was thoroughly beaten, but he entered the race for LBJ's vacated seat, took advantage of a large field that included two well-known liberal candidates, and won a runoff against a reactionary Democrat whom many liberals would not support. Tower was thus the first Republican since Reconstruction, not only in Texas but in the South, to win a Senate seat.

Until then, the Texas Republicans were more a paper party than anything else, although ticket-splitting in rich urban precincts was already common in presidential elections and spread further down the class structure after Eisenhower had twice carried the state. But the establishment saw no need for a two-party state. Indeed, like Creager and his able pupil, the elder Bentsen, it saw much to be gained by one-partyism. Not only did the one-party arrangement obscure class issues, but under the old seniority system Democratic congressmen, lacking serious opposition, worked their way up to powerful committee chairmanships where they did a world of good for the tightly knit upper class, whatever party the rich paid public homage to.

Tower's victory, followed by the Goldwater movement over the next three years, augured a new day in Texas. Just as the events of 1944 within the Democratic party had given rise to a liberal movement culminating in

Ralph Yarborough's Senate career and LBJ's Great Society, the very triumph of liberalism nationally, as well as the many excesses of the political and cultural "revolutionaries" of the 1960s, gave rise to a powerful countermovement.[3]

The scope of this movement can be seen in three trends. The first is the growing electoral successes of Republicans in a traditionally Democratic state, which underscore the extent of party realignment. The second is the influence on Texas Republicanism of its extreme Right—those elements that in the McCarthy period were known as the "Radical Right." The third is the staying power of racial politics, which will be examined in the next chapter.

Texas Republicanism has had a remarkable history. After 1928, none of its presidential candidates carried Texas again until 1952; yet in the nine elections between 1952 and 1984, the GOP ticket took the state's popular vote five times. At the senatorial level, Tower proved his 1961 victory was not happenstance by winning every succeeding election he contested until he bowed out in 1984. He was succeeded by Republican Phil Gramm, a congressman recently converted to the party whose conservatism proved to be even more hard-line than that of Tower. The governor's mansion was captured by the Republicans in 1978 with Bill Clements's upset victory over Democrat John Hill. Clements lost to Democratic moderate-conservative Mark White in 1982 and then defeated him in 1986. The Republican groundswell continued to grow.

True, by the mid-1980s the GOP had failed to win any important statewide offices below the level of governor—including the powerful lieutenant governorship—and had captured less than 10 percent of the five thousand or so county-level offices. But it had made deep inroads into the state legislature and congressional delegation, as figure 10.1 demonstrates.[4] At the time of Tower's 1961 election, only a tiny fraction of Republicans were in either body. The change was gradual, although Nixon's 1968 and 1972 victories, along with Reagan's smashing landslides in 1980 and 1984, were accompanied by sharp Republican gains among Texas lawmakers.

What is the significance of this important and long-prophesied evolution toward a two-party state? What is the nature of Texas Republicanism? How does it compare with the Democratic party from which it sprang? And how does it accord with the expectations of V. O. Key?

Sources of Texas Republicanism

When the liberals set out in the 1940s to reform the state's Democratic party, they appeared to believe that if they were successful, conservatives would migrate to the Republicans. The resulting two-party system would

FIGURE 10.1

Republican Elected Officials, Texas, 1960–1986

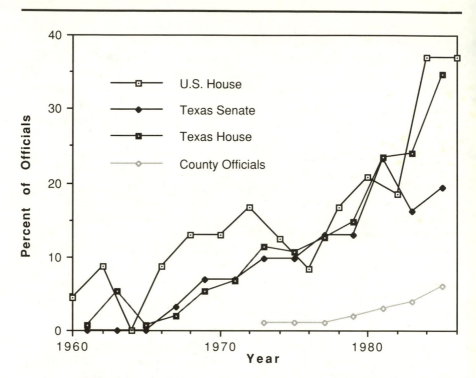

Sources: Calculated from data in *The Book of the States*, vols. 13–26 (Chicago: Council of State Governments, 1960–1984); *Texas Almanac and Industrial Guide* (Dallas: A. H. Belo Corp., 1959–1985); *Congressional Quarterly's Guide to U.S. Elections*, 2d ed. (Washington, D.C.: Congressional Quarterly Inc., 1985); and data supplied by the Texas Republican party.

resemble that of the nation. In those days the national Republican party was dominated by eastern moderates on the order of Thomas Dewey and, later, Nelson Rockefeller—a dominance that continued into the early 1960s. The idea that realignment might give rise to a different kind of Republican party locally seemed not to have occurred to Texas liberals then. Nor, for that matter, was this possibility mentioned by Key in *Southern Politics*.

In retrospect, liberals' failure to anticipate this possibility is curious, because the very logic of their argument pointed to it. The coming realignment in Texas, they had explained, would result from the liberalization of the Democratic party, which would drive economic conservatives and unreconstructed racists into the arms of the GOP. But the Texas Republicans, unlike many northern state parties, did not have a liberal wing to moderate the excesses of the converts. The newly constituted Republican party, one might have anticipated, would be something quite different from the GOP found in New York, Pennsylvania, or Massachusetts. Of course, the liberals could not have been expected to foresee that the conservative movement, beginning in earnest with the 1964 presidential candidacy of Barry Goldwater, would dramatically transform even the Republicanism of the Eastern Seaboard. *Thought NC would moderate SW GOP?*

The realignment that actually came about owed much to the rapid growth of a Texas Republicanism that was deeply reactionary, when seen in the light of optimistic liberal expectations. In a number of elections in the 1960s, many liberals had either refused to vote rather than support conservative Democrats against Republicans such as Tower, or they had tried to rally fellow liberals to Republican candidates, for the tactical purpose of driving conservatives out of the Democratic primaries and conventions. This, they had hoped, would enable liberal candidates to win the party's nomination more easily.[5]

"I want you to realize [that] there are no liberals in this party," outgoing Texas Republican chair Chet Upham told his state committee in April 1983, and "there are no moderates. We're all conservatives."[6] It was a statement the committee obviously wanted to hear. And it was at least true of the party's activist core. A study of Republican delegates to their 1978 state convention found that 90 percent called themselves conservatives; 5 percent, middle-of-the-roaders; and the remaining 5 percent were liberals. And while the right-wingers and "moderates" often talked as though a vast chasm separated them, their differences were small indeed when compared to those that separated liberal Democrats from the Republican Right.[7]

There were of course factions, some of which coalesced around personalities. John Tower, George Bush, James Baker, and Anne Armstrong were among those whom less well-connected Republicans accused of being part of the country club set, and this seemed to imply a conservatism more attuned to considerations of wealth and status than, for example, their positions on race, homosexuality, "secular humanism," or abortion.

To be sure, there were stylistic differences that sometimes distinguished the social elite. Bush and Baker, important members of Reagan's team in the 1980s, were more pragmatic in temperament and more adept in the give-and-take of American politics than were ideologues like Henry Grover, Clymer Wright, or Nancy Palm in Houston or Jim Collins in Dallas.

But it is doubtful that the country club set as a whole was more moderate in its basic values than were its "populist" critics. When Bush, who as a congressman represented an extremely wealthy district that included

Houston's River Oaks, announced his intention in 1968 to vote for a federal open housing provision—one of the few liberal stands he took during his tenure—his office was deluged with hate letters and anonymous death threats, many from his district. After the vote, he had to face down his own crowd—a group of angry businessmen at the exclusive Ramada Club.[8] Bush himself, in spite of being continually attacked by the Radical Right as a "moderate," never scored above twelve (out of a possible hundred) on the liberal Americans for Democratic Action's scorecard while in Congress. One year he scored zero.[9]

The differences that split Republicans involved disputes over means as often as ends. For example, Bush, humane in his personal views, nonetheless was an ardent Goldwaterite in 1964 and attacked that year's Civil Rights Act in its entirety, arguing that the strong George Wallace vote in the Wisconsin presidential primary was not so much a sign of extremism as of general concern over government civil rights measures.[10] In the same campaign he criticized Medicare as "socialized medicine."[11] As vice president he eagerly sought the endorsement of the religious firebrand Jerry Falwell—praising his "moral vision for America"—and other right-wing leaders and fringe groups in his quest for the 1988 presidential nomination, reminding them of his earlier Goldwater support.[12]

Another member of the country club set, Peter O'Donnell of Dallas, once a Republican state chairman, was one of Goldwater's earliest and most enthusiastic supporters. He switched tactics sharply after Goldwater's 1964 disaster, however, and with Tower engineered a moderate state platform in 1966 in the belief that a hard right-wing approach would not work at that point. This belief remained widespread among country club Republicans until 1976. Previous Goldwaterites among them counseled support for Gerald Ford that year out of the fear that Ronald Reagan was too far out of the political mainstream. Austin party activist and Ford's Texas campaign director, Beryl Buckley Milburn, a cousin of William F. Buckley, expressed fear that under Reagan the party might "develop too narrow a base or get too far out in right field." She added, "His philosophy certainly doesn't bother me, but I'm afraid it would be a repeat of the Goldwater election."[13] When Reagan demonstrated his widespread appeal in 1980, however, most of the country club set jumped aboard his bandwagon.

Tower, despite his talk between 1964 and 1976 of Republicans' capturing the center, had a Senate voting record during those days that placed him at the right edge of his own national party. As Texas's favorite son at the Republican convention in 1968, he supported Reagan's candidacy before finally backing Nixon.[14] Houston millionaire Theodore Law, who in the more cautious 1970s sided with Ford in his losing fight for Texas dele-

26. John Tower. A Republican activist and college professor in the 1950s, Tower won an upset victory in the
1961 special election for Lyndon Johnson's recently vacated U.S. Senate seat. He held that post until 1985.
Courtesy of Alan Pogue and the *Texas Observer*.

gates, was a big contributor to Far Right North Carolina Senator Jesse
Helms's 1984 reelection campaign in his home state, along with Texas
millionaires Oscar Wyatt, Jr., Roy H. Cullen, James Lyon, and Walter
Mengden.[15]

If there was a spectrum of Texas Republican beliefs, its "Left" was
firmly anchored in what might be called the establishment conservatism
of John Connally, who had migrated from the Tory Democratic wing in
the 1970s. The Republicans' right flank consisted of militant religious fundamentalists, racial bigots, current or former members of the John Birch
Society, homophobes, financial backers of mercenary anti-Sandinista
troops, and advocates of conspiracy theories linking the Illuminati with
the Trilateral Commission.[16]

Somewhere between these two poles, numerous Texans took up political residence in the decades following Tower's election to the Senate.

Many of the new Republicans were decent Americans worried or frightened by the economic and social problems of the times, who hoped for a return to "traditional" values. Others were apostles of discord: paranoid, anti-intellectual, intemperate, full of hatred for outgroups, and contemptuous of fair play. While probably a minority, the latter were influential in setting the tone of Texas Republican politics in the early 1960s, the formative years of the modern party. Although as a group their influence declined after Goldwater was buried in the LBJ landslide of 1964, they returned to prominence as part of the New Right—sometimes under the same leaders—in the late 1970s. In consequence, the Texas GOP developed into an unabashedly right-wing party.

Where did the recruits who swelled the GOP rolls come from? Two separate groups of "immigrants" accounted for much of the increase. The first consisted of erstwhile Democrats who found their party too liberal for their liking. They included the rich and the upper-middle class whose families had been "presidential Republicans" for decades and who made up the establishment. They also included those less-affluent Texans who had left the party in 1968 and 1972, many voting for George Wallace under the American party label before moving into Republican ranks.[17]

Wallace, an erstwhile economic liberal in Alabama who later tried to turn the racial backlash to his advantage, drew substantial support in his 1968 presidential bid in the South from Birchers, former Goldwaterites, and Democrats who had sat out the 1964 presidential race. In Texas, half of Wallace's state executive committee consisted of John Birch Society members, according to the organization's state chairman.[18] It was to the Wallace supporters, among others on the Far Right, that Reagan's forces in Texas made strong overtures in 1976, and they attributed Reagan's stunning defeat of Ford in the state's primary to Reagan's appeal to these groups.

The nature of the second "immigrant group" is suggested by the fact that the number of Texas whites born outside the South rose from 9 percent in 1950 to 20 percent in 1980. Among the latter were a disproportionate number of Republicans from other states. Many had moved to Texas from the Midwest during the boom years of the late 1970s and early 1980s. The immigrants seemed to be somewhat less conservative than natives[19] but were unwilling to challenge the rightward drift of the Texas Republican party.

The growth of Republicanism was also a result of broad social currents sweeping across Texas and the nation, and it laid claim to the allegiance of a disproportionate number of new voters as well.[20] Key's theory of southern realignment seemed premised on the assumption of continuing, perhaps expanding, support for New Deal or similar principles. Yet many developments created crosscutting loyalties among New Deal constituencies. The Cold War and McCarthyism gave rise to an emotional anticommunism in America beyond anything warranted by Russian threats to American interests at the time. Anticommunist jingoism was at the heart of the Radical Right revival in the 1950s.[21]

At the same time, the civil rights movement was gathering force. Its epochal achievements were first expressed in Supreme Court decisions: *Smith v. Allwright*, which struck down the exclusively white Democratic primary in Texas; and *Brown v. Board of Education*, which declared state-enforced school segregation unconstitutional. After much travail and violence, Congress passed the Civil Rights Act of 1964 and the Voting Rights Act of 1965, the first abolishing Jim Crow and the second enfranchising hundreds of thousands of new black voters. Many white southerners were deeply alienated from the national Democratic party that, through passage of these two measures, reluctantly, then with increasing purpose, imposed a second Reconstruction on the South.

Another contemporary political current was the conservative reaction to the 1960s—including political excesses of the Left and the "counterculture"—and to subsequent social and economic trends that the Right blamed on the Democrats, particularly liberals. High on their bill of particulars were the women's equal rights movement, including the right to abortion; the perceived decline in religion; the rising divorce rate; the alleged permissiveness of the courts toward criminals; the homosexual rights movement; and America's failure to win the Vietnam War. These perceived results of liberal culture fueled both traditional conservatism and the Radical Right. The Republicans capitalized on the fear, anger, and uncertainty these factors engendered across the socioeconomic spectrum.

The Radical Right

The distinction between the radical and the traditional Right is sometimes fuzzy. In Texas, historically both groups have opposed racial desegregation, inveighed against "big government" as the defender of the disadvantaged and against labor unions, and vehemently attacked the USSR as a military threat to the United States. According to David W. Reinhard, a student of the Republican Right, "it is the Radical Right's all-encompassing conspiratorial view of American politics that places it apart from Right Wing Republicans, who may themselves entertain limited conspiratorial notions."[22] Earlier students of the Radical Right such as historian Richard Hofstadter referred to a "paranoid style"—a tendency to imagine Communists around every corner, to harbor theories of vast conspiracy, and to use ethnic minorities and other outgroups as scapegoats for their problems.[23] Their simplistic views of the world and even more simplistic solutions to its problems set them apart from sophisticated conservatives. Even so, both types of rightists have often worked together in common cause.

It is the thesis of this chapter that the Radical Right in Texas, always a minority but sometimes including rich and influential members of the elite, has had a marked influence on the state's modern Republican party. It has not taken over the party, but its influence is significant and gives the Texas Republicans their particular stridency and, at times, their appearance of a Know-Nothing movement. This influence is wielded by virtue of the radicals' importance in winning elections. Given the Republican decision, for all practical purposes, to write off minority voters, their party relies more heavily than it otherwise would on the radicals.

Until the end of World War II, the Radical Right in Texas operated primarily within the Democratic party. Since then, it has often tied its hopes to third parties—such as Strom Thurmond's Dixiecrats and Wallace's American party—or joined with the Republicans. The John Birch Society, to take one example, was firmly ensconced in the Texas GOP by the early 1960s. Its founder was Massachusetts candy manufacturer Robert Welch, who was keenly interested in the Republican party. In his book, *The Politician*, he concluded that Dwight Eisenhower was "a dedicated conscious agent of the Communist conspiracy."[24]

Birch Society organizational operations in the 1950s and 1960s were quite similar to those of the American Communist party a generation earlier. Membership was largely secret; front groups were used to infiltrate respectable organizations; local chapters were "designed to operate as isolated islands, impervious to penetration by outsiders"; members were expelled if they did not follow the official line; "dirty tricks" were employed against opponents; and a grand conspiratorial theory of evil forces explained events. But instead of Wall Street bankers, as the Communists had believed, communism itself had taken control of American government, in the Birchers' version. At its height, the Birch Society had numerous chapters in Texas. Several thousand members were reported in Houston, Dallas, and the Panhandle.[25] Uniquely Texan were teenage chapters in high schools. By the mid-1960s, the Birch magazine, *American Opinion*, had a press run per issue of about 50,000. Among the magazine's owners was Nelson Bunker Hunt of Dallas.[26]

Historian George Norris Green asserts that it was easier for the Birchers to gain entry to the state's Republicans than it was for the Democrats because there was no connection between the liberal wing of the national Republican party and the local GOP activists. In addition, the state party's fast expansion made it vulnerable to Birch infiltration. By the time Tower was elected to the Senate, the state Republican party, especially in West Texas, was heavily influenced by the society. And while there were liabilities for public officials in becoming openly identified with it, the leading elected Republicans of the time—Dallas congressman Bruce Alger and Tower—"maintained voting records indistinguishable from the Birch line," according to Green.[27]

The extensive interconnections between the Birch Society and the Goldwater movement are well known. The Birchers were extremely enthusiastic about the Arizona senator and were active in the movement to nominate him. Goldwater refused to disavow the society in his 1964 campaign, calling many members he knew "fine . . . citizens."[28] The society claimed that 100 of the 1,300 delegates to the Republican national convention who nominated Goldwater were Birch members. The proportion in the Texas delegation was probably larger, as suggested by a prominent Birch official's claim that the organization was "strong" in that state.[29]

Three Texans in particular exemplify the nature of the Radical Right and its evolution as an integral part of the state Republican party: J. Evetts Haley, H. L. Hunt, and the Reverend W. A. Criswell. Haley, a West Texas rancher and writer, was active in the Jeffersonian Democrats, an anti-Roosevelt organization in the 1930s founded by businessmen with Republican leanings. He was the group's chief propagandist, and in the organization's newspaper he often accused FDR of complicity with communism. During the 1936 campaign, Haley charged Postmaster General Jim Farley with "Catholicizing" the Post Office in an attempt to help Roman Catholics "wipe out Protestantism." He attacked New Deal supporters on the University of Texas faculty as "so-called liberals . . . who advocate communist doctrines destructive of all religion" and "who believe in the communist doctrine of racial equality and practice it in the University neighborhood on occasion."[30] Despite the efforts of some Jeffersonians to enlist the support of the Ku Klux Klan and to identify FDR with all types of evil, the president carried the state in November 1936 with 87 percent of the popular vote.

Haley called himself a Democrat, but in 1948 he ran as a Republican for Congress in the Amarillo district. He was trounced by the Democratic incumbent. For a time he wrote a column for the *Wichita Daily Times*, calling for such things as the impeachment of the entire U.S. Supreme Court and attacking the Marshall Plan and the United Nations. In the 1956 Democratic primary, he ran for governor on a segregationist platform that had strong White Citizens' Council backing. He promised, if elected, to call out the Texas Rangers to repel, at the state's borders, federal officials trying to enforce desegregation. He attacked the progres-

sive income tax and government intervention in the marketplace and ex-
tolled right-to-work laws. At one stop he told a labor unionist to quit his
job if he was unhappy with it.

> If after you do quit, you think you have the right to keep somebody else off that
> job let me tell you this: If, on my ranch, a bunch of my hands quit and you
> fellows came up there and tried to interfere with the fellows I then hire to flank
> a bunch of yearlings on my land, I'll meet you at the fence with a .32 and, if
> necessary, I'll draw a bead on you and rim a shell and leave you lying on the
> fence line.[31]

Unfortunately for Haley, the old demagogue W. Lee "Pappy" O'Daniel
tried to make a comeback that same year—1956—and received most of
the Far Right's support. Haley received less than 6 percent. Together, he
and O'Daniel got 28 percent in the first Democratic primary. After this,
Haley organized a group called Texans for America, which Green credits
with being more successful than any of Haley's radical competitors at that
time, although some of them—Birchers and the "Minute Women," another militant group—also belonged to it. The organization sounded many
of Haley's earlier themes.[32]

As a regent of Texas Technological College in Lubbock, Haley was alleged to be instrumental in the 1957 firing of three professors, including
Byron Abernethy, who had addressed a reform Democratic group a short
time before. The firings led to the university's censure by the American
Association of University Professors. Haley's attack on Southern Methodist University in 1960 as a hotbed of leftist radicals failed—no doubt because of the preposterous nature of the charge—in spite of his mailing to
alumni and parents of students eight thousand reprints of an article from
the reactionary magazine *American Mercury*.[33]

Haley next took up the cudgels in the Texas "school textbook wars."
Rallying several groups, including the Birch Society, he appeared before
the state textbook committee and proposed "deleting from all textbooks
any favorable mention of the income tax, social security, TVA, federal
subsidies to farmers and schools, the U.N., disarmament, integration, and
the Supreme Court." The committee made numerous concessions to the
Haley group.[34]

When Goldwater challenged Johnson for the presidency in 1964, Haley
wrote and published *A Texan Looks at Lyndon*, a careless and inaccurate
attack on LBJ as seen from the vantage point of the Radical Right. Some
of the "research" for the book was done by one of Haley's neighboring
rancher friends who had connections to the American Nazi party. Selling
for one dollar a copy—and for much less in bulk—the book supposedly
sold over seven million copies, an impressive though probably inflated
figure. It was distributed by, among others, Birch Society members, Re-

publicans, and oilmen. Although the book did not endorse Goldwater, the senator emerged from its pages as a principled hero. Haley vilified Johnson's commitment to civil rights. Consistently he refused to capitalize the word *Negro*. He predicted that the 1964 Civil Rights Act would "end the American Republic." The Supreme Court was reviled for its "pro-communist school integration and subversion cases." Martin Luther King, Jr., was the "darling of the Communists." Haley ended his book by assailing "Johnson's humanistic leanings," as exemplified by LBJ's statement "that man's 'best hope lies in the realm of reason.' "[35]

After Goldwater's defeat, Haley was not heard from much in the media. But in 1976 the West Texan gained attention as an ardent supporter of Reagan—himself a Goldwater backer in 1964—in the battle between Ford and Reagan in the state Republican primary. Elected as an at-large Reagan delegate by the same state convention that denied Tower a seat in retaliation for his having backed Ford, the aging reactionary spoke poetically of the Reagan sweep, made up, as he perceived it, of "little shopkeepers, filling station owners, waitresses and cooks and school teachers . . . farmers, truck drivers, cowboys."[36] Haley's life had come full circle: From the Jeffersonian Democrats to the Texas Reaganites, he had finally joined a movement that was destined to win at the polls—if not that year, then in 1980 and beyond.

The Political Legacy of H. L. Hunt

Another link between the old Right and the new was oil billionaire H. L. Hunt—who had backed Republican causes as far back as the New Deal—and his son Nelson Bunker Hunt. H. L. was convinced by the early 1950s that the national Democratic party, with the exception of the Dixiecrat wing, was "the instrument of socialism and communism," and in 1951 he organized a tax-exempt foundation called Facts Forum, which grew rapidly in conjunction with the rise of Senator Joseph McCarthy, Hunt's personal friend. The media empire that purveyed Hunt's bizarre views continued into the 1970s.[37]

Although initially modest in scope, by the fall of 1952 Facts Forum was receiving outside contributions totaling about $1 million annually. Within a year and a half of its founding, it claimed a listening and viewing audience "of at least five million," which was probably exaggerated. Activities included "Answers for Americans," a half-hour weekly panel discussion "carried by 360 radio stations and 22 television stations"; two kinds of nationwide weekly radio broadcasts heard on 315 and 222 stations respectively; and "a half-hour TV version of Facts Forum filmed in Washington and carried by 58 stations." Facts Forum also had a "free circulating" library program that mailed free copies of right-wing books and pamphlets to "participants"; among its titles were *We Must Abolish the United Nations, Hitler was a Liberal, Behind the Lace Curtains of the Y.M.C.A.*, and *Traitors in the Pulpit. Facts Forum News*, with a claimed circulation of sixty thousand, urged its readers to get involved in the hunt for "subversives" and reprinted anticommunist tracts—including a famous piece by William Buckley entitled "The Liberal Mind." The board of directors of Facts Forum included the popular TV figure Norman Vincent Peale; Sears, Roebuck chairman Robert E. Wood; Allan Shivers; and movie star John Wayne. Like Hunt, both Shivers and Wayne were McCarthy's friends and supporters.

In 1958, when his interest took a religious turn, he founded a new organization called LIFE LINE (always spelled with capital letters) that journalist Harry Hurt has described as "basically a reincarnation of Facts Forum in religious clothing." Its most influential staff members were former FBI men and fundamentalist preachers. By 1969 its programs were carried on 547 stations. At the height of its popularity in 1962 its newspaper, *Lifelines*, had thirty-five thousand subscribers.[38] The organization claimed that "just about every city in the state of Texas" was in listening range of the program. In Abilene, for example, the site of three Christian colleges, there were five opportunities a day to tune in to a LIFE LINE program. Like its predecessor, Facts Forum, LIFE LINE enjoyed tax-exempt status in spite of its blatantly one-sided political propaganda. Among its heroes were Wallace and Reagan. It declined rapidly after Hunt's death in 1974.[39]

The day of JFK's assassination in Dallas, Hunt's LIFE LINE broadcast an anticommunist harangue. An ad entitled "Welcome, Mr. Kennedy, to Dallas," which H. L.'s son Bunker had helped to purchase, appeared in the *Dallas Morning News* and contained a harsh attack on the president.[40] Negative publicity stemming from these Hunt-related events in the wake of Kennedy's assassination played a role in the respectable Right's distancing itself from the old man. However, his ad was hardly more unseemly, per se, than earlier incidents in Dallas, such as when right-wingers had hit, heckled, and spit on U.N. ambassador Adlai Stevenson, who had been visiting the city on United Nations Day 1963, or when Lyndon Johnson and Lady Bird had been jostled by an ugly, threatening crowd of Republican women in 1960.[41] But Hunt soon bounced back, and by 1965 he had set up a speakers' program, "District Speakers, Inc.," with Robert H. Stewart III, a prominent member of Dallas's banking establishment, as its secretary-treasurer. It included on its executive committee, among others, the singer Pat Boone and Jack Kemp, who at the time was a football player.[42]

When Hunt died, news commentators tended to dismiss the media empire he had built as ineffective and out of touch with political reality. Yet the constant bombardment of the airwaves with diatribes against "the

27. H. L. Hunt. A Dallas oilman reputed to be one of
the world's richest men, he was a patron of the Radical
Right, as is his son Nelson Bunker Hunt. Courtesy of the
Texas Observer.

Communist menace"—internal as well as external—for a period of over
two decades surely helped keep a crude and credulous reactionary spirit
alive at the grass roots. This spirit returned to prominence in the 1970s
among those "populist" supporters of Reagan who voiced many of the
same paranoid themes that were Facts Forum and LIFE LINE staples. Far
from being inimical to the respectable Right, as William Buckley argued
at the time, Hunt's efforts probably aided it in ways that could only be
fully appreciated in the 1980s, when the respectable Right and its radical
brethren joined forces. A key broker in this alignment was Hunt's son,
Nelson Bunker Hunt.

Bunker was early enamored of the John Birch Society. Founder Robert
Welch "became a kind of surrogate ideological father" for him, according
to Harry Hurt. Bunker's biggest known donation to a political campaign

went to the Wallace presidential effort in 1968. Bunker's personal involvement was so great that a Wallace operative charged "that the John Birch Society was trying to take over the campaign in Texas." The Wallace camp officially denied the charge, but three years later it was disclosed that Hunt had given Wallace's running mate, General Curtis LeMay, "a $1 million investment fund as an incentive to become" Wallace's vice presidential candidate.

Bunker Hunt continued to fund right-wing and religious fundamentalist enterprises, including such organizations as Campus Crusade for Christ. In 1982, he and a group of more than fifty friends raised $350,000 for the National Conservative Political Action Committee (NCPAC). In 1984, he hosted a huge barbecue at his ranch outside Dallas for fellow Republicans then attending the party's national convention, again to raise money for NCPAC. "A total of 1,650 people paid $1,000 a head to attend what was certainly the most elaborate of many social extravaganzas related to the Republican National Convention," in the words of a reporter. Among the entertainers were Pat Boone and Bob Hope. Falwell gave the invocation. Guests included Senators Jesse Helms and Orrin G. Hatch, millionaires Lamar Hunt and John Murchison, actor Charlton Heston, the Osmond Brothers, Danny White of the Dallas Cowboys, and Howard Phillips, chairman of the Conservative Caucus.[43] The elder Hunt would have been immensely gratified that his son and the ideas they both stood for had finally become acceptable in the highest ruling circles of the land.

God, Politics, and the Reverend Criswell

The Reverend Dr. W. A. Criswell, longtime pastor of the First Baptist Church of Dallas, to which H. L. Hunt belonged (and members of the Hunt families still do), has been called "the best-known, most heeded, most influential preacher of the Southern Baptist persuasion." The Southern Baptists are the largest Protestant denomination by far in Texas and, in the aggregate, the most conservative of the major religious groups. In the mid-1980s, an estimated 2.3 million Texans were Southern Baptists. Their state newspaper, the *Baptist Standard*, was mailed in 1984 to 350,000 subscribers.[44]

A majority of Baptists, Criswell among them, are fundamentalists, believing that the entire Bible is literally true, or "inerrant," as they say. "I believe that a fish literally swallowed Jonah," Criswell has said. "And if there isn't a fish big enough to do that, I believe that God could have made a fish for that purpose. If He'd wanted to, He could have made it big enough to have a whole suite of rooms in his belly for Jonah."[45] Criswell is a "premillennialist" as well, interpreting certain scriptures to predict a seven-year period of wars, natural disasters, and scourges by the Anti-christ—who will unfortunately rise to power in the guise of a peace-maker—to be followed by Jesus' thousand-year reign on earth. Like many Baptists, Criswell sees no point in working for social betterment or preaching a "social gospel." The end is near, and the task of the true Christian is to save souls before Armageddon.

Raised in a farm family in hardscrabble West Texas, Criswell imbibed the true faith early. "I was brought up to love God and hate the Method-ists," he once said. Licensed to preach at age sixteen, he worked his way through Baylor, a Baptist college, and then obtained a doctorate from seminary. After preaching in Oklahoma, he was called in 1944 to the First Baptist Church in Dallas, where Carr P. Collins, a prominent layman in the church, an insurance millionaire, and bankroller of "Pappy" O'Daniel, helped smooth over initial opposition in the congregation to Criswell's premillennarian doctrines.[46]

The First Baptist Church of Dallas is a wonder in its own right. It houses the world's largest Southern Baptist congregation, with a member-ship of twenty-five thousand, and sits on real estate valued at $200 million. It counts evangelist Billy Graham among its more distinguished mem-bers. In 1986 the church had a budget of $12 million. Criswell's salary was $90,000. He was also given money for his wardrobe and a new car each year.[47]

The flamboyant minister gained renown in the days following *Brown v. Board of Education* by using his pulpit to attack school integration as evil and contrary to biblical command, thus aligning himself against that group of Baptists that "steadfastly refuses to believe that God is behind the identifiable streams of brutality, bigotry, and vicious chauvinism that course their way through the Bible," as a Texas professor of religion—also a Baptist—put it. In 1956 Criswell declared that "the idea of the universal brotherhood of man and the fatherhood of God is a denial of everything in the Bible." The same year he thundered against desegregation before the South Carolina legislature, where he had been introduced by Senator Strom Thurmond. The speech gained national press coverage. During the days of the civil rights struggle, he was one of its most outspoken and vituperative opponents. Billy Graham, a racial moderate, took care to dis-tance himself from Criswell over the matter.[48]

John F. Kennedy's presidential race created a stir among Protestant Evangelicals in 1960. Southern Baptists, in particular, had a long history of anti-Catholic hostility, and until JFK met with Baptist ministers in Houston that summer and somewhat defused the issue, his candidacy was a fertile ground for religious bigotry. Criswell, who only months earlier had publicly endorsed H. L. Hunt's newly created LIFE LINE, delivered a sermon in July asserting that "the election of a Catholic as President would mean the end of religious liberty in America." He added that "the institution of Roman Catholicism is not only a religion, it is a political tyranny. . . . like an octopus, [that] covers the entire world." H. L. Hunt "reproduced" the sermon and sent out two hundred thousand copies.[49]

Later in the summer, Criswell told reporters that Kennedy was "lying" when he said he would not take orders from the Catholic hierarchy. The preacher advocated barring all Catholics from public office and endorsed Nixon. Nonetheless, when the November votes were tallied, the Kennedy-Johnson ticket swept most Texas counties with the largest Baptist concentrations.[50]

By 1968 a spirit of moderation was evident among Southern Baptists who controlled the annual convention in Houston. The group issued "the strongest statement" ever on racial discrimination by the denomination, which had split from its northern counterpart in 1845 over the slavery issue. It committed its members to "open" church membership and urged them to work for equality in "employment, housing and education."[51] Almost three-quarters of the voting delegates supported the statement in a secret ballot, after defeating an amendment that blamed racial tension on "Communist infiltration."[52]

At this meeting, Criswell was elected president of the convention, which coincided with the hundredth anniversary of his church. Given his reputation on race, this development struck many observers as incongruous. Within weeks of his election, his church opened its doors to blacks, although Criswell denied that this had anything to do with his attempt to win the presidency. He also pledged to support the convention's statement on race. However, in a book published as late as 1979, Criswell was still preaching the notorious doctrine of "the curse of Ham"—visited on one of Noah's sons and his descendants—a doctrine that the Southern Baptist tradition long employed to justify racial segregation of blacks, who are purported to be the accursed "sons of Ham."[53]

Like J. Evetts Haley, Criswell at one time called himself a Democrat, but it is not clear if he has ever backed a Democratic presidential candidate. When asked in 1960 if he had voted for FDR, he said "yes and no," and he refused to clarify the answer when probed. Beyond that, he would not name a Democrat he had voted for. He admitted not liking Truman and voting for Eisenhower.[54]

As the decade progressed, Criswell preached against Vietnam War protesters and asserted that " 'hippies, beatniks, peaceniks and others' were traitors." By the 1970s, it was clear that Criswell was firmly in the Republican camp. At a time when Jimmy Carter's Evangelical background was getting widespread attention, Criswell endorsed Ford, an Episcopalian, in the 1976 presidential race, criticizing Carter's proposed social programs and the "social policies of the Democratic party."[55] When Clements was first elected governor, Criswell presided at an inaugural prayer service, and on that cold January day in 1979 delivered what a reporter described as a "thunderous diatribe against the welfare state and government intrusion."[56]

It was an auspicious year for Criswell. A deep schism was developing in the Southern Baptist convention between conservatives on one side and moderates and liberals on the other. The battle was fought ostensibly on theological grounds over inerrancy, but it clearly had political overtones that spilled into the secular realm. Indeed, the rise of a militant right-wing faction within the convention coincided with the rise nationally of the New Religious Right, whose most prominent spokesman was Falwell, an independent Baptist who founded the Moral Majority with help from Richard Viguerie, a Republican direct-mail expert and erstwhile Goldwater supporter from Houston.[57]

Working behind the scenes, Houston judge Paul Pressler, an ardent fundamentalist, Baptist theologian Paige Patterson, president of the Criswell Center for Biblical Studies, and a handful of other conservative Baptists met in Atlanta in 1978 to plan a takeover of the Southern Baptist Convention, a process that Pressler predicted would take a decade to complete. Their purpose was to purge Southern Baptist seminaries of moderates and liberals by gradually taking control of the key institutions within the convention. The next year Criswell nominated for president Adrian Rogers of Tennessee, "the Patterson-Pressler faction's chosen man," who won amidst charges of voting irregularities, "hardball" political tactics, and "religious McCarthyism." The vote for Rogers, an inerrantist, was 51 percent.[58]

The split deepened at each succeeding convention, with the factions becoming more polarized and the conservatives increasing their winning margins. In 1984 the Criswell faction engineered the election of Charles Stanley, a founder and former vice president of the Moral Majority. Stanley, who had earlier called the Equal Rights Amendment "a satanic attack upon the American home," was also a leader in the American Coalition for Traditional Values, a national clearinghouse for the religious Right that delivered millions of copies of "morality scorecards" on candidates in the early 1980s. Preparing for the reelection battle of Stanley in 1985, Criswell sent out thirty-five thousand letters to pastors supporting him. The next year, he denounced Baptist seminary professors as infidels. When inerrantist Rogers was reelected president by a 55-45 percent vote in 1986, Reagan sent the delegates a letter of greeting, assailing "the proud liberal myths about man's self sufficiency."[59]

In addition to supporting inerrancy, the conservative Baptist faction opposed homosexuality, the ordination of women, the Equal Rights Amendment, abortion (even in cases involving rape or incest), the nuclear freeze proposal, and the banning of state-sanctioned prayer in the schools. They endorsed teaching "creation science" as a legitimate competitor of scientific cosmology and evolutionary theory. And they backed other issues closely identified with the political New Right. Indeed, the overlap between theological and secular conservatives was so great that a top convention official—moderate Wilmer C. Fields—argued that inerrancy was "merely a flag of convenience to march under." In his view, "the major issue is not theology, but politics by a small group who want to take over the convention and more or less hijack it."[60]

The 1980s were good to Criswell. Not only did his faction within the convention come to prevail, but in the world of temporal powers so did his party—and a presidential candidate he obviously admired. As the crowning political honor to the aging preacher's career, he was asked to give the benediction at the Republican convention in Dallas in the summer of 1984, following President Reagan's acceptance speech. The Sunday after the convention, Criswell preached a sermon to his congregation. His theme was homosexuality: "In our lifetime we are scoffing at the word of God . . . and opening up society and culture to the lesbian and sodomite and homosexual . . . and now we have this disastrous judgement . . . the disease and sin of AIDS."[61]

To those who thought along Criswellian lines—and many did—the AIDS epidemic was literally a godsend, both politically and morally. Coming to prominence as the doctrine of the Curse of Ham was in decline, AIDS provided a new rationale for bigotry against an outgroup. Indicative of the Right's influence on the Texas Republican party was the fact that Gramm, its winning candidate for Tower's vacated Senate seat, would make homosexuality a major theme that year, running what one Republican columnist called a "virulently anti-gay campaign."[62] In 1986 the state Republican platform demanded strict "enforcement of all laws regarding homosexual conduct. . . . a perversion of natural law [that] . . . is biologically, morally and medically unsound." The platform also called for "public health agencies to quarantine" AIDS victims, and urged mandatory blood tests before marriage.[63] The same year Criswell enthusiastically endorsed Bush for the presidency, as had Falwell a short time before.[64]

The Radical Right and the Respectable Right

The modern Texas Republican party was not wholly or primarily made up of reactionary fringe groups, even though it was overwhelmingly a right-wing party, as Reinhard uses the term: that is, one "in arch opposition to the domestic, foreign, and political changes wrought by Franklin Roosevelt and later the Great Society of Lyndon Johnson."[65] Nonetheless, the radicals' fervor, organizing talents, showmanship, and energy—not to mention the money of right-wingers like the Hunts and the institutional prominence of Criswell and some of his fellow zealots—gave them an important voice in the party's affairs. Their numbers, while difficult to estimate precisely, were large enough to make them an essential part of any serious effort by Republicans to win statewide, so long as the party wrote off potential converts among minority groups and moderates.

Moreover, the respectable Right and the Radical Right often intermingled. The shriller evangelists had become an integral part of the Republican party in Texas, as in the nation. Both Clements and former state chairman George Strake were publicly associated with Falwell—as was Bush —and attempted to use him for their political purposes, just as he tried to use them for his.[66]

A meeting in 1981 to form a Houston chapter of the Roundtable—a vehicle for the Religious Right—exemplified the close ties between Republican officialdom and the more extreme fringes of the party. The audience was treated to a speech by Texas evangelist James Robison, whom H. L. Hunt had once called "the most effective communicator I have ever heard." Robison informed reporters that when liberals "are defeated at the ballot box, [they] will be the first to take up bullets." Among those attending were several Republican legislators and congressmen, as well as the party's county chairman.[67] Robison had already been involved in Reagan's 1980 Texas campaign and would be asked to give the invocation at the opening of the same 1984 convention in Dallas at which Criswell would give the benediction.[68]

A year earlier, John Connally was a featured speaker at the Religious Roundtable political action seminar in Dallas, which also drew presidential candidate Reagan, Helms, Phyllis Schlafly, Falwell, Robison, and evangelist Pat Robertson. In 1979 Connally had met with Falwell and other right-wingers at his ranch and agreed to participate in Robison's TV special, "Wake Up America."[69] Robison was known at the time for his public attacks on "queers," as he called homosexuals, and for his definition of an anti-Semite as "someone who hates Jews more than he's supposed to."[70]

Another example of the easy familiarity among the various "Rights" within the party was the picnic that ideologue Jim Collins threw every year at his family's farm. It was "the longest-running and best-attended Republican social function in Dallas County," according to journalist Paul Burka. Collins, a millionaire congressman and son of Carr Collins (who, as previously noted, was influential in bringing Criswell to Dallas) ran against Bentsen in 1982, calling him a liberal. When challenged by incredulous reporters, Collins cited an analysis of the senator's voting record in a magazine associated with the John Birch Society.[71]

The close connections between the respectable and the Radical Right among the Republicans was captured by a *New York Times* photograph taken in Dallas during the 1980 presidential campaign as luminaries of the New Right convened to hear candidate Reagan address the Roundtable. The picture showed Reagan and Robison shaking hands, while Collins and Connally looked on, smiling. Later in the day, Reagan spoke of the "great flaws" in the theory of evolution and suggested that public schools should also teach the creation story from the Bible.[72]

Especially noteworthy about the intimacy between the Radical Right and the respectable Right was the virtual absence among the Texas party's mainstream of any outspoken opposition to this confluence—opposition like that voiced in 1986 by Republican news columnist Doug Harlan of San Antonio who wrote that "religious fundamentalists are to Republicans what LaRouchites are to Democrats, but the threat to Republicans from the religious right is far greater than the threat to Democrats from [right-wing demagogue Lyndon] LaRouche."[73] Harlan—who earlier had criticized Gramm for homosexual baiting in his 1984 senatorial contest—was a lonely voice in the Republican wilderness. Perhaps the extent of radical right-wing influence in the state's party was no better illustrated than by the fact that it was almost unthinkable, by the mid-1980s, that a Republican candidate would make a statement such as that of Harlan.

The perpetual tendency of the Texas Radical Right to move as far on the fringes of the political spectrum as they could go pulled the entire party in their direction. The result was that one day's traditional rightists were always in danger of becoming the next day's "liberals," at least as the radicals saw it. Thus in 1984, a faction of "prolife" and antihomosexual fundamentalists—called ultraconservatives by the press—openly chastised the party leadership for being out of touch with the grass roots. Two years later, fundamentalists tried to persuade the state convention to proclaim the party a Christian party, in effect, and most party leaders were "careful to bend over in conciliation to their concerns," according to reporter Jane Ely.[74] This solicitude occurred in spite of the fact that the conservative Christian activist candidate for party chair got only 18 percent of the vote.[75]

The extent of Texas Republican conservatism is suggested by the voting record of its elected officials. Tables 10.1 and 10.2 contain a comparison of Democratic and Republican key votes in the 1985 state legislative session in the house of representatives and the senate, respectively. The twelve votes in the house and the eight in the senate were chosen by the *Texas Observer*, the liberal journal, as most representative of a liberal-conserva-

Table 10.1
Liberal Voting Record on Twelve Key Votes, Texas House of Representatives, 1985 (12 = perfect liberal score)

Score	Democrats (N = 98)	Republicans (N = 52)
10–12	32%	0%
7–9	25	0
4–6	16	14
0–3	24	85
No data	1	2
Total	98%	101%

Sources: Key votes were chosen by editors of the *Texas Observer* 77 (14 June 1985): 17–21. Party membership was derived from *Texas State Directory*, 28th ed. (Austin: Texas State Directory, Inc., 1985), 25–81. Column percentages do not sum to 100 due to rounding.

Table 10.2
Liberal Voting Record on Eight Key Votes, Texas Senate, 1985 (8 = perfect liberal score)

Score	Democrats (N = 25)	Republicans (N = 6)
6–8	32%	0%
3–5	44	84
0–2	24	17
Total	100%	101%

Source: Data calculated from sources cited in table 10.1.

tive split. A perfect liberal score would be twelve and eight, respectively. Among the bills voted on were one to include farmworkers under state workers' compensation insurance, a National Rifle Association–backed measure restricting the ability of local governments to regulate firearms, a bill funding health care programs for indigents, another one constitutionally prohibiting a personal or corporate income tax, and bills that would have weakened environmental regulation and laws governing the use of pesticides around agricultural workers.

The tables reveal that Democrats in both houses varied widely in their support of the measures. Around one-third tended to vote liberal, and one-quarter voted conservative. The remaining 40 percent or so were in the moderate category. The Republicans' overall difference from the Democrats was striking. In neither house was a single one of the fifty-eight Republicans in the liberal category. In the senate, which contained only six Republicans, five were in the moderate category, and one was in the most conservative one. In the house, where most of the Republican legislators were concentrated, the overwhelming majority—85 percent— were in the most conservative category compared to 24 percent of the Democrats; and another 14 percent were in the more conservative of the two "moderate" categories. Twenty-two percent of the fifty-two House Republicans did not cast a single liberal vote on the twelve issues, and another twenty-six percent cast only one.

Table 10.3
Liberal Voting Record, Texas Congressional Delegation,
1985–1986 (100 = perfect liberal vote)

		Scores					
		0–20 (%)	21–40 (%)	41–60 (%)	61–80 (%)	81–100 (%)	Mean (%)
Democrats	(N = 17)	11.8	17.6	41.2	17.6	11.8	53.3
Republicans	(N = 9)ᵃ	100.0	0.0	0.0	0.0	0.0	4.7
Delegation total	(N = 26)	42.3	11.5	26.9	11.5	7.7	35.8

Source: Calculated from information supplied by Americans for Democratic Action, Washington, D.C.

ᵃ One newly elected Republican omitted for lack of a voting record.

An even clearer pattern is revealed by the Republican voting record of Texas congressmen in 1985 and 1986. The measure of liberal voting is the scorecard of the Americans for Democratic Action, a national liberal group that also tallies votes on key issues.

As table 10.3 demonstrates, the congressional Democrats, much like their counterparts in the Texas legislature, ranged from liberal to conservative. Their voting proclivities, as a matter of fact, are described by an almost perfect normal curve, with most congressmen falling into the moderate category. The Republicans stood in marked contrast, with all nine in the most conservative category. Like the core Texas party membership generally, there were no liberals among these Republican representatives. Perhaps more important, there were no congressional moderates. They represented the far right wing of Texas—and American—politics in the 1980s.

11

Race and Realignment

> Black and white Americans had begun to take
> their bitterness into the streets and country
> lanes, into the piney-woods ambuscades and
> slum-alley butchering places. This revolution
> was to overhang the entire election of 1964—
> and will intrude in all the elections of the fore-
> seeable future.
>
> (Theodore H. White, *The Making of the Pres-
> ident, 1964*)

> If there's a southern strategy, I'm part of it.
>
> (Ronald Reagan, quoted in Ronnie Dugger,
> *On Reagan: The Man & His Presidency*)

> The conservative political revolution in America
> was conceived in the Goldwater movement
> prior to 1964 and was consummated by Ronald
> Reagan's victory in 1980.
>
> (F. Clifton White and William J. Gill, *Why
> Reagan Won: A Narrative History of the Con-
> servative Movement, 1964–1981*)

STANDING waist-deep in a Houston apartment swimming pool, Bob and Al
argued politics one muggy August evening in 1985. The garden apart-
ments that the pool serviced catered primarily to retirees, widows, lower-
middle-class singles, students, and young married couples unable to afford a house.

Both in their thirties, Bob and Al were friends. Al, who worked for a
lie-detector firm, had lived in the complex with his wife, who was an insurance adjuster, for two years. He was a large, barrel-chested man who
affected a hearty manner, although he sometimes complained to his
neighbors about the stress of his job—especially when it involved firing
subordinates, which the company occasionally asked him to do as a periodic "house cleaning" function, as Al called it.

Bob was a slender man with a mustache and a pockmarked face. He had
moved into the complex a few months earlier. He was a union electrician

who had lost a good job with a construction firm on the ship channel "because of Reagan," he said. Bob lived with a girlfriend who was a bartender. He advertised his electrician's services in the local "green sheet"—a person-to-person weekly advertising throwaway—and he got occasional odd jobs. He spent most of the summer days in the swimming pool, standing at the edge sipping from a beer can and smoking menthol-tipped cigarettes. To anyone who would listen, he talked about his trouble finding steady work and his problems with alcohol.

On this Saturday evening, he and Al had both been in the pool for quite some time, and both were tipsy. Neighbors had gathered in the wrought-iron chairs that bordered the pool to chat and listen to the political debate.

"I had me a good job," Bob was saying. "I come from a union family, and I grew up believing in the union. My dad got me a union job, and I've been a journeyman electrician for ten years. And now I can't even make child-support payments for my daughter in Illinois. And my ex-wife's lawyer knows it, but he's putting the screws to me anyway."

The kibbitzers were silent.

"What the hell kind of a country is this," Bob went on, "when a good electrician can't even get a job that will pay the rent on a one-bedroom apartment?"

"The papers say the economy is picking back up," Al said, encouragingly.

"The papers have been printing that shit for a year," Bob retorted. "Reagan's been saying it for at least that long. But don't tell that kind of bull to me and all my buddies that got laid off—don't tell it to those guys that used to work for Cameron Iron Works. Man, we can't find any *work*."

"Well," Al said, "We're starting to give more lie detector tests now than we did a couple of months back. That's a good sign the economy is picking back up."

Bob stared at his beer can for a moment, and then, savagely, to no one in particular, he said, "That son-of-a-bitch Reagan put me out of a job. That's who did it."

Al stiffened. "Wa-a-a-it a minute," he said. "You're talking about my man, now. You're talking about my man."

"I don't care if he's your man. That son-of-a-bitch is the reason I'm standing in this goddamn pool tonight, drunk on my ass, the IRS is after me, my ex-wife's lawyer is after me. He may be your man, but he's a son-of-a-bitch to me." Al moved a step closer, his eyebrows raised in anger.

"Just a minute," he said. "You don't talk about the president like that."

"To hell with the president!"

"Look here, Bob," Al said, trying another tack. "This country was built on the free market. If you leave the market alone, it'll take care of itself.

There will be a job for everyone, after the wrinkles get smoothed out. That's what Reagan did—he was just trying to get the market running smoothly again."

One of the people near the pool piped up. "Okay, you guys, enough politics. Talk politics when you're sober."

"I know who's messing me over, drunk or sober," Bob shot back. "I used to work for the union. We've lost 200,000 union members in Texas since 1980, and don't try to tell me Reagan wasn't behind that. The bastard's a union buster."

"Listen, Bob," Al said, suddenly calm. "You've got it wrong. You've got it all wrong. You want me to tell you who's taken your job away? You really want to know?"

Bob glared at him.

"It's the goddamn niggers, who'll work for lower wages. And it's these goddamn wetbacks. That's who's taken your job. You can't blame that on Reagan."

Bob was silent for what seemed like a long time, staring straight at Al. "Now you're talking sense," he said, finally. "Now you're talking something that I can relate to. You've put your finger on something now."

There was a murmur of assent among the group at pool side. The debate was over, the tension dispelled. In a moment, the talk had turned to the prospects for the Houston Oilers in the coming season.[1]

A Republican Racial Strategy Emerges

The decline of the Democratic party since the 1964 election is the result of numerous factors, some of which were described in the previous chapter. One of these factors, however—continuing racial polarization—stands out among the others. As Theodore White's prediction suggests, the best-informed observers of the 1964 campaign sensed that there was something fundamentally different about that election year from previous ones. The crisis toward which the nation's racial conflict had been heading for at least a generation was at hand, and the turmoil it created in the presidential campaign indicated that its effects would not soon disappear. Instead, race would "intrude in all the elections of the foreseeable future," as White predicted.

This fact did not jibe with the received wisdom of liberal thought that had prevailed since World War II. In the conventional view, racial struggle, an integral part of our history for over three centuries, would soon come to an end once Americans saw that a caste system was in fundamental conflict with the nation's basic commitment to equal rights. This conflict between equal rights and black oppression had been the central

CHAPTER 11

theme of Swedish scholar Gunnar Myrdal's detailed study of American race relations, *An American Dilemma*, in 1944. Myrdal believed that the conflict could soon be resolved in favor of "the American Creed" of equality. *"Not since Reconstruction,"* he wrote, *"has there been more reason to anticipate fundamental changes in American race relations, changes which will involve a development toward the American ideals."*[2]

V. O. Key's *Southern Politics*, which appeared shortly after the publication of *An American Dilemma*, shared its optimism. In particular, Key held out hope for a speedy resolution of racial inequality in Texas, where the black percentage was lower than in any other southern state and where economic conflict seemed to be more important than that between the races. But fundamental change does not come easily. As in the other states of the old Confederacy, *Brown v. Board of Education* provoked an immediate reaction in Texas. The Republican State Executive Committee met on June 14, 1954, barely a month after U.S. Supreme Court chief justice Earl Warren had announced the Court's unanimous decision. The Republican gubernatorial candidate, Tod R. Adams, told the committee he could state "flatly that regardless of the nine politicians on the Supreme Court, if I'm governor, we'll continue to have segregation in schools."[3]

Governor Shivers, the Democrats' standard-bearer, was hardly more receptive; but at least his nomination was opposed that year by fellow Democrat Ralph Yarborough, who, although he initially waffled on the school desegregation issue, would emerge as the chief spokesman for a significant faction dissenting on both race and economics. That faction gradually gained influence in the party. No such organized dissent ever developed among the Republicans. An editorial in the *Dallas Morning News*, commenting on the Republican candidate's remarks, made a perceptive distinction that would become even more appropriate with time. "It once would have been a phenomenon for a Republican to stand for states' rights or segregation of the races, but it is no longer so. In recent years the Republican party [has done] more to defend states' rights than the Democratic party."[4]

Opposition to school desegregation quickly became a cause within the state Republican party. At its 1958 convention, John Tower, then a little-known political science professor in Wichita Falls, read the state party platform to the assembled delegates. That document came out strongly against federal enforcement of desegregation laws and urged that "the gradual solution for problems relating to desegregation in Texas be left to the people, the school boards, and the courts, within this state."[5] Given the popular mood in Texas at the time, such a policy would have been tantamount to the perpetuation of segregation indefinitely.

By 1960, the civil rights movement had created a serious conflict within the national GOP. That year New York governor Nelson Rockefeller met secretly with presidential candidate Richard Nixon at the former's apartment on Fifth Avenue, in part to get a more progressive civil rights plank in the national platform then being constructed, and he succeeded. When the results of the meeting became known, however, a controversy erupted.

Many conservative Republicans were appalled by the revision of the civil rights plank to commit the party to "aggressive action to remove the remaining vestiges of segregation or discrimination in all areas of national life." Indeed, they believed that the plank dictated in the "Compact of Fifth Avenue" would obliterate the difference between the Republicans' proposed civil rights plank and the one the Democrats had already accepted and that the Republicans' competitive edge in the South would therefore disappear. Senator Barry Goldwater, the leading spokesman of the party's right wing, was outraged and called the Compact the "Munich of the Republican Party."[6]

Texans on the Right threatened to bolt to Goldwater and to lead a floor fight against the platform at the national convention. Goldwater was already known for his stand on "states' rights," the contemporary code word for, among other things, opposition to school desegregation and to the destruction of the southern Jim Crow system in general. Nixon succeeded in convincing the 103-member platform committee to accept the basic substance of Rockefeller's civil rights proposal; but Tower, a "states' rights" candidate challenging Lyndon Johnson in the U.S. Senate race that year, was credited with keeping the committee from writing all of Rockefeller's civil rights proposals into the platform—a performance that earned him a standing ovation from the Texas delegation to the convention.[7]

Nixon, whose moderate civil rights stance in the 1960 presidential race was not significantly different from that of John Kennedy, lost narrowly in November. Blacks had rallied strongly behind the Democratic ticket, and Nixon later attributed his loss to his failure to campaign hard enough for the black vote.[8] But the lesson that the Republican Right, including Goldwater, drew from the 1960 campaign was that Nixon's "me-tooism" had hurt his cause.[9] In their view, this strategic lesson was soon confirmed. The most significant event of the 1962 elections, according to Theodore White, was that an Alabama Republican almost won a U.S. Senate seat. "There was a Southern strategy to be shaped—if the Republican Party did indeed want to court the South," he observed not long afterward. Eliot Janeway, a New York economic consultant, coined the term *backlash* in 1963 to indicate the possibility of whites revolting against blacks as their struggle for equality gained momentum, and it became a catchphrase among political pundits.[10]

The point was not lost on the Republican Right, whose leaders believed there were also votes to be gotten from whites outside the South if the race issue was exploited deftly. Academic research findings also provided them with grounds for hope. Analyzing University of Michigan survey data, political scientist Philip Converse wrote in 1963 that in the South the race issue came closest to having "those characteristics necessary if a political issue is to form the springboard for large-scale partisan realignment."[11] Up to that point, however, as Converse observed elsewhere, "the Republicans have [not] come forth to champion the Southern white. Instead, their gestures toward the Southern Negro have come close to matching those of the Northern Democrats. If we doubt that partisan realignment is likely to occur, it is to say that we expect no dramatic change in this state of affairs."[12]

The Goldwater Movement

For a brief, fateful moment, the Republicans hovered between two choices, each with monumental consequences. They could adopt a progressive line on civil rights policy and attempt to put the rhetoric of racism behind them, as the national Democrats, however tentatively, were doing. This was the course urged by Republican liberals and moderates, including Rockefeller, who had given money to Martin Luther King's Southern Christian Leadership Conference and had even arranged a loan to the more controversial Student Nonviolent Coordinating Committee.[13] Or the Republicans could offer the nation "a choice, not an echo," in the memorable phrase popularized by militants such as Phyllis Schlafly. The rapidly growing Right pushed hard for this option, arguing that blacks would not vote for Republicans in any case.

The evidence suggested the opposite. On average, only 51 percent of blacks called themselves Democrats in the election years of 1952, 1956, and 1960. Fifteen percent called themselves Republicans, 18 percent independents, and 16 percent were apolitical.[14] Eisenhower had gotten a significant minority of black votes in 1956 when Adlai Stevenson had backpedaled on civil rights issues. Indeed, majorities or near majorities of blacks in several southern cities had gone over to Eisenhower in 1956, and significant numbers of them voted for Nixon in 1960.[15]

Goldwater, urged along by the southern GOP, was the first major-party presidential candidate since the race issue became prominent after World War II to pursue a southern white-oriented strategy that appealed to racial animosity. Albert Fay, a rich Houston Republican, had called Goldwater the day after Nixon lost to Kennedy and offered his support. Soon thereafter, Dallas Republican organizer Peter O'Donnell, Jr., Alabamian John Grenier—who would become Goldwater's southern regional chairman—and others secretly began planning for his 1964 campaign.[16]

Speaking in Atlanta in 1961, Goldwater told his listeners, "We're not going to get the Negro vote as a bloc in 1964 and 1968, so we ought to go hunting where the ducks are." He candidly revealed to the audience the issues most likely to bring his southern white ducks to earth. High on his list was school integration, which, he averred, was "the responsibility of the states. I would not like to see my party assume it is the role of the federal government to enforce integration in the schools."[17] This sop to southern racism was ladled out four years after President Eisenhower, by mobilizing federal troops to ensure the desegregation of Little Rock High School in Arkansas, had done just the opposite of what Goldwater now apparently was advocating. Goldwater and his followers seemed to want to turn back the clock.[18]

But things had changed in the South since the 1940s, when crude racist demagoguery was tolerated and often encouraged. A presidential election strategy designed to appeal to whites would now have to operate behind a cloak of hypocrisy. Even southern politicians were aware of the need to eschew old-style race-baiting. They understood that their actions were being scrutinized by a national audience.

The behavior of Republican James Martin, the ardent Goldwater admirer who had almost defeated moderate Lister Hill in the 1962 Alabama senatorial race, set an example for practitioners of the emerging southern strategy. In early fall, the Kennedy administration had reluctantly used federal troops to suppress a riot at the University of Mississippi over the admission of James Meredith, a black man. This event, in the words of political scientist Donald Strong, had "whipped segregationist sentiment to a fever heat." But Martin, in trying to mobilize whites by pinning responsibility for federal civil rights policy on Senator Hill, "did not yell 'nigger' at every crossroads," wrote Strong. "He held forth earnestly on 'states' rights' and 'constitutional government.' Both expressions had become code words for segregation. The use of federal troops in Oxford to uphold the supreme law of the land was somehow a violation of 'constitutional government.' "[19] Goldwater, too, used the prevailing code words for racism. The Republican Right would thenceforth employ this highflown rhetoric to justify the low road the party had taken.

In 1964, Goldwater was traveling it doggedly. His focus was on the South and West, and the epochal Civil Rights Act of 1964 gave him an issue he believed would deliver the South to him. Part of this legislation, which would dismantle much of the South's Jim Crow system, was, in Goldwater's view, an unconstitutional violation of states' rights. One of his most vocal supporters that year, Reagan of California, agreed with him and also voted in favor of a state ballot proposition that struck down an open-housing law.[20]

South Carolina's senator Thurmond, the former Dixiecrat presidential candidate and a symbol of unabashed southern white racism, switched to the Republican party that year and enthusiastically clambered onto the Goldwater bandwagon.[21] In July, Wallace withdrew his third-party candidacy in deference to Goldwater and then crossed party lines to support the Republican ticket.[22] Tower, who had attacked the public accommodations section of Kennedy's civil rights bill in 1963, was the only Republican in the Senate to join the southern Democrats' filibuster against the bill in 1964. George Bush, in his campaign against Yarborough that year, also came out against the bill.[23]

Republicans in Texas were enthralled by Goldwater. They had already evinced a giddy enthusiasm for him in 1960; in 1962, the state convention "went on record" supporting his nomination in 1964.[24] Now his reactionary campaign rallied the state's Republicans to unprecedented efforts. According to a party activist and scholar who came of political age during this period, the Goldwater movement, along with Goldwater's book *The Conscience of a Conservative* and William Buckley's highly popular *Up From Liberalism*, had an electrifying effect on the new generation of collegiate Republicans throughout the state.[25]

GOP officials and candidates were ardently behind Goldwater; these included oilmen Bush and Jack Cox, who were opponents in the primary contest for the U.S. Senate nomination.[26] Bush, the victor, told the August state convention that he would take Yarborough's "Reuther dominated left wing voting record and wrap it around his neck." And he attacked the courageous stand Yarborough had recently made on behalf of the Civil Rights Act of 1964.[27]

At the Republican convention in San Francisco, there was a bitter fight in the platform committee over the civil rights plank submitted by Pennsylvania governor William Scranton. When it was over, Tower told the seven hundred southern delegates (only seven of whom were not Goldwaterites): "I have always been proud to be a Southerner, but never so proud as I am today. The backbone of Barry Goldwater's strength on the platform committee was Southern delegates," who beat back liberal efforts "to include a harsh and punitive civil rights plank."[28] The scrappy Republican senator from Texas had become an important figure in the Goldwater movement's efforts to build a southern base—efforts that "seemed to many . . . [to be] an attempt by Texas and other Southern Republican leaders to build a 'lily white' party," in the words of historian Paul Casdorph.[29]

A few days later, the platform was presented for adoption by the convention, and the central issue was the civil rights plank. When the Scranton forces proposed amendments, the delegates overwhelmingly defeated them as well as ones that would have condemned extremism of the kind exemplified by the John Birch Society. The civil rights amendments were defeated by a vote of 897 to 409, with all fifty-six Texas delegates voting against them.[30]

Black delegates and alternates issued a statement "challeng[ing] Senator Goldwater's fitness to carry out" the newly passed Civil Rights Act that he and Tower had voted against. The black group "declared political war" on proponents of "a lily-white Republican party." The next day former president Eisenhower expressed unhappiness over the defeat of the civil rights plank and condemned the tactics of Goldwater delegates, intimating that their booing, cursing, and general rowdiness on television had hurt their candidate's image in the electorate.[31]

The unamended civil rights plank, weaker in some respects than the 1960 version, tepidly supported "full implementation and faithful execution" of the new law, while opposing "inverse discrimination." A *New York Times* editorial noted laconically that "the party of Abraham Lincoln is now cautious on civil rights, criticizing the Justice Department for 'police state tactics' despite mounting evidence that some states cannot or will not control lawlessness and anarchy."[32] Columnist Robert Novak was more forthright, describing the "unabashed hostility toward the Negro rights movement" as "fully shared by the overwhelming majority of convention delegates." Conservative though he was, Novak was deeply dismayed.[33]

After the convention was over, hardly a Texas Republican voiced public dissent from the party's policy. A noteworthy exception was University of Texas law professor Charles Alan Wright, who wrote in the *Texas Observer* that he would cross party lines for the first time in his life that November to disavow "a candidate whose election would be regarded as a mandate to slow down on civil rights."[34]

Goldwater's defeat was massive, both in Texas and in the nation. But the election results did not unambiguously argue for scrapping opposition to civil rights as a potent issue in 1968. Goldwater's strategy had netted him the five states of the Deep South. Before Goldwater, Republican presidential candidates had received their highest southern support in traditional Republican areas that traced their GOP allegiance back to the nineteenth century, and they had received their next highest support from the metropolitan suburbs. Goldwater reversed this pattern. His strongest support in the South as a whole came from the Black Belt counties, which gave him 59.6 percent of their vote—a 100 percent increase over their support for Nixon in 1960. These were counties where few blacks at the time were allowed to vote. In the Black Belt of the five Deep South states, Goldwater obtained 72.7 percent, and the correlation between his support and Thurmond's 1948 Dixiecrat support was greater than that between Goldwater's support and that of Nixon in 1960, indicating that the racial issue was a key factor in Goldwater's southern support.[35]

Not long before, Philip Converse had foreseen no attempt by the Republicans to capitalize on the southern race issue. Now he interpreted

University of Michigan survey data in this light: "The capture of the Republican Party by the Goldwater faction led to a 1964 campaign strategy attempting to make a Republican bastion of the South, largely by appealing to southern whites on the civil rights issue. . . . [The 1964 survey data] collected in the South during the 1964 campaign leaves no doubt that Goldwater was perceived by southern whites as a defender of segregation, even to a point well beyond any which the Senator actually took." It was the first time since the Reconstruction era that the Democratic ticket received a smaller percentage of the vote from the South than from any other region.[36]

Class realignment in the cities of the Deep South was especially remarkable. There was already a well-established tradition of presidential Republicanism among the upper classes, and it was no surprise that the silk-stocking precincts surged toward Goldwater. But the working-class whites had previously either voted Democratic or, in some of the more racially tense cities, had given far less of a margin to the GOP than had upper-class whites. That changed in 1964.

In Jackson, Mississippi, 60.9 percent of the upper-class whites had voted for Nixon in 1960, but only 35.4 percent of the lower-class whites had. In 1964, 90.7 percent of the upper class backed Goldwater *as did 81.5 percent of the lower class.* Similar patterns were evident in Shreveport, Birmingham, Mobile, and Montgomery.[37] Reviewing the data in Alabama cities, Donald E. Strong concluded: "Here was a white man's front rather than a class politics."[38] Coming from Strong, a co-worker with Key on *Southern Politics,* this observation deserves emphasis. At a point when, Key might have thought, the race issue should have been evaporating, it was suddenly endowed with new life by a Republican party bent on capitalizing on the white backlash. True, the "white man's front" did not develop that year in Texas cities, where the names of LBJ and Ralph Yarborough on the ballot helped stem the tide of racial reaction in spite of Republican efforts to keep race at the forefront of the campaign. The long-term effects of the Republican southern strategy in Texas are another matter.

Analyzing the 1964 election-year survey data, Converse and his colleagues pointed out that the gradual decline in the South's Democratic support—a trend going back to the early 1950s—was reversed somewhat in 1964. But the reversal, they discovered, could be traced entirely to the votes of southern blacks, who for the first time voted overwhelmingly for the Democrats. Among whites, the gradual downward trend continued at roughly the same rate.[39]

Moreover, as Bernard Cosman noted, the Goldwater campaign left behind it in the Deep South "a number of state and local Republican parties demonstrably stronger than at any time in the past, whether measured by votes, contests entered and won, organization, money, motivation, or even conversion of Democratic officeholders to Republicanism." Southern Republican leaders, he added, would benefit greatly "to the extent that racial tensions remain at a high level."[40]

If anything, tensions increased. In 1968 Nixon—pressed on the race issue by Wallace's American party—made overtures to Thurmond and other southern reactionaries by vowing that, if elected, he would appoint a different brand of Supreme Court justice, all the while denying publicly that he was continuing to pursue a southern strategy. Thurmond gave crucial support to Nixon at a time when Wallace's third-party bid, the most successful one in more than half a century, threatened to destroy Nixon's southern base. The result, according to University of Michigan analysts, was a presidential election probably "as sharply polarized along racial lines as at any time during American history."[41] Converse and his colleagues spoke of Nixon and Wallace voters in their nationwide sample as "lily-white" in composition.[42]

Once in office, Nixon repaid his debt to southern whites by nominating two southern conservatives to the Supreme Court (both were rejected by the Senate), by attempting to slow down school busing for desegregation purposes, and by diluting amendments to the bill extending the Voting Rights Act of 1965.[43] His use, with modifications, of Goldwater's southern strategy had worked.

The Phillips Thesis

It remained for a young Republican activist, Kevin Phillips, to provide the party with a plausible, clearly stated interpretation of Nixon's success and, in doing so, to set forth a long-term southern strategy designed to evade charges of racism or extremism. But it was more than a southern strategy. Phillips urged fellow Republicans to go North, West, and to the "Outer South" as well as to the Deep South to reap the benefits of the white backlash.

Phillips had offered his statistics and his analysis to the 1968 Nixon campaign. In 1969 he published a revision of both that was entitled *The Emerging Republican Majority* and dedicated it to Nixon and his campaign chief, Attorney General John Mitchell. *Newsweek* dubbed the book the "political Bible of the Nixon era." In tone and argument it is an exemplary statement of Republican racial strategy from the 1960s to the present. Its pervasive influence over the years was underscored by right-wing columnist and political activist William A. Rusher, writing in the 1980s. Phillips's "central analysis in *The Emerging Republican Majority*," Rusher asserted, "became the Bible of subsequent discussions among thoughtful conservatives as to the essential strategy of their movement, and it remains highly influential."[44]

Phillips began from Goldwater's basic premise that the party's future lay in successfully capitalizing on the racial division that had become so intense by the 1960s. Like Goldwater, he saw no profit in trying to attract black voters. His book was an updated and expanded manual on how to hunt Goldwater's white ducks.

"One of the greatest political myths of the decade—a product of liberal self-interest," he wrote, "is that the Republican Party cannot attain national dominance without mobilizing liberal support . . . gaining substantial Negro support and courting the affluent young professional classes of 'suburbia.' " On the contrary, "the GOP can build a winning coalition without Negro votes. Indeed, Negro-Democratic mutual identification was a major source of Democratic loss [in 1968]." This loss, moreover, was part of a long-term trend, and the Republicans' resultant gain was virtually foreordained, he believed. As Phillips put it, "given the midcentury impact of Negro enfranchisement and integration, reaction to this change almost inevitably had to result in political realignment." Freed of any dependence on liberals or "urban Negroes," the Republicans had "the political freedom to disregard the multitude of vested interests which have throttled national urban policy."

In a passage reverberating with optimism, Phillips envisioned the American future, once Republicans had gained control of it, in terms of "a revitalized countryside, a demographically ascendant Sun Belt and suburbia, and new towns—perhaps mountainside linear cities astride monorails 200 miles from Phoenix, Memphis or Atlanta."[45] Leave the liberals and the blacks in their metropolitan enclaves, Phillips seemed to say, where they could work out their problems as best they could, bereft of federal "commitment to the political blocs, power brokers and poverty concessionaires of the decaying central cities of the North."[46]

Even as late as 1969, the first year of the Nixon administration, there were significant voices of moderation within Republican ranks that still argued strongly against the emerging strategy of political apartheid. The postelection analysis of the Ripon Society—a moderate-to-liberal Republican group—recalled the significant Republican vote of blacks in elections prior to 1964: 39 percent in 1956 and 32 percent in 1960. Moreover, the society pointed out, there was an appreciable move in the Republican direction among black middle-class voters in those years, approaching 50 percent in some locales. Even after the Goldwater debacle, liberal Republicans at the state level—Jacob Javits in New York, Winthrop Rockefeller in Arkansas—were able to rack up impressive black support when Nixon was heading the party's ticket.[47] The voice of Republican racial moderates, however, grew feebler after Phillips's book appeared. In Texas, this voice was nonexistent where party strategy was concerned.

On many fundamental points relating to goals and means, Phillips and Goldwater were in accord. Wherein lay their differences? On racial matters, these consisted, first, in Phillips's belief that the white backlash was not a peculiarly southern phenomenon. "Some Northern cities are nearly half Negro," he argued, "and new suburbia is turning into a bastion of white conservatism; moreover, growing Northern-based Negro political influence has prompted not only civil rights measures obnoxious to the South but social legislation and programs anathema to the sons and daughters of Northern immigrants."[48]

He provided ample documentation of racial polarization and violence in the North and special antiblack hostility among northern white ethnic groups. He also pointed to racial unrest in the Outer South. These trends augured well for the newly reconstituted Republican party, Phillips argued, and provided the same opportunities that the older racial hostilities did in the Deep South that Goldwater had captured.

A second point was Phillips's belief that Goldwater's campaign was too conservative: "His platform—quite conservative to begin with—was quickly propagandized as barely disguised racism in the Deep South vein." Goldwater thus sacrificed votes that a "moderate" candidate could have picked up.[49] Phillips, however, did not clarify the distinction between a platform that was "quite conservative" and one that was "moderate." He implied that the difference was one of tone or emphasis rather than substance. His ostensive definition of a moderate candidate in this context was Nixon in 1968, who quite clearly had a southern strategy of his own.

One explicit distinction between "moderate" and "conservative" strategies, however, was contained in Phillips's insistence that Republicans should not attack the Voting Rights Act of 1965 presumably in the way that Goldwater had attacked the Civil Rights Act of 1964. "Maintenance of Negro voting rights in Dixie . . . is essential," he argued, "if southern conservatives are to be pressured into switching to the Republican party—for Negroes are beginning to seize control of the national Democratic Party in some Black Belt areas."[50] Elsewhere he pointed to the increase in white turnout in the wake of black enfranchisement in the Deep South following implementation of the Voting Rights Act, counting it as an added benefit to Republicans.[51] As they came through in his book, Phillips's motives for urging the GOP to support the Voting Rights Act were deeply cynical. The sole benefit of that act, as he portrayed it, was further backlash.

The Emerging Republican Majority was, in brief, a handbook for Republicans on how to capitalize on—and how to encourage—racial polarization along party lines without appearing to be racists "in the Deep South vein." In addition, it was full of reassurances that a racial strategy of this sort would increase the party's chances of electoral success.

The tract was influential in Republican circles, although clearly it reflected an existing strategy. In Texas, for example, political scientists had already written in 1964 that state and local Republicans "as indicated by their conduct and pronouncements . . . have virtually written off that one-fourth of the electorate composed of Negroes and Latin Americans."[52]

The Tower Era

While he was a U.S. senator, John Tower, the only Republican in Texas history to hold statewide office for twenty-three years, was the embodiment of the modern Texas party. A book devoted to that party is subtitled *The John Tower Era, 1961–1984.*[53] As has been shown, Tower early identified with efforts to thwart the 1954 school desegregation decision and to gut the 1960 and 1964 Republican national platforms of progressive civil rights planks. He was a leading opponent of the Civil Rights Act of 1964 and the Voting Rights Act of 1965. In 1965 he crossed swords with Yarborough, one of forty-five senators supporting a measure to abolish the poll tax as a voting barrier in Texas and the three other states where it was still on the books. In 1972 Tower opposed passage of a Senate compromise bill strengthening prohibition of employment discrimination.[54]

In both 1970 and 1975, Tower opposed extension of the nonpermanent features of the Voting Rights Act of 1965, the major vehicle for protecting minority voting rights in areas of the country—especially the South—with particularly bad histories of electoral discrimination. Only in 1982, when extension of the act again came before the Senate, which passed it by an overwhelming majority, did Tower finally vote for it. Even then, some Texas Republicans did not. Congressman James Collins, challenging Senator Bentsen that year, strongly opposed it.[55] In 1983 Tower, only months from retirement, joined twenty-one other senators who lined up behind Jesse Helms of North Carolina to oppose creation of a national holiday honoring Martin Luther King, Jr.[56]

Lyndon Johnson as Senate majority leader engineered the first civil rights act of this century in 1957 and another in 1960. As president, he skillfully guided through both the Civil Rights Act of 1964 and the Voting Rights Act of 1965. Ralph Yarborough voted for every civil rights bill to come before the Senate during his thirteen years in office. John Tower, on the other hand, opposed almost all progressive racial measures during his more than two decades in office. Such was the "southern strategy" as practiced by the state's leading Republican officeholder.

Despite his conservatism, Tower was often viewed with suspicion, if not contempt, by many Republicans on *his* right. In 1976 he received the

most humiliating rebuke of his senatorial career for supporting President
Ford against Reagan in a bitter Texas primary election that Reagan won.
The infuriated Reaganites denied him an at-large position with the delega-
tion to the national convention while giving one to J. Evetts Haley on the
Far Right. (Reagan backers went on to taunt and harass Ford and his fam-
ily at the Kansas City convention.)[57]

Tower was not alone among Texas Republican leaders in pursuing the
southern strategy. Indeed, there was virtually no public dissent in state
Republican ranks on this point. The one notable exception was Paul
Eggers, the gubernatorial candidate who in 1972 opposed incumbent
Preston Smith, a conservative Democrat. Eggers developed "moderate to
progressive stands on education and racial issues" and was endorsed by
the Texas Observer.[58] It is true that party leaders occasionally made per-
functory statements about the desirability of building a minority base.[59]
Referring to such statements, Joe Nolan, the political editor of the Houston Chronicle, observed in 1980 that "there is little real [Republican] effort aimed at recruiting blacks."[60] This might seem only logical. What use,
one might ask, would it be for a party whose policy was so manifestly
inimical to the needs and aspirations of blacks to try to recruit the victims
of that policy? "Blacks supporting the Republican Party is like a bunch of
chickens getting together to support Col. Sanders," Congressman Mickey
Leland observed in 1982.[61]

Texas Republicans—and indeed the national party—violated Kevin
Phillips's purely pragmatic injunction to steer clear of attempts to prevent
blacks from voting. Their primary method of intimidating minority voters
was to saturate a neighborhood with pamphlets or radio advertisements in
the days immediately preceding the election and then to send white suburban poll watchers into black and Hispanic polling places. The ads often
contained false information as well as dire warnings of punishments that
awaited anyone who committed voting fraud. Some were designed to convince the uneducated that even going to the polls was a risky act. Thus a
1964 Republican pamphlet distributed in Houston's black neighborhoods
claimed, falsely, that anyone who so much as had a family member with an
unpaid parking ticket or unpaid child-support obligation could be arrested
after voting.[62]

The history of this harassment goes back to the beginning of the modern
Republican party in Texas. In 1960, for example, Republican poll watchers were charged with harassing black voters—even as Republicans were
accusing white Democrats of using the same tactic against them.[63]

In the years that followed, Republicans were continually involved in
efforts to monitor minority precincts, always under the umbrella of uncov-
ering voting fraud. On election day, well-dressed whites from the suburbs
would descend on black and Hispanic polling places, "observing" voters

and stirring intense hostility among blacks. A $1,000 reward was offered by Republicans in 1980 "for information leading to . . . prosecution for voter fraud." No one claimed it. Four years later, the amount was increased to $250,000 as a "ballot security" fund to be paid to anyone exposing voter fraud. None of that money was disbursed, either. The Republicans that year also coordinated a statewide plan to supply poll watchers in minority precincts, provoking black Democratic state senator Craig Washington to threaten to send out "big, black and burly" ex-felons to watch the poll watchers.[64] In 1986 Russ Mather, the Harris County Republican chairman, dispatched between one hundred and two hundred poll watchers to inner-city minority precincts. Mickey Leland called him a "racist bastard."[65]

Republicans denied any racist motives for their obsession with minority precincts, a claim made dubious by evidence in a lawsuit that led the Republican National Committee (RNC) in 1987 to scrap an ambitious plan to monitor black precincts nationwide. The RNC's Middle West regional director, Kris Wolfe, had written the southern regional director, Lanny Griffith, during the 1984 campaign to urge the adoption of a "ballot integrity" program in Louisiana. "I would guess that this program will eliminate at least 60–80,000 folks from the rolls," Wolfe said. "If it's a close race . . . which I'm assuming it is, this could keep the black vote down considerably."[66]

One of the most successful uses of a racial issue by Republicans occurred as court-ordered busing plans were imposed to achieve school desegregation. An unsuccessful Republican legislative candidate formed the Austin Anti-Busing League in 1970 and gathered twenty thousand signatures on a petition delivered to Washington.[67] Dr. George Willeford, Republican state chairman, called the White House and other party leaders in Washington to exert pressure. In a letter to National Republican chairman Robert Dole, Willeford wrote, "I can assure you that no single issue, be it Vietnam or the economy, has the attention of the people of Texas ahead of this busing issue. . . . If we are strong-armed by a runaway department of HEW, Republicans will not work for Nixon, Conservative Democrats will not work for Nixon, and we will all suffer the consequences."[68] Republican author John Knaggs commented, "That language may seem a bit tough in retrospect, but it was measured and mild compared to what grass roots Republicans were saying."[69] Tower, in the meantime, had sponsored a proposed constitutional amendment barring "forced busing" and used the issue deftly in his 1972 senatorial campaign against Democratic moderate Barefoot Sanders.[70] In 1976 the state Republican party added a referendum on "forced busing" to its May 1 primary. Ninety percent of the vote opposed it. The Democrats refused to place the issue on their primary ballot.

Republicans, of course, were not alone in their antibusing stance. Bentsen used it effectively to defeat Yarborough in the 1970 primary, thus blunting Bush's antibusing rhetoric in the general election. But for the Republicans, unlike the Democrats, it was not an issue that split the party into factions. The specter of busing continued to be invoked by the Texas GOP in the 1980 election campaigns even though federal judges by then had largely put a halt to new court-ordered plans.

The Texas party did make some effort to recruit Mexican Americans, who occupy an intermediate rung on the caste ladder between Anglos and blacks and whose growing middle class is receptive to conservative appeals on pocketbook issues. During his first term as governor, Clements appointed 143 (5.2 percent) Mexican Americans to state office, a record number for a Texas governor at that time, although smaller in percentage terms than his conservative Democratic predecessor, Dolph Briscoe (who appointed 134 Hispanics, or 6.2 percent, to state office).[71] In 1986 Roy Barrera, Jr., a Republican Mexican American judge with backing from party leaders, ran a strong race against Democratic attorney general Jim Mattox, who had been indicted (but later acquitted) on criminal charges earlier in his term. Barrera received 39 percent of the Hispanic vote, an unusually high figure for a Republican.[72] Whatever goodwill the party may have created among the Mexican American rank and file as a result of Barrera's race, however, was dampened a few weeks after the election when the party executive committee voted to press for constitutional amendments making English the official language of Texas and the United States, a measure vehemently opposed by Hispanic leaders across the state.[73]

The prevailing attitude of Texas Republican officials toward minorities was symbolized by an event in 1983. The state committee, led by its outspoken new chairman, oilman George Strake, sharply rejected a subcommittee's proposal to recruit blacks, Hispanics, working women, and senior citizens. "I don't want to be called a racist," said committeeman Robert Pigg, expressing the majority's opposition to the recruitment plan. "But I think we're missing the boat by chasing the Democrats. We ought to accuse them of what they're really doing—exploiting these people."[74]

Race and Realignment

From the vantage point of the 1980s, the results of the southern strategy in Texas were obvious. Liberal national Republicans as early as 1961 warned that such a strategy, "built on the backs of the Negro," would lead to a "lily-white" racist GOP.[75] The prediction came true. Whether one looks at minority participation in party primaries and conventions, minority voter support for candidates in partisan contests, or minority elected officials, it is obvious that the Texas Republican party was "the party of the white race" as surely as the Democratic party had been so from the rise of the all-white primary to the Supreme Court decision in 1944 that declared that primary unconstitutional. And just as clearly, the previously all-white Democratic party was now increasingly the refuge of black and brown voters, as many whites continued to flee that party much as they fled neighborhoods when black and brown homeseekers moved in.

Republican conventions were overwhelmingly white Anglo affairs. One percent of the Texas delegates to the 1984 national Republican convention were black and 9 percent were Hispanic, compared to 24 and 20 percent, respectively, of Democratic delegates. A study of the Texas Republican gubernatorial primary electorate in 1978 revealed that blacks and Mexican Americans made up less than 1 percent of the voters. Ten years later, blacks constituted 1 percent of the Republican presidential primary electorate and slightly more than one-half of 1 percent of the state Republican convention.[76] The minority proportion of the Democratic primary electorate in the 1980s may sometimes have exceeded 35 percent.

By the mid-1980s, only one minority official had been elected to statewide office—a Mexican American Democratic supreme court judge who was first appointed by Governor White. The overwhelming majority of black and Hispanic officeholders at lower levels were Democrats. In the state legislature, for example, none of the 58 Republicans in 1985 was a Mexican American, and 1 was black. Among the 123 Democrats, 22 were Mexican American and 13 were black, for a total of 28 percent of the party's legislative strength. In the Texas delegation to the U.S. House of Representatives elected in 1986, none of the 10 Republicans belonged to a minority group; of the 17 Democrats, 4 were Hispanic and 1 was black, for a total of 29 percent. This was the politics of racial polarization—with a vengeance.[77]

The Republican party's hard-line racial policy had accomplished two goals. It had drawn large numbers of racially conservative Democrats and erstwhile supporters of George Wallace into its ranks. (A 1984 postelection poll showed more than half of white Texas voters identified with the Republican party, compared to one-fourth who aligned themselves more closely to the Democrats.)[78] And it had strengthened the commitment of blacks and Mexican Americans to the Democrats. The gradual realignment that resulted was one in which the Radical Right combined with the respectable Republican Right in a party of whites. The working-class base of the Democrats was crumbling as less-affluent whites in increasing numbers either split their ticket, adopted the Republican party as their new home, or did not vote at all.

V. O. Key's hoped-for realignment along economic cleavage planes did not occur. Instead, the spirit of the Old South reasserted itself to prove once more, if proof were needed, that racial hatreds die hard. Realignment did occur. Many white Texans at all socioeconomic levels moved toward the Republicans. Racial polarization in state and many local elections remained intense and in fact sometimes increased over what it had been in the early 1960s.[79] University of Michigan voting data revealed a gap of 62 percentage points between blacks and whites nationally in the 1968 presidential race, a gap that political scientists described as "substantially larger than class differentiation or other social cleavages or partisanship within the United States in recent history, or for democracies in Western Europe."[80] By comparison, in 1984 blacks in Texas gave the Mondale-Ferraro ticket 95 percent of their vote. Whites gave it 26 percent, a 69-point difference.[81] Race, rather than class, turned out to be the driving force behind party realignment.

12

Race and Class in Texas Politics

Most of the conservatives like myself had to be
dragged kicking and screaming into the upper
half of the 20th century.
  (William Blanton, Democratic state district
judge, 1983)

THE ESSENTIAL dynamic of Texas politics, according to V. O. Key's theory, was a modified class conflict that periodically burst into the open, as during the Populist era and the post–New Deal years. In normal times, a small, tightly knit upper class managed to run the government in its own interests, often at the expense of those of the lower third of the population, a group Key called the "have-nots." The power of the upper class was aided greatly, Key believed, by the one-party system that for many decades had prevented the emergence of articulate spokesmen for the interests of the have-nots. And when, in unusual circumstances, a crisis brought forward such leaders, the upper class was able to play on the racial antagonisms of the have-nots, a group that contained large numbers of both whites and blacks. The result of this divide-and-conquer strategy was a demoralized and credulous working class prey to the appeals of spurious issues and demagoguery. Under the circumstances, the have-nots saw little reason to participate in politics and left even minimal acts of involvement like voting to the middle and upper classes.

Key portrayed the forces unleashed by the New Deal and the industrializing South as progressive over the long term. Urbanism and the growth of organized labor would foster a new sense of solidarity among the have-nots. These forces, he believed, were most advanced in Texas among the eleven southern states. The development there of a sharp split between liberal and conservative factions among the Democrats portended a genuine two-party system. All of these developments—but particularly the growth of party competition—would serve to bring Texas more into line with the nation as a whole.

This would mean, first, that southern racial attitudes would dissipate, thus encouraging blacks and whites at the same socioeconomic level to work together for the same goals. Interracial cooperation would be aided in Texas, Key predicted, by the low black percentage and the existence of a third ethnic group, Mexican Americans. The nationalization of state politics would also mean the less affluent would participate more, not only because long-standing disfranchising measures were crumbling under legal assault but because the disadvantaged of all races could better match up their interests with liberal candidates, thanks to the clarifying function of a two-party system.

Increased participation would give the have-nots greater electoral influence than ever before. Seeing what they could accomplish through unity, they would put behind them the irrationalities of race and sectional chauvinism, relics of a more primitive age. Class conflict, while still continuing, would be managed by two competitive parties, each with different but overlapping platforms, in the manner of national partisan competition and compromise. This, in essence, was Key's hopeful vision of Texas politics.

Key's Theory in Retrospect

Key's analysis was in many respects penetrating, even brilliant. The existence of two groups—one a small, powerful, and cohesive upper class, the other a large, racially heterogeneous mass of have-nots—is still a fundamental fact of the state's political life. Almost as soon as the liberal-conservative battle broke out, Key understood it as the renewal of a conflict with strong racial and class overtones that had shaken the state's political structure in the 1890s and then had disappeared in the wake of the Bourbon reaction. He saw that the struggle had the potential to endure as an important phenomenon beyond the 1940s. That potential, we have seen, has been realized in succeeding decades, as liberals and conservatives continue to oppose each other in election after election.

Key's description of the bases of factional support went against the conventional wisdom of his day, and it is still widely ignored or misunderstood. But the evidence vindicates his description for three reasons. First, contrary to the conceit that Texas is an overwhelmingly conservative state except for a smattering of middle-class liberals, most Texans, when asked, call themselves moderates, and they shift to the right or left under different conditions. Second, large numbers of voters—sometimes a majority—have supported liberal candidates in statewide Democratic primaries as well as general elections, and their support would sometimes have been even greater if turnout among the have-nots had approached the national norm. Third, liberal voting is closely correlated with socioeconomic status and, independently, with ethnicity: Blacks, Hispanics, and the Anglo poor and near-poor traditionally give a majority of their votes to the liberals, as Key's theory predicted.

These patterns have existed, with some recent exceptions, at least since the 1940s. The size of the liberal coalition, which includes segments of the middle class in addition to large numbers of the less affluent, has made it a force to be reckoned with in electoral politics, a fact underscored by the continuing efforts of conservatives to restrict voter turnout among the liberals' core constituencies.

Key understood well that class conflict in Texas, as it had been historically played out, worked to the disadvantage of the have-nots. The rich have long been potent in Texas, but the consolidation of oil, cotton, cattle, and manufacturing fortunes during and after World War II gave a new meaning to political clout. In contrast, the have-nots have lacked organization, in part because until quite recently the one-party system controlled by the establishment concealed issues from the disadvantaged: issues of tax fairness, educational opportunities, job safety, and public utility regulation, to name but a few. A two-party system, Key thought, would remedy the disorganization of the have-nots. Furthermore, he recognized the liberal-conservative split among Texas Democrats for what it was—the first stage of a fission process that would result in two competitive parties. His grasp of the split's significance only a few years after it occurred was prescient. When his interpretation was published in 1949, it provided a blueprint for a two-party system that both liberal Democrats and conservative Republicans used for their own purposes.

The basic premise supporting Key's belief in a two-party Texas was the decline of racial antagonism that had been such a stumbling block to cooperation within the working class. Following the decline, he believed, the Democrats would give special consideration to that class as well as to ethnic minorities and their allies. And the party would compete on a more equal basis with the numerous organizations of the rich.

Key was certainly justified in his hope that the Jim Crow system would be destroyed. And, despite bitter resistance from conservatives, the principle of equal access to the ballot was largely realized, a culmination of the civil rights cause growing out of World War II. The conservatives fought a desperate rearguard action on that issue that ultimately failed. In its aftermath, the decent people among them admitted, as did Judge Blanton in an interview from which the quotation at the beginning of this chapter was taken,[1] that the liberals had redeemed the political process.

Key was also correct in his perception that the Democrats would become a party of liberals and moderates who would better represent the working class and the ethnic minorities. The liberal-moderate coalition gained control of the Democratic party machinery in 1976, after having worked toward that end for a generation. And it was clear by the 1980s that candidates for the Democrats' nomination for important statewide offices could seldom succeed unless they were moderates or liberals. They could be more conservative than liberal, to be sure, as were Mark White and Lloyd Bentsen; but the hard-line conservatism of Allan Shivers, John Connally, or Dolph Briscoe was unacceptable to the Democratic primary electorate by the late 1970s. It was no accident that the two most powerful conservative Democratic leaders in the 1980s were both Speakers of the House, elected by fellow representatives—Democratic and Republican—without being nominated in a statewide Democratic primary.

Actually, Texas Democrats in the 1980s were very much as Key would have expected: Conservatives were still numerous, but they were counterbalanced by moderates and liberals. Minority voters were a major component. The party was also the natural home of organized labor, the environmental movement, and advocates of consumers' interests. It was left of center, compared with the state's electorate, but not so far left as to be outside the mainstream, even though the New Right claimed otherwise. In short, the "realigned" Democratic party in Texas was quite similar to the one limned by Key as a possibility.

The new Republicans, however, were different. Key's schema seemed to imply a moderately conservative party overall, much like the national party of the 1940s. Instead, modern Texas Republicanism, with few exceptions, was an amalgam of the Right and the Far Right, with the latter exercising influence out of proportion to its size. In addition, continued racial conflict gave Republicans a chance to "wave the bloody shirt" as the conservative Democrats had done earlier. The Goldwater campaign of 1964 first tested this strategy and succeeded only in the Deep South. Nixon employed it with more subtlety in 1968 and succeeded nationwide, capitalizing on the Johnson administration's failure on various fronts, including Vietnam. It might also have succeeded that year in Texas had not Wallace's rabble-rousing attracted much of Nixon's potential vote. Nixon used the strategy again in 1972. Reagan continued to use it in 1976, 1980, and 1984.

Texas Republicans such as Tower were in the vanguard of racial reaction a few years earlier than were those in the national party. They continued on this course into the 1980s, persistently badgering minority voters through their "ballot security" programs, advocating an "official English" policy, and implying that street crime, poverty, unemployment, and welfare programs were preeminently minority problems. The result was an almost complete absence of Republican minority elected officials and minuscule proportions of blacks and Hispanics in their rank and file.

Key's vision had another blind spot. He gave no thought in *Southern Politics* to the possibilities that Evangelical fundamentalism presented to demagogues. Yet, a generation later, from the late 1970s on, militant fundamentalist opposition to full rights for women in the church and the family, to abortion rights, to homosexuals, to the principle of the separation

28. Phil Gramm. A right-wing Democrat-turned-Re-
publican, Gramm succeeded John Tower in the U.S.
Senate in 1985. Here he shared the podium at a GOP
convention with his wife, Wendy Gramm, an economist
like her husband. In 1988 she became chair of the Commodities Futures Trading Commission in the Reagan administration. Courtesy of Dave Denison and the *Texas
Observer*.

of church and state, and to the theory of evolution gave Texas Republicans
an important boost and obscured class issues, just as racial conflict had
done. These two tendencies—racial reaction and politicized fundamentalism—undoubtedly helped explain the Democrats' narrowing white working-class base.[2]

Finally, Key's measured optimism about the two-party system stemmed
from his hypothesis that inclusive registration and voting laws, together
with the reconstituted Democratic party's ability to nominate more liberal
candidates who could appeal directly to the party's grass-roots constituency, would help the Democrats compensate for the inevitable losses of
conservative party members to the Republicans. These two developments, he thought, would serve to activate nonvoters, mostly racial or
economic liberals who previously had been disfranchised or who had been
alienated by the one-party system.

But the mass of nonvoters were not activated following the realignment
process and voting law reforms. And whatever influence the union movement had had on turnout was sharply curtailed by the steep decline in
organized labor's overall membership during the 1980s.

Thus, in spite of a significant realignment in Texas, the relative political
position of the have-nots and the upper class appeared to have changed

little, if at all. This is one possible interpretation of table 12.1, which compares the percentage of liberals, moderates, and conservatives in the state congressional delegation in 1960–1961—before the realignment had really begun in earnest—and 1985–1986, three-quarters of the way through the Reagan administration. The scores, compiled by the liberal group Americans for Democratic Action (ADA), ranged from 0 to 100, with 100 indicating "most liberal."

The data in table 12.1 can most quickly be understood by focusing on averages. In 1960–1961, the mean ADA score for the entire Texas delegation was 36, indicating moderate conservatism. In 1985–1986, it was still 36. The Democrats' score, however, jumped from 38 to 55, while the Republicans' remained virtually constant, rising only from 0 to 5.

Scattered evidence suggests that much the same pattern exists in the legislature: a more liberal and moderate voting record among Democrats than a generation earlier; a hard-line conservatism among Republicans replacing the much larger conservative Democratic vote of earlier times; and a propensity for the conservatives of both parties to vote together on major class issues—and a number of social issues as well.

Reform through Federal Intervention

Key thought that a realignment, combined with an increase in voting among the have-nots, could very well lead to the election of more liberals to state government and thus result in policies that would help the disadvantaged. Tables 10.1 and 10.2 indicate, however, that liberals were heavily outnumbered in the state legislature in the 1980s. Table 12.1, limited to the state's congressional delegation, indicates that the same is true of that group and also that congressional liberal strength has not increased in the last twenty-five years. This evidence arguably goes against Key's thesis.

On the other hand, congressional and legislative voting records such as the ones contained in these tables are open to various interpretations. One view is that liberals have not gained relative to conservatives in recent decades; but another is that liberals have achieved many goals that are now supported by the majority and have gone on to embrace new and still controversial goals that put their leaders once more in the minority when confronting the establishment.

Take the case of the poll tax as a voting prerequisite, for example. The tax was a project of turn-of-the-century conservative Democrats to exclude blacks and impoverished whites from the electorate. Its abolition was a major goal of Texas liberals well into the 1960s, but hardly anyone advocates its use any more. Today's liberals and conservatives alike sup-

Table 12.1

Realignment of Ideological Voting Patterns, Texas Congressional Delegation, 1960–1961 and 1985–1986 (U.S. House of Representatives only)

		Percent Distribution of ADA Scores; Two-Year Mean					
			1960–1961				
		0–20	*21–40*	*41–60*	*61–80*	*81–100*	*Total*
Democrats	(N = 21)	28.6	28.6	23.8	19.0	0.0	100.0
Republicans	(N = 1)	100.0	0.0	0.0	0.0	0.0	100.0
Total	(N = 22)	31.8	27.2	22.7	18.2	0.0	99.9
			1985–1986				
Democrats	(N = 17)	11.8	17.6	41.2	17.6	11.8	100.0
Republicans	(N = 9)[a]	100.0	0.0	0.0	0.0	0.0	100.0
Total	(N = 26)	42.3	11.5	26.9	11.5	7.7	99.9

Source: Calculated from information supplied by Americans for Democratic Action, Washington, D.C. (100 = perfect liberal vote.)

[a] One newly elected Republican omitted for lack of a voting record.

port the liberal position of the past. The same is true, by and large, of such issues as social security insurance, Medicaid and Medicare, and a host of other measures that in their time were opposed by the conservative establishment. If this is so, then the tables are misleading, and Key may have been right on this point after all. Was he?

There are two issues here. One is whether the liberals' past goals have been achieved and new ones placed on their agenda. The second is whether, assuming their past goals were achieved, this was the result of state government's being pushed in a liberal direction by a realigned Texas electorate, as Key anticipated, or by other forces.

To answer the first question, detailed questionnaires were sent to a small sample of liberal leaders active at the state and local level at least as far back as the 1940s. The sample was designed to include only those liberals and progressives who were widely known among political insiders as having long been active in the Democratic party and who were still active in 1985, when the survey was made.

The twenty-two who responded included inhabitants of all the state's major regions; ten of them were current or former officeholders—including two officials elected statewide and several legislators. The group contained men and women, Anglos and minorities (though mostly Anglos), professionals and housewives. Most had been active in numerous capacities: as fund-raisers, party officials, precinct organizers, journalists, civil rights workers, election judges, convention delegates, lawyers for plaintiffs in liberal causes, and union organizers. The officeholders had typically held more than one kind of elective office. The oldest respondents had first voted for president in 1928; the youngest in 1960. Half had first voted in 1944 or before. In sum, they represented the organizational core of the state's liberal movement. Among the questions they were asked was this one:

> Of all the public issues or problems during your years of political involvement that have come before the Texas public—either through the legislature, the courts, referenda, or by any other route—which, in your view, were the five most significant ones?

The following issues were mentioned by more than one-fourth of the respondents:

Desegregation, equal rights for minorities (82 percent)
Fair political representation (50 percent)
Equal rights for women (36 percent)
Guarantees of a decent standard of living (32 percent)
Educational reform (32 percent)
Fair taxation (32 percent)
Fair treatment of workers, unions (27 percent)
Environmental protection (27 percent)
Coping with "big government" and/or "big business" (27 percent)

The respondents were asked to indicate, for each issue they mentioned, if it had been resolved and, if so, whether in a more liberal, conservative, or neutral direction. The answers—heavily qualified, to be sure—generally indicated a belief that significant progress had been made on minority civil rights, fair representation, and women's rights.

Yet this progress was primarily the result of federal intervention—often over the fierce resistance of the conservative-dominated state and local governments. The U.S. Supreme Court, beginning with *Smith v. All-wright* in 1944 and then *Brown v. Board of Education* in 1954, provided the legal framework for the civil rights revolution that continued with the Civil Rights Acts of 1957, 1960, and 1964 (Title VII of the latter being crucial in fighting sex discrimination), the "reapportionment cases"— *Baker v. Carr* and *Reynolds v. Sims* in 1962 and 1964, respectively—and the Voting Rights Act of 1965.

The same is true of the women's rights movement. Texas feminists worked hard in the 1960s and 1970s both locally and at the national level, and their efforts paid off in dramatic ways. But the mechanism by which their efforts achieved success was largely federal laws written by Congress and interpreted by federal judges or, as in the abortion case, *Roe v. Wade*—although originating in Texas and argued by Texas attorney Sarah Weddington—through the Supreme Court's interpretation of the Constitution. The same is true of the environmental movement that, with the creation of the Environmental Protection Agency, has made headway in

Texas. And the limited progress in Texas workplace safety is largely the result of federal initiatives. Social safety nets for the disadvantaged, whether Medicare, Medicaid, Head Start, the food stamp programs, Legal Aid, or Community Development, also were federal solutions to local problems that were opposed by the state's conservative power structure.

The federal government, and not state government, in short, has provided the solutions to these pressing problems. This point is implicit in Numan V. Bartley's observation that in "the politics of the post–World War II South . . . the sporadic battle between haves and have-nots seems to have had limited observable influence on policy formation."[3]

Progress in civil rights illustrates Bartley's point. "The movement" in Texas was widespread and included significant numbers of blacks, Hispanics, and Anglos. They played many roles: demonstrators, fund-raisers, donors to legal and political causes, journalists who wrote fairly and aggressively on the treatment of minorities, legislators and congressmen, lawyers who developed and argued legal strategies, and judges who wrote landmark decisions. Lyndon Johnson himself, as responsible as any single official for the Civil Rights Acts of 1957 and 1964 and the Voting Rights Act of 1965, not to mention many aspects of his "Great Society" program, was a product of the culture of Texas progressivism, and along with the liberal coalition, he helped carry the state for the Kennedy-Johnson ticket in 1960 in one of the closest contests on record. The Texas liberal movement, in short, played an important role during the civil rights decade. The success of that movement, however, finally depended on the force of federal law to overcome local resistance marshaled by the establishment that controlled the governor's mansion and the state capitol.

The Representation of Minorities

Recent developments illustrate both the strength and the weakness of Key's theory. Successes on the civil rights front, which grew out of the bitter struggles of earlier decades, were considerable. As the above ranking of major issues by veteran liberal leaders suggests, civil rights was their single greatest preoccupation over the long haul, and in this area outstanding victories were achieved.

Most important, de jure school desegregation collapsed under federal assault. In the largest cities, this was followed by de facto resegregation as whites fled to the suburbs. In smaller cities and towns, much racial integration took place and remains the norm. Yet whatever the gains and losses as measured statistically, the principle that a state or its political subdivisions can legally exclude children of a minority race from its schools has been demolished beyond hope of resurrection. Indeed, the principle of legal racial exclusion from any area of public life was decisively destroyed by the civil rights revolution.

One index of the rising strength of minorities and their allies is the increase in black and Hispanic officeholders. In 1970, 29 elected public officials in Texas were black; in 1975, 298 elected *and appointed* officials were Hispanic. By 1984, the figures for black and Hispanic elected officials alone were 228 and 1,427 respectively—still a relatively low percentage of all elected Texas officials but nonetheless indicative of the inroads minority leaders were making in the political elite. One black and three Hispanics in 1985 belonged to the Texas congressional delegation of 27; in addition, 14 blacks and 18 Hispanics sat in the 150-member house of representatives, while one black and four Hispanics belonged to the 31-member senate.[4]

Many minority officials were elected in the larger towns and cities as a result of the legal attack on at-large or multimember election structures, an attack based on the Fourteenth and Fifteenth Amendments and the Voting Rights Act. Plaintiffs in these cases were usually represented by the civil rights bar and legal services lawyers, and funding typically came from minority group organizations and labor unions. A study of the change in minority representation on the forty-one Texas city councils and other governmental units that switched from pure multimember to district-based elections in the 1970s revealed a 290 percent increase in black and Hispanic officials. After the switch, the proportion of minority officeholders on those governmental bodies rose almost to the same level as the proportion of minority persons living in the political jurisdictions.[5]

Increased representation is symbolized by changes in several cities formerly dominated by conservative business interests either through informal networks of the rich—such as Houston's fabled "8F Crowd" or Fort Worth's "Seventh Street Gang"—or through so-called nonpartisan slating groups that selected and funded conservative city council candidates who won easily in at-large elections where money was a big factor in the outcome. Groups such as San Antonio's Good Government League and Dallas's Citizens Council were able to control election results for decades, thus insuring that city government was run by conservative insiders. A number of factors—not the least of which was the advent of single-member-district elections—curtailed the influence of such groups in the 1970s and paved the way for the election of more representative local governments.[6]

Kathy Whitmire won the mayorship of Houston by building a coalition of blacks, Hispanics, women, homosexual rights groups, and traditional liberals in her 1981 campaign. (Roy Hofheinz and his son Fred, mayors in the 1950s and 1970s, respectively, had already established the tradition of a liberal coalition in Houston city politics.) As a result of litigation funded by labor unions and minority groups and subsequent intervention by the U.S. Justice Department under the Voting Rights Act, the city had voted in 1979 to change from an eight-member council elected entirely at large to a fourteen-member one, nine seats of which were elected from districts. The result was a council that contained several liberals, including blacks and a Mexican American. Two women were elected to council for the first time in the city's history—one conservative, the other liberal.[7] One of Whitmire's first major appointments was a black police chief, Lee Brown, who imposed new standards of professionalism on a force that had had a long history of racism and factional strife. Whitmire and her council allies were able to win reelection against conservative challengers funded by the downtown business establishment throughout the decade.

In San Antonio, Henry Cisneros, a moderate Mexican American Democrat with alliances in the business community, also won a mayorship in 1981. There, too, the creation of single-member districts under pressure from the U.S. Justice Department in 1976 gave Cisneros a council he could work with.[8] In Dallas another moderate Democrat, Annette Strauss, was able to win the mayorship in that city in 1987 against the former chairman of the Dallas County Republican party and former Republican congressman Jim Collins. Dallas had been forced by the federal courts to adopt several district-based council seats in 1975. Commentators were quick to note that a city dogged by an image of intolerance now had a Jewish woman as mayor and a black as city manager. The school superintendant hired soon after Strauss's election was also black. "The day that [John F.] Kennedy was killed," reminisced black councilman Al Lipscomb, a plaintiff in the case that resulted in district elections, "I was a bartender out at Brookhaven Country Club. And today I'm sitting at the same table at times with the man who owns the club. I couldn't in all truthfulness say it's the same city today as it was then."[9]

The access to city hall that minorities gained, however, was primarily the result of two factors: relief granted by federal courts to plaintiffs in voting rights suits, and the growing minority percentages within the municipal boundaries as whites fled to the suburbs.[10] For example, between 1960 and 1980 the combined black-Hispanic population percentage rose in Dallas from 23 to 42, in Houston from 29 to 45, and in San Antonio from 49 to 61. Thus, while increasingly fair representation was not a fact to be minimized, it was not quite what it seemed on the surface. When the suburban whites joined forces in metropolitan-wide or statewide elections, their strength was usually sufficient to overwhelm the city-based coalitions. This was even more true as the traditionally Democratic counties in West Texas began to vote Republican, along with the metropolitan suburbs.

Developments within the cities, therefore, illustrate a central thesis of this chapter: While Key's hope that civil rights victories would lead to the growth of a two-party state has been realized, this came about primarily *from without*—albeit with liberals' help from within—over the opposition of a conservative-dominated state and local government system.

Party Conflict and Intraparty Tensions

The Compromise of 1877, by which northern Republicans, in exchange for the South's acceptance of their presidential candidate, Rutherford B. Hayes, agreed to remove federal troops from the South, marked the end of the first Reconstruction and allowed the dominant southern white oligarchy to settle the race question by disfranchising the recently emancipated blacks and reducing them to a status not far removed from their previous servitude. "One is driven by the evidence to the conclusion," C. Vann Woodward wrote of the northern Reconstructionists, "that the radicals committed the country to a guarantee of equality that popular convictions were not prepared to sustain."[11]

The Civil Rights Act of 1964 and the Voting Rights Act of 1965 symbolized the abrogation of the Compromise of 1877. Coming at the end of an increasingly conflictual civil rights movement that had begun during World War II, these two epoch-making laws overcame the adamant refusal of the southern white oligarchy to accord blacks their full American citizenship. The acts signaled the willingness of influential national leaders in both parties to guarantee basic citizenship rights for blacks.

Yet no sooner had these rights been secured through law than a hardening of attitudes between the races occurred. James Sundquist, citing opinion poll data, places the pivotal turning point in August 1965, following the outbreak of the Watts riot in Los Angeles. White support for the civil rights movement began to diminish. The first electoral sign of this was the 1966 midterm congressional elections, when the Democrats lost forty-seven seats, more than the Republicans had lost in 1964. Polling data clearly pointed to a white backlash among core Democratic constituencies.[12] The separatist impulse behind the black power slogans of that era—and La Raza Unida party in Texas—indicated both a growing fear among many Americans of color that they would never gain full equality, and a reaching out for something beyond mere assimilation into the dominant white culture. The fear and anger among many whites, reinforced by continued rioting in following summers and the radical directions taken within the black and brown power movements, in turn, hardened the already widespread resistance to further acts of racial reconstruction.[13]

Resistance was greatest in the South. Jim Crow institutions were suddenly illegal. Black Belt whites' control of the southern legislatures was under attack. Insurgents were storming the gates of the Democratic party, long the bastion of the white oligarchs. The old order was toppling.

For a moment it looked to some as though the race issue might finally be exorcised from the region's politics, just as Key had hoped. Others were skeptical. Harlem congressman Adam Clayton Powell, Jr., privately spoke of "two phases of the black revolution." One was the southern phase, ending with the passage of the Civil Rights Act, which addressed middle-class concerns. "The 'Northern,' 'proletarian,' 'rough,' phase" remained to be fought. Northern blacks already had most of the rights their southern compatriots had been struggling for. Looming in the future was the "gut issue of who gets the money." Powell added, ominously, "watch out."[14]

The "northern" phase of the civil rights struggle still had to be fought in the South as well. It was this phase that optimists had largely ignored in their prognosis of southern politics. The "Negro problem" that had so bedeviled the South was transformed, but not in the way liberals had hoped. Racial politics did not disappear from the American scene; they simply shifted to a different terrain. The barriers to equality no longer resulted from formal prohibitions against voting, attending school with whites, or using public accommodations but from handicaps that blacks suffered as a result of past injustice and from continuing but more subtle forms of discrimination.

Extreme racial polarization at the polls, which observers first pointed to after Goldwater's presidential campaign, continued unabated in Texas. Such polarization derived from two sources. One was a legacy of old racial hatreds that had existed ever since Anglo slaveholders came to Texas, breaking Mexican antislavery law in the process. The second source was resistance by many whites to measures, often conveniently if inaccurately lumped under the rubric of "affirmative action," designed to deal with the seemingly intractable problems of blacks and Hispanics that resulted from their many years of victimization by Texas's racial caste system. These were the measures with which advocates of full equality for people of color were attempting to fight the "second phase" of the civil rights revolution.

Opposition, encouraged by the Reagan administration's concerted attack on many of these measures, was in some respects analogous to the popular reaction to Radical Republicans' efforts in the first Reconstruction to go beyond mere black emancipation by securing the basic economic rights that freedmen desperately needed to give meaning to their legal liberation.

The race issue, then, posed grave problems for the progressive movement in Texas despite the undeniable existence of both a sizable liberal contingent in the state and an array of pressing issues, the successful exploitation of which would ordinarily allow liberals to mobilize voters. Liberals and their allies constituted approximately 35 to 55 percent of the statewide electorate, depending on the issues, the contested office, the candidates, and the year. They were still hampered by low turnout and a lack of political interest among the have-nots. Their ranks were thinned as whites left the party or dropped out of the electorate, and popular liberal candidates for major statewide office ran less often. To have any chance of winning, such candidates had to work together with the Tory wing of the party, which in the aggregate had become somewhat more moderate as the hardliners switched to the Republicans. In recent years, this cooperation was encouraged by centrist Democratic party leaders such as Calvin Guest, Billy Goldberg, and Robert Slagle—the state chairs since the mid-1970s—and a state executive committee comprised of all factions in the party who worked fairly well together.

The 1982 off-year elections were a model of how the factions of the reconstituted party could cooperate to benefit both liberals and moderates. Popular disenchantment with "Reaganomics" encouraged old enemies such as Yarborough and Bentsen to join ranks and urge unity against Republicans, with stunning success. Elected to statewide office that year were four progressives—Attorney General Jim Mattox, Treasurer Ann Richards, Agriculture Commissioner Jim Hightower, and Land Commissioner Gary Mauro—and a moderate governor, Mark White. All except White were reelected in 1986.

Many of the Texas liberals' aims in the 1980s would not have surprised Key. Progressive groups around the state opposed the increasingly regressive state sales tax and favored, instead, a progressive personal and corporate income levy. They fought for a more equal distribution of public school financing, workplace safety, stricter regulation of utility rates, higher payments to recipients of Aid to Families with Dependent Children, and higher salaries for school teachers.

Other, more recent liberal causes included protection of the rights of the handicapped, prisoners, and AIDS patients; representation of women and ethnic minorities in public office and in the higher-paying professions; protection of women's right to abortion; strict separation of church and state; registration of handguns; abolition of the death penalty; and government regulation of environmental pollution.

Yet such a list underscores the Achilles' heel of Texas progressivism: the heterogeneity of the issues and the potential for fractures of many kinds. The challenge to liberal leaders was to keep their coalition intact. In shorthand, this meant unifying economic liberals and "social-issues" liberals. One of the most innovative and successful organizations devoted to this endeavor achieved statewide influence in the 1980s. Coordinated by Ernesto Cortes, Jr., a gifted grass-roots organizer, the Texas Industrial Areas Foundation Network was created on principles advocated by the

29. Jim Mattox campaigns. A populist legislator, congressman, and attorney general, Mattox here courts the "yellow dog Democrat" vote. He lost his bid for the 1990 Democratic gubernatorial nomination to Ann Richards. Courtesy of Frederick Baldwin and the *Texas Observer*.

late Saul Alinsky. Its various branches scored notable victories at the local and state levels.[15]

The conservatives also had problems building stable coalitions, but they had a somewhat larger initial base. In cooperation with moderates, they constituted perhaps 45 to 65 percent of the Texas electorate, again depending on the circumstances in a given year. Unlike the liberals, they were split between two parties, some comprising the Tory faction of the Democrats and others making up the GOP.

The conservatives were vulnerable to fractures along several cleavage planes. The rich had long provided both an ideological and a financial

30. Pleading the people's cause. State legislator Frank Tejeda (left) listens to Ernie Cortes. Trained at the Industrial Areas Foundation established by Saul Alinsky in Chicago, Cortes is the organizing genius behind several local neighborhood-based multi-ethnic pressure groups that formed in the 1970s and 1980s under names such as Communities Organized for Public Services (COPS) in San Antonio, Valley Interfaith in the Rio Grande Valley, and The Metropolitan Organization (TMO) in Houston. Courtesy Alan Pogue and the *Texas Observer*.

base. Joining with them in the 1970s were many erstwhile Wallace supporters and, in the late 1970s and 1980s, religious fundamentalists who had been solid Democrats. The three-way vote in 1968 for Humphrey, Nixon, and Wallace prefigured the emergence of a "third force" of lower- to middle-income Texans cross-pressured between economic liberalism and social reaction. This third force gave Carter, a southern Evangelical, a sizable vote in 1976 and then switched massively to Reagan in the next two presidential elections. The conflict between social and economic issues had numerous sources. David B. Hill, an employee of Republican pollster V. Lance Tarrance, noted in 1985 that the infusion of in-migrants from other states and of younger voters were two contributing factors. "The new people tend to be more liberal on social issues than native Texans, but perhaps even more conservative on free-market issues."[16]

The conservative strategy for holding together their subcoalitions was to play up racial and "family" issues. The Republican attack on homosexuals in the 1980s, for example, was couched in terms of family values. Anti-homosexuality has long been a staple of demagogues. Orville Bullington, a leading Texas Republican, raised a controversy during the Rainey affair at the University of Texas in the 1940s by falsely charging the embattled president with coddling a "nest of homosexuals" on campus. A university regent appointed by W. Lee O'Daniel, Bullington later tried to make homosexuality a major issue in Texas senate hearings over Rainey's firing. Senator Joe McCarthy resorted to homophobic tactics in the 1950s.[17] Both the use to which W. A. Criswell—among other conservative ministers— put the AIDS issue regarding the "sinfulness" of homosexuality and the homophobic appeal Phil Gramm made in his 1984 Senate campaign have been noted previously.

The explosive criticism that greeted the Houston city council's enactment of an ordinance in 1984 forbidding municipal hiring practices that discriminated on the basis of sexual preference was orchestrated by Republican notables, including former mayor Louie Welch, at that time president of the Houston Chamber of Commerce. The most striking exception to the partisan nature of the anti-ordinance leadership was Democratic councilman Ben Reyes, a Catholic Hispanic who was liberal on many issues.[18] The ordinance was rejected by a vote of four to one in a referendum, a vote that followed a campaign as ugly and menacing as school desegregation controversies had been in the 1950s and 1960s.[19] Like Gramm in his Senate race, ordinance critics falsely characterized their opponents' antidiscrimination proposal as an "affirmative action" measure that would give preference to homosexuals in hiring and promotion.

The evidence pointed to widespread grass-roots hostility toward homosexuals. Data from a survey of Houston's registered voters revealed that only 16 percent claimed to "like" homosexuals "even a little," and only a narrow majority believed they should be allowed to hold a public demonstration.[20] Nonetheless, campaigns in which homosexuality was only one of several issues offered a more restricted opportunity for demagoguery.

Too crude an appeal to homophobia might even backfire in a close contest. In the Houston mayoral race in 1985, for example, Welch, encouraged by the outcome of the Houston "gay-ordinance referendum," challenged incumbent mayor Kathy Whitmire, who had supported the ordinance. Working closely with Republican organizations and militantly homophobic groups on the Far Right, Welch mounted a well-financed campaign, but Whitmire beat him decisively. One reason, undoubtedly, was a joke he uttered to a televison crew into what he mistakenly thought was a dead microphone. His policy to contain AIDS, he said, would be to "shoot the queers."[21] Effective gay-baiting by Republican politicians conformed to the same rules as effective racism: Code words and innuendo were preferable to crude epithets, and it had to be justified in terms of widely held values, such as those denoted by the phrase "the traditional family."

If these rules were followed, however, the Republican Right seemed likely to capitalize on the widespread prejudice against gays, and the Texas party probably would continue to exploit this theme, just as it had exploited the subject of race. Both issues appealed to a wide spectrum of groups. The homophobic viewpoint, moreover, appealed to blacks and Mexican Americans as well as Anglos. In the 1984 Houston referendum, the antidiscrimination ordinance was defeated in every section of town but the Montrose area, which is disproportionately populated by homosexuals.[22]

Other issues that conservatives would continue to use included the standard class issues of the Bourbons: anti-unionism; low taxes overall with a preference for "broad-based" ones requiring the poor to pay the highest taxes proportionally; minimal government help for the needy; generous government subsidies and tax loopholes for the large corporations and the rich; and modest to minimal government expenditures on public education, hospitals, and public health facilities. "We are a low-tax, low-service state," Jared Hazelton of the business-financed Texas Research League told a reporter in 1985.[23] To liberals, the statement was a fact to bemoan. Conservatives applauded it.

Regarding social issues, the conservatives opposed handgun registration—aided by lobbying efforts of the powerful National Rifle Association—and supported the death penalty, both in the name of "law and order." They were against the prison reforms required by federal judge William Wayne Justice in the landmark case of *Ruiz v. Estelle*, decided in 1980, which mandated better treatment and more adequate living space for prisoners. They opposed regulation of the environment and supported a Cold War position in international affairs. They advocated government prohibition of abortion, official prayer in the schools, and teaching biblical "creation science" to students as an alternative to evolutionism, geology, and scientific cosmology.

Keeping a coalition together on election day was a problem for conservatives (just as it was for liberals), few of whom were conservative on all the issues. Sociologist Stephen Klineberg's annual Houston Area Survey in the 1980s revealed noteworthy Republican support for progressive views on several social issues, including abortion rights for women.[24] Class issues, too, always posed a danger to the GOP, for they could drive a wedge between blue collarites and the country-club wing.

Nevertheless, the tensions within Texas Republicanism were significantly eased by the racial solidarity of their lily-white party; and it was the race issue, perhaps more than any other, that undercut the potential soli-

31. William Wayne Justice. Before becoming a U.S. district judge in East Texas, Justice was a supporter of Ralph Yarborough during his statewide campaigns. After Justice's appointment to the federal bench, he wrote widely influential decisions on voting rights and prison reform, among other topics. Courtesy of Paul Blankenmeister and the *Texas Observer*.

darity of the Democrats. For, despite gradually changing attitudes, Texas was still a state in which blacks and whites faced each other with suspicion, fear, and animosity.[25] The situation was complicated by the presence of Mexican Americans, themselves long the victims of Anglo discrimination and hostility. Blacks continued to live in largely segregated enclaves, although survey evidence indicated that they would greatly prefer to live in racially mixed areas. Hispanics were more dispersed, but many still clustered in urban barrios.[26] Both groups contained huge numbers of the poor, a population that contributed disproportionately to violent crime statistics and the epidemic of serious drug abuse in the cities.

The Republicans' strategy was premised, first, on the continued existence of social and political barriers between the races and, second, as

Kevin Phillips had argued in 1969, on the Democrats' efforts to overcome these barriers through "civil rights measures obnoxious to the South [and] social legislation and programs anathema to the sons and daughters of Northern immigrants."[27] Devising a successful countervailing strategy remained the liberals' challenge.

Epilogue

IN THE SUMMER of 1989, 101 years after Joshua Hicks in the prohibitionist *Advance Advocate* debated the Reverend Cranfill on the color line in politics, a journalistic event of a different kind occurred in Austin's municipal auditorium. The *Texas Observer* held a fund-raiser honoring Ralph Yarborough.[1]

Over one thousand people came. Some were not much younger than Yarborough. Others were activists in their teens and twenties who had come to see the legendary man. Liberal organizers, trade unionists, lawyers, and journalists were there. Representatives of the state legislature, the U.S. Congress, and the state and federal benches sat on the dais. Officials long retired and famous old war-horses of the liberal movement were sprinkled through the crowd. But for the most part, the auditorium was filled with the rank and file who had worked for Yarborough in his campaigns from 1952 to 1972.

Molly Ivins, the master of ceremonies, introduced Senator Edward Kennedy of Massachussets, who spoke warmly of Yarborough's Senate days when Yarborough fought alongside the Kennedy brothers to enact the Democratic reforms of the 1960s. Then Yarborough himself, still recovering from heart surgery and helped to the podium by his old ally Bob Eckhardt, delivered a rousing speech. It was laced with righteous anger and humor, with satire and moral uplift; and it brought the crowd to its feet again and again, whooping and laughing.

Then came testimonials, sometimes tearfully rendered, of the speakers' debt to "the Senator." The tributes of some of the ethnic leaders were particularly emotional. State senators Carlos Truan and Eddie Bernice Johnson, a Mexican American and a black, respectively, spoke of Yarborough's impact on them personally and on the lives of their people. Barbara Jordan, referring to the widening scandal in the Department of Housing and Urban Development under the Republicans, opined that "Ralph Yarborough would not be caught cribbing around the edges of the public trough for private gain. He would not do that!"

Later, as the affair came to an end and people streamed out into the sweltering Austin night, it was obvious that the "Yarborough crowd," those who had rallied to him during his campaigns and who had made up the core of the progressive movement in those years, was undoubtedly meeting for the last time under one roof with their leader. It was a bit like the last encampment of veterans of an ancient war. The Yarborough era was over.

32. Barbara Jordan. A college debating champion and lawyer, Jordan twice ran unsuccessfully for the state legislature from a Houston multimember district. In 1966, after court-mandated redistricting, she won a state senate seat from a single-member district with a sizable minority makeup, thus becoming Texas's first black senator since 1881 and the state's first minority woman legislator ever. In 1972 she ran for Congress and won, becoming the South's first black U.S. representative since Reconstruction. Courtesy of the *Texas Observer*.

The New Era

What was the nature of the new era that would take its place? The 1980s was a decade of political retrogression and uncertainty in both Texas and the nation. But in Texas there was economic crisis as well. In 1981 the price of crude oil rose at one point above $40 a barrel, and there was talk of a continuing boom that could lead to prices of $60 or higher. By December 1982, however, oil had fallen to $30, and a recession that witnessed the destruction of the state's petroleum-based economy was under way. At one point in 1986, the year of Texas's sesquicentennial anniversary, the price of oil dropped to less than $10 a barrel.

Thousands of companies dependent on petroleum revenues collapsed. "The Great Oil Era Ends in Texas," announced a 1984 headline in the *New York Times*.[2] Oilmen demanded government help. Michel T. Halbouty expressed anger at his erstwhile hero, Ronald Reagan, for refusing to give sufficient backing to the Texas oil industry. Halbouty called for "a tax credit on new production, restoration of the 27 1/2 percent depletion allowance or—I hate to say it—even an import fee."[3] The crisis was so acute that Billie Carr, the Houston liberal leader, urged Massachusetts governor Michael Dukakis to back an oil import fee in his presidential campaign.[4]

Not only the oilmen were in trouble. The state's big banks, transformed in the 1970s from local enterprises to statewide multibank holding companies, had made lavish and often poorly secured loans during the boom. These banks collapsed, as did many smaller ones: 103 between 1982 and 1987, and 113 in 1988 alone. The once-proud Texas holding companies were ignominiously merged with larger out-of-state banks, usually with restructuring by the Federal Deposit Insurance Corporation.[5] Savings-and-loan institutions were, if anything, even less fortunate than the banks. Fraud and shaky loans led many into insolvency, and the result was a gargantuan federal bailout at taxpayer expense.[6]

For a while it looked as though the entire state economy had caved in. Almost one-quarter of a million jobs in oil and gas extraction and manufacturing were lost in the first half of the decade.[7] Thousands of other jobs were also lost, as enterprises of every sort disappeared, along with the fortunes of not a few of the rich and famous. In the Houston area alone, 1,688 businesses went bankrupt in 1987.[8]

John Connally's reversals dramatized the plight of many of the high rollers. In the 1970s and early 1980s, trading on his establishment connections, he had launched vast, highly leveraged real estate ventures with former lieutenant governor Ben Barnes. When the bubble burst, the two men suddenly found themselves "at least $215 million" in debt, at one point facing "more than 35 lawsuits charging non-payment of debts or failure to meet contractual obligations . . . in at least 13 Texas counties." Incredibly, Connally had not incorporated his main businesses, apparently in the belief that he simply could not fail. Therefore, most of his personal property was not shielded from creditors.[9] He and Barnes filed for bankruptcy in 1987.[10] The auction of the Connallys' personal effects at the Hart Galleries in January 1988 was Houston's social and media event of the decade, rivaling in symbolism the demolition at about the same time of the city's Shamrock Hotel, built by wildcatter Glenn McCarthy in the late 1940s.[11]

For millions of Texans the situation was more grim, even though their fall was less spectacular. Texas's unemployment rate increased from 5.3 percent in 1981, when it was the lowest among the eleven most populous states, to over 10 percent in some months in 1986, when it was the highest.[12] The ranks of the poor increased by about one million persons between 1980 and 1986. Requests for emergency food handouts skyrocketed, reaching 3.6 million in 1986, an increase of more than 100 percent over the previous year.[13] In September 1987, the homeless population in San Antonio was estimated at ten thousand, 1 percent of the city's people.[14] Not surprisingly, those suffering most seriously from the depression were minorities and the poor.[15]

By mid-decade it was clear that oil would no longer play the central role in the state's economy and politics. The catchword now was "diversification," a word linked in the public mind to "high tech." The pressure that Texas politicians and opinion makers put on Congress to fund a supercollider—a high-energy particle accelerator—near Waxahatchie symbolized the desire of the state's leaders to move aggressively away from petroleum dependence.

The impact of the oil collapse on public finance was ominous. Tax revenues from petroleum profits dropped sharply. Liberals, moderates, and the more enlightened business lobbyists in the legislature fought a bitter battle in 1987 against Governor Clements, who had won reelection in 1986 on a no-new-taxes pledge, to pass a tax bill that would raise enough revenues to protect public education and other human services programs from drastic cuts. They won, thanks in large measure to Bill Hobby, the lieutenant governor, whose leadership and bargaining skills ultimately overcame the maneuvering of Clements and his followers, mostly Republicans.

But despite the legislative victories of the liberal-moderate coalition during the state's worst fiscal crisis since the Great Depression, the state's political structure remained unchanged. The new tax bill barely maintained the tenuous status quo; it was not a sign of liberal-moderate resurgence. Further, the class structure appeared to emerge intact from the oil crisis.

The Texas economy was always more than an oil fiefdom and by the 1970s it was fairly diversified. So the crisis, even though it caused the destruction of some great fortunes, did not result in the breakup of the Texas upper class. While the Murchison brothers went broke and Bunker and William Hunt were hounded by hundreds of creditors as well as by

33. Bill Hobby. A moderate Democrat, Hobby has been lieutenant governor and presiding officer of the Texas senate longer than anyone in history. Courtesy of Vic Hinterlang and the *Texas Observer*.

the Internal Revenue Service, the Bass family retained vast wealth, as did branches of the Hunt families, the Cullen clan, and titans outside the energy industry such as H. Ross Perot and Trammell Crow. Indeed, recent research on the very rich suggests that many members of "the ninety-nine," the richest individuals in Texas circa 1980, were much better off by the end of the decade than they had been at the beginning.[16]

This stratum was still overwhelmingly Republican, and many of the most prominent members were deeply involved in right-wing politics. In 1989 Clayton Williams announced his intention to run in the next year's governor's race to succeed Clements, charging that the legislature was controlled by "liberals and socialists."[17] Both men were members of the ninety-nine. Robert Mosbacher, Jr., whose father was also a member, decided to run for the lieutenant governor's race to succeed Hobby. The senior Mosbacher meanwhile had become President Bush's secretary of commerce, after having "directed the raising of $60 million for the Bush campaign and another $25 million for the Republican National Committee."[18]

The Reverend W. A. Criswell announced that the Hunt family in Dallas had donated $3 million to buy land on which to build Criswell College for aspiring Baptist ministers who would presumably carry on his politico-religious crusade.[19] The year before, 1988, billionaire Robert M. Bass of

Fort Worth, also a member of the ninety-nine, gave $100,000 apiece to the Republicans and the Democrats during the presidential campaign, while Perot was helping fund Republican Pete Dawkins's race in New Jersey for the U.S. Senate.[20]

The Texas upper class had survived the tumultuous 1980s, although its leading members gradually and inevitably were replaced by others, as death and occasional misfortunes took their toll. The influence on the political process of the Texas-based corporate elite may have declined somewhat, as a result of mergers between local banks and out-of-state institutions. But in 1987, the same year reporter Paul Burka mentioned this possibility, the Pennzoil Corporation alone had twenty-six lobbyists on its payroll, including Billy Clayton, former speaker of the Texas House of Representatives.[21] The big Texas-based corporations were still huge economic institutions, the interests of which were closely linked to the legislature and usually to several state regulatory agencies as well.

In the cities, it was true that many of the businessmen's pressure groups, such as the Houston "8F Crowd" and the San Antonio Good Government League, were long gone. But in its analysis of the Dallas Citizens Council, on that organization's fiftieth anniversary in 1987, the *Dallas Times Herald* discovered that the city's ten most influential people, as identified in a survey of its business leaders, were all millionaires (including the mayor, Annette Strauss), and eight were members of the tightly knit Citizens Council described in chapter 5. Four were members of the ninety-nine.

While reporter Jim Henderson stressed the importance of Strauss's election in democratizing the city's power structure (she was only the second mayor since 1932 who was not the establishment candidate), he also observed that "the oligarchy that once ruled Dallas is still a political force and future mayors are likely to come from its ranks." His summation of the progress that had come about was appropriately guarded: "Dallas may never again be completely safe from democracy."[22] Texas, too, was "less safe from democracy," primarily as a result of the generation-long political mobilization of minority voters and the continuing efforts of the liberal coalition. But the 1988 presidential campaign raised questions about the direction in which Texas democracy was heading.

Presidential Politics in 1988

Race was a crucial issue in Texas, as it was in the nation. The battle leading to the U.S. Senate's rejection in 1987 of Robert Bork, Reagan's Supreme Court nominee, was fought along racial lines, among others. Bork's contemporary opposition to the civil rights bill of 1964 played a large role in the vote that denied him a seat on the Court, a fact foreshadowing the importance racial issues would have in 1988. However, the battle over Bork's nomination occurred in the Democratic-controlled Senate, where it was politic for Bork's opponents to emphasize his position in 1964 on the civil rights bill. It was indicative of the Dukakis campaign's pessimistic evaluation of the racial climate in the electorate at large that it decided to ignore Bush's militant opposition to the bill during his 1964 U.S. Senate race.

Two intertwined factors gave the campaign its unique racial character: the Reverend Jesse Jackson's presidential quest and the Republicans' decision to base a major advertising campaign on Willie Horton, a black convicted murderer who, while out on a weekend furlough from a Massachusetts prison, had fled and raped a white Delaware woman and stabbed her fiancé. Bush tried to link the tragedy to Dukakis, who was governor when the event occurred.

Jackson's decision to contest the Democratic nomination delighted Texas Republicans, some of whom likened the Democrats' "Jackson problem" to their own "Pat Robertson problem," a reference to the evangel of the Religious Right who was campaigning for the GOP nomination. And many white liberal and moderate Texas Democrats, and some blacks, were angry that Jackson, who as a left-wing liberal black had absolutely no chance of obtaining the nomination, would launch a campaign that was bound to leave his followers hostile toward the party that had denied their hero its nomination. But no prominent Texas liberal was willing to voice this anger. Indeed, there was very little Democratic criticism of Jackson at any point during the presidential campaign period, even when his bid for the nomination was over and he refused for some time to rally behind the Democratic ticket. Barbara Jordan was virtually alone among Texas liberals in criticizing his recalcitrance.[23]

Indicative of Jackson's trouble in Texas early on was the fact that one of his most vocal spokesmen was Houston legislator Al Edwards, a black who had no important allies—and a good many enemies—outside the central city district he represented, and who was not even on good terms with some of the other black political leaders in the campaign. Edwards was known for his difficulties in working within the liberal coalition and for his eccentric behavior as a legislator. *Texas Monthly* magazine's biennial ranking of state lawmakers placed him in the "perennial Worst" category.[24] Edwards had been Jackson's 1984 state chairman, and apparently resented the Jackson campaign's designating Congressman Mickey Leland as the state chairman in 1988. Yet Edwards remained a vocal Jackson supporter to the end of the campaign, highly critical of the Democratic party.

In spite of Jackson's talk of a "rainbow coalition," he had little success with Mexican Americans, getting only about one-fourth of their votes in the Democratic primary. His candidacy also split white liberals. Some backed him, but many others did not, either because they doubted his presidential abilities, thought a vote for him would be wasted, or believed his candidacy would create an even deeper split in the Democratic coalition. Among white elected officials of note, only Agriculture Commissioner Jim Hightower endorsed Jackson's nomination. In the Texas Democratic primary, Dukakis won a plurality of 33 percent, followed by Jackson with 25 percent. Mexican Americans gave Dukakis between 50 and 60 percent of their votes, while blacks gave Jackson almost 95 percent of theirs.[25]

With the Jackson issue smoldering in the Democratic camp, the Republicans launched a campaign in which race was a major theme. The centerpiece of their strategy was an advertisement that ran for twenty-eight days on national television during the fall. The ad featured Willie Horton and the associated issues of crime, "permissiveness," and neighborhood safety, issues that had been essential to the Republican southern strategy since 1964. "The Horton case," Bush campaign manager Lee Atwater said in the summer of 1988, "is one of those gut issues that are value issues, particularly in the South, and if we hammer at these over and over, we are going to win."[26] The irony of the Willie Horton advertising strategy was that Dukakis, who personally had nothing to do with Horton's furlough, was administering a program established by his Republican predecessor. But the ads, along with massive mailings from the Republican party, tried to link Dukakis to the black criminal.

In Texas the presidential race was "even meaner and more negative, largely fought over emotional issues defined by the Bush campaign," according to reporter Peter Applebome, who traveled with the vice president. In Bush's visit to Longview, a city deep in East Texas imbued with the traditions of the Old South, he gave "a made-for-Texas speech, full of sneering references to 'the liberal Governor of Massachusetts' that centered on the Pledge of Allegiance, school prayer, gun control and abortion. 'What in the world is his problem with the Pledge of Allegiance to the flag?' Bush asked, biting off his words like a man in a state of permanent pique. 'I simply cannot understand the kind of thinking that lets first-degree murderers out of jail on a furlough and won't deal with the Pledge of Allegiance.' "[27]

What made Bush's Willie Horton ploy in Texas even more cynical was that the state had long had a prison furlough program—an expansion of which was signed into law in 1979 by Clements, then in his first term as governor. By the time of Bush's Longview speech, Clements was almost two years into his second term, during which the Texas prison bureaucracy had furloughed nearly 5,000 inmates, including 517 murderers. The program was similar to the one in Massachusetts before Dukakis had gotten it changed the previous January to prevent furloughs of first-degree murderers. The Texas program allowed all but death-row inmates a

34. Lloyd Bentsen, Jr. A wealthy conservative businessman, he has been a congressman, U.S. senator, and presidential candidate. In 1988 Bentsen successfully campaigned for reelection to the Senate while he was the running mate of the Democratic presidential nominee, Massachusetts governor Michael Dukakis, with whom he is shown here. Courtesy of Bill Leissner and the *Texas Observer*.

chance for furlough. When the matter of the Texas program came to public attention during the campaign, Clements professed not to have known about it.[28]

To make matters worse for Dukakis, his organization persisted in sending to Texas Massachusetts campaign workers whose ineptitude and ignorance of Texas politics and folkways quickly made them the butt of the Democratic regulars' scorn. The Dukakis workers even shunned operatives of vice presidential candidate Bentsen, the magnitude of whose get-out-the-vote machine was unparalleled in Texas.[29]

At the same time, Texas blacks were still fuming over Jackson's failure to win the presidential or vice presidential nomination and the "insult" of him by Dukakis, who had not let Jackson know in advance of Dukakis's vice presidential choice. Edwards, Jackson's man in Texas, told reporters he was not sure blacks would support the Democratic ticket. Houston's black radio stations' talk shows sizzled with rage at Dukakis, often expressed in sulfurous language.

On election day, Texans gave Bush 56 percent of their vote—almost 8 points less than they had given Reagan in 1984. Mexican Americans gave Dukakis 83 percent. Over 90 percent of blacks who went to the polls voted for Dukakis, but great numbers of them did not go. Black turnout in 1988 was lower than in 1984, and the decrease probably offset the rise in Democratic voting among whites that year. One analyst found that "an increase of about 5,000 Democratic votes in predominantly white [Houston] precincts was swallowed up by a loss of about 24,000 black votes."[30]

The most significant Texas GOP victories were in four statewide races, the first such races below the governorship ever won by Republicans in this century. These included three seats on the nine-member Texas Supreme Court. Republicans especially savored the court victories because they capped a decade of change within what had been one of the most business-oriented courts in the nation. The court in the 1980s had issued decisions that tended to favor consumers, injured workers, and organized labor, among others. Plaintiffs' attorneys had spent lavishly in these low-profile races on candidates of liberal or moderate persuasion. Two of their candidates, incumbent justices, were rebuked in 1987 by the Texas Commission on Judicial Conduct for questionable ties to lawyers. One was among the three Democrats defeated. Pundits predicted that the new court would take a distinctly more conservative tack.[31]

The battle between Texas Democrats and Republicans assumed national significance a few months later when John Tower's former colleagues in the U.S. Senate rejected his nomination as Bush's secretary of defense amid charges of drinking problems, "womanizing," and dubious financial dealings with Pentagon contractors. Soon thereafter, the U.S. House of Representatives pressured Speaker Jim Wright into resigning after its investigation of his multifarious financial dealings revealed improprieties that broke House rules. The evidence pointed to serious infractions by both Texans, but the controversies had highly partisan overtones.

The Enduring Political Themes

As the end of the 1980s approached, Texas was still torn by race and class conflict. Because the racial issue and the complex social questions connected with it—poverty, crime, drugs, and abortion, among others—had not subsided and, indeed, showed little signs of doing so, the possibility of an ascendant liberal-moderate coalition seemed remote.

From the viewpoint of the needy, this was a tragedy of major proportions. For in spite of the state's great natural resources, its prowess as a major industrial center, and its growth in aggregate income since World War II, its social programs for the disadvantaged were among the worst in the nation, still reflecting the influence of the conservative establishment.

On a per capita basis, Texas in 1987 ranked last among the states, for example, in general government revenue and general expenditures. It ranked twenty-ninth in education expenditures and forty-ninth in public welfare spending. In 1988 it ranked fiftieth in funding for alcohol and drug abuse services. The same year, it ranked forty-third on Medicaid health assistance for the poor. In 1986 it ranked thirty-eighth on community mental health funding and forty-fourth on community mental retardation services.[32] These low per capita rankings had almost no connection to the state's economic problems of the 1980s—they were largely unchanged from the previous decade.

Such miserly expenditures occurred in a state with one of the largest poverty populations in the nation; with great numbers of homeless, many of whom were mentally ill; with a growing health-care crisis as small hospitals shut down, leaving towns without medical facilities; with probably the largest number of pregnant adolescents in the United States and the fourth largest number of reported AIDS patients; and with a rapidly increasing school population whose teachers were underpaid and whose school facilities were woefully unequal and often inadequate.[33] Texas in the 1980s failed to meet the standards of public social service provisions for the disadvantaged that most Western democratic societies for decades had required as a basic mimimum and that large numbers of Texans clearly wanted and needed but were prevented from having. What would it take to change this situation?

V. O. Key, speculating forty years ago on "a way out" of this long-standing problem, saw that it required the abatement of racial politics. Texas Populists such as Joshua Hicks before him were of the same opinion. Numerous writers have reiterated the idea since Key.

But how could the exorcism of racial issues from Texas politics be achieved when racial antagonisms were still tightly woven into the fabric of everyday life? How could one ignore race when every step forward by racial minorities was resisted by numerous whites who perceived this progress as being at their expense? How could a moratorium be declared on the subject when one of the two major political parties saw an advantage in keeping it before the public, fanning the embers of old racial hostilities? These were questions to which there were no good answers.

Notes

Preface

1. Richard Hamilton, *Restraining Myths: Critical Studies of U.S. Social Structure and Politics* (New York: John Wiley & Sons, 1975), 281.

2. Raymond E. Wolfinger and John Osgood Field, "Political Ethos and the Structure of City Government," *American Political Science Review* 60 (June 1966): 307n.6.

3. Hamilton, *Restraining Myths*, 281.

4. Peirce has written fascinating accounts of the states, in geographical groupings, which have appeared occasionally since 1972. The latest, containing chapters on all fifty states, is in Neal R. Peirce and Jerry Hagstrom, *The Book of America: Inside Fifty States Today* (New York: Norton, 1983).

Prologue

1. Joshua Hicks Scrapbook, Texas Labor Archives, University of Texas at Arlington.

2. Ibid.

3. Ibid.

4. Lawrence Goodwyn, *Democratic Promise: The Populist Moment in America* (New York: Oxford University Press, 1976). See especially chap. X.

5. Louis Hicks, Joshua Hicks's son, interview with George N. Green, 26 April 1977, Joshua Hicks Scrapbook, Texas Labor Archives, University of Texas at Arlington.

6. Hicks Scrapbook.

7. Louis Hicks interview.

8. *Congressional Quarterly's Guide to U.S. Elections* (Washington, D.C.: Congressional Quarterly Inc., 1975), 676; Bruce Palmer, historian, expert testimony in *Velasquez v. Howard*, CA 1-80-57 (N.D. Tex. 1982), trial transcript pp. 44, 72–73, 79–80.

9. Hicks Scrapbook.

10. Ibid.

11. John L. Moore, ed., *Congressional Quarterly's Guide to U.S. Elections*, 2d ed. (Washington, D.C.: Congressional Quarterly Inc., 1985), 347–49.

12. James Weinstein, *The Corporate Ideal in the Liberal State: 1900–1918* (Boston: Beacon Press, 1968), 17; James A. Tinsley, "The Progressive Movement in Texas" (Ph.D. diss., University of Wisconsin, 1953), 200.

13. Louis Hicks interview.

14. Hicks Scrapbook; Louis Hicks interview.

15. Hicks Scrapbook; Louis Hicks interview; Nicholas von Hoffman, "The Third Man Theme," *New York Times Magazine*, 28 September 1980, p. 100.

James Weinstein lists seventeen Socialist newspapers published in Texas between 1912 and 1918. See *The Decline of Socialism in America, 1912–1925* (New York and London: Monthly Review Press, 1967), 101–2. Another researcher discovered forty-three references to Socialist newspapers in Texas between 1900 and 1916. See James R. Green, "Tenant Farmer Discontent and Socialist Protest in Texas, 1901–1917," *Southwestern Historical Quarterly* 81 (October 1977): 138n.14.

16. *Abilene Daily Reporter*, 17 December 1910; ibid., 8 January 1911.

17. Ibid., 19, 31 January 1911; *City Directory of Abilene, Texas*, 1905.

18. *Abilene Daily Reporter*, 26 March, 10 April 1911.

19. Ibid., 16 April 1911.

20. Ibid.

21. Ibid., 17 April 1911.

22. Hicks Scrapbook.

23. *Abilene Daily Reporter*, 21 April 1911.

24. Louis Hicks interview; George E. Mowry, *Theodore Roosevelt and the Progressive Movement* (New York: Hill & Wang, 1946), 267. Generational links between the Populists, the Socialists, and a later generation of liberals are suggested by these men and their fathers or sons. E. R. Meitzen was the son of former Judge E. O. Meitzen of Hallettsville, a veteran Alliance and Populist leader who, like his son E. R., converted to Socialism. Hicks's son Louis, a typographers' union official, was among the liberals led by Maury Maverick, Sr., who bolted the state Democratic convention in May 1952 to protest the refusal of conservative Governor Allan Shivers's forces to commit themselves to supporting the party's presidential nominee. Henry Faulk of Austin, a judge, was the father of John Henry Faulk, an entertainer, writer, and outspoken defender of First Amendment freedoms active in Texas liberal causes until his death in 1990. See Weinstein, *Decline of Socialism in America*, 17–18; and Louis Hicks interview. For an account of John Henry Faulk's experience with blacklisting during the McCarthy era see his *Fear on Trial* (New York: Simon & Schuster, 1963).

25. Hicks Scrapbook. The article appeared 20 March 1915.

26. Darlene Clark Hine, *Black Victory: The Rise and Fall of the White Primary in Texas* (Millwood, N.Y.: KTO Press, 1979), 44–45 (quotation on p. 44).

1. V. O. Key's Theory of Texas Politics

1. Alexander Gerschenkron, Arthur Maass, Robert G. McCloskey, Don K. Price, Jr., and Merle Fainsod, "In Memoriam," *American Political Science Review* 58 (March 1964): 204–5.

2. Key was brought to the project through the assiduous efforts of Roscoe Martin, a fellow Texan who was chairman of the Department of Political Science and director of the Bureau of Public Administration at the University of Alabama. For a reminiscence of the events leading to Key's involvement, see Alexander Heard, "The Making of *Southern Politics*," in *Perspectives on the American South: An Annual Review of Society, Politics and Culture*, vol. 2, ed. Merle Black and John Shelton Reed (New York: Gordon and Breach Science Publishers, 1984), 5–11; see also Alexander P. Lamis and Nathan C. Goldman, "V. O. Key's *Southern Politics*:

The Writing of a Classic," *Georgia Historical Quarterly* 71 (Summer 1987): 261–85.

3. C. Vann Woodward, "Behind The Facade of Southern Politics," *Yale Review* 39 (Winter 1950): 375. Woodward's own book, *Origins of the New South: 1877–1913* (Baton Rouge: Louisiana State University Press, 1951), which appeared shortly after Key's work, had a similar impact on the historiography of the post-Reconstruction South. "The two books differed in emphasis and conflicted on specific points," writes a leading southern historian, "but, in the main, they were overwhelmingly complementary." See Numan V. Bartley, "Beyond *Southern Politics*: Some Suggestions for Research," in *Perspectives on the American South*, Vol. 2, ed. Merle Black and John Shelton Reed, p. 36.

4. This quotation appears on the back cover of V. O. Key, Jr., *Southern Politics in State and Nation* (New York: Alfred A. Knopf, 1949).

5. Key owed some of his major insights not only to the southern insurgent tradition but to academic precursors such as Paul Lewinson, whose work was influential among students of southern politics in the 1930s. See Paul Lewinson, *Race, Class & Party: A History of Negro Suffrage and White Politics in the South* (New York, London, and Toronto: Grosset & Dunlap, 1932). Many of Key's ideas were expanded and new ones developed in Alexander Heard, *A Two-Party South?* (Chapel Hill: University of North Carolina Press, 1952).

Certain of the emphases in *Southern Politics* shifted noticeably in Key's works published only a few years later. See David R. Mayhew, "Why Did V. O. Key Draw Back from His 'Have-Nots' Claim?" in *V. O. Key, Jr., and the Study of American Politics*, ed. Milton C. Cummings, Jr. (Washington, D.C.: American Political Science Association, 1988), 24–38.

6. Key, *Southern Politics*, 307 (all three quotations).

7. Ibid., 5.

8. Ibid., 666.

9. Ibid., 5. Emphasis added.

10. Ibid., 5–7.

11. Ibid., 8 (first and third quotations), 7–8 (second quoted phrase).

12. Ibid., 8 (first, second, and third quoted phrases), 9 (fourth and fifth quoted phrases).

13. Ibid., 8–9.

14. Ibid., 11.

15. Ibid., 15 (both quotations).

16. Ibid., 299 (first quotation), 301 (second quotation).

17. Ibid., 307 (both quotations).

18. Ibid., 310–11.

19. Ibid., 550.

20. Ibid., 517.

21. Ibid., 507.

22. Ibid., 646.

23. Ibid., 664.

24. Ibid., 669.

25. Ibid., 670.

26. Ibid., 510–11.
27. Ibid., 673.
28. Ibid., 674–75 (first quotation), 675 (second quotation).
29. Ibid., 7 (for statistics), 254 (quotation).
30. Ibid., 260.
31. Ruth Allen, *Chapters in the History of Organized Labor in Texas* (Austin: University of Texas, 1941), 10–11.
32. Key, *Southern Politics*, 255. Emphasis added.
33. Ibid., 259 (both quotations).
34. Ibid., 255.
35. Ibid.
36. For a discussion of this strategy, see Richard F. Hamilton, *Class and Politics in the United States* (New York and other cities: John Wiley & Sons, 1972), chap. 1; and Donald A. Wittman, "Parties as Utility Maximizers," *American Political Science Review* 67 (June 1973): 490–98.
37. Key, *Southern Politics*, 655.
38. Ibid., 470 (first quotation), 472 (second quotation).

2. The Myth of Overwhelming Conservatism

1. James P. Sterba, "Texas Is City Country; Conservatism Is King," *New York Times*, 25 April 1976, sec. 4, p. 4; "Political Intelligence," *Texas Observer* 69 (9 September 1977): 15; and "Lib-Baiting," ibid., 76 (18 May 1984): 11.
2. Walter L. Buenger, *Secession and the Union in Texas* (Austin: University of Texas Press, 1984), 174.
3. Rupert Norval Richardson, Ernest Wallace, and Adrian N. Anderson, *Texas: The Lone Star State*, 3d ed. (Englewood Cliffs, N.J.: Prentice-Hall, 1970), 298 (quotation). See, however, the claim by other historians that populism was more "interest" politics than "class" politics: T. R. Fehrenbach, *Lone Star: A History of Texas and the Texans* (New York: Macmillan, 1968), 617; and C. Vann Woodward, *Origins of the New South: 1877–1913* (Baton Rouge: Louisiana State University Press, 1951), 192–94. Woodward, however, refers to southern populism in general in this passage and makes his tentative claim on the basis of evidence from the South Carolina Farmers' Alliance. With respect to Texas populism, especially in its more radical manifestations, Lawrence Goodwyn's evidence tends to support the class politics interpretation. See Lawrence Goodwyn, *Democratic Promise: The Populist Moment in America* (New York: Oxford University Press, 1976), especially 51–86, 232–43. For a somewhat different interpretation from Goodwyn's that stresses internal conflicts within the Texas Farmers' Alliance and Populist party, see Donna A. Barnes, *Farmers in Rebellion: The Rise and Fall of the Southern Farmers Alliance and People's Party in Texas* (Austin: University of Texas Press, 1984), 20, 91–92.
4. See Goodwyn, *Democratic Promise*, 10–32, 52.
5. J. Morgan Kousser, *The Shaping of Southern Politics: Suffrage Restriction and the Establishment of the One-Party South, 1880–1910* (New Haven, Conn., and London: Yale University Press, 1974), 197–98. There were, to be sure, Demo-

cratic reformist tendencies during this period under the leadership of James S. Hogg. There is much evidence that Hogg's progressivism was heavily interlarded with flim-flam. As T. R. Fehrenbach put it, "Hogg was a flaming reformer on the hustings, standing against everything the embattled farmer hated, inventing some things the farmer had not yet imagined. But Hogg was no fool, nor was he really radical. He was a flamboyant, but deeply folk-conservative man; he knew how to survive in party politics, whom to fight, and with whom to make a deal." *Lone Star*, 620–21. After his stint in politics, Hogg became a corporation lawyer and an oil investor.

6. Roscoe C. Martin, *The People's Party in Texas: A Study in Third Party Politics* (Austin: University of Texas Press, 1933), 62–66.

7. Kousser, *Shaping of Southern Politics*, 199–200; and Lawrence D. Rice, *The Negro in Texas: 1874–1900* (Baton Rouge: Louisiana State University Press, 1971), 68–85. The Democrats were not the only party to engage in fraud; but given their power, they were probably the most successful.

8. Kousser, *Shaping of Southern Politics*, 199.

9. Bruce Palmer, *"Man Over Money": The Southern Populist Critique of American Capitalism* (Chapel Hill: University of North Carolina Press, 1980), 185–86.

10. C. Vann Woodward, *The Strange Career of Jim Crow*, 2d rev. ed. (New York: Oxford University Press, 1966), 61.

11. Palmer, *"Man Over Money,"* 182 (first quotation), 184 (second quotation). The relative tolerance of Texas populism is documented in detail by Donald Graham in his work on Texas and Oklahoma radicals' attitudes toward blacks. "The Populists of Texas," he writes, "in their appeals to ethnic minorities, their rejection of sectional prejudices and their subordination of states rights to the interests of the 'laboring class' were acting as conscious agents of the 'Solid South's' decline." Yet it is well to keep in mind Graham's caveat. "There was no typical Populist. Appeals for disfranchisement and 'Jim Crow' legislation emanating from suballiances deep in the black belt showed clearly that the response to local conditions could overcome verbal support for the State Platform." Donald Ralph Graham, "Red, White, and Black: An Interpretation of Ethnic and Racial Attitudes of Agrarian Radicals in Texas and Oklahoma, 1890–1920" (M.A. thesis, University of Saskatchewan, Regina Campus, 1973), 88 (first quotation), 121 (second quotation).

12. V. O. Key, Jr., *Southern Politics in State and Nation* (New York: Alfred A. Knopf, 1949), 553 (quotation). Fraud and violence perpetrated by the Democrats did not begin in 1896. The party had used these to control the vote throughout the last quarter of the nineteenth century. See also Alwyn Barr, *Reconstruction to Reform: Texas Politics, 1876–1906* (Austin and London: University of Texas Press, 1971), chap. 13; Goodwyn, *Democratic Promise*, 553; and Lawrence C. Goodwyn, "Populist Dreams and Negro Rights: East Texas as a Case Study," *American Historical Review* 76 (December 1971): 1435–56.

13. Kousser, *Shaping of Southern Politics*, 201–3 (both quotations on p. 202).

14. Ibid., 205; as Key's research makes clear, the precipitous decline in Texas voter turnout following the collapse of populism began *before* the poll tax went into effect in 1904. However, it seems clear that the tax and other features of the Terrell Election Law were designed to ensure that the Populist phoenix did not

rise from the ashes after it had been crushed by terror, coercion, and threat. As Key put it, "In some states at least, and perhaps in all, the formal limitation of the suffrage was the roof rather than the foundation of a system of political power erected by a skillful combination of black-belt whites, financial and trade interests, and upper-class citizens of the predominantly white counties." See Key, *Southern Politics*, 534–35, 553. Kousser has shown, moreover, that while the vote dropped sharply before the tax was put into effect, it continued to drop afterward, suggesting that the poll tax did, in fact, play a role in disfranchisement. See Kousser, *Shaping of Southern Politics*, 208.

15. Cited in Woodward, *Origins of the New South*, 336 (first quotation). See also Frederic D. Ogden, *The Poll Tax in the South* (University, Ala.: University of Alabama Press, 1958), 20–29; and Palmer, "*Man over Money*," 187 (second quotation).

16. Laura Snow, "The Poll Tax in Texas: Its Historical, Legal, and Fiscal Aspects" (M.A. thesis, University of Texas at Austin, 1936), 50; and Kousser, *Shaping of Southern Politics*, 200–201. Lawrence Rice, the leading student of Texas blacks in the latter part of the nineteenth century, disagrees with the interpretation that disfranchisement was aimed at both blacks and populism. In his view, blacks were the only targets of the disfranchisers. See Lawrence D. Rice, *The Negro in Texas: 1874–1900* (Baton Rouge: Louisiana State University Press, 1971), 132–39. Rice couches the question of the disfranchisers' purpose in terms of two mutually exclusive hypotheses: it was either to bar blacks from the polls or to bar "poor whites who were swept along by the tide of Populism in the 1890's" (p. 133). Given the fact that a significant number of blacks were swept along by the Populist tide as well, the idea that both blacks and whites—of the kind who would join forces in a biracial movement for economic justice—were the twin targets of the disfranchisers seems at least as plausible as Rice's view, although there is no question that blacks were one of the targets.

17. See Key, *Southern Politics*, 533–35; Kousser, *Shaping of Southern Politics*, 249; Snow, "The Poll Tax in Texas," 50; and Barr, *Reconstruction to Reform*, 205. Kousser argues persuasively that official returns showing support for the tax in some heavily black and Republican counties were the result of fraudulent counting (pp. 206–7).

The pattern of support for repeal of the poll tax in a 1949 referendum was similar to the pattern of opposition to its institution in 1902. Counties with a strong labor base—especially the Gulf Coast counties where the CIO had made inroads—and South Texas counties with high Mexican American concentrations were strongest in their opposition. See Ogden, *Poll Tax in the South*, 215–24.

18. *The Breweries and Texas Politics*, Vol. 1 (San Antonio: Passing Show Printing Co., n.d.), 294. At the time a man's summer suit cost five dollars.

19. For discussions of the Fergusons see Richardson et al., *Texas*, 304–7; and Key, *Southern Politics*, 264–65. James A. Tinsley's entry in the *Dictionary of American Biography, Supplement 3, 1941–45*, ed. Edward T. James and others (New York: Charles Scribner's Sons, 1973), on pages 266–67, gives a rather negative assessment of Ferguson. More in keeping with Key's favorable evaluation is that of Jack Lynn Calbert, "James Edward and Miriam Amanda Ferguson: The

'Ma' and 'Pa' of Texas Politics" (Ph.D diss., University of Indiana, Bloomington, 1968), 273–96.

20. Monroe Lee Billington, *The Political South in the Twentieth Century* (New York: Charles Scribner's Sons, 1975), 57.

21. For a detailed account of events surrounding the Rainey firing see Alice Carol Cox, "The Rainey Affair: A History of the Academic Freedom Controversy at the University of Texas, 1938–1946" (Ph.D. diss., University of Denver, 1970).

22. An incisive account of the liberal-conservative conflict from the vantage point of the early 1960s is found in James R. Soukup, Clifton McCleskey, and Harry Holloway, *Party and Factional Division in Texas* (Austin: University of Texas Press, 1964). It should be noted that the terms *liberal* and *conservative* do not always do justice to the complexity of popular political ideology, especially from the 1970s on. Chapter 10 of this book makes this clear. For now, however, it is sufficient to point out that the two ideological poles in Texas from the 1940s to the 1970s at least, as represented by major candidates opposing each other in statewide elections, were liberal and conservative.

23. See "Yarborough Concedes," *Houston Post*, 5 May 1970, sec. 1, p. 3, for estimates on Bentsen's expenditures; see "GOP 'in principle,' " *Texas Observer* 49 (13 December 1957): 6, for Yarborough's lack of newspaper support; and Robert Sherrill, *The Accidental President* (New York: Pyramid Books, 1968), 104, for the number of newspapers.

24. Dave Denison, "On the 'Liberal Primary,' " *Texas Observer* 78 (18 April 1986): 12.

25. Ronnie Dugger, "Tower Steps Down," *Texas Observer* 75 (16 September 1983): 3–4 (quotation on p. 3).

26. Lyndon Johnson, a liberal during his New Deal days in Congress, shifted to the center and, on some issues, to the right as his senatorial ambitions began to surface in the early 1940s. He was convinced, on good evidence, that the powerful economic establishment of that day—which included some of his close friends and benefactors—would not allow a liberal to win statewide. The difference between Johnson's statewide basis of support and that of other liberal candidates is revealed in the virtual absence of a correlation between the support for liberal gubernatorial candidate Homer Rainey in the 1946 primary runoff and that for Johnson two years later in the runoff for U.S. senator or between Johnson's 1948 support and that of Ralph Yarborough in the 1952 primary. See Numan V. Bartley and Hugh D. Graham, *Southern Politics and the Second Reconstruction* (Baltimore and London: Johns Hopkins University Press, 1975), 42.

Not just Johnson's middle course but his betrayal of liberals in Texas convention politics and even, on occasion, his red-baiting, led to a deep schism between him and much of the state's liberal leadership during the 1950s and 1960s. On Johnson's red-baiting see Ronnie Dugger, *The Politician: The Life and Times of Lyndon Johnson: The Drive for Power, from the Frontier to Master of the Senate* (New York: W. W. Norton, 1982), 350–55. Once in the White House, Johnson's domestic and racial liberalism again came forth, for he was then no longer politically dependent on the Texas establishment.

27. Sam Kinch, Jr., "Yarborough Isn't Through Yet," *Dallas Morning News*

Southwest Scene Sunday Magazine 122 (11 October 1970), 6–10 (quotation on p. 7).

28. William G. Phillips, *Yarborough of Texas* (Washington, D.C.: Acropolis Books, 1969), 9. This book, a campaign biography, is partial to Yarborough. However, it contains a useful summary of his major accomplishments.

29. On Yarborough's role in cancer legislation, see Solomon Garb, M.D., Citizens' Committee for the Conquest of Cancer, to Ralph Yarborough, 25 January 1970; and U.S. Senate, 92 Cong., 1st sess., Doc. no. 92–9; *Report of the National Panel of Consultants on the Conquest of Cancer . . . Prepared for the Committee on Labor and Public Welfare . . .* (Washington, D.C.: U.S. Government Printing Office, 1971), xiii.

On occupational safety, see Phillips, *Yarborough of Texas*, 123; and Bryan Wooley, "Ralph Yarborough," *Westward* Sunday magazine, *Dallas Times Herald*, 5 June 1983, p. 25. For Yarborough's account of his involvement in passage of the Occupational Safety and Health Act, see Ralph W. Yarborough interview with the author, 26 June 1982, 182–84.

On community health, see Phillips, *Yarborough of Texas*, 123; and on aid to children and on other health issues, see ibid., chap. 8; Macdonald Critchley, *The Dyslexic Child*, 2d ed. (London and Tonbridge: The Whitefriars Press Ltd., 1970), ix; and U.S. Senate, 90 Cong., 2d sess., Doc. no. 90–108: *Committee on Labor and Public Welfare, United States Senate. 100th Anniversary, 1869–1969* (Washington, D.C.: U.S. Government Printing Office, 1970), 79.

On veterans, poverty, and the disadvantaged, see Phillips, *Yarborough of Texas*, chap. 8, and p. 100; and U.S. Senate Committee on Labor and Public Welfare, *100th Anniversary, 1869–1969*, 147–49.

30. Tyrus G. Fain, ed., *National Health Insurance* (New York and London: R. R. Bowker, 1977), x.

31. " 'A Prophet Is Not Without Honor . . . ,' " *Austin Times*, 20 December 1970, sec. B, p. 4.

32. Mark W. Oberle, "Endangered Species: Congress Curbs International Trade in Rare Animals," *Science* 167 (9 January 1970): 153; and Yarborough interview with the author, 26 June 1982, 155.

33. Phillips, *Yarborough of Texas*, 130. For Yarborough's account of passage of these bills, see Yarborough interview with the author, 26 June 1982, 148–55.

34. Thomas N. Schroth, ed., *Congress and the Nation, 1945–1964: A Review of Government and Politics in the Postwar Years*, vol. 1 (Washington, D.C.: Congressional Quarterly Service, 1965), 74a, 81a, 93a; and William B. Dickinson, Jr. and David Tarr, eds., *Congress and the Nation, 1965–1968: A Review of Government and Politics*, vol. 2 (Washington, D.C.: Congressional Quarterly Service, 1969), 15a, 40a.

35. "Notes from Chicago," *Texas Observer* 60 (6 September 1968): 8; and Yarborough interview with the author, 26 June 1982, 99–101.

36. Robert A. Diamond, ed., *Congress and the Nation, 1969–1972: A Review of Government and Politics*, vol. 3 (Washington, D.C.: Congressional Quarterly Service, 1973), 8a, 19a; and Kaye Northcott and Ronnie Dugger, "The Yarborough Defeat: Anti-Nigger, Anti-Mexican, Anti-Youth," *Texas Observer* 62 (15 May 1970):1.

37. For a summary of Yarborough's accomplishments in education, see Phillips, *Yarborough of Texas*, chap. 7. On Yarborough's involvement with the National Defense Education Act, see Yarborough interview with the author, 26 June 1982, 169–72.

38. Phillips, *Yarborough of Texas*, 102–5; and U.S. Senate Committee on Labor and Public Welfare, *100th Anniversary, 1869–1969*, 147–48. On the three presidents' opposition, see Yarborough interview with the author, 26 June 1982, 172.

39. Phillips, *Yarborough of Texas*, 101–2; and " 'A Prophet Is Not Without Honor . . .' " *Austin Times*, 20 December 1970, sec. B, p. 4.

40. James Presley, *A Saga of Wealth: The Rise of the Texas Oilmen* (New York: Putnam, 1978), 306–7.

41. According to official campaign reports, Lloyd Bentsen, Jr., and George Bush each spent about $1 million in the primary and general elections of 1970, or almost $3 million each in 1985 dollars. Reporter Bryan Wooley, without citing sources, claims that the Texas "establishment" spent $6 million (or what would be about $17 million in 1985 purchasing power) to defeat Yarborough. See Bryan Wooley, "Ralph Yarborough," *Dallas Times Herald* Sunday supplement, 5 June 1983, p. 19. Among large donors to the Senate candidates that year, the *Washington Post* identified only five who gave at least $5,000 to Yarborough. "But businessmen's contributions of $5,000 and more seemed to fall like confetti into the coffers of [Bentsen and Bush]." See "Where Did All the Money Go? . . . Not to Yarborough!" *Austin Times*, 17 December 1970, sec. B, pp. 1, 4 (quotation on p. 4).

42. The term *folk conservatism* appears throughout Fehrenbach's book. The paradigm of the Texan who embodies this outlook or culture is found in chap. 37. The idea of a uniquely Texas brand of conservatism is rendered all the more plausible by Fehrenbach's device—never made explicit—of using "Texan" in this chapter to mean the *male Anglo native Texan*. Thus he writes at one point, "Texans were indeed gracious to ladies, but preferred not to have ladies dabbling in warriors' business." See Fehrenbach, *Lone Star*, p. 713. A few sentences later he writes, "Votes for Negroes, desegregation, welfare, and various forms of the so-called civil rights for the non-peer group were forced down the Texan throat from outside." (Ibid.) And further: "The Texan despised Mexicans." (Ibid., p. 717.) It is still common today for writers generalizing about "Texans" to consciously or unconsciously limit the concept to Anglo males, as Fehrenbach did twenty years ago. Even limited thus narrowly, the concept can be seriously misleading.

43. Daniel J. Elazar, *American Federalism: A View from the States* (New York: Thomas Y. Crowell, 1966), 79 (quotation). An enlightening discussion of the problems involved in the notion of political culture is found in Lucian W. Pye, "Culture and Political Science: Problems in the Evaluation of the Concept of Political Culture," *Social Science Quarterly* 53 (September 1972): 285–96. Pye concludes with the guarded if not faintly damning prediction that "in spite of the difficulties in rigorously applying the concept, political culture will continue to attract attention among political scientists" (p. 296).

44. Elazar, *American Federalism*, 14 n–15 n.

45. Quoted in Robert Graham Porterfield, Jr., "The Early History of Abilene up to 1920" (M.A. thesis, Hardin-Simmons University, 1969), 24 (first, second,

third, and fourth quotations); *Abilene Daily Reporter: Illustrated Edition,* Abilene: Abilene Printing Company, 15 May 1900.

46. Mody C. Boatright, "The Myth of Frontier Individualism," *Southwestern Social Science Quarterly* 22 (June 1941): 14–32 (quotation on p. 17).

47. Ibid., 17.

48. David Gottlieb, "Texans' Responses to President Carter's Energy Proposals," unpublished paper, 1977, 4; see Art Wiese, "Connally Losing Voter Influence, Poll Reveals," *Houston Post,* 16 May 1976, sec. B, p. 1. Gottlieb, a sociologist at the University of Houston, polled Texans' attitudes on the oil crisis over several years.

49. Some of the data from the CSEP that I report have been published. See Roderick Bell, "Texas," in *Explaining the Vote: Presidential Choices in the Nation and the States, 1968,* pt. 2, *Presidential Choices in Individual States,* ed. David M. Kovenock et al. (Chapel Hill: Institute for Research in Social Science, University of North Carolina, 1973), 425–65.

50. A *New York Times*/CBS national poll of blacks and Hispanics in 1986, for example, showed that 16 and 17 percent of Hispanic and black respondents, respectively, said they were liberal while Hispanics had given Walter Mondale 61 percent of their vote two years earlier and blacks had given him 89 percent. See Adam Clymer, "Poll Studies Hispanic Party Loyalties," *New York Times,* 18 July 1986, sec. A, p. 7.

51. See table headlined "Texas and the Nation," *New York Times,* 9 October 1980, sec. B, p. 10.

52. Ibid.

3. The Basis of the Liberal Coalition

1. V. O. Key, Jr., *Southern Politics in State and Nation* (New York: Alfred A. Knopf, 1949), 259–61.

2. Presidential elections include all those between 1948 and 1980. Senatorial primaries include the first primaries in 1958, 1964, and 1970; and the second primary in 1972. Ralph Yarborough was the liberal in all cases. Gubernatorial primaries include the second one in 1946 (Rainey); the first in 1952 (Yarborough); the second in 1954 (Yarborough); the second in 1956 (Yarborough); the first in 1962 (Don Yarborough); the first in 1964 (Don Yarborough); the first in 1966 (Woods); the second in 1968 (Don Yarborough); the second in 1972 (Farenthold); and the first in 1974 (Farenthold). The percentage base is the vote for all candidates—not simply the leading candidates.

3. James R. Soukup, Clifton McCleskey, and Harry Holloway, *Party and Factional Division in Texas* (Austin: University of Texas Press, 1964), 73–74. The authors also found a sharp decrease between 1926 and 1956 in county-by-county deviation from the statewide vote received by winning gubernatorial candidates (p. 74).

4. Survey research data are sometimes preferable to precinct returns in sorting out demographic factors in voting. Unfortunately, only in recent years has reliable survey research been conducted regularly in Texas. To get a picture of trends over

the long term, therefore, one must rely for the early years on returns from voting precincts containing a few thousand registered voters, so for consistency precinct data are used for the later years as well.

Precinct analysis involves making inferences about individual voters' behavior on the basis of aggregate precinct returns. Thus students of precinct behavior try to limit their investigations to fairly homogeneous precincts. These are most numerous in the larger cities, and the bulk of the existing information on racial and class voting derived from returns is consequently most applicable to the metropolitan population.

Since 1936 several studies have been carried out in Texas urban areas in which heavily black, Mexican American, and Anglo precincts were isolated and analyzed. Anglo precincts were sorted into different socioeconomic categories, and the voting propensities of each social class determined. Usually class analysis has not been applied to minority precincts either because they lacked sufficient diversity of social class to warrant investigation or because rich and poor neighborhoods existed side by side within the same precincts.

In such studies, the categories to which Anglo precincts are assigned are usually determined by a measure of socioeconomic status such as median family income, percentage of the work force in manual occupations, median number of years of schooling completed, or an index of these census variables. Then the precincts are ranked and grouped into "class" categories. Researchers may use different socioeconomic variables for classification purposes or may weight them differently in deriving a socioeconomic index. They may separate the "classes" at different points on the scale and choose different numbers of them. Given these different measures, comparisons of the findings in several cities in various election years allow only tentative conclusions about intercity differences or temporal trends.

Typically, Hispanic precincts are less homogeneous than black precincts, which has led some writers to doubt whether inferences about Hispanic voting from these precinct returns are valid. Statewide exit polls of Hispanic voters in the 1984 presidential elections conducted by the three major television networks, ABC, CBS, and NBC, indicated an average Democratic vote of 69 percent, compared with 76 percent derived from homogeneous precinct analysis in Houston. See Robert R. Brischetto, Southwest Voter Registration Education Project, "Latinos in the 1984 Election Exit Polls: Some Findings and Some Methodological Lessons," paper presented at a conference on "Ignored Voices: Public Opinion Polls and the Latino Community," Center for Mexican American Studies, The University of Texas at Austin, October 1985, p. 8.

There are other potential problems with data of this sort. One problem stems from the fact that, in theory at least, people of a given type who make up a homogeneous precinct may differ in their voting from people of the same type who live outside those precincts. For example, Mexican Americans in the heavily Mexican American precincts may not be representative of all Mexican Americans in the city.

Too, as noted, precincts sufficiently homogeneous to warrant analysis are most likely to be in cities of some size. Thus precinct analysis usually must ignore voters in small towns and rural areas. If voters outside cities differ in their political preferences, the focus on city precincts may bias the findings. It is not clear that systematic bias exists, however. An analysis of southern voters in 1964 revealed no clear correlation between city size and party preference or ideology. The most conservative voters were found in middle-sized cities as compared to large cities and small towns. See Richard F. Hamilton, *Class and Politics in the United States* (New York: John Wiley & Sons, 1972), 286–88.

5. In the text I use interchangeably lower-income, lower socioeconomic status, less-affluent, and disadvantaged to refer to the precincts at the bottom of the class scale. The same holds for wealthy and upper-income at the other end of the scale.

6. See Bernard Cosman, *Five States for Goldwater: Continuity and Change in Southern Presidential Voting Patterns* (University, Ala.: University of Alabama Press, 1966), 87.

7. Donald S. Strong, "Alabama: Transition and Alienation," in *The Changing Politics of the South*, ed. William C. Havard (Baton Rouge: Louisiana State University Press, 1972), 441.

8. Raymond E. Wolfinger and Steven J. Rosenstone, *Who Votes?* (New Haven and London: Yale University Press, 1980), 34.

9. Ibid., 35–36 (quotations on p. 36).

10. Charles E. Johnson, Jr., *Nonvoting Americans* (Washington, D.C.: U.S. Department of Commerce, Bureau of the Census, Current Population Reports, Special Studies, Series P–23, No. 102 [1980]); and Frances Fox Piven and Richard A. Cloward, *Why Americans Don't Vote* (New York: Pantheon Books, 1988), 178–80.

11. "Survey Reveals Firms' Policies on Voting Time," *Houston Post*, 14 October 1975, sec. D, p. 8.

12. Jerry T. Jennings et al., *Voting and Registration in the Election of November 1980* (Washington, D.C.: U.S. Department of Commerce, Bureau of the Census, Current Population Reports, Population Characteristics, Series P–20, No. 370, April 1980), 81.

13. Darrell Hancock, "Briscoe Counts on Small Vote," *Houston Post*, 26 May 1972, sec. A, p. 10.

14. Jim Craig, "Non-Voters Called Key to Clements' Election Victory," *Houston Post*, 19 December 1978, sec. A, p. 10.

15. For a history of the white primary in Texas, see Darlene Clark Hine, *Black Victory: The Rise and Fall of the White Primary in Texas* (Millwood, N.Y.: KTO Press, 1979).

16. Luther Wayne Odom, "The Effect of Texas Laws on Voter Participation," report prepared for the Texas Urban Development Commission (Austin, Texas, 1970), 2, 8.

17. U.S. Bureau of the Census, *Statistical Abstract of the United States, 1986* (Washington, D.C.: U.S. Government Printing Office, 1985), 255.

18. "The Special Session," *Texas Observer* 58 (18 February 1966): 7.

19. "The Free Vote: Halting 'Chaos,' " ibid. (4 March 1966): 3.

20. "The Amendments," ibid. (28 October 1966): 9; "An Editorial: The Right to Vote in Texas," ibid. (9 December 1966): 2.

21. Odom, "Effect of Texas Laws on Voter Participation," 9.

22. Allen M. Shinn, Jr., "A Note on Voter Registration and Turnout in Texas, 1960–1970," *Journal of Politics* 33 (November 1971): 1128–29.

23. Henry B. Gonzalez, "Poll Tax Primer: The Behead Tax," *Texas Observer* 55 (18 October 1963): 3.

24. Charles Caldwell, interview with the author, 21 November 1983; "Act I: Four Year Terms for Governor," *Texas Observer* 57 (30 April 1965): 1.

25. "Connally for Governor, 1966–1970?" *Texas Observer* 57 (16 April 1965): 4–6; "Act I: Four Year Terms for Governor," ibid. (30 April 1965): 1–4; "The Governor's Mood," ibid. (14 May 1965): 6; "Connally, Business vs. Liberals, Labor," ibid. (29 October 1965): 9–10; "Voters Refuse the Governor," ibid. (12 November 1965): 8–9.

26. Oscar Mauzy, interview with the author, 13 June 1986.

27. "The Amendments," *Texas Observer* 64 (3 November 1972): 3.

28. Texas was not alone in its shift of gubernatorial elections to off years. See Walter Dean Burnham, "V. O. Key, Jr., and the Study of Political Parties," in *V. O. Key, Jr., and the Study of American Politics*, ed. Milton C. Cummings, Jr. (Washington, D.C.: American Political Science Association, 1988), 9.

29. Robert Brischetto, "The Hispanic Electorate," in *The Hispanic Almanac* (Washington, D.C., 1984), 142.

30. Adam Clymer, "Poll Studies Hispanic Party Loyalties," *New York Times*, 18 July 1986, sec. A, p. 7.

31. James DeNardo, "Turnout and the Vote: The Joke's on the Democrats," *American Political Science Review* 74 (June 1980): 406–20. While Harvey Tucker and Arnold Vedlitz take issue with DeNardo's methods and findings, their own analysis—and that of Thomas Holbrook-Provow—indicate no consistent correlation between turnout levels and Democratic advantage. See Harvey J. Tucker and Arnold Vedlitz, "Does Heavy Turnout Help Democrats in Presidential Elections?" *American Political Science Review* 80 (December 1986): 1291–98. (See DeNardo's response [pp. 1298–1304] in the same issue.) See also Thomas M. Holbrook-Provow, "The Political Impact of Turnout in Gubernatorial Elections" (Paper delivered at the Southwestern Political Science Association Annual Meeting, Houston, March 1988).

32. Neil R. McMillen, *The Citizens' Council: Organized Resistance to the Second Reconstruction, 1954–64* (Urbana, Chicago, and London: University of Illinois Press, 1971), 353 (quotation).

33. Roderick Bell, "Texas," in *Explaining the Vote: Presidential Choices in the Nation and the States, 1968*, pt. II: *Presidential Choices in Individual States*, ed. David M. Kovenock, et al. (Chapel Hill: Institute for Research in Social Science, University of North Carolina, 1973), 439 (quotation and statistics).

4. The Upper Class

1. John Bainbridge, *The Super-Americans* (New York, Chicago, and San Francisco: Holt, Rinehart & Winston, 1961), 2.

2. "Mad Eddie," *Time* 115 (26 May 1980): 46.

3. James R. Soukup, Clifton McCleskey, and Harry Holloway, *Party and Factional Division in Texas* (Austin: University of Texas Press, 1964), 11.

4. The classic formulation of the theory of separation of ownership and control is that of Adolf A. Berle, Jr., and Gardiner C. Means, *The Modern Corporation and Private Property* (New York: Macmillan, 1933). See especially their summing up on pages 352–57. Among the several assessments of the "managerial revolution" that cast doubt on the development of a split between the perceived interests of corporate owners and managers are Philip H. Burch, Jr., *The Managerial Revolution Reassessed: Family Control in America's Large Corporations* (Lexington, Mass.: D.C. Heath, 1972), 102; Maurice Zeitlin, "Corporate Ownership and Control: The Large Corporation and the Capitalist Class," *American Journal of Sociology* 79 (March 1974): 1073–1119; and David R. James and Michael Soref, "Profit Constraints on Managerial Autonomy: Managerial Theory and the Unmaking of the Corporate President," *American Sociological Review* 46 (February 1981): 1–18.

5. Wealth, like height, is distributed along a gradient, and where one draws the line between the rich or the tall and the rest depends largely on the reason for the classification. There is no official list of the wealthy nor even an agreement on how wealth should be measured. A common measure is personal net worth—assets minus liabilities. The advantage of this measure is that various financial journalists have made something approximating a systematic effort to identify people who are rich in terms of net worth. The disadvantage is that two individuals, A and B, may have a grossly different net worth, and yet A, who is richest by this measure, nonetheless has far less control over important assets than B. Indeed, a man may have vast holdings that enable him to buy politicians, to manipulate the news, and to bully his enemies into submission while actually owing debts greater than his assets. It is not the favorable balance between assets and debts that confers economic power, so much as it is the scope and kind of holdings. Of course, if debts become so large that they sully one's credit rating and cast a shadow over his or her holdings, the liability side of net worth becomes relevant. But up to that point, debt may be a sign of an economic empire's growth. Be this as it may, since those who compiled the lists of the very rich used in this study took worth as a measure of wealth, I have adopted it also.

6. The 2 percent figure is a rough guess, as data on wealth distribution for individual states are hard to come by. A study by the Federal Reserve found that about 2 percent of all families in the country had a net worth of $500,000 or more in 1983. See Robert B. Avery et al., "Survey of Consumer Finances, 1983: A Second Report," *Federal Reserve Bulletin* 70 (December 1984): 862. I thus used the same percentage for Texas, assuming that wealth there was not distributed much differently from that in the rest of the United States.

Actually, the concentration of top wealth holders may be somewhat greater in Texas. See Marvin Schwartz, "Estimates of Personal Wealth, 1982: A Second Look," *Internal Revenue Service. Statistics of Income Bulletin* (Washington, D.C.: U.S. Government Printing Office, Spring 1988), 33. Schwartz defines top wealth holders as individuals (rather than as families in the above Federal Reserve study) with gross assets (rather than net worth) of $325,000. Using the estimated number of such wealth holders he provides (p. 44), I have calculated their concentration as a percentage of the population age eighteen and over in 1982 as 2.6 percent in the United States and 3.2 in Texas. If this higher concentration applies to family net worth, then the 2 percent figure I use in the text may be a bit low.

Top wealth holders own a large percentage of the nation's private wealth, but here again I was unable to uncover precise data on Texas. It is suggestive that in 1962 43 percent of the nation's private wealth was held by the top 2.5 percent of wealth-holding consumer units. See Thomas Osman, "The Role of Intergenerational Wealth Transfers in the Distribution of Wealth over the Life Cycle: A Preliminary Analysis," in *The Distribution of Economic Well-Being*, ed. F. Thomas Juster (Cambridge, Mass.: Ballinger Publishing, 1977), 409.

7. C. Wright Mills drew the line between "mere millionaires" and the "fabulously rich" at $30 million—although he did not correct for changes in the value of the dollar over the more than half a century encompassed by his study. I chose a net worth of $50 million in 1979 dollars—which still falls considerably short of the more than $90 million in 1979 buying power represented by $30 million in 1950, the last benchmark year in the Mills study. See C. Wright Mills, *The Power Elite* (New York: Oxford University Press, 1956), 377.

Having established this criterion, I first tried culling the standard social and economic histories of great American fortunes for names of rich Texans. This produced practically no information on those living after World War II. I also read many journalistic accounts—including obituaries—of the Texas rich, which eventually resulted in a card file on several dozen people. What soon became obvious, however, was that while the names of the putative big rich appeared frequently— along with wildly varying estimates of their net worth—no systematic inquiry into the subject had been made. An exception was the ongoing study of the national big rich reported occasionally in *Fortune* magazine by financial reporters Richard Austin Smith and Arthur M. Lewis. But these articles, while sometimes mentioning Texans, concerned wealth holders nationally, and the net worth threshold was usually so high as to exclude all but a few Texans.

The problem was solved, to the extent that it is likely to be, by the appearance of two articles, one of which resulted from a systematic effort to discover exclusively Texas fortunes, and the second of which, while devoted to the United States, cast a wide enough net to land several very rich Texans.

"The Wealthiest Texans," by Dan Rottenberg, appeared in the September 1979 issue of *Town & Country* magazine (pp. 131–42). It is a list of both individuals and some extended families whose net worth was conservatively estimated to be at least $30 million and was classified into wealth categories, including those of $50 million and over. From the list, I extracted the names of all individuals—not extended families—with a net worth of at least $50 million, which came to a total of 60.

"The Forbes Four Hundred," by Harold Seneker, Jonathan Greenberg, and John Dorfman, in *Forbes* 130 (13 September 1982): 99–180, lists four hundred individuals and a few families who were judged to be the wealthiest in the country. The least-wealthy individuals had a net worth conservatively estimated at around $100 million. There were sixty-five individual Texans, including thirty-nine who were not on the *Town & Country* list three years earlier. Thus by integrating the two lists, I arrived at ninety-nine individuals estimated to be worth at least $50 million at some point between 1979 and 1982.

Rottenberg's figures, like those in the *Fortune* series, "were arrived at after extensive research through multitudes of proxy statements, Securities & Exchange Commission filings, foundation reports, books, magazines, newspapers and conversations with dozens of knowledgeable insiders: bankers, lawyers and investment counselors" (p. 132). In a letter to me, Rottenberg said that he, like *Fortune*, counted the net worth of individuals as including trusts, foundations, and holdings of spouses and children. The *Forbes* list was compiled in much the same way (see page 101). However, its compilers were a bit more self-conscious than Rottenberg in deciding how to treat the wealth of an individual's spouse and children.

There are numerous problems associated with any such list of big wealth holders. In Texas, in particular, the fact that unexploited mineral assets constitute a large part of individual wealth should give one pause, because the value of underground reserves is notoriously hard to estimate. It should also be noted that estimates of the worth of the big rich in the two studies vary greatly—more, presumably, than the passage of three years could explain. Such problems bedevil all lists of the great fortunes. Indeed, it is a commonplace that the rich themselves can only speculate about the value of their holdings.

8. See "Top Ranking as Apartment Builder-Operator Surprised Farb," *Houston Post*, 6 August 1978, sec. C, p. 18.

9. See John Huey, "The Giant Developers of Dallas Began Small, Took Enormous Risks," *Wall Street Journal*, 24 March 1986, sec. 1, pp. 1, 14; and Joseph Nocera, "The Eccentric Genius of Trammell Crow," *Texas Monthly* 12 (August 1984): 118–22, 202–16, 222.

10. National figures were calculated from data in *Historical Statistics of the United States: Colonial Times to 1957* (Washington, D.C.: U.S. Bureau of the Census, U.S. Government Printing Office, 1960), 210–11.

11. "Krueger's Dollars," *Texas Observer* 70 (17 March 1978): 5. The four Cullen clan members on the *Forbes* list in 1982 were each estimated to be worth $500 million, but further research led the staff to revise their estimates to less than $125 million for each. "The Forbes Four Hundred," *Forbes* 132 (Fall 1983, sp. issue): 162.

12. See Harry Hurt III, "The Most Powerful Texans," *Texas Monthly* 4 (April 1976): 73–77, 107–23 (see p. 119 for details on Robertson).

13. A woman claiming to be Hunt's second wife, Frania Tye Lee, emerged from obscurity in Louisiana after his death and successfully claimed a portion of his estate. Hunt had sired four other children by her, and Mrs. Lee testified that she believed she and Hunt were married at the time. The first and third families, chronologically speaking, lived in Dallas and were known as the "first" and "second" families, respectively. See Harry Hurt III, *Texas Rich: The Hunt Dynasty from the Early Oil Days through the Silver Crash* (New York and London: W. W. Norton, 1981), 17–21, 350.

14. Harry Hurt III, "Silver Finger," *Playboy*, September 1980, 132.

15. "The Forbes Four Hundred," *Forbes* 136 (28 October 1985, sp. issue): 115, 120–21, 132–34.

16. Seneker, Greenberg, and Dorfman, "The Forbes Four Hundred," 102.

17. "The Forbes Four Hundred," *Forbes* 136 (28 October 1985, sp. issue): 126.

18. Ann Crittenden, "The Hunt Brothers: How They Deal," *New York Times*, 6 January 1980, sec. 3, pp. 1, 4–5 (all quotations on p. 1).

19. "Texas on Wall Street," *Time* 77 (16 June 1961): 80.

20. Ibid., 83.

21. Tony Castro, "Mr. Brown of Brown & Root," *Texas Observer* 67 (25 July 1975): 15.

22. Gerald Egger, "$40 Million for 32 Blocks," *Houston Post*, 26 April 1970, sec. 1, pp. 1, 2.

23. See David Welsh, "Building Lyndon Johnson," *Ramparts* 6 (December 1967): 53–64, for an account of Brown and Root's involvement in Vietnam.

24. James Conaway, *The Texans* (New York: Alfred A. Knopf, 1976), 106.

25. Annual Report, First City Bancorporation of Texas, Inc., for the fiscal year ended 31 December 1973.

26. Tenneco's internal structure is described in its 1974 Annual Report, 8–20.

27. The criteria for choosing the largest economic institutions were these: They had to be headquartered in the state; they could not be subsidiaries of out-of-state firms; and they had to be publicly held. Data for ranking them were obtained from *Texas Parade* magazine, July 1974, and *The Foundation Directory*, 5th ed. (New York: The Foundation Center, 1975). Depending on the kind of institution, ranking was by 1973 sales, assets, or deposits; or, in the case of foundations, 1972 or 1973 assets.

28. *Historical Statistics of the United States*, 74.

29. *Texas Almanac and State Industrial Guide, 1986–87* (Dallas: A. H. Belo Corp., 1985), 629. The data on religious adherents for the entire state are for 1980.

30. Names and salaries are given by William G. Smith, "The Compensation Countdown," *Texas Business* 8 (September 1983): 68–71, 125–26 (Dixon's salary given on p. 68; Mackin's on pp. 70–71).

31. Paul Blumberg, "Another Day, Another $3,000: Executive Salaries in America," *Dissent* 25 (Spring 1978): 158–59.

32. Ibid., 160.

33. Wilbur G. Lewellen, *The Ownership Income of Management* (New York: National Bureau of Economic Research, 1971), 105.

34. Unless otherwise noted, estimates of personal worth in these sketches of "the ninety-nine" are from *Forbes*'s annual issue on the "richest 400 Americans," beginning 13 September 1982; or Dan Rottenberg, "The Wealthiest Texans," *Town & Country* (September 1979): 131–42. On Perry Bass and sons, see Eric Gelman et al., "The Bass Dynasty," *Newsweek* 104 (19 November 1984): 72–78; Ann Crittenden, "Even for Texans, the Basses Are Rich," *New York Times*, 13 December 1981, sec. 3, pp. 1, 17; and "Billionaires Funnel $84,000 to White," *Houston Post*, 24 March 1986, sec. A, p. 6.

35. "The Forbes Four Hundred," *Forbes* 136 (28 October 1985, sp. issue): 140; John Makeig, "A&M Loyalist," *Houston Chronicle*, 31 March 1985, sec. 1, p. 43;

Rowland Evans and Robert Novak, "GOP Needs Faith Leap to Buy Hance," *Houston Post*, 29 October 1985, sec. B, p. 2; and "Gramm Picks Committee as Prelude to Senate Bid," *Austin American-Statesman*, 14 September 1983, sec. B, p. 6.

36. See "How Much Financial Does a Financial Disclosure Disclose?" *Texas Observer* 64 (12 May 1972): 3; and "Unfair to Dolph," ibid. 65 (19 October 1973): 15; Arthur Wiese, "Regional Council Blasts Briscoe on Health Agencies," *Houston Post*, 29 July 1977, sec. A, p. 7 (quotation); and "Gov. Briscoe Feted," ibid., 17 June 1978, sec. B, p. 1 (for appreciation dinners).

37. Waldemar A. Nielsen, *The Big Foundations* (New York and London: Columbia University Press, 1972), 166.

38. See Saralee Tiede, "Clements' Assets at $29.4 Million," *Dallas Times Herald*, 9 October 1978, sec. A, p. 12; Rottenberg, "The Wealthiest Texans," 138; biographical information sheet contained in Clements's file in the *Dallas Times Herald* library; Margaret Mayer, "Dallas Executive in Line for No. 2 Pentagon Job," *Dallas Times Herald*, 30 November 1972, sec. A, p. 1; "Clements Formally Named," *Houston Post*, 27 August 1976, sec. A, p. 7; Doug Harlan, "A Cool Look at the Big Spenders," *Texas Observer* 71 (2 February 1979): 9–10; Saralee Tiede, "Clements Second to Helms in Campaign Spending," *Dallas Times Herald*, 12 December 1978, sec. D, pp. 1, 2 (for 1978 campaign expenditures); "White Spent $7.2 Million in Governor's Campaign," *Dallas Times Herald*, 3 December 1982, sec. B, p. 3; and "Gramm Picks Committee as Prelude to Senate Bid," *Austin American-Statesman*, 14 September 1983, sec. B, p. 6.

39. Darrell Hancock, "Governor Hopes to Take Reins of Democratic Party Saturday," *Houston Post*, 2 May 1974, sec. A, p. 18 (for Crow's support of Briscoe in 1974); Art Wiese, "Ford, Reagan Battle Lines Already Forming in State," *Houston Post*, 12 January 1976, sec. A, pp. 1, 17 (for Crow's support of Ford); and Charlotte Curtis, "The Dallas Billionaires," *New York Times*, 14 August 1984, sec. C, p. 12 (for Crow's support of Reagan).

40. Rowland Evans and Robert Novak, "Ford's Texas Dropouts," *Houston Post*, 2 January 1976, sec. D, p. 2 (for Halbouty's switch to Reagan); Sam Fletcher, "Halbouty Says Administration Will Move on Gas Deregulation," ibid., 10 October 1981, sec. B, p. 2 (for Halbouty as Reagan's energy adviser); Jim Craig, "Halbouty Withdraws as Cabinet Candidate," ibid., 20 December 1980, sec. A, p. 4 (in which Halbouty declines to be secretary of the energy department); and "Halbouty to Head Mosbacher's Campaign Panel," ibid., 19 November 1983, sec. A, p. 15 (for Halbouty's participation in Mosbacher campaign).

41. "The Forbes Four Hundred," *Forbes* 136 (28 October 1985): 144; Robert I. Vexler, *The Vice-Presidents and Cabinet Members* (Dobbs Ferry, N.Y.: Oceana Publications, 1975), 704–5; Garland A. Smith, *Men of Achievement in Texas* (Austin, Texas: Garland A. Smith Associates, 1972), 230; *Who's Who in the South and Southwest, 1975–76*, 14th ed. (Chicago: Marquis Who's Who, 1975), 325; Juan R. Palomo, "Lt. Governor Hobby's Term in Office Now Longest in State's History," *Houston Post*, 18 September 1983, sec. D, pp. 1, 2; Eleanora W. Schoenebaum, ed., *Political Profiles: The Eisenhower Years* (New York: Facts on File, 1977), 271–72; and Theodore H. White, "Texas: Land of Wealth and Fear (Part II:

Texas Democracy—Domestic and Imported Models)," *The Reporter* 10 (8 June 1954): 33, 37.

42. See Ann Crittenden, "The Hunt Brothers: How They Deal," *New York Times*, 6 January 1980, sec. 3, pp. 1, 4–5; Judy Klemesrud, "A Texas Gala at $1,000 a Head," ibid., 23 August 1984, sec. C, p. 12 (quotation); "Don't Count Hunts Out, Despite Hefty Setbacks," *Houston Post*, 31 March 1985, sec. E, pp. 1, 14; George Kuempel, "Bentsen Turned Tables on Right-Wing PAC," *Dallas Morning News*, 8 November 1982, sec. A, pp. 1, 5 (for $350,000 figure); Hurt, "Silver Finger," 138, 162; *Dallas Times Herald*, 25 January 1975; Hurt, *Texas Rich*, 264; and John S. Saloma III, *Ominous Politics: The New Conservative Labyrinth* (New York: Hill & Wang, 1984), 53, 89.

43. "The Forbes Four Hundred," *Forbes* 136 (28 October 1985): 190; Hurt, *Texas Rich*, 335; Jim Atkinson, "Downtown," *Texas Monthly* 14 (February 1986): 18–20 (especially p. 18); Richard Fly, "Gramm Edges Closer to Race for Senate," *Dallas Times Herald*, 14 September 1983, sec. C, p. 3 (for Hunt's membership on Gramm's "exploratory finance committee"); and "With Two You Get Eyesore," *Texas Observer* 72 (3 October 1980): 15.

44. Rottenberg, "The Wealthiest Texans," 137.

45. See "Anderson Plans Affect 4 Clayton Daughters," *New York Times*, 2 June 1986, sec. D, p. 2 (for information on the Clayton women); and anonymous interview with friend of Mrs. McAshan. She contributed $2,000 to liberal Frances Farenthold's gubernatorial campaign in 1972. See Herbert E. Alexander and Katharine C. Fischer, eds., *CRF Listing of: Political Contributors of $500 or More in 1972 to Candidates and Committees in Twelve States* (Princeton, N.J.: Citizens' Research Foundation, 1974), 137; and Dave Denison, "Friends of the 'Freedom Fighters,' " *Texas Observer* 79 (7 March 1986): 8.

46. Jack Z. Smith and Ron Hutcheson, "Governor's Spending Sets Record," *Fort Worth Star Telegram*, 5 October 1982, sec. A, pp. 1, 2 (Tex Moncrief's donation to Clements listed on p. 2); Tom Morganthau, Julia Wallace, and Kim Royal, "Jim Wright's Politics of Oil," *Newsweek* 96 (11 August 1980): 31–32 (relation of Moncriefs to Jim Wright; quotation on p. 32); Rottenberg, "The Wealthiest Texans," 135; John R. Knaggs, *Two-Party Texas: The John Tower Era, 1961–1984* (Austin, Texas: Eakin Press, 1986), 175.

47. See Linda Charlton, "Fund-Raiser for Ford: Robert Adam Mosbacher," *New York Times*, 8 December 1975, sec. 1, p. 20 (quotation); Lesley Wayne, "The New Face of Business Leadership," ibid., 22 May 1983, sec. 3, pp. 1, 8–9 (especially p. 8 for Mosbacher's heavyweight status); Jim Simmon, "Tower's Seat Sought by Mosbacher," *Houston Post*, 15 September 1983, sec. A, p. 10 (for Robert, Jr.'s campaign against Gramm); and Clifford Pugh, "The SO Asks: How Rich *Are* They?" *Houston Post*, 19 August 1984, sec. A, p. 21 (for information on both the Eagles and the $1,000-a-plate luncheon hosted by Mosbacher).

48. Virginia Ellis, "Business Unfinished," *Dallas Times Herald*, 2 June 1981, sec. A, pp. 1, 11; Felton West, "Studies Shouldn't Be Funded by Rich," *Houston Post*, 12 April 1985, sec. B, p. 2 (quotation); Jack Z. Smith and Ron Hutcheson, "Governor's Spending Sets Record," p. 2 (Perot's donation to Clements listed); "Welfare Pays Perot's Dues," *Texas Observer* 64 (14 April 1972): 3–5; "Perot Close

to AG," ibid. (12 May 1972): 6; Chan McDermott, "The Checkered Career of H. Ross Perot," ibid. 75 (8 July 1983): 4–5; and "Texan of the Year," *Texas Business*, December 1984, 33–40.

49. Paul Burka, "The King of the Forest," *Texas Monthly* 10 (August 1982): 114–22, 196–208, 214 (see pp. 203 and 205–6); "The Forbes Four Hundred," *Forbes* 136 (28 October 1985): 298; Rottenberg, "The Wealthiest Texans," 140; *Texas Observer* 72 (23 May 1980): 19; "The Bright New Winners," ibid., 74 (21 May 1982): 4; and John C. Henry, "Temple's Father Tops Political Spender List," *Austin American-Statesman*, 2 June 1982, sec. B, p. 1 (for details of 1982 campaign).

50. Soukup et al., *Party and Factional Division*, 10.

51. Barbara D. Paul et al., eds., *CRF Listing of: Political Contributors and Lenders of $10,000 or More in 1972* (Princeton, N.J.: Citizens' Research Foundation, 1975).

52. "Mandate, Mandate, Who's Got the Mandate?" *Texas Observer* 66 (24 May 1974): 3.

53. "Funny Money," ibid. (29 November 1974): 5.

54. Herbert E. Alexander, *Financing the 1972 Election* (Lexington, Mass.: D.C. Heath, 1976), 472.

55. V. O. Key, Jr., *Southern Politics in State and Nation* (New York: Alfred A. Knopf, 1949), 655.

56. Robert Engler, *The Politics of Oil: A Study of Private Power and Democratic Directions* (Chicago: University of Chicago Press, 1961), 349–50.

5. Upper-Class Institutions

1. Stanley H. Brown, *Ling: The Rise, Fall and Return of a Texas Titan* (New York: Atheneum, 1972), March 22 quotation, p. 169; March 24 quotation, p. 172 (first paragraph), p. 173 (second paragraph); April 9 quotation, pp. 176–77 (first paragraph), p. 177 (second paragraph); April 10 quotation, pp. 182–83; April 16 quotation, p. 186; April 17 quotation, p. 188; May 1 quotation, pp. 190–91; May 2 quotation, p. 194; May 3 quotation, p. 194; May 8 quotation, p. 201; June 27–28 quotation, p. 205 (first paragraph), pp. 206–7 (second and third paragraphs); July 8–12 quotation, p. 207; July 19 quotation, p. 216; August 19 quotation, pp. 217–18; August 23 quotation, p. 233; and September 5 quotation, p. 234. Hereinafter the corporation will be referred to as LTV Corporation.

2. Brown, *Ling*, 4–5.

3. Patricia Linden, "San Antonio," *Town & Country* May 1977, 138–47 (quotation on p. 147).

4. John Bainbridge, *The Super-Americans* (New York, Chicago, and San Francisco: Holt, Rinehart & Winston, 1961), 198.

5. Paul M. Sweezy, "Power Elite or Ruling Class?" in *C. Wright Mills and The Power Elite*, ed. G. William Domhoff and Hoyt B. Ballard (Boston: Beacon Press, 1968), 130.

6. Lyn Bracewell, "Sanctuaries of Power," *Houston City Magazine*, May 1980, 50–55 (see p. 50 for details on John Bookout).

7. "Recession Is a Non-Existent Word for Many Upper-Class in Highland Park," *Houston Post*, 24 March 1975, sec. A, p. 22.

8. "Ex-policeman Paid Not to Press Charges," *Houston Post*, 20 July 1983, sec. A, p. 12 (all quotations).

9. George Diaz-Arrastia, "Is There an Upper Social Class in Houston?" (Undergraduate paper, Rice University, in a class taught by the author in 1980).

10. Robert Coles's research on this early socialization process among the rich nationally (based on interviews with children, including some from Texas families) is essential reading on this point. See Robert Coles, *Privileged Ones: The Well-Off and the Rich in America*, vol. 5 of *Children of Crisis* (Boston and Toronto: Little, Brown and Company, 1977).

11. Peter W. Cookson, Jr., and Caroline Hodges Persell, *Preparing for Power: America's Elite Boarding Schools* (New York: Basic Books, 1985), 22.

12. Iver Peterson, "Prep Schools' Rolls Are Rising Steadily," *New York Times*, 19 October 1975, sec. 1, pp. 1, 40 (quotation on p. 40).

13. For an account of the origins of the secession effort, see Dave Precht, "Westheimer Breakaway," *Texas Observer* 69 (11 March 1977): 18–21.

14. "An ULTRA Guide to the Top Private Schools of Texas," *ULTRA* 1 (August 1982): 77–78, 80, 83–84, 86, 88, 91–92, 94, 96 (St. Stephen's is on p. 78; Hockaday is on pp. 78 and 80; St. Mark's, p. 80; Trinity Valley is on pp. 84 and 86; Kincaid is on p. 88; and St. John's, pp. 88 and 91).

15. Prudence Mackintosh, "The Greatest Experience of Your Life," *Texas Monthly* 3 (May 1975): 55–59, 107–11.

16. G. William Domhoff, "The Women's Page as a Window on the Ruling Class" (Paper prepared for "Women and the Media," a symposium sponsored by the Institute for Scientific Analysis and the National Science Foundation, San Francisco, 26–27 April 1975), p. 5b.

17. Nancy Holmes, "The Texas Deb," *Town & Country*, June 1974, 77, 98–99 (see especially p. 77).

18. D. Susan Barron, "The Reviving Rituals of the Debutante," *New York Times Magazine*, 15 January 1984, 26–37 (quotation on p. 34).

19. Ibid., 36 (for quotation and cost estimates of a season).

20. Allegro Club membership list booklet, 1975: "A Fiftieth Anniversary Message from F. Carrington Weems, Chairman, General Committee."

21. Bracewell, "Sanctuaries of Power," 50.

22. Prudence Mackintosh, "My Life and Hard Times in the Junior League," *Texas Monthly* 7 (December 1979): 157–60, 229–40 (quotation on p. 234).

23. Bracewell, "Sanctuaries of Power," 50 (for Ramada, Coronado, and Tejas clubs' memberships see p. 50; for exclusion of women, Jews, Hispanics, and blacks see pp. 50 and 55).

24. Harry Hurt III, "The Most Powerful Texans," *Texas Monthly* 4 (April 1976): 73–77, 107–23 (quotations on pp. 122–23). Hurt's observations lend substance to the emphasis various sociologists have placed on the importance men's clubs play in integrating the interests of "gentlemen of property and standing." See for example E. Digby Baltzell, *Philadelphia Gentlemen: The Making of a National Upper Class* (Glencoe, Ill.: The Free Press, 1958); G. William Domhoff, *Who Rules*

America? (Englewood Cliffs, N.J.: Prentice-Hall, 1967), 19; and Gwen Moore, "The Structure of a National Elite Network," *American Sociological Review* 44 (October 1979): 687–89.

25. See "The 500 Largest U.S. Industrial Corporations," *Fortune* 113 (28 April 1986): 182–201.

26. Mark V. Nadel, *Corporations and Political Accountability* (Lexington, Mass.: D. C. Heath & Company, 1976), 6.

27. Duane Windsor, "Regulation and the Corporate Environment: Strategies for Business," *Texas Business Review* 57 (January-February 1983): 1–5 (quotations on p. 2).

28. Anonymous employee of Coastal States, interview with the author, 19 May 1978. This person gave the author a packet of printed material in a folder entitled "Coastal Action Program," containing brochures prepared in-house as well as by the Advertising Council.

29. Ira Glasser, "You Can Be Fired for Your Politics," *Civil Liberties* (April 1979): 8; and Loren Siegel, "ACLU Launches New Task Force on Rights in the Work Place," ibid. (Spring 1989): 3.

30. Senate Subcommittee on Consumer Affairs, *Final Report of the Senate Subcommittee on Consumer Affairs Into [sic] the Activities of Southwestern Bell Telephone Company* (Published for the Texas Senate Subcommittee on Consumer Affairs, 11 May 1976), 45 (first quotation), 47 (second quotation).

31. Tim Mahoney, "Texas Commerce Bancshares, Inc.," *Texas Observer* 69 (29 July 1977): 12. For a useful general discussion of the corporate elite's involvement in elections and lobbying, see James W. Lamare, *Texas Politics: Economics, Power and Policy*, 2d ed. (St. Paul, New York, and other cities: West Publishing 1985), chaps. 5–6.

32. Mark Sanders, "HL&P Bases Bonuses on Contacts of Local Officials," *Houston Post*, 2 July 1986, sec. A, p. 3 (quotation). See "HL&P Parent Taps Lindsay to be Director," ibid., 28 April 1988, sec. A, p. 8, for the story of how, in 1988, Houston Lighting and Power Company's parent firm, Houston Industries, Inc., broke new ground in corporate-public official relations when it nominated the chief executive officer of Harris County (Republican county judge Jon Lindsay) to serve on its board of directors; the job paid "an estimated minimum of $21,000 a year" (ibid.).

33. James R. Soukup, Clifton McCleskey, and Harry Holloway, *Party and Factional Division in Texas* (Austin: University of Texas Press, 1964), 87 n. 9.

34. House Bill 246, Texas Education Code 21.101.

35. "Speakers!" Atlantic Richfield Speakers Bureau brochure, Houston, n.d. (early 1980s).

36. See "Students Busy in Economic Program," *Bellaire Texan*, 23 November 1977, p. 10 (quotation). See also Matthew Lyon, "And Now The Word from Our Sponsor," *Texas Observer* 70 (3 November 1978): 2–9.

37. Dave Precht, "HISD Won't Withdraw Antiunion Pamphlets," *Houston Post*, 5 May 1977, sec. A, pp. 1, 27 (first two quoted phrases are on p. 1; last two quoted phrases are on p. 27). Don Horn, secretary-treasurer of the Harris County Central Labor Council, interview with author, 24 May 1977.

38. Jane Wolfe, "The Corporate Image Scrimmage," *ULTRA* 3 (January 1984): 73, 94–99 (quotation on pp. 97–98).

39. Olive Talley, "Longstanding Houston Law Firm Hit by Rash of Defections," *Houston Post*, 22 June 1986, sec. D, pp. 1, 6 (the table on p. 6D entitled "Eight Largest Houston Law Firms" gives the number of attorneys then employed nationwide by each firm. Figures for the Big Three total 1,063; figures for the remaining five firms total 640).

40. Jim Newkirk, "Public-Sector Attorneys Hard to Keep," *Houston Post*, 12 April 1987, sec. A, p. 10 (for salaries of firm lawyers versus salaries of city attorneys).

41. "Busy Law Firms' Profits Leap," *New York Times*, 2 July 1987, sec. D, pp. 1, 4 (see especially the table on p. D1 entitled "The Leading Law Firms Ranked by Revenues" for the names and revenues of the twenty-one law firms referred to here).

42. Lee Jones, "Big Three Pay Well and Lay Down the Law," *Fort Worth Star-Telegram*, 11 December 1983, sec. A, pp. 29, 32 (salaries are on p. 29).

43. Geraldine R. Segal, *Blacks in the Law: Philadelphia and the Nation* (Philadelphia: University of Pennsylvania Press, 1983), 159. At the time of the book's publication, two blacks reportedly had been made partners—a larger number, it should be added, than the number of professors who held a tenured position at the author's university in the same city.

44. James B. Stewart, *The Partners: Inside America's Most Powerful Law Firms* (New York: Simon & Schuster, 1983), 14.

45. Griffin Smith, Jr., "Empires of Paper," *Texas Monthly* 1 (November 1973): 53–60, 62–63, 98–109 (quotation on p. 101).

46. Bob Meckel, "Lawyers Recruited for Project," *Houston Post*, 16 May 1985, sec. A, p. 14.

47. "Houston Attorney Named Texas' Top Young Lawyer," *Houston Post*, 4 July 1989, sec. A, p. 18 (for Barbara Radnofsky); Douglas Freelander, "Death Row Indigents Get Help," ibid., 7 August 1988, sec. B, pp. 1, 3 (for both Scott Atlas and Houston law firms' efforts); and "Big Firms Offer Death Row Defense," *New York Times*, 8 July 1988, sec. B, p. 20 (which discusses the work of Houston's and other Texas law firms).

48. Smith, "Empires of Paper," 57.

49. For details see Nicholas Lemann, "Taking Over," *Texas Monthly* 11 (October 1983): 130–37, 209–20 (see especially p. 219).

50. Quoted in James Willard Hurst, *The Growth of American Law: The Law Makers* (Boston: Little, Brown and Company, 1950), 342–43.

51. See "Lawyer-Directors Continue to Flourish," *Business Week*, 16 July 1979, 40–41.

52. The information on Texas law firm–corporation interlocks is derived from data contained in Stephen A. Glasser, ed., *Outside Counsel: Inside Director: The Directory of Lawyers on the Boards of American Industry*, rev. ed. (New York: Law Journal Press, 1976).

53. Tom Goldstein, "Book Gives Look at Legal World," *New York Times*, 1 December 1974, sec. 1, p. 59 (information in this article pertains only to Baker & Botts).

54. Al Reinert, "Not Guilty," *Texas Monthly* 3 (June 1975): 53–57, 98–110 (quotation on p. 98).

55. Lee Jones, "Counsel to the Powerful," *Fort Worth Star-Telegram*, 11 December 1983, sec. A, pp. 1, 12 (PAC figures on p. 12).

56. Ibid., 12 (quotation).

57. Smith, "Empires of Paper," 106.

58. Ibid., 108.

59. Jones, "Counsel to the Powerful," especially p. 12.

60. See Smith, "Empires of Paper," 54–55, for a discussion of influence through state and local bar associations; and "Less than Democratic," *Texas Observer* 69 (25 March 1977): 23–24.

61. Smith, "Empires of Paper," 107.

62. Jones, "Counsel to the Powerful," 12 (quotation).

63. "New Corporate Clout in the Capital," *Time* 110 (4 July 1977): 63. See also Mary Alice Davis, "Crossing the Bar," *Texas Observer* 69 (25 February 1977): 3–6.

64. Janet Elliott, "Discreet Search Led to Griffin," *Houston Post*, 26 January 1986, sec. E, pp. 1, 2.

65. "Akin, Gump Law Firm Gets Breather from Frenetic Pace," *Houston Post*, 6 February 1983, sec. B, p. 4 (for information on Akin, Gump).

66. Arthur Wiese, "City Legal Firms Expand, Open Washington Offices," *Houston Post*, 25 September 1977, sec. B, p. 6.

67. Stuart Taylor, Jr., "Senator Baker and the Art of Making Rain," *New York Times*, 11 December 1984, sec. B, p. 12.

68. "Texas Lawyer Hinted for Key Energy Post," *New York Times*, 6 September 1977, sec. 1, p. 25.

69. "Political Intelligence," *Texas Observer* 77 (3 May 1985): 10.

70. Neal R. Peirce and Jerry Hagstrom, *The Book of America: Inside 50 States Today* (New York and London: W. W. Norton, 1983), 625.

71. Lee Jones, "Lobbyists Use Money, Varied Tactics to Sway Legislators," *Houston Post*, 28 June 1978, sec. A, p. 6. The definition of lobbyist varies from state to state, and that employed in Texas statutes may be broader than normal. This same point was made in the 1960s, when research revealed over five thousand registered Texas lobbyists, more than in any other state. See Arnold S. Rose, *The Power Structure: Political Process in American Society* (New York: Oxford University Press, 1967), 376 n. 23.

72. Jim Hightower, "Lobbyists," *Texas Observer* 73 (13 February 1981): 2. For a more recent estimate of the role played by the business lobby in Austin, see Keith E. Hamm and Charles W. Wiggins, "The Transformation of Texas Interest Group Politics: From Personal to Informational Lobbying" (unpublished paper). The authors, political scientists at Rice University and Texas A&M University, respectively, examined lobbyist registration records filed with the secretary of state in February 1987, and concluded that 63 percent of Texas lobbyists at that time were representing business, exclusive of the professions. (See Table 1, p. 34).

73. See Bill Cryer, "Study: Lobbyists Spent $1 Million," *Longview Daily News* (Texas), 11 June 1982, sec. A, p. 10 (for $5,500 figure).

74. Willie Morris, "Political Profile: Harris' Eckhardt," *Texas Observer* 54 (15 June 1962): 3.

75. For an account of one such chamber's involvement see Joe R. Feagin, *Free Enterprise City: Houston in Political-Economic Perspective* (New Brunswick, N.J., and London: Rutgers University Press, 1988), 134–38; and Chandler Davidson and Stephen J. Reilly, "Upper Class Mobilization of Bias in Houston" (Paper presented to the annual meeting of the Southwestern Social Science Association, Houston, April 1977), 8–12. On the political role of the Texas Research League see Beryl E. Pettus and Randall W. Bland, *Texas Government Today*, 3d ed. (Homewood, Ill.: Dorsey Press, 1984), 388–92.

76. George Norris Green, *The Establishment in Texas Politics: The Primitive Years, 1938–1957* (Westport, Conn., and London: Greenwood Press, 1979), 11.

77. As one illustrative example of the influence of powerful men in 1972, see Felton West, "Lobbyists Urged to Support Briscoe, Connally," *Houston Post*, 13 May 1972, sec. D, p. 7.

78. Richard West, "Inside the Lobby," *Texas Monthly* 1 (July 1973): 42–49 (see p. 47 for quotation and for Whitworth's support of Barnes).

79. Joe Holley and Geoffrey Rips, "Tracking the Chemical Lobby," *Texas Observer* 75 (6 May 1983): 5.

80. Lee Clark, "May the Lobby Hold You in the Palm of Its Hand," *Texas Observer* 60 (24 May 1968): 3. It should be noted that Clark was scandalized by the lobby in general. Day, she believed at the time she wrote, was an exception. Day was convicted of scheming to defraud Libya, one of his clients. He was also given a probated sentence in 1979 for his plea of guilty on two counts of bank and savings and loan fraud. For details of James C. Day, Jr.'s case, see "Ex-legislator Gets Probation in Fraud Case," *Houston Post*, 31 May 1979, sec. A, p. 22; and "Texan Given 4–Year Term for Fraud," ibid., 11 February 1981, sec. C, p. 20 (for Day's conviction and sentencing).

81. Ronnie Dugger, *The Politician: The Life and Times of Lyndon Johnson: The Drive for Power, from the Frontier to Master of the Senate* (New York and London: W. W. Norton, 1982), 128.

82. Dugger, *The Politician*, 128; Robert A. Caro, *The Years of Lyndon Johnson: The Path to Power* (New York: Alfred A. Knopf, 1983), 220.

83. Caro, *The Years of Lyndon Johnson*, 269.

84. Ibid., 373.

85. Ibid., 375.

86. Ronnie Dugger, "What Corrupted Texas?" *Harper's*, March 1957, 72.

87. Dugger, *The Politician*, 290.

88. Ibid., 291.

89. The *Reader's Digest* citation is quoted in Dugger, *The Politician*, 290; "Nouveau Republicans," *Texas Observer* 64 (4 August 1972): 9.

90. Larry Goodwyn, "This New Vision into My Land and My Society," *Texas Observer* 56 (11 December 1964): 5.

91. "Strange New Turn in Texas Politics," *Texas Observer* 48 (5 September 1956): 8.

92. "Skating on Thin Ice," *Texas Observer* 53 (13 May 1961): 4.

93. Molly Ivins, "New Hopes, Old Problems: *Houston Chronicle*," *Texas Observer* 64 (18 February 1972): 7.

94. Information obtained from the Secretary of State, Enforcement Division, 29 January 1976. On Bracewell's involvement in the Public Utilities Commission bill see Jack Hopper, ed., *Southwest Energy & Utility Watch*, September 1982, p. 2.

95. Jo Clifton, "George Christian: The lobby's Mr. Big," *Texas Observer* 71 (2 February 1979): 5.

96. Mark Sanders, "Ex-Speaker Clayton Undergoes Quiet Transformation," *Houston Post*, 30 March 1986, sec. A, p. 17 (both quotations).

97. For journalistic accounts of some of Texas's philanthropists, see Kathryn Means, "The Biggest Givers," *ULTRA* 4 (December 1985): 88–89, 160–61; and Anne Lowrey Bailey, "In Philanthropy, Ross Perot Style, There's No Room for Bureaucracy," *Chronicle of Higher Education*, 2 March 1988, sec. A, pp. 1, 28.

6. Blue-Collar Texans

1. Details on the Spradling case are in Harold Scarlett, "Lawsuits Blame Phosgene Plant for Death, Injuries," *Houston Post*, 22 May 1983, sec. A, pp. 1, 23. These and other facts on the phosgene problem at Upjohn reported in the introductory section of this chapter are taken from a remarkable series of articles on the subject by environmental reporter Scarlett, appearing in the *Post* 22–26 May 1983.

2. Ibid. (all quotations and the suit settlement amount are on p. 23).

3. Ibid. (all quotations and figures are on p. 23).

4. Ibid., 1 and 23 (first quotation), 23 (remaining quotations).

5. This incident is outlined in Harold Scarlett, "Worker's Death in '81 Only Phosgene Fatality at Upjohn Co.'s Plant," *Houston Post*, 25 May 1983, sec. B, p. 4.

6. This incident is detailed in Harold Scarlett, "Chemical Plant Official Discounts Possibility of Gas Reaching Park," *Houston Post*, 23 May 1983, sec. A, p. 4.

7. See Scarlett, "Lawsuits Blame Phosgene Plant for Death, Injuries," p. 23.

8. See Scarlett, "Worker's Death in '81 Only Phosgene Fatality at Upjohn Co.'s Plant."

9. Scarlett, "Lawsuits Blame Phosgene Plant for Death, Injuries," p. 23.

10. Ibid. (quotations are on p. 23).

11. Andrew Levison, *The Working-Class Majority* (New York: Coward, McCann & Geoghegan, 1974), 78.

12. The census classifies manual work separate from farm occupations, yet over half the people in farm jobs are manual laborers. If they are included in the manual category, the percentage of the work force belonging to it is slightly larger than is suggested by census figures classified according to "nonmanual," "manual," and "farm" occupations (as in table 6.1). But this is not a major problem in recent years because the farm population is a small percentage of the total—in Texas, only 3 percent in 1980. Nonetheless, to preclude misunderstanding, one must distinguish between urban manual workers and the slightly larger group of manual workers that includes rural manual workers as well.

13. See William Form, *Divided We Stand: Working-Class Stratification in America* (Urbana and Chicago: University of Illinois Press, 1985), chap. 2.

14. Richard F. Hamilton, *Class and Politics in the United States* (New York and other cities: John Wiley & Sons, 1972), 34–46, especially p. 42. See also Herbert H. Hyman and Charles R. Wright, "Trends in Voluntary Association Memberships of American Adults: Replication Based on Secondary Analysis of National Sample Surveys," *American Sociological Review* 36 (April 1971): 191–206.

15. Compiled from data in Michael T. Kingston and Ruth Harris, eds., *The Texas Almanac and Industrial Guide, 1984–1985* (Dallas: A. H. Belo Corp., 1983), 654–55.

16. Margaret Carter, interview with the author, for the Southern Oral History Project, University of North Carolina at Chapel Hill, 25 October 1975.

17. The Massachusetts statistics are in Mary Jo Bane, "The Poor in Massachusetts," in *The State and the Poor in the 1980s*, ed. Manuel Carballo and Mary Jo Bane (Boston: Auburn House Publishing Company, 1984), 2.

18. For details see Kathy Kiely, "Plan Aims to Improve Colonias Along Border," *Houston Post*, 18 May 1988, sec. E, p. 5. For a useful account of Mexican Americans in the Southwest economy from the Great Depression to the 1970s, see Mario Barrera, *Race and Class in the Southwest* (Notre Dame and London: University of Notre Dame Press, 1979), 104–56. For a more general treatment of Mexican Americans in Texas, see David Montejano, *Anglos and Mexicans in the Making of Texas, 1836–1986* (Austin: University of Texas Press, 1987).

19. Jeffrey S. Passel and Karen A. Woodrow, "Geographic Distribution of Undocumented Immigrants: Estimates of Undocumented Aliens Counted in the 1980 Census by State," *International Migration Review* 18 (Fall 1984): 642–71; and Jeffrey S. Passel, "Undocumented Immigrants: How Many?" (Paper presented at the 1985 Annual Meeting of the American Statistical Association, Las Vegas, Nevada, August 1985). Passel and Woodrow estimate that the 1980 census counted 186,000 undocumented persons in Texas, of whom 147,000 were from Mexico (p. 657). Passel accepts an estimate that in the nation as a whole, the census counted 56 percent of undocumented Mexican aliens (Passel, p. 14). If that percentage applied to Texas, then approximately 262,000 such aliens were in Texas. Passel also estimates that 110,000–235,000 undocumented persons—from Mexico and elsewhere—entered the United States annually between 1979 and 1983 (Passel, p. 17). As Texas contained only 13.02 percent of the nation's undocumented aliens in the 1980 census count (Passel and Woodrow, p. 660), perhaps 10,000 to 25,000 more undocumented Mexicans were added annually in the state. Passel's estimates appear to be among the lowest of those derived from careful demographic analysis.

20. Carey McWilliams, *Brothers Under the Skin*, rev. ed. (Boston and Toronto: Little, Brown & Company, 1964), 130.

21. Thomas H. Petzinger, Jr., et al., "Illegal Immigrants Are Backbone of Economy in States of Southwest," *Wall Street Journal*, 7 May 1985, pp. 1, 10 (first quotation on p. 10; second quotation on p. 1). For two different views of the economic impact of Mexican immigrants, see Donald L. Huddle, "The Undocumented Worker: A Valuable Participant in the Texas Economy or Merely 'Cut-

Rate' Competition for the 'Legal' Labor Force?" The Victoria College Social Sciences Symposium, *The Texas Frontier: Illegal Immigration* (Victoria, Texas: Victoria College Press, 1987), 91–127; and Sidney Weintraub et al., *The Use of Public Services by Undocumented Aliens in Texas: A Study of State Costs and Revenues* (Austin: Lyndon Baines Johnson School of Public Affairs, University of Texas at Austin, 1984).

22. See Lydia Chavez, "Fears Prompted Hispanic Votes in Bill's Support," *New York Times*, 11 November 1986, sec. A, p. 12; poll results are found in Jim Craig, "Poll Shows Hispanics, Blacks See Aliens as Threat," *Houston Post*, 3 August 1983, sec. A, p. 12 (quotation). A poll conducted in 1986, during Texas's deep recession, found that 54 percent of the state's Latinos favored and 35 percent opposed employer sanctions—a key feature of the controversial immigration reform bill passed by Congress. This feature was opposed by many Mexican American leaders. See Robert R. Brischetto, *The Political Empowerment of Texas Mexicans, 1974–1988* (San Antonio, Texas: Southwest Voter Research Institute, 1988), 14.

23. See Harry Bernstein, "Illegal Aliens—Where to Draw the Line," *New York Times*, 13 December 1978, sec. A, p. 28 (reprint of an article that originally ran in the *Los Angeles Times*).

24. For the deep ideological split within the southern working class as a whole, see Earl Black and Merle Black, *Politics and Society in the South* (Cambridge, Mass.: Harvard University Press, 1987), 66–72.

25. U.S. Department of Health and Human Services, "Selected Health Characteristics by Occupation, United States, 1975–76," DHHS Publication No. (PHS) 80–1561 (Hyattsville, Md., May 1980), table 12.

26. George Orwell, *The Road to Wigan Pier* (London: Victor Gollancz, 1937), 21.

27. Hoyt Gimlin, ed., *America's Needy: Care and Cutbacks* (Washington, D.C.: Congressional Quarterly, 1984), 144.

28. Ruth Graves, "Labor, Migrant," in *The Handbook of Texas: Supplement*, vol. 3, ed. Eldon Stephen Branda (Austin: Texas State Historical Association, 1976), 488.

29. For Clements's veto of Uribe's bill, see Felton West, "Veto of Stoop-Labor Bill a Low Blow," *Houston Post*, 23 June 1987, sec. B, p. 2; and Jane Juffer, "UFW Pushing for Sanitation in the Fields," *Texas Observer* 80 (3 June 1988): 4.

30. For statistics supporting this high agricultural death rate in Texas, see table 1, *Texas Preventable Disease News*, 15 December 1984 (week no. 50), p. 3.

31. For the story, see *Civil Liberties* (Austin: Texas Civil Liberties Union, Spring 1985), 9; Jorjanna Price, "House Tentatively Passes Jobless Pay for Farm Workers," *Houston Post*, 11 April 1985, sec. D, p. 18; and Dave Denison, "A Victory for Farmworkers," *Texas Observer* 77 (17 May 1985): 6–7. For a recent account of laws affecting Texas farm workers, see Annmarie Jensen, *The Hidden People: Farmworkers in Texas* (Austin, Texas: Texas Conference of Churches and Texas IMPACT, November 1984), 7–14.

32. Sonia Jasso and Maria Mazorra, "Following the Harvest: The Health Haz-

ards of Migrant and Seasonal Farmworking Women," in *Double Exposure: Women's Health Hazards on the Job and at Home*, ed. Wendy Chavkin (New York: Monthly Review Press, 1984), 86–99.

33. *Regulating Pesticides in Texas* (Austin, Texas: Lyndon B. Johnson School of Public Affairs, University of Texas, 1984), 245.

34. Ibid., 211.

35. Geoffrey Rips, "How It Ended," *Texas Observer* 77 (14 June 1985): 5–6.

36. Robin Baker and Sharon Woodrow, "The Clean, Light Image of the Electronics Industry: Miracle or Mirage?" in Chavkin, *Double Exposure*, 24–25.

37. For this story, see David Burnham, "Asbestos Workers' Illness—and Their Suit—May Change Health Standards," *New York Times*, 20 December 1977, sec. 1, p. 30.

38. Paul Brodeur, *Expendable Americans* (New York: Viking Press, 1974), 250. The story of the Pittsburgh Corning plant is told in full in Brodeur's book.

39. Daniel M. Berman, *Death on the Job: Occupational Health and Safety Struggles in the United States* (New York and London: Monthly Review Press, 1978), 122–23.

40. See Richard Severo, "Dispute Arises over Dow Studies on Genetic Damage in Workers," *New York Times*, 5 February 1980, sec. A, p. 1, sec. B, p. 10; Tom Curtis, "Danger: Men Working," *Texas Monthly* 6 (May 1978): 129–33, 182–202 (especially for information on Velsicol Chemical Corp. and Phosvel); Harold Scarlett, "Velsicol Reported Storing Phosvel at Bayport Site," *Houston Post*, 6 August 1977, sec. A, p. 4; and ibid., "Radiation Board Calls for Prosecution of Gulf Nuclear," *Houston Post*, 6 September 1983, sec. A, pp. 1, 12.

41. National Institute for Occupational Safety and Health, "National Traumatic Occupational Fatalities, 1980–1984" (Morgantown, W. Va.: NIOSH, Division of Safety Research, 27 April 1987, rev. 11 June 1987), table 3.

42. Texas Department of Health, "Occupational Safety in Texas" (Austin, Texas: n.d., c. 1984), attachment 1.

43. Nicholas Askounes Ashford, *Crisis in the Workplace: Occupational Disease and Injury. A Report to the Ford Foundation* (Cambridge, Mass., and London: MIT Press, 1976), 10; and Roy R. Evans, *Tragedy at Work* (Austin, Texas: Futura Press, 1979), 156.

44. *Congressional Quarterly Almanac: 91st Congress, 2nd Session . . . 1970* 26 (Washington, D.C.: Congressional Quarterly, 1971), 675–82.

45. David P. McCaffrey, *OSHA and the Politics of Health Regulation* (New York and London: Plenum Press, 1982), 171–74.

46. "The OSHA Bone in Labor's Throat," *New York Times*, 30 May 1985, sec. A, p. 22 (for quoted word and information on Robert Rowland); and William Glaberson, "Is OSHA Falling Down on the Job?" *New York Times*, 2 August 1987, sec. 3, pp. 1, 6 (see table on p. 1 for figures on OSHA inspectors in 1980 and 1987).

47. *Preventing Illness and Injury in the Workplace* (Washington, D.C.: Congress of the United States, Office of Technology Assessment, OTA-H-256, April 1985), see especially pp. 264–69.

48. Ray Marshall and Arnold H. Packer, *An Interim Report to Congress on*

Occupational Diseases (Washington, D.C.: U. S. Department of Labor, 1980), 112 (second quotation), 114 (first, third, and fourth quotations); and Lloyd Criss, "Poor Work Place Safety Costs Us All," *Houston Post*, 24 December 1987, sec. E, p. 3 (for information on and number of OSHA inspectors [eighty-seven] in Texas).

There are several categories of OSHA violations. "Serious ones" are "those that involve a substantial probability of causing death or serious physical harm and that the employer either knew about or could reasonably have been expected to know about." See John Mendeloff, *Regulating Safety: An Economic and Political Analysis of Occupational Safety and Health Policy* (Cambridge, Mass., and London: MIT Press, 1979), 2. For a more general critique of OSHA, see Charles Noble, *Liberalism at Work: The Rise and Fall of OSHA* (Philadelphia: Temple University Press, 1986).

49. Clifton McCleskey, E. Larry Dickens, and Allan K. Butcher, *The Government and Politics of Texas*, 5th ed. (Boston: Little, Brown and Company, 1975), 335; and Evans, *Tragedy at Work*, 11, 16. Ralph Yarborough, chairman of the Senate Labor and Public Welfare Committee, was active in getting the OSHA bill passed at the federal level in 1970 in spite of fierce opposition from many employer groups. Like the Texas act, the federal one was the result of a compromise between business and labor. Richard Nixon signed it into law only months after Yarborough had been defeated by Lloyd Bentsen in the Democratic primary. See Evans, *Tragedy at Work*, 12.

50. Berman, *Death on the Job*, 56.

51. State Health Department, "Occupational Safety in Texas," 1–2, and table entitled "Occupational Safety in Texas."

52. "Report and Recommendations of the Governor's Task Force on Work-Related Accidents," sent to Governor William F. Clements by Dr. Richard McBurney, chairman of the task force created by Executive Order WPC-31B, 15 March 1982, (Austin: n.d.); and "Recommendations of Governor's Job Injury Interagency Council and Advisory Committee," sent to Governor Mark White by Allen Parker, Sr., chairman of the council created by Executive Order MW-22, 17 May 1984 (Austin: December 1984).

53. "Report and Recommendations of the Governor's Task Force," 7.

54. "Safety Bill Fought," *Texas Observer* 52 (25 February 1961): 1.

55. Fred Bonavita, "Job Safety Conditions in State 'Intolerable'?" *Houston Post*, 3 January 1987, sec. A, p. 5.

56. For evidence of the link between strong unions and workers' remuneration, see Beth A. Rubin, "Class Struggle American Style: Unions, Strikes and Wages," *American Sociological Review* 51 (October 1986): 618–33.

57. See Richard B. Freeman and James L. Medoff, *What Do Unions Do?* (New York: Basic Books, 1984). For a summary of their findings, see pp. 19–25. See also Derek C. Bok and John T. Dunlop, *Labor and the American Community* (New York: Simon & Schuster, 1970).

58. On labor discrimination against blacks nationally, see Philip S. Foner, *Organized Labor and the Black Worker, 1619–1981*, 2d ed. (New York: International Publishers, 1982), especially chaps. 21–26; and Ray Marshall, *The Negro and Organized Labor* (New York: John Wiley & Sons, 1965). On Texas union discrimina-

tion, see F. Ray Marshall and Vernon M. Briggs, Jr., *The Negro and Apprenticeship* (Baltimore: Johns Hopkins University Press, 1967), 175–81. Harry Hubbard, president of the Texas AFL-CIO, admitted in 1984 that while apprenticeship programs in 1984 were more open to minorities than ten years before, there was still resistance. Interview with the author, 1 August 1984.

59. "Houston Lawmakers Respond to Daniel Charter Criticism," *Houston Post*, 6 August 1974, sec. A, p. 8.

60. Harry Hubbard interview; and Robert Garland Landolt, *The Mexican-American Workers of San Antonio, Texas* (New York: Arno Press, 1976), 135–38.

61. Harry Hubbard interview.

62. F. Ray Marshall, *Labor in the South* (Cambridge, Mass.: Harvard University Press, 1967), 25.

63. Ibid., 27.

64. Interview with the author, 19 June 1984.

65. George Norris Green, *The Establishment in Texas Politics: The Primitive Years, 1938–1957* (Westport, Conn., and London: Greenwood Press, 1979), 58–60.

66. Ibid., 62, 90; and J. Earl Williams, *Plantation Politics: The Southern Economic Heritage* (Austin, Texas: Futura Press, 1972), 120.

67. Marshall, *Labor in the South*, 256; and Green, *Establishment in Texas Politics*, 70.

68. Don E. Carleton, *Red Scare! Right-wing Hysteria, Fifties Fanaticism, and Their Legacy in Texas* (Austin: Texas Monthly Press, 1985), 19. On labor's philosophy, see Selig Perlman, "The Basic Philosophy of the American Labor Movement," *Annals of The American Academy of Political and Social Science* 274 (March 1951): 57–63 (quotation on p. 61).

69. Carleton, *Red Scare!* 19–20, 28. The distinction between Communist influence and Communist domination is obvious, although the CIO's enemies preferred to ignore it.

70. Green, *Establishment in Texas Politics*, 103.

71. Wilbourn E. Benton, *Texas: Its Government and Politics*, 3d ed. (Englewood Cliffs, N.J.: Prentice-Hall, 1972), 352.

72. Chris Dixie, interview with the author, 12 February 1987.

73. Ronnie Dugger, *The Politician: The Life and Times of Lyndon Johnson: The Drive for Power, from the Frontier to Master of the Senate* (New York and London: W. W. Norton, 1982), 290.

74. Interview with the author, August 1984.

75. Marshall, *Labor in the South*, 299.

76. *The Handbook of Texas: A Supplement* 3 (1976): 489.

77. U.S. Bureau of the Census, *Statistical Abstract of the United States, 1988* (Washington, D.C.: U.S. Government Printing Office, 1987), 401.

78. Freeman and Medoff, *What Do Unions Do?*, 31.

79. Robert Coles, *Privileged Ones: The Well-Off and the Rich in America*, vol. 5, *Children of Crisis* (Boston and Toronto: Little, Brown and Company, 1977), chap. 3.

80. Freeman and Medoff's data on union membership came from the 1977 Cur-

rent Population Survey of the Bureau of Labor Statistics, while their data on work-ers' desire to join a union were from the 1977 Quality of Employment Survey conducted by the Institute of Social Research, University of Michigan. Both sam-ples were constructed to represent the nation's private-sector employees.

81. Robert W. Glover and Allan G. King, "Organized Labor in Texas," in *Dy-namics of Growth: An Economic Profile of Texas*, ed. Louis J. Rodriguez (Austin, Texas: Madrona Press, 1978), 142.

82. Ibid., 152.

83. Ibid.

7. Money and Politics

1. This research project was carried out by the author and two Rice undergrad-uate students, David Fleischer and Becky Mathre. Data from the Texas secretary of state's office were used. The results were reported in Chandler Davidson, David Fleischer, and Becky Mathre, "The Influence of Money on Elections: The Texas Case" (paper presented at the annual meeting of the Southwestern Sociolog-ical Association in Dallas, Texas, 30 March–2 April 1977).

2. David F. Prindle, *Petroleum Politics and the Texas Railroad Commission* (Austin: University of Texas Press, 1981), 168–79. Prindle believes that the influ-ence of money may be particularly great in railroad commission contests because of their low profile.

The influence of money in Texas elections is even more plausible in light of the research of Murray and Tedin, whose study of vote switching during the 1978 gubernatorial campaign found that multimillionaire Bill Clements, who began with virtually no name identification, was able, through massive spending on ad-vertising, to win over large numbers of voters who had planned to vote Demo-cratic. The authors conclude that "electoral success . . . comes to depend more than ever on the personal attributes of the candidates, and their ability to raise funds and exploit modern campaign technologies." See Kent L. Tedin and Richard W. Murray, "Dynamics of Candidate Choice in a State Election," *Journal of Poli-tics* 43 (May 1981): 455.

3. Ann Arnold and Ron Hutcheson, "Consultants Thriving on Election," *Fort Worth Star-Telegram*, 10 October 1982, sec. A, pp. 29, 36 (media expenditures are on p. 29).

4. Ibid., p. 36.

5. Arthur Wiese and Rosalind Jackler, "Houston Executive Top Political Con-tributor," *Houston Post*, 29 November 1981, sec. D, p. 8.

6. James E. Anderson, Richard W. Murray, and Edward L. Farley, *Texas Poli-tics: An Introduction*, 4th ed. (New York and other cities: Harper & Row, 1984), 51–52.

7. Virginia Ellis, "Clements Quietly Organizing Move to Reform Campaign Fi-nancing Laws," *Houston Post*, 10 July 1988, sec. A, p. 13.

8. For the amount of political contributions Manges made in 1982, see Michael Holmes, "Recipients of Manges' Largesse Eye Next Step," *Houston Post*, 12 June 1988, sec. B, p. 4; for other details on Manges, see Mike Cochrane, "The Desert

Fox," ibid., sec. B, pp. 1, 4; and *Dallas Times Herald*, 3 October 1982. For information on Robert J. Perry, see Virginia J. Ellis, "Houston Builder Gives but Says He'll Never Seek Office," *Dallas Times Herald*, 3 October 1982, sec. A, p. 7.

9. Larry L. Berg, Larry L. Eastland, and Sherry Bebitch Jeffe found in their study of a sample of 175 California donors of $500 or more to state or national elections between 1968 and 1972 that most were quite affluent by standards of the day. See their "Characteristics of Large Campaign Contributors," *Social Science Quarterly* 62 (September 1981): 412.

10. Bernard Rapoport, one of the few liberal Texas big spenders today, told a reporter in 1974 that he spent about "$25,000 per election year, more in Presidential years." This would come to about $55,000 in 1985 dollars. See Jon Ford, "Texas: Big Money," in *Campaign Money: Reform and Reality in the States*, ed. Herbert E. Alexander (New York: Free Press, 1976), 93.

11. "Contributions to the 1944 campaign in the state of Texas of $500.00 or over in amount," Walter G. Hall papers, Woodson Research Center, Rice University.

12. Ford, "Texas: Big Money," 87.

13. In recent years, Clinton Manges, another big donor to liberals, has emerged in the public arena. Manges, a South Texas rancher and oilman who was involved in the notoriously corrupt politics of the counties bordering the Rio Grande River, is not particularly liberal himself. His antics have proved an embarrassment to some of his beneficiaries. Some hard-pressed liberals, however, have swallowed hard and taken money from Manges, who may dispense great quantities in a given election year. Several moderate-to-liberal candidates who won office in 1982 were indebted to him, and at least three—Land Commissioner Garry Mauro, Attorney General Jim Mattox, and Texas supreme court justice William W. Kilgarlin—subsequently took actions (entirely legal) in their official capacities that added several million dollars to Manges's fortune. See Richard H. Kraemer and Charldean Newell, *Texas Politics*, 2d ed. (St. Paul, Minn.: West Publishing Company, 1984), 107; and for Manges's donations to Mauro, Mattox, and Kilgarlin see "Study Reveals Source of Political Donations," *Houston Post*, 15 October 1982, sec. A, p. 9.

14. George Thayer, *Who Shakes the Money Tree? American Campaign Financing Practices from 1789 to the Present* (New York: Simon & Schuster, 1973), chap. 7.

15. Herbert E. Alexander et al., *Financing the 1972 Election* (Lexington, Mass., Toronto, and London: D. C. Heath, 1976), 460–61, for background on Watergate events; see J. Anthony Lukas, *Nightmare: The Underside of the Nixon Years* (New York: Viking Press, 1976), 141, for Gulf Resources' problems with the Environmental Protection Agency. Robert Allen's laundering was at the time legal; and so was the amount contributed, arriving as it did before the Federal Election Campaign Act went into effect.

16. Alexander, *Financing the 1972 Election*, 461.

17. Ibid., 472 and 475.

18. Details on the Murchisons' gift are outlined in James R. Polk, "Murchison Is Said to Link Nixon to Role in Donation," *New York Times*, 19 July 1974, sec. 1, p. 19.

19. Alexander et al., *Financing the 1972 Election*, 194, 198.

20. All contribution amounts are given in Art Wiese, "Nixon's Texas Fund-Raising Relied on Big Donors," *Houston Post*, 3 October 1973, sec. A, p. 3.

21. John R. Knaggs, *Two-Party Texas: The John Tower Era, 1961–1984* (Austin, Texas: Eakin Press, 1986), 291.

22. See Michael C. Jensen, "9 Corporate 'Political Action' Units Gave 20% of Aid in '76 Campaigns," *New York Times*, 14 September 1977, sec. D, p. 1.

23. Helen Jardine, "Business PACs—The Real Majority," *Texas Observer* 70 (1 December 1978): 7–10.

24. Ibid., 8–9.

25. Jim Landers, "Voters Deal Major Defeat to Oil Industry PACs," *Dallas Morning News*, 7 November 1982, sec. A, p. 25.

26. This information on HOUPAC is taken from Kathy Lewis, "Houston PACs," *Houston Post*, 1 November 1982, sec. A, p. 9.

27. See Brent Manley, "Texans Pouring Big Bucks into N.C. Campaigns," *Houston Post*, 4 November 1984, sec. B, p. 7.

28. All information and quotations on the Tenneco PAC are taken from Lewis, "Houston PACs."

29. Virginia Ellis, "Lobbyists' Coalition Packs Clout," *Dallas Times Herald*, 18 July 1982, sec. A, pp. 1, 28 (numbers and expenditures are on p. 28).

30. Ibid., 28 (all quotations).

31. See "Ex-Gulf Lobbyist Says LBJ Used as Conduit," *Houston Post*, 2 June 1978, sec. A, pp. 1, 19 (for figures and details of Wild's activities); Arthur Wiese, "Former Gulf Lobbyist Details Contributions to Politicians," ibid., 3 June 1978, sec. B, p. 5 (for more details on Wild); "Phillips Co. Fined $30,000 by U.S. Judge," *Houston Post*, 23 November 1977, sec. F, p. 10 (for Phillips Petroleum's activities); "U.S. Fines Gulf Oil $229,500 for Gifts in Political Drives," *New York Times*, 12 November 1977, sec. D, p. 27 (gives amount Gulf Oil donated to politicians in United States and overseas); Darrell Hancock, "Gulf's Texas Gifts Reported Untouchable," *Houston Post*, 7 January 1976, sec. C, p. 15 (for statement that politicians receiving Gulf funds did not know the source of the contribution); Art Wiese, "Illegal Political Links Revealed in Testimony," ibid., 14 December 1975, sec. B, p. 9 (for details on the relationship between Texas oil companies and the state's politicians in the 1960s and early 1970s); "Occidental Report 'Amazes' Permian Corp. Official," ibid., 22 April 1978, sec. A, p. 23 (for details on Occidental Petroleum's involvement in illegal political contributions); Sam Fletcher, "Tenneco Admits Illegal Gifts," ibid., 15 February 1976, sec. A, pp. 1, 2 (for details of Tenneco's illegal political contributions); "Tenneco Named in Stockholder Suits," ibid., 24 March 1976, sec. A, p. 7 (for lawsuits stemming from company's illegal political contributions); for illegal political contributions made by Zale Corp. see "Zale Slapped with SEC Suit," ibid., 20 August 1977, sec. C, p. 6; and "Louisiana Expects No Tenneco Actions," ibid., 16 February 1976, sec. A, pp. 1, 19 (for details of Tenneco's illegal political contributions in Louisiana). See also Herbert E. Alexander, *Financing the 1976 Election* (Washington, D.C.: Congressional Quarterly Press, 1979), 573–79, 583–97.

32. Jardine, "Business PACs—The Real Majority," 7; and Jim Hightower, "Lobbyists," *Texas Observer* 73 (13 February 1981): 2, 18.

33. Harvey Katz, "The First Time I Saw Ben Barnes . . . ," *Texas Observer* 64 (21 July 1972): 9.

34. Ford, "Texas: Big Money," 90–91, 97.

35. Ibid., 97–98.

36. Berg, Eastland, and Jeffe, "Characteristics of Large Campaign Contributors," 418–19.

37. Mark Sanders, "Money Given to Politicians Well-Spent, Utility Says," *Houston Post*, 9 February 1986, sec. A, pp. 1, 18 (quotations are on p. 1).

38. For Ford fund-raiser, see "Ford Draws Dollars," ibid., 25 September 1975, sec. C, p. 1.

39. See "Biggest White Contributors on Best Boards, Paper Reports," ibid., 7 October 1985, sec. A, p. 5.

8. The Struggle for Control of the Democratic Party

1. Quoted in Hawkins Henley Menefee, Jr., "The Two-Party Democrats, the Study of a Texas Political Faction" (M.A. thesis, University of Texas at Austin, 1970), 11.

2. Clifton McCleskey, E. Larry Dickens, and Allan K. Butcher, *The Government and Politics of Texas*, 5th ed. (Boston and Toronto: Little, Brown and Company, 1975), 56.

3. "Dear Reader . . . ," *Texas Observer* 68 (4 June 1976): 13.

4. Pendleton Herring, *The Politics of Democracy: American Parties in Action* (New York and Toronto: Rinehart & Company, 1940), 229.

5. Stuart Long, interview with the author, 3 June 1976 (Texas Oral History Project, Rice University), 3–4.

6. While Alexander Heard depicted the Regulars as being motivated primarily by economics, their leaders made what use they could of the race issue to fragment liberal opposition. See Heard's *A Two-Party South?* (Chapel Hill: University of North Carolina Press, 1952), 258–59.

7. For an account of New Dealer state party chairman Harry Seay's efforts in this regard, see his letter to Walter G. Hall, 15 November 1945 (Walter G. Hall Papers, Woodson Research Center, Rice University).

8. Ronnie Dugger, *The Politician: The Life and Times of Lyndon Johnson: The Drive for Power, from the Frontier to Master of the Senate* (New York and London: W. W. Norton, 1982), 262.

9. Walter G. Hall to Charles E. Hawes, Jr., et al., 27 September 1944 (Hall Papers).

10. James L. Gibson, John P. Frendreis, and Laura L. Vertz, "Party Dynamics in the 1980s: Change in County Party Organizational Stength, 1980–1984" (Paper delivered at the annual meeting of the Midwest Political Science Association, Chicago, 1985), 2.

11. Harry L. Seay to Walter G. Hall, 15 November 1945 (Hall Papers).

12. Ibid.

13. Wilbourn E. Benton, *Texas: Its Government and Politics*, 2d ed. (Englewood Cliffs, N.J.: Prentice-Hall, 1966), 114.

14. George Norris Green, *The Establishment in Texas Politics: The Primitive*

Years, 1938–1957 (Westport, Conn., and London: Greenwood Press, 1979), 141. See also Eugene W. Jones, ed., *The Texas Country Editor: H. M. Baggerly Takes a Grass-Roots Look at National Politics* (Cleveland, Ohio, and New York: World Publishing Company, 1966), 156–58.

15. Green, *Establishment in Texas Politics*, 145.

16. O. Douglas Weeks, *Texas Presidential Politics in 1952* (Austin: Institute of Public Affairs, University of Texas, 1953), 46.

17. Green, *Establishment in Texas Politics*, 146.

18. Weeks, *Texas Presidential Politics in 1952*, 90–91.

19. For an account of the *Observer's* founding, see Larry Goodwyn, "Dugger's *Observer*," *Texas Observer* 66 (27 December 1974): 3–8. Since 1963 the paper has been issued biweekly.

20. Billie Carr, "Memories of Conventions Past," *Texas Observer* 68 (1 October 1976): 5.

21. Allan Shivers, interview with Joe B. Frantz, 29 May 1970 (Lyndon Baines Johnson Oral History Project, Lyndon Baines Johnson Library, Austin), 12, 14.

22. Green, *Establishment in Texas Politics*, 173.

23. Margaret Carter of Fort Worth explained why liberal organizers—many of whom were women—were so strongly opposed to the election of Bentsen's wife as committeewoman:

> [Before the 1956 convention opened] I found out that Lyndon was pushing Mrs. Lloyd Bentsen for national committeewoman. So, we got up to Ed Levy's suite. . . . I knew some of the people . . . and as soon as I came in, they quit talking to each other. So, as soon as I got a drink in my hand, I said, "Who is going to be national committeewoman?" They were sure I was pledged to Frankie Randolph and so nobody would rise to the bait and there was a long pause and then somebody said, "Well, who do you think it is going to be?" I said, "Well, I don't know, but it sure isn't going to be Lloyd Bentsen!" Poor old Ed realized that there was tension at his party, so he came wandering over with about his fifth drink in his hand and he said, "Lloyd Bentsen can't be the national committeewoman, he's a man."

At that moment in the interview, Mrs. Carter laughed. "That was the feminist point we tried to make during a good part of the convention," she said. "Whichever woman became the national committeewoman should be someone who had worked hard in the campaign, not someone whose husband was given the committeewoman's seat as a consolation prize." See Margaret Carter, interview with the author, 25 October 1975 (Southern Oral History Program, University of North Carolina at Chapel Hill), 58.

24. Green, *Establishment in Texas Politics*, 177.

25. Ibid., 177–78.

26. O. Douglas Weeks, *Texas in the 1960 Presidential Election* (Austin: Institute of Public Affairs, University of Texas, 1961), 7; and George Fuermann, *Reluctant Empire* (Garden City, N.Y.: Doubleday, 1957), 72.

27. Weeks, *Texas in the 1960 Presidential Election*, 11.

28. Ibid., 27.

29. "Delegation to L.A.," *Texas Observer* 52 (1 July 1960): 3.

30. Weeks, *Texas in the 1960 Presidential Election*, 34.

31. "Brotherhood in El Paso," *Texas Observer* 54 (21 September 1962): 1.

32. Jim Clark, "The Democratic Party in Atlantic City," ibid., 56 (4 September 1964): 4.

33. Greg Olds, "Democrats Feign Unity and Harmony," ibid., 58 (30 September 1966), 9.

34. Herbert S. Parmet, *The Democrats: The Years after FDR* (New York: Macmillan, 1976), 230. Watson had been an employee and political lieutenant of E. B. Germany—a steel magnate, former Texas Regular, and conservative campaign donor—for many years.

35. Quoted in Parmet, *The Democrats*, 231.

36. John S. Saloma III and Frederick H. Sontag, *Parties: The Real Opportunity for Effective Citizen Politics* (New York: Alfred A. Knopf, 1972), 6.

37. Paul T. David, Ralph M. Goldman, and Richard C. Bain, *The Politics of National Party Conventions*, rev. ed. (Gloucester, Mass.: Peter Smith, 1972), 236–37 (quotations on p. 236).

38. Greg Olds, "Connally Retains Control," *Texas Observer* 60 (10 May 1968): 4.

39. "John Connally, Favorite Son," ibid. (21 June 1968): 1.

40. Greg Olds, "Liberal Lunacy," ibid., 14.

41. "A Fourth Party," ibid. (12 July 1968): 11.

42. "Showdown in Chicago," ibid. (23 August 1968): 1.

43. "Vice President Connally?" ibid. (9 August 1968): 8.

44. Author's estimate from the delegates' list in "The Competing Delegations," ibid., 60 (23 August 1968): 3.

45. Fred Bonavita, "Demo Panel Votes to Drop Unit Rule," *Houston Post*, 24 August 1968, sec. 1, pp. 1, 13 (for larger picture); and "Connally Backers Fear Trouble on Unit Rule," ibid., sec. 1, p. 13 (for specific details on Connally and the Texas delegation).

46. "The Opening Skirmish against Boss Rule," *Texas Observer* 60 (6 September 1968): 2.

47. Bonavita, "Demo Panel Votes to Drop Unit Rule," sec. 1, pp. 1, 13 (quotations on p. 13). Erwin was the only speaker in two days of testimony before the rules committee to support the unit rule. See ibid.

48. Ibid., 13 (for threat to support Johnson).

49. "Amidst the Wreckage, Hubert," *Texas Observer* 60 (6 September 1968): 1.

50. Saloma and Sontag, *Parties*, 14.

51. Fred Bonavita, "Unit Rule Death Means More Work," *Houston Post*, 31 August 1968, sec. 4, p. 8.

52. Saloma and Sontag, *Parties*, 19.

53. Ibid., 21.

54. Parmet, *The Democrats*, 295.

55. Ronnie Dugger, "Observations," *Texas Observer* 64 (7 July 1972): 19.

56. Molly Ivins, "How Texas Voted and, More or Less, Why," ibid., 64 (4 August 1972): 5.

57. Molly Ivins, "Everything You Ever Wanted to Know About the September State Conventions," ibid. (6 October 1972): 5.

58. For 1972 Texas delegation makeup, see R. W. Apple, Jr., "Texas Yields Boon to McGovern," *New York Times*, 15 June 1972, sec. 1, p. 36.

59. James W. Davis, *National Conventions: Nominations under the Big Top* (Woodbury, N.Y.: Barron's Educational Series, 1972), 31; *Congressional Quarterly Weekly*, (16 August 1975), p. 1, 118.

60. "A Class Challenge," *Texas Observer* 60 (6 September 1968): 5.

61. *The Activist* (Cleveland, Ohio: Committee for New Political Initiatives, January 1976).

62. Liberal discontent with Guest's chairmanship had festered since he was first appointed by Briscoe after his election in 1972. Guest was challenged in 1974 by Houston city controller Leonel Castillo, who garnered over 40 percent of the vote in the contest. See Felton West, "Castillo Boosted for State Democratic Leader," *Houston Post*, 16 September 1974, sec. A, pp. 1, 18 (quotation on p. 1).

63. Bo Byers, "Liberals Gain on Democrat Executive Panel," *Houston Chronicle*, 17 September 1978, sec. A, pp. 1, 6 (quoted phrase on p. 1).

64. Matthew Lyon, "The Democratic Convention," *Texas Observer* 72 (4 July 1980): 6.

65. Bo Byers and Joe Nolan, "Carter Gains 104 Texas Delegates; Kennedy but 38," *Houston Chronicle*, 22 June 1980, sec. 1, p. 23 (for Texas liberals' support of Carter); "SDEC Expected to Keep Liberal-Moderate Flavor," *Houston Post*, 28 September 1980, sec. A, p. 21 (for quotation and listing of committee members); and Jane Ely and Monica Reeves, "State's Democrats Elect Sherman Lawyer," ibid., sec. A, pp. 1, 23.

66. For Carr's description of the 1982 Texas state convention, see Jane Ely and Fred Bonavita, "Democrats Close State Convention United in Harmony," *Houston Post*, 12 September 1982, sec. B, p. 2.

67. Ibid.

68. Alexander P. Lamis, *The Two-Party South*, expanded ed. (New York and Oxford: Oxford University Press, 1988), 208.

69. Nene Foxhall, "Frankie," *Houston Chronicle Texas Magazine*, 3 July 1983, pp. 6–10 (quotation on p. 10).

9. The Year of the Liberal Breakthrough

1. Billie Carr, interview with the author, 29 August 1974.

2. "Bentsen of Texas 5th Democrat in Race," *New York Times*, 18 February 1975, sec. 1, pp. 1, 15.

3. Darrell Hancock, "Primary Election Law Change Eyed to Aid Bentsen," *Houston Post*, 18 February 1975, sec. A, p. 6.

4. State Representative Sarah Weddington, interview with the author, 3 January 1977. In 1972 liberals had criticized Bentsen and other conservatives, including Robert Strauss, national party treasurer, and John Connally, still a Democrat at the time, for having modified state party rules to include a winner-take-all provision as a functional equivalent of the old unit rule. Bentsen denied such equiva-

lence and stated, "I want to see Texas Democrats conform fully to the new party rules in substance and in spirit . . . we should have nothing less than proper, proportional representation for these groups." See "Bentsen Reiterates Strong Opposition Over 'Unit Rule,' " *Houston Post*, 5 February 1972, sec. A, p. 11. The previous year, liberals criticized conservatives who were considering using the "favorite son" gambit in 1972 as another substitute for the unit rule, because it denied voters the chance to choose among serious candidates for the nomination. Bentsen was mentioned as a potential favorite son at that time. See Fred Bonavita, "Democratic Group Raps Favorite Sons," ibid., 10 October 1971, sec. A, p. 8.

5. "Rep. Hall to Head Democratic Panel," *Houston Post*, 11 February 1975, sec. A, p. 4.

6. "Winning and Losing with LBJr.," *Texas Observer* 67 (14 March 1975): 3.

7. Felton West, "State Committee Passes Primary Bill," *Houston Post*, 27 March 1975, sec. A, p. 16. Some of the more discriminatory features of the bill were gradually deleted during the legislative fight for its approval. For example, uncommitted slates were allowed, and presidential candidates were not required to qualify in all thirty-one districts.

8. "Bentsen Defends Presidential Primary Proposal," ibid., 25 March 1975, sec. C, p. 18 (all three quotations); and Darrell Hancock, "Primary Bill Revisions Supported," ibid., 25 February 1975, sec. A, pp. 1, 17 (for how bill would benefit Bentsen). An activist of moderate persuasion told the author that in her view the Bentsen measure was far more unfair than the old unit rule. "At least the unit rule required the 'winner' to obtain a majority before he could 'take all,' " she said. Anonymous interview with the author, 16 September 1976.

9. "Winning and Losing with LBJr.," *Texas Observer* 67 (14 March 1975): 3–4; and see Darrell Hancock, "Primary Bill Battered," *Houston Post*, 26 February 1975, sec. A, pp. 1, 13.

10. "Winning and Losing with LBJr.," *Texas Observer*, 4.

11. "Primary for 1976 Is Voted in Texas," *New York Times*, 10 May 1975, p. 27.

12. The account of the September Scholz Garten meeting is based on notes taken by the author.

13. Darrell Hancock, "Harris to Run; Liberals Fail to Unify Strategy," *Houston Post*, 14 December 1975, sec. A, pp. 1, 2 (quotation on p. 2).

14. Billie Carr, interview with the author, 27 July 1976. There is obvious irony in a Carter organizer's not wanting "Baptist" delegates. Among Texas liberals, some of them Baptists, the word has a special connotation: right-wing fundamentalists.

15. Ibid.

16. John Pouland, interview with the author, 14 December 1976.

17. Richard Vara, "Delegate Threat Planned for Bentsen, Wallace," *Houston Post*, 11 January 1976, sec. A, p. 13.

18. "Labor Group Won't Endorse," *Houston Post*, 23 January 1976, sec. B, p. 1.

19. The Bentsen delegates were mistakenly described by reporter Paul Burka as "the most balanced delegate slate in Texas history." He contended that "as recently as 1968 the Texas delegation was composed almost exclusively of conser-

vative Democrats, but Bentsen gave a piece of the action to labor, blacks, Mexican-Americans, white liberals, and women." This offer "was no token gesture, either—liberals were included in large numbers." See Paul Burka, "Gearing Up," *Texas Monthly* 4 (May 1976): 12–14 (quotation on p. 14). There followed a list of ten names of members of these groups, one of whom was moderate-to-conservative. But the entire statewide Bentsen slate was composed of ninety-eight people, and the liberal contingent thus constituted about 10 percent. John Connally's 104-member delegation to Chicago in 1968, stacked with conservatives as it was, actually contained a slightly larger percentage of liberals.

20. Carrin Patman, interview with the author, 16 September 1976.

21. It is not clear whether the $2.3 million included money spent in Bentsen's simultaneous campaign for reelection to the Senate. See *Presidential Pre-Nomination Receipts and Expenditures, 1976 Campaign*, FEC Disclosure Series, no. 1 (Washington, D.C.: U.S. Federal Election Commission, September 1976).

22. Darrell Hancock, "Sen. Bentsen Calls Off Presidential Campaign," *Houston Post*, 11 February 1976, sec. A, pp. 1, 13 (quotation on p. 1).

23. "Unitary Primary?" *Texas Observer* 68 (16 July 1976): 9.

24. Notes of the author, taken at the conservative caucus.

25. Carrin Patman is quoted in Felton West, "Texas Sending Fresh Faces to N.Y.," *Houston Post*, 10 July 1976, sec. A, p. 4.

26. Cecile Harrison, interview with the author, 10 February 1977.

27. Billie Carr, interview with the author, 27 July 1976.

28. Ibid.

29. Ibid. This was a voice vote that was not possible to tabulate. On two other litmus-test issues to reach the floor, proportional representation and 15 percent committee member support of reports, the Texans voted 58 to 45 and 70 to 56, respectively, for the more progressive point of view. See Felton West, "Democrats Ban Winner-Take-All Presidential Primaries," *Houston Post*, 16 July 1976, sec. A, p. 17.

30. Cragg Hines, "Carter Blasts Texas Primary Law," *Houston Chronicle*, 1 May 1976, sec. 1, p. 4 (first quotation); and Tony Castro, "Texas Political Establishment Troubles Seen in Reagan Win," *Houston Post*, 8 May 1976, sec. A, p. 4 (second quotation).

31. Letter from Frank Moore to all delegates, 11 August 1976.

32. Cited in Fred Bonavita, "Bullock Backs Bid by Tatum, Assails Guest," *Houston Post*, 20 August 1976, sec. A, p. 9.

33. "Guest's Indications Differed from Ledger," *Fort Worth Star-Telegram*, 2 September 1976, sec. B, p. 4.

34. Ibid.

35. Accountant's report circulated by Guest at the convention.

36. Leonel Castillo, interview with the author, 13 December 1976.

37. Calvin Guest and John Henry Tatum, interviews with the author, 18 September 1976.

38. Billie Carr, interview with the author, 18 September 1976; and Jane Ely and Fred Bonavita, "Guest Beats Tatum," *Houston Post*, 19 September 1976, sec. A, pp. 1, 2 (quotation on p. 2).

39. Ben Reyes and John Brunson, interviews with the author, summer 1978.

10. The Rise of Right-Wing Republicanism

1. Jan Jarboe, "Lord of the Valley," *Texas Monthly* 14 (January 1986): 184–85, 232 (quotation on p. 232).

2. There is a difference of opinion among scholars of Republicanism on the actual point when the new Republican party came into being in Texas. See Roger M. Olien, *From Token to Triumph: The Texas Republicans Since 1920* (Dallas: Southern Methodist University Press, 1982), 153 ff.

3. On the causes of this countermovement, see James L. Sundquist, *Dynamics of the Party System: Alignment and Realignment of Political Parties in the United States*, rev. ed. (Washington, D.C.: Brookings Institution, 1983), chap. 17; Donald S. Strong, *Issue Voting and Party Realignment* (University, Ala.: University of Alabama Press, 1977), chap. 4; and Allen J. Matusow, *The Unraveling of America: A History of Liberalism in the 1960s* (New York and other cities: Harper & Row, 1984), pt 3.

4. The party had also developed a well-staffed and well-funded headquarters. By 1986 the Republican party budget for the year was $2.5 million (as compared with the Democrats' budget of between $700,000 and $800,000) and it had fifteen full-time staff workers, "70 volunteers who work[ed] the phone banks, and all of the names of the state's eight million registered voters on computer." See Dave Denison, "Are We There Yet?" *Texas Observer* 78 (13 June 1986): 7. The actual number of Republican elected officials, moreover, may understate the change in party identification among voters, thanks to the tendency of incumbent Democrats to have an advantage in reelection bids. See Richard G. Hutcheson III, "The Inertial Effect of Incumbency and Two-Party Politics: Elections to the House of Representatives from the South, 1952–1974," *American Political Science Review* 69 (December 1975): 1399–1401.

5. "Political Intelligence," *Texas Observer* 58 (2 September 1966): 14.

6. Jim Simmon, "GOP Elects Strake to Head State Panel Amid Pleas for Unity," *Houston Post*, 1 May 1983, sec. A, p. 26.

7. Tom Pardue and Sharon T. Thomas, "The Republican Party in Texas: The Elites and Their Effect on Party Strength" (Paper delivered at the annual meeting of the Southwestern Social Science Association, Houston, 1980), p. 14 and table 3.

8. Harry Hurt III, "George Bush, Plucky Lad," *Texas Monthly* 11 (June 1983): 139–43, 192–208 (especially p. 198).

9. Cragg Hines, "Bush's Career Spent Fighting Labels," *Houston Chronicle*, 17 July 1980, sec. 1, p. 15.

10. Stewart Davis, "Don Labels McLendon Connally's Hatchet Man," *Houston Chronicle*, 9 April 1964, sec. 1, p. 13.

11. Ronnie Dugger, "The Substance of the Senate Contest," *Texas Observer* 56 (18 September 1964): 5.

12. See Jack W. Germond and Jules Witcover, "Bush's Effort to Broaden Base Could Hurt His Image," *Houston Post*, 7 February 1986, sec. B, p. 2 (for Bush's support of Goldwater); Bush's remark regarding Falwell's "moral vision" for America is cited in Phil Gailey, "Bush Salutes Falwell Conservatism," *New York Times*, 25 January 1986, p. 8; and Gerald M. Boyd, "The Front-Runner," *New York Times Magazine*, 23 February 1986, pp. 28–30, 80–84 (quotation is on p. 80).

13. Art Wiese, "Ford, Reagan Battle Lines Already Forming in State," *Houston Post*, 12 January 1976, sec. A, pp. 1, 17 (first quotation on p. 1; second quotation on p. 17).

14. Griffin Smith, "Little Big Man," *Texas Monthly* 5 (January 1977): 84–87, 130–38 (especially pp. 131–32); for Tower's support of both Reagan and Nixon see "Highlights of Tower's Life, Career," under the "May 2, 1968" paragraph in *Houston Post*, 24 August 1983, sec. A, p. 18.

15. On Republican fund-raisers, see Art Wiese, "Ford, Reagan Battle Lines Already Forming in State," *Houston Post*, pp. 1, 17 (especially p. 17); Brent Manley, "Texans Pouring Big Bucks into N.C. Campaigns," ibid., 4 November 1984, sec. B, p. 7; and "Contributors of $1,000 or More to Race Listed," ibid.

16. Austin heiress Ellen Clayton Garwood, both a wife and a mother of Texas Supreme Court judges, was among several right-wing Republicans who funded mercenaries fighting Communists in various parts of the world. In 1986 she attracted national attention by spending $65,000 to recondition a helicopter named "the Lady Ellen" for use by the Nicaraguan Contras. See Dave Denison, "Friends of the 'Freedom Fighters,' " *Texas Observer* 79 (7 March 1986): 1, 7–13 (helicopter anecdote and quotation are on p. 8).

The Illuminati, a secret Masonic society founded in 1776, has been a favorite target since the 1790s of American conspiracy theorists, who have held it responsible for everything from the French Revolution to the Poor People's March on Washington. Robert Welch, founder of the John Birch Society, popularized the theory again in the 1960s. See Seymour Martin Lipset and Earl Raab, *The Politics of Unreason: Right-Wing Extremism in America, 1790–1970* (New York, Evanston, Ill., and London: Harper & Row, 1970), 252–53. In 1981 oil heir Cullen Davis, one of the ninety-nine richest Texans described in chap. 4, explained to a reporter his view of the Illuminati as a worldwide plot against the family, religion, patriotism, and free enterprise. Davis's views of the Illuminati are contained in Jim Asker, "Davis, Wife Telling the World They've Found a Better Life," *Houston Post*, 5 September 1981, sec. AA, p. 5.

17. Southerners who had voted for Wallace in 1968 voted for Nixon three-to-one in 1972. See Alexander P. Lamis, *The Two-Party South*, expanded ed. (New York and Oxford: Oxford University Press, 1988), 30.

18. Lipset and Raab, *The Politics of Unreason*, 354 (for percentage of Birch Society members), 379 (for supporters of Wallace).

19. Earl Black and Merle Black, *Politics and Society in the South* (Cambridge, Mass., and London: Harvard University Press, 1987), 17. On the ideological makeup of "immigrants" compared with natives, see Joe Nolan, "New Texans Have Good News for GOP," *Houston Chronicle*, 13 August 1979, sec. 1, p. 16. On the disproportionate number of nonnative Texas Republicans, see James A. Dyer, Arnold Vedlitz, and David B. Hill, "New Voters, Switchers, and Political Party Realignment in Texas," *Western Political Quarterly* 41 (March 1988): 155–67 (see especially p. 164).

20. Dyer, Vedlitz, and Hill, "New Voters," 159.

21. The "Minute Women" in Houston, mostly wives of professionals and managers from upper-middle-class neighborhoods who staged the city's red scare in the 1950s, exemplified the radicals' hysteria. See Don E. Carleton, *Red Scare!*

Right-Wing Hysteria, Fifties Fanaticism and Their Legacy in Texas (Austin: Texas Monthly Press, 1985), 111–34.

22. David W. Reinhard, *The Republican Right since 1945* (Lexington: University Press of Kentucky, 1983), vii.

23. Richard Hofstadter, *The Paranoid Style in American Politics and Other Essays* (New York: Alfred A. Knopf, 1965).

24. Reinhard, *Republican Right since 1945*, p. 174.

25. For an account of an inquiring newsman's encounter with the John Birch Society in Houston, see Willie Morris, *North Toward Home* (Boston: Houghton Mifflin, 1967), chap. 8.

26. Benjamin R. Epstein and Arnold Forster, *Report on the John Birch Society: 1966* (New York: Vintage Books, 1966), 1–6, 84 (for details on the society in Texas), 90 (for data on *American Opinion*).

27. George Norris Green, "The Far Right Wing in Texas Politics, 1930's–1960's" (Ph.D. diss., Florida State University, 1966), 254 (first four quoted words and phrases), 255 (fifth quotation).

28. Goldwater disavowed the Birch Society in 1965, however, after his defeat. Reinhard, *Republican Right since 1945*, p. 176.

29. Reinhard, *Republican Right since 1945*, p. 194 (for number of delegates who were Birch Society members); and Epstein and Forster, *Report on the John Birch Society: 1966*, p. 82 (quoted word).

30. Lionel V. Patenaude, "The New Deal and Texas" (Ph.D. diss., University of Texas, 1953), 146–60.

31. Green, "Far Right Wing in Texas Politics," 210–11 (for biographical information on Haley), 213 (quotation); and Haley sketch in "The Six Who Want to Be Governor," *Texas Observer* 48 (25 July 1956): 8.

32. See Green, "Far Right Wing in Texas Politics," 214–16, for details.

33. Ibid., 215–18 (information on *American Mercury* is on p. 218).

34. Ibid., 219–21 (quotation on p. 219).

35. Ibid., 238–39 (first quoted word is on p. 238; figures on the book's sales are on p. 239); and J. Evetts Haley, *A Texan Looks at Lyndon: A Study in Illegitimate Power* (Canyon, Texas: Palo Duro Press, 1964), 172 (for Haley's comment on the Civil Rights Act), 173 (for Haley's comments on the Supreme Court), 217 (for his comments on Martin Luther King, Jr.), 253 (for last two comments on Johnson).

36. Quoted in Darrell Hancock, "Conservative Texas Delegation 100 Per Cent Reagan," *Houston Post*, 16 August 1976, sec. A, p. 8.

37. Unless otherwise noted, the following material on H. L. Hunt is taken from the investigative reportage contained in Harry Hurt III, *Texas Rich: The Hunt Dynasty from the Early Oil Days through the Silver Crash* (New York and London: W. W. Norton, 1981), 154, 179–87, 221, 245, 253, 264–65, 346–47, and 376.

38. For a brief history of the newspaper, see "H. L. Hunt's Paper Ends Publication," *New York Times*, 6 July 1975, p. 39.

39. Martin Waldron, "The Right-Wing 'Life Line' Program, Lacking H. L. Hunt's Aid, Has Lost Radio Outlets and Revenues," *New York Times*, 3 April 1975, p. 19.

40. Harry Hurt III, *Texas Rich*, 227–28.

41. On Stevenson, see "An Early Halloween in Big D," *Texas Observer* 55 (1

November 1963): 6; on the Johnsons, see Lawrence Wright, *In the New World: Growing up with America, 1960–1984* (New York: Alfred A. Knopf, 1988), 24–28.

42. See "Hunt's New Project," *Texas Observer* 57 (15 October 1965): 10. For an account of Hunt in the months after the assassination, see Robert G. Sherrill, "H. L. Hunt: Portrait of a Super-Patriot," *Nation* 198 (24 February 1964): 182–95.

43. See George Kuempel, "Bentsen Turned Tables on Right-Wing PAC," *Dallas Morning News*, 8 November 1982, sec. A, pp. 1, 5, for details of NCPAC; for a description of the Hunt barbecue, see Judy Klemesrud, "A Texas Gala at $1,000 a Head," *New York Times*, 23 August 1984, sec. C, p. 12 (quotation).

44. Dick J. Reavis, "The Politics of Armageddon," *Texas Monthly* 12 (October 1984): 162–66, 235–46 (quotation is on p. 162; see p. 164 for number of Texas Baptists and figures on the weekly newspaper circulation).

45. George Dugan, "Baptists Release Integration Vote," *New York Times*, 7 June 1968, sec. 1 (national edition).

46. Reavis, "Politics of Armageddon," 166, 235–38 (for biographical details).

47. Ibid., 162 (for membership figure), 165 (for real estate value); and "Criswell Seeking Young Successor," *Houston Post*, 11 January 1986, sec. C, p. 6 (quotation).

48. Joe Edward Barnhart, *The Southern Baptist Holy War* (Austin: Texas Monthly Press, 1986), 132–33; and Reavis, "Politics of Armageddon," 166 (second quotation), 243 (for Criswell's stance on civil rights); and John W. Storey, *Texas Baptist Leadership and Social Christianity, 1900–1980* (College Station: Texas A&M University Press, 1986), 183–84.

49. "Hunt's New Forum," *Texas Observer* 51 (1 January 1960): 1–3 (Criswell's endorsement of LIFE LINE is on p. 2); and "Criswell Reproached," ibid., 52 (22 July 1960): 5 (for Criswell's quotation regarding Kennedy's Catholicism as political tyranny). The story of H. L. Hunt sending out Criswell's sermon is included in "Criswell Seeking Young Successor," *Houston Post*, 11 January 1986, sec. C, p. 6.

Hunt endorsed the Democratic ticket on November 3, apparently convinced that it could better protect the oil depletion allowance. See O. Douglas Weeks, *Texas in the 1960 Presidential Election* (Austin: Institute of Public Affairs, University of Texas, 1961), 58.

50. Criswell's negative comments about Kennedy can be found in "Criswell's Attack," *Texas Observer* 52 (30 September 1960): 1–2 (quoted word on p. 2); and for Criswell's repudiation of Kennedy and support for Nixon, see Darrell Hancock, "Dallas Pastor Gives Blessing to President," *Houston Post*, 11 October 1976, sec. A, pp. 1, 3 (especially p. 3).

51. George Dugan, "Southern Baptists Approve a Strong Racial Stand," *New York Times*, 6 June 1968, p. 65.

52. George Dugan, "Baptists Release Integration Vote," ibid., 7 June 1968, p. 40.

53. See Reavis, "Politics of Armageddon," 243–44; and Storey, *Texas Baptist Leadership and Social Christianity*, 197–99. Leavis (pp. 243–44) claims that Criswell talked his board of deacons into agreeing to desegregate his church only a week before the convention elected him president, and announced the deacons' decision to his congregation on the Sunday following his election. Storey (p. 197)

puts the church's decision "a few months before the convention." In any event, when asked by reporters at the Houston convention how many black members his church had, Criswell "first avoided the question but later said that there were three." (G. Dugan, "Baptists Release Integration Vote," *New York Times*, 7 June 1968, p. 40.)

54. "Criswell's Attack," 1–2 (quoted words on p. 1).

55. Hancock, "Dallas Pastor Gives Blessing to President," 1, 3 (quotations on p. 3).

56. Charles Deaton, ed., *Texas Government Newsletter* 7 (22 January 1979): 1.

57. "Religion Dividing North, South?" *Houston Post*, 2 March 1985, sec. G, p. 6.

58. Reavis, "Politics of Armageddon," 245–46 (for information on Patterson and Pressler); and Jim Asker, "Southern Baptists Vote for Rogers," *Houston Post*, 13 June 1979, sec. A, p. 6 (for first quoted phrase and Rogers's percentage of the vote); and Jim Asker, "Southern Baptist Investigator Says Rules of Convention Were Violated," ibid., 20 September 1979, sec. A, pp. 1, 27 (for alleged voting irregularities; second quoted phrase is on p. 27).

59. John Buchanan, "Reagan Should Repudiate Demagoguery of Moral McCarthyism," *Houston Post*, 9 February 1985, sec. B, p. 3; Michael Berryhill, "The Baptist Schism," *New York Times Magazine*, 9 June 1985, pp. 90–95, 99 (Criswell's support of Stanley is detailed on p. 99); "Bad Blood Over the Good Book," *Texas Monthly* 13 (May 1985): 122–26 (for details of conflict at the 1985 Southern Baptist Convention); Barnhart, *Southern Baptist Holy War*, 71, 235; and Richard Vara, "Baptists Elect Fundamentalist," *Houston Post*, 11 June 1986, sec. A, p. 7 (for Rogers's percentage of vote in election).

60. Jim Asker, "Baptist Official Says Group Trying to 'Hijack' SBC," *Houston Post*, 8 June 1981, sec. C, p. 24.

61. V. S. Naipaul, "Among the Republicans," *New York Review of Books*, 25 October 1984, p. 5.

62. Joe Herzenberg, "Gay-Baiting in Southern Politics," *Southern Exposure* 13 (September/October 1985): 17–18 (especially p. 18); and Doug Harlan, "Gramm May Be Planting Time Bomb on Gay Issue," *Houston Post*, 25 September 1984, sec. B, p. 3.

63. Felton West, "State GOP Sticks to Fundamentals," *Houston Post*, 10 July 1986, sec. B, p. 2.

64. See "Criswell Backs Bush," *Houston Post*, 9 March 1986, sec. A, p. 2 (for Criswell's endorsement of Bush); and Phil Gailey, "Bush Salutes Falwell Conservatism," *New York Times*, 25 January 1986, p. 8.

65. Reinhard, *Republican Right since 1945*, vii.

66. William Martin, "Onward Christian Voters," *Texas Monthly* 8 (June 1980): 90–93 (for Falwell's influence in Texas); and Phil Gailey, "Bush Salutes Falwell Conservatism," *New York Times*, 25 January 1986, p. 8.

67. William Martin, "God's Angry Man," *Texas Monthly* 9 (April 1981): 152–57, 223–35 (first quotation on p. 152). Jim Asker describes the founding meeting in "Conservatives Hope to Start Roundtable," *Houston Post*, 19 July 1981, sec. A, p. 10 (second quotation).

68. See Thomas Ferguson and Joel Rogers, "The Reagan Victory: Corporate

Coalitions in the 1980 Campaign," in *The Hidden Election: Politics and Economics in the 1980 Presidential Campaign*, ed. Thomas Ferguson and Joel Rogers (New York: Pantheon Books, 1981), 4; and see John Herbers, "Ultraconservative Evangelicals a Surging New Force in Politics," *New York Times*, 17 August 1980, sec. 1, pp. 1, 52 (for broad overview).

69. John S. Saloma III, *Ominous Politics: The New Conservative Labyrinth* (New York: Hill & Wang, 1984), 56 (for Religious Roundtable information), and 62 (for data on Connally and Robison).

70. Martin, "God's Angry Man," 223–24 (for Robison's use of the word "queer"); and Anthony Lewis, "Cross and Flag," *New York Times*, 8 October 1984, sec. A, p. 19 (quotation).

71. Paul Burka, "Jim Collins and the Armies of the Faithful," *Texas Monthly* 10 (October 1982): 24–27, 204–18 (quotation on p. 213).

72. Photograph accompanies Howell Raines, "Reagan Backs Evangelicals in Their Political Activities," *New York Times*, 23 August 1980, sec. 1, p. 8.

73. Quoted in Doug Harlan, "Test of Fundamentalists' Power in GOP 5 Weeks Off," *Houston Post*, 25 May 1986, sec. B, p. 3.

74. Fred Bonavita, "Texas GOP 'Ultra' Sensitive about New Faction," ibid., 18 June 1984, sec. A, pp. 1, 3 (for prolife, anti-abortion, pro-Reagan GOP stance); Jane Ely, "State GOP's 'Religious Right' Loses Early Convention Battle," ibid., 26 June 1986, sec. A, p. 9 (for proposed statement to make Republican party a Christian party); and Jane Ely, "Religious Right Loses Test Vote," ibid., 28 June 1986, sec. A, p. 6 (quotation).

75. In 1988, however, he got 38 percent. See Louis Dubose, "Invisible Army," *Texas Observer* 80 (1 July 1988): 10.

11. Race and Realignment

1. This confrontation was observed by the author. The names of the two men are fictitious.

2. Gunnar Myrdal, *An American Dilemma: The Negro Problem and Modern Democracy* (New York and London: Harper & Brothers, 1944), xix (italics are in the original).

3. Paul Casdorph, *A History of the Republican Party in Texas, 1865–1965* (Austin, Texas: Pemberton Press, 1965), 200.

4. Cited in ibid., 201.

5. Cited in ibid., 214.

6. Theodore H. White, *The Making of the President, 1960* (New York: Atheneum Publishers, 1961), 389 (first quotation), 199 (second and third quotations); see pp. 388–90 for the text of the "Compact of Fifth Avenue"; and Hugh Scott, *Come to the Party* (Englewood Cliffs, N. J.: Prentice-Hall, 1968), 170, for more details.

7. O. Douglas Weeks, *Texas in the 1960 Presidential Election* (Austin: Institute of Public Affairs, University of Texas, 1961), 41–43; Casdorph, *A History of the Republican Party in Texas*, 218–19 (for details of the ovation); see "Highlights of Tower's Life, Career," *Houston Post*, 24 August 1983, sec. A, p. 18, under "September 1963" paragraph for details of Tower's role in Goldwater campaign.

8. Monroe Lee Billington, *The Political South in the Twentieth Century* (New York: Charles Scribner's Sons, 1975), 144.

9. White, *Making of the President, 1960,* p. 203.

10. Theodore White, *The Making of the President, 1964* (New York: Atheneum, 1965), 92–93 (first quotation), 233 (for a discussion of Janeway and the term *backlash*).

11. Philip E. Converse, "A Major Political Realignment in the South?" in Allan P. Sindler, ed., *Change in the Contemporary South* (Durham, N.C.: Duke University Press, 1963), 220.

12. Philip E. Converse, "On the Possibility of Major Political Realignment in the South," in Angus Campbell, Philip E. Converse, Warren E. Miller, and Donald E. Stokes, *Elections and the Political Order* (New York, London, and Sydney: John Wiley & Sons, 1966), 240. *Realignment* is a technical term that has acquired various meanings since V. O. Key elaborated the concept in the 1950s. It is used in this chapter simply to mean the growth of Republican voting at the expense of the Democrats in presidential, state, congressional, and local races. For a broader definition, see David W. Brady and Patricia A. Hurley, "The Prospects for Contemporary Partisan Realignment," *PS* 18 (Winter 1985): 63–68.

13. White, *Making of the President, 1964,* p. 74.

14. E. M. Schreiber, "Where the Ducks Are: Southern Strategy Versus Fourth Party," *Public Opinion Quarterly* 35 (Summer 1971): 159.

15. Numan V. Bartley and Hugh D. Graham, *Southern Elections: County and Precinct Data, 1950–1972* (Baton Rouge and London: Louisiana State University Press, 1978), pt 2, as quoted in James L. Sundquist, *Dynamics of the Party System: Alignment and Realignment of Political Parties in the United States,* rev. ed. (Washington, D.C.: Brookings Institution, 1983), 362.

16. "Random Glances At the New Republicans," *Texas Observer* 56 (21 August 1964): 3.

17. Goldwater's candidacy was that of a man who did not seem to be personally bigoted trying to capitalize on the bigotry of others. He steered clear of direct appeals to racial passion in 1964, although many people took his statements on "crime in the streets" and "law and order" to apply to racial matters. At one point in his campaign, Goldwater scotched a film that Citizens for Goldwater had slated for television containing pictures of black rioters, calling it "racist." See David W. Reinhard, *The Republican Right since 1945* (Lexington: University Press of Kentucky, 1983), 201; and Allen J. Matusow, *The Unraveling of America: A History of Liberalism in the 1960s* (New York and other cities: Harper & Row, 1984), 146. Yet Goldwater's southern strategy obviously was an appeal to the whites most immediately affected by the civil rights movement's assault on legally enforced racial apartheid.

Former Mississippi congressman Frank Smith, a moderate, described a Goldwater appearance in East Tennessee in September 1964:

> When Senator Goldwater spoke . . . a large Confederate flag dominated the platform, and smaller Rebel pennants were waved throughout the crowd. Here was a candidate who spoke of "states' rights," and the people with Confederate flags know that "states' rights" means segregation. . . . The same year that saw all the segregation barriers finally broken,

at least in token fashion, roused the first real hope in the Southern bastions of resistance that the tide would actually change in their favor.

Frank E. Smith, *Look Away from Dixie* (Baton Rouge: Louisiana State University Press, 1965), 71–72.

18. Quoted in Jack Bass and Walter DeVries, *The Transformation of Southern Politics: Social Change and Political Consequence Since 1945* (New York: Basic Books, 1976), 27.

19. Donald S. Strong, "Alabama: Transition and Alienation," in *The Changing Politics of the South*, ed. William Havard (Baton Rouge: Louisiana State University Press, 1972), 438, 439 (both quotations). The "code" also had nonverbal aspects. South Carolina representative Albert Watson, a Thurmond-backed Republican running in the 1970 gubernatorial race against John West, a moderate Democrat, wore a white tie throughout his campaign to keep voters mindful of his racial views. See Bass and DeVries, *Transformation of Southern Politics*, 39. Even Wallace, whose 1968 presidential campaign was the most blatantly racist campaign by a major presidential candidate in the modern era—and who was still openly identified with the White Citizens' Council—"skillfully substituted such code words as 'law and order' for his more customary brand of strident Negrophobia," historian Neil McMillen writes. Wallace's campaign chairman had early predicted that "when you get right down to it, there's really only going to be one issue, and you spell it n-i-g-g-e-r." See Neil R. McMillen, *The Citizens' Council: Organized Resistance to the Second Reconstruction, 1954–64* (Urbana, Chicago, and London: University of Illinois Press, 1971), 353. A Lou Harris poll found that *73 percent* of all Wallace supporters wanted progress for blacks to be halted. See Seymour Martin Lipset and Earl Raab, *The Politics of Unreason: Right-Wing Extremism in America, 1790–1970* (New York, Evanston, Ill., and London: Harper & Row, 1970), 346.

20. Lou Cannon, *Reagan* (New York: Perigee Books, 1982), 111.

21. Bass and DeVries, *Transformation of Southern Politics*, 24.

22. See McMillen, *Citizens' Council*, 350–51.

23. See "Highlights of Tower's Life, Career," p. 19, under "July 1963" paragraph (for attack on civil rights bill); and "Houston Dailies and the Senate Race," *Texas Observer* 56 (15 May 1964): 10 (on Tower and the southern filibuster); George Bush's opposition to the civil rights bill is described in Stewart Davis, "Don Labels McLendon Connally's Hatchet Man," *Houston Chronicle*, 9 April 1964, sec. 1, p. 13.

24. Casdorph, *History of The Republican Party in Texas*, 229.

25. Robert Eubank, interview with author, 8 July 1983. See also Robert Eubank, "Understanding Texas Republicans," in Wendell M. Bedichek and Neal Tannahill, eds., *Public Policy in Texas* (Glenview, Ill., and other cities: Scott, Foresman, 1982), 170–81.

26. Casdorph, *History of the Republican Party in Texas*, 238.

27. Ibid., 242 (quotation), 244.

28. "Random Glances at the New Republicans," *Texas Observer* 56 (21 August 1964): 3–4.

29. Casdorph, *History of the Republican Party in Texas*, 247.

30. Tom Wicker, "Goldwater Backers Vote Down Scranton's Anti-Bircher Plank and His Rights and A-Bomb Plans: Platform Voted," *New York Times*, 15 July 1964, sec. A, p. 1 (for overall vote count); and "Roll-Call of Convention on Rights Amendment," ibid., p. 20 (for Texas delegates' vote).

31. Quotations cited in John D. Morris, "Negro Delegates Drop Plans to Walk Out as a Demonstration against Goldwater," *New York Times*, 16 July 1964, sec. A, p. 19. For Eisenhower's views, see Felix Belair, Jr., "Eisenhower Hints Doubts on Ticket," ibid., 17 July 1964, sec. A, p. 12.

32. Reinhard, *The Republican Right since 1945*, p. 194 (first two quotations); and "The Goldwater Platform," *New York Times*, 13 July 1964, sec. A, p. 28 (last quotation).

33. Robert D. Novak, *The Agony of the G.O.P., 1964* (New York: Macmillan, 1965), 201.

34. Charles Alan Wright, "A Republican Makes Up His Mind," *Texas Observer* 56 (21 August 1964): 2.

35. Bernard Cosman, *Five States for Goldwater: Continuity and Change in Southern Presidential Voting Patterns* (University, Ala.: University of Alabama Press, 1966), 55 (first percentage), 61 (second percentage), 74 (importance of race to Goldwater).

36. Campbell et al., *Elections and the Political Order*, 240 n–241 n.

37. Percentages are taken from Cosman, *Five States for Goldwater*, 87 (table 7).

38. Strong, "Alabama," 441.

39. Philip E. Converse, Aage R. Clausen, and Warren E. Miller, "Electoral Myth and Reality: The 1964 Election," *American Political Science Review* 59 (June 1965): 330.

40. Cosman, *Five States for Goldwater*, 128 (first quotation), 129 (second quotation).

41. Quoted in Reg Murphy and Hal Gulliver, *The Southern Strategy* (New York: Scribner's, 1971), 218.

42. Philip E. Converse et al., "Continuity and Change in American Politics: Parties and Issues in the 1968 Election," *American Political Science Review* 63 (December 1969): 1086 n.

43. See Murphy and Gulliver, *Southern Strategy*, 2–3; Reinhard, *Republican Right since 1945*, p. 221; Billington, *Political South in the Twentieth Century*, 150; and Richard Harris, *Decision* (New York: E. P. Dutton, 1971) on the Carswell nomination to the Supreme Court. Also see Nixon aide Harry S. Dent's account of Nixon's "pro-southern" policy in *The Prodigal South Returns to Power* (New York and other cities: John Wiley & Sons, 1978), chap. 8.

44. William A. Rusher, *The Rise of the Right* (New York: William Morrow and Company, 1984), 226.

45. Kevin P. Phillips, *The Emerging Republican Majority* (Garden City, N.Y.: Anchor Books, 1970), 467–68, 470, 472–74.

46. Ibid., 272. In a preface to the paperback version of his book, Phillips denied his critics' claims that he "wrote off" blacks and the Northeast. He argued that his

remarks about these aggregates and about American voting blocs in general were not prescriptive, but were merely projections of existing trends. See ibid., p. 23. However, the prescriptive nature of the book is obvious throughout. The tone is set at the very beginning: "This book is respectfully dedicated to the emerging Republican majority and its two principal architects: Richard M. Nixon and Attorney General John N. Mitchell." The implication of this passage is that there were trends—including those of white racial reaction to the civil rights movement—but it took "architects" to refashion the Republican party so as to profit from them.

47. Ripon Society, *The Lessons of Victory* (New York: Dial Press, 1969), 175–80 (percentages on p. 175).

48. Phillips, *Emerging Republican Majority*, 39.

49. Ibid., 204.

50. Ibid., 464.

51. Ibid., 205–6. Phillips's view was shared by Wallace supporters as well. In 1965 an official in Governor Wallace's office told a reporter, "This voting bill is not going to affect Alabama the way many people think. What it is going to accomplish is the biggest registration of whites in our history." See Harold W. Stanley, *Voter Mobilization and the Politics of Race: The South and Universal Suffrage, 1952–1984* (New York and other cities: Praeger, 1987), 50.

52. James R. Soukup, Clifton McCleskey, and Harry Holloway, *Party and Factional Division in Texas* (Austin, Texas: University of Texas Press, 1964), 64.

53. See John R. Knaggs, *Two-Party Texas: The John Tower Era, 1961–1984* (Austin: Eakin Press, 1986).

54. See pertinent paragraphs in "Highlights of Tower's Life, Career," *Houston Post*, 24 August 1983, sec. A, p. 19.

55. Arthur Wiese, "Sen. Tower Expects to Support Extension of Voting Rights Act," ibid., 9 June 1982, sec. A, p. 12.

56. For details of Helms's fight against the King holiday see "Holiday for King Approved," ibid., 20 October 1983, sec. A, pp. 1, 27 (especially p. 27).

57. See both Knaggs, *Two-Party Texas*, 196–97; and Griffin Smith, Jr., "Little Big Man," *Texas Monthly* 5 (January 1977): 136.

58. Roger M. Olien, *From Token to Triumph: The Texas Republicans since 1920* (Dallas: Southern Methodist University Press, 1982), 215–16.

59. Roy Reed, "G.O.P., Aided by Agnew, Surges in South," *New York Times*, 7 December 1969, sec. A, pp. 1, 60; and Art Wiese, "GOP Told to Woo Latins," *Houston Post*, 13 September 1970, sec. A, p. 15.

60. Joe Nolan, "State Democrats Facing Serious Problems," *Houston Chronicle*, 23 June 1980, sec. 1, p. 7.

61. "Blacks, Prosecutors, Union Campaigning for White," *San Antonio Express*, 29 October 1982, sec. B, p. 4.

62. Chandler Davidson, "Negro Politics and the Rise of the Civil Rights Movement in Houston, Texas" (Ph.D. diss., Princeton University, 1968), 202.

63. " 'Irregularities' Are Charged," *Texas Observer* 52 (11 November 1960): 1, 3 (allegations of GOP poll watchers harassing black voters are on p. 3).

64. For amounts of reward money, see Brent Manley, "White Says Voter Fraud Reward Plan Ridiculous," *Houston Post*, 19 October 1984, sec. A, p. 16 (quoted

sentence and first quoted phrase); the same figures are also cited in William Pack, "Ex-felons Will Watch Polls Tuesday," ibid., 5 November 1984, sec. A, pp. 1, 11 (Washington's quoted remark is also on both pages). See also George Strake, Jr., telephone interview with the author, 1 November 1988.

65. See David Ellison, "GOP to Place Poll Watchers at 100 Democratic Precincts," *Houston Post*, 23 October 1986, sec. A, p. 4; and Allan C. Kimball and Guy Cantwell, "Democrats Plan Poll-Watcher Watchers," ibid., 26 October 1986, sec. A, p. 1 (for Leland quotation).

66. Brent Manley, "White Says Voter Fraud Reward Plan Ridiculous"; John Whitmire, "9 'Big, Burly' Athletes to Watch Polls," ibid., 6 November 1984, sec. A, p. 12; Mark Sanders, "Democratic Chief Says Republicans Attacked Offices," ibid.; "The Measure of Republican 'Integrity,'" *New York Times*, 1 November 1986, 30 (all quotations); and Bernard Weintraub, "Suit Charging G.O.P. Sought to Cut Black Vote Is Settled," ibid., 24 July 1987, sec. A, p. 15.

67. Knaggs, *Two-Party Texas*, 166.

68. Ibid.

69. Ibid.

70. Ibid., 173.

71. Ibid., 269; and Felton West, "Many 'Firsts' in White Appointees," *Houston Post*, 6 January 1987, sec. B, p. 2 (for numbers and percentages of both Clements's and Briscoe's appointments).

72. *Southwest Voter Research News* 1 (November 1986). Published by the Southwest Voter Research Institute, San Antonio.

73. See "State GOP to Back 'English Only' Constitutional Amendment," *Houston Post*, 16 November 1986, sec. A, p. 3.

74. See "State Republican Panel Rejects Proposal to Target Minorities for Recruitment," *Houston Post*, 3 October 1983, sec. A, p. 3.

75. Reinhard, *Republican Right since 1945*, p. 169.

76. Sam Attlesey, "The Texas Delegation," *Dallas Morning News*, 15 July 1984, sec. G, p. 1 (for percentages of blacks and Hispanics in Texas Democratic delegation); and Christy Hoppe and Sam Attlesey, "Color Texas Green," *Dallas Morning News*, 19 August 1984, sec. A, p. 35 (for percentages of blacks and Hispanics in Texas Republican delegation). I am indebted to Professor Jeanie Stanley for calling these articles to my attention. James E. Anderson, Richard W. Murray, and Edward L. Farley, *Texas Politics: An Introduction*, 4th ed. (New York and other cities: Harper & Row, 1984), 80; Richard S. Dunham, "Gephardt Suffers Big Losses," *Dallas Times Herald*, 9 March 1988, sec. B, p. 1, 6 (chart on p. 6 gives percentage of black vote for Republicans in the 1988 national election); and "Political Intelligence," *Texas Observer* 80 (1 July 1988): 16.

77. Of those Texans eighteen years old and older in 1986 who identified themselves as Democrats or Republicans, 39 percent of the Democrats were black (18 percent) or Hispanic (21 percent), and 10 percent of the Republicans were black (2 percent) or Hispanic (8 percent). See James A. Dyer, Arnold Vedlitz, and David B. Hill, "New Voters, Switchers, and Political Party Realignment in Texas," *Western Political Quarterly* 41 (March 1988): 164.

78. See poll data cited in Dennis S. Ippolito, "Texas," in *The 1984 Presidential*

Election in the South: Patterns of Southern Party Politics, ed. Robert P. Steed, Laurence W. Moreland, and Tod A. Baker (New York and other cities: Praeger Publishers, 1986), 179.

79. Richard Murray and Arnold Vedlitz, "Racial Voting Patterns in the South: An Analysis of Major Elections from 1960 to 1977 in Five Cities," *The Annals of the American Academy of Political and Social Science* 439 (September 1978): 34.

80. Quoted in Murphy and Gulliver, *Southern Strategy*, 218.

81. Data supplied by the Voter Education Project, Atlanta.

12. Race and Class in Texas Politics

1. Nene Foxhall, "Frankie," *Houston Chronicle Magazine, Texas*, 3 July 1983, pp. 6–10 (quotation on p. 10).

2. See chap. 11 above on the racial factor generally; more specifically see Roderick Bell, "Texas," in *Explaining the Vote: Presidential Choices in the Nation and the States, 1968*, pt 2, *Presidential Choices in Individual States*, ed. David M. Kovenock et al. (Chapel Hill: Institute for Research in Social Science, University of North Carolina, 1973), 425–65 (especially p. 439), for the extent of working-class Texans' defection to Wallace in 1968.

The toll Evangelical and fundamentalist politics has taken on traditional Democratic support is suggested by the decline in white Evangelical support for the Democratic ticket nationally: from 56 percent for Carter—himself an Evangelical—in 1976, to 61 percent for Reagan in 1980 and 81 percent for Reagan in 1984. As two students of Evangelical voters in the 1984 elections put it, "Outside of their religious beliefs, this group of highly religious citizens had characteristics that one normally associates with Democrats, but [they] supported mostly Republican candidates." Their subjects were "disproportionately Southern, less educated, and holders of lower status occupations." See Gary W. Copeland and Jeffrey L. Brudney, "Ronald Reagan and the Religious Vote: Trends, Continuities, and Discontinuities" (Paper delivered at the Annual Meeting of the American Political Science Association, Washington, D.C., September 1988), 5. A poll conducted by Texas A&M University in 1985 found that "born again" Texans were more likely to be poorly educated and from low-income households. Information on the Texas poll is in David Hill, "Religion Actively Promoted by Texans," *Houston Chronicle*, 1 April 1985, sec. 1, p. 10.

3. See Numan V. Bartley, "Beyond *Southern Politics*: Some Suggestions for Research," in *Perspectives on the American South: An Annual Review of Society, Politics and Culture*, vol. 2, ed. Merle Black and John Shelton Reed (New York and other cities: Gordon and Breach Science Publishers, 1984), 35–47 (quotations on p. 42).

4. Joint Center for Political Studies, Washington, D.C.; National Association of Latino Elected and Appointed Officials, Washington, D.C.; data collected by the author; and House Committee on the Judiciary, prepared statement by George Korbel, *Hearings Before the Subcommittee on Civil Rights and Constitutional Rights H.R. 9939 . . .* , 94th Cong., 1975, p. 467.

5. See Chandler Davidson and George Korbel, "At-Large Elections and Minor-

ity-Group Representation: A Re-Examination of Historical and Contemporary Evidence," *Journal of Politics* 43 (November 1981): 982–1005 (see especially p. 1001).

6. See Chandler Davidson and Luis Ricardo Fraga, "Slating Groups as Parties in a 'Nonpartisan' Setting," *Western Political Quarterly* 41 (June 1988): 373–89 (see especially pp. 384–87).

7. Chandler Davidson, "Reforming a Reform: The Attack on Multimember Districts," in *Perspectives on the American South: An Annual Review of Society, Politics and Culture*, vol. 1, ed. Merle Black and John Shelton Reed (New York, London, and Paris: Gordon and Breach Science Publishers, 1981), 143–49; and Robert D. Thomas and Richard W. Murray, "Applying the Voting Rights Act in Houston: Federal Intervention or Local Political Determination?" in *Publius* (symposium issue entitled *Assessing the Effects of the U. S. Voting Rights Act*) ed. Charles L. Cotrell, 16 (Fall 1986): 81–96.

8. John A. Booth, "Political Change in San Antonio, 1970–82: Toward Decay or Democracy?" in *The Politics of San Antonio: Community, Progress, & Power*, ed. David R. Johnson, John A. Booth, and Richard J. Harris (Lincoln, Neb., and London: University of Nebraska Press, 1983), 193–211.

9. Quoted in Peter Applebome, "25 Years after the Death of Kennedy, Dallas Looks at Its Changed Image," *New York Times*, 21 November 1988, sec. A, p. 14. For a detailed journalistic account of the history of the Dallas Citizens Council, see Bryan Woolley, "The Dallas Way," *Dallas Times Herald*, 15 November 1987, special sec. H, pp. 1, 16.

10. Charles Cotrell, *Status of Civil Rights in Texas*, vol. I: *Participation of Mexican-Americans, Blacks and Females in the Political Institutions and Processes in Texas. 1968–1978* (San Antonio: Texas Advisory Committee to the United States Commission on Civil Rights, January 1980), 255.

11. C. Vann Woodward, *The Burden of Southern History*, rev. ed. (Baton Rouge: Louisiana State University Press, 1968), 83.

12. James L. Sundquist, *Dynamics of the Party System: Alignment and Realignment of Political Parties in the United States*, rev. ed. (Washington, D.C.: Brookings Institution, 1983), 402; Alan Draper, "Labor and the 1966 Elections," *Labor History* 30 (Winter 1989): 77.

13. Allen J. Matusow, *The Unraveling of America: A History of Liberalism in the 1960s* (New York and other cities: Harper & Row), 345–75, 438–89.

14. Eric F. Goldman, *The Tragedy of Lyndon Johnson* (New York: Alfred A. Knopf, 1969), 173 (all quotations).

15. Ernesto Cortes, Jr., is profiled in Peter Applebome, "Changing Texas Politics at Its Roots," *New York Times*, 31 May 1988, sec. A, p. 16; for details on the Texas Industrial Areas Foundation Network, see John Gravois, "Dukakis Focuses on Texas Electorate," *Houston Post*, 4 March 1988, sec. A, p. 18; and for an account of one branch's beginnings in San Antonio in the early 1970s, see Paul Burka, "The Second Battle of the Alamo," *Texas Monthly* 5 (December 1977): 139–43, 218–38.

16. Robert Reinhold, "As Texas Republican Party Grows, So Do Rifts," *New York Times*, 23 August 1985, sec. A, p. 8 (quotation).

17. On Bullington, see George Norris Green, *The Establishment in Texas Poli-*

tics: The Primitive Years, 1937–1958 (Westport, Conn.: Greenwood Press, 1979), 88; and Alice Carol Cox, "The Rainey Affair: A History of the Academic Freedom Controversy at the University of Texas, 1938–1946" (Ph.D. diss., University of Denver, 1970), 76–80, 114–15. For examples of McCarthy's homosexual-baiting see Edwin R. Bayley, *Joe McCarthy and the Press* (Madison: University of Wisconsin Press, 1981), 79, 161–62.

18. See John Gravois, "City Hall Blitzed by Phone Calls," *Houston Post*, 19 June 1984, sec. A, p. 4 (for details on the gay rights amendment to Houston's civil service ordinance); Bill Coulter, "No Referendum on City's Gay Amendment," ibid., 27 June 1984, sec. A, p. 3 (for Reyes's opposition to the original ordinance); John Gravois, "Group Opens Petition Drive for Gay Rights Referendum," ibid., 4 July 1984, sec. B, p. 4; Emily Grotta and John Gravois, "Business Leaders Back Anti-Gay Vote," ibid., 12 January 1985, sec. A, pp. 1, 5; and Houston Chamber of Commerce "Action Alert," January 1985, signed by Louie Welch (which describes the ordinance as an affirmative action program for gays).

19. See John Gravois and Emily Grotta, "Gay Measures Rejected 4-to-1," *Houston Post*, 20 January 1985, sec. A, pp. 1, 18; see also Jane Ely, "City Turns Out to Repudiate Gay Lifestyle," ibid., sec. A, p. 18, for comments on the negativism of the whole referendum episode.

20. James L. Gibson and Kent L. Tedin, "Political Tolerance and the Rights of Homosexuals: A Contextual Analysis" (paper delivered at the Annual Meeting of the Midwest Political Science Association, Chicago, 1986). See also James L. Gibson and Kent L. Tedin, "The Etiology of Intolerance of Homosexual Politics," *Social Science Quarterly* 69 (September 1988): 587–604.

21. See Jim Simmon and John Gravois, "Welch Gaffe Talk of Town—and Beyond," *Houston Post*, 26 October 1985, sec. A, pp. 1, 22, for the story of the controversy.

22. See Gravois and Grotta, "Gay Measures Rejected 4-to-1," sec. A, p. 1, for Montrose's support.

23. Robert Reinhold, "Texas Scrambles for Revenue as Oil Glut Cuts State Funds," *New York Times*, 22 May 1985, sec. A, p. 1; sec. B, p. 4 (quotation on p. B4).

24. Stephen Klineberg, Houston Area Survey, 1988, unpublished data (Rice University Department of Sociology).

25. The extent of these changes in attitude—changes not necessarily correlated with changes in behavior, unfortunately—is indicated in Arnold Vedlitz, James A. Dyer, and David B. Hill, "The Changing Texas Voter," in *The South's New Politics: Realignment and Dealignment*, ed. Robert H. Swansbrough and David M. Brodsky (Columbia, S.C.: University of South Carolina Press, 1988), 41.

26. On blacks' preference for integrated neighborhoods, see Stephen Klineberg, Houston Area Survey, 1986, unpublished data (Rice University Department of Sociology). Segregation data on Texas cities in 1980 are found in Sean-Shong Hwang and Steve H. Murdock, "Residential Segregation in Texas in 1980," *Social Science Quarterly* 63 (December 1982): 737–48.

27. Kevin P. Phillips, *The Emerging Republican Majority* (Garden City, N.Y.: Anchor Books, 1970), 39.

Epilogue

1. The author attended this event and the following description is based on his notes.

2. See Robert Reinhold, "The Great Oil Era Ends in Texas," *New York Times*, 16 September 1984, sec. 3, pp. 1, 8.

3. Quoted in Sam Fletcher, "Reagan Angers Oilmen," *Houston Post*, 7 May 1987, sec. F, pp. 1, 2 (quotation on p. 1).

4. "Political Intelligence," *Texas Observer* 79 (9 October 1987): 18–19.

5. See Jane Baird, "Texas Banking Woes Show No Sign of Ending," *Houston Post*, 28 February 1988, sec. A, pp. 1, 16; and "2 More Banks Push Failures to 101 in State," ibid., 4 August 1989, sec. B, p. 1.

6. See Pete Brewton and Gregory Seay, "S&L Probe Grew—and Grew Again," ibid., 13 March 1988, sec. A, pp. 1, 15.

7. For job loss figures, see the *Texas Research League Analysis* 8 (January/February 1987): 1.

8. The number of Houston bankruptcies is given in Carl Hooper, "87 Business Failures Reach High in Houston, Study Says," *Houston Post*, 29 February 1988, sec. D, p. 2.

9. Details of Connally's travails are in Robert Reinhold, "John Connally's Texas-Sized Troubles," *New York Times*, 14 September 1986, sec. 3, pp. 1, 8 (quotation on p. 1).

10. James Drummond, "Beleaguered Connally, Pal File for Bankruptcy," *Houston Chronicle*, 1 August 1987, sec. A, pp. 1, 12.

11. Details of the auction are in Michael Haederle, "Connally 'Numb' at Finish of Sale," *Houston Post*, 27 January 1988, sec. A, p. 8.

12. Texas unemployment rates for 1986 are given in Peter Applebome, "Problems With Budget Pose Painful Choices for Texans," *New York Times*, 13 July 1986, sec. 1, p. 14.

13. Ronnie Dugger, "Appeal to the Gut," *Texas Observer* 79 (14 August 1987): 4–5 (especially p. 5).

14. San Antonio's homeless population size is given in "Shelter for the Homeless a Model of Cooperation," *New York Times*, 16 September 1987, sec. D, p. 31.

15. For effects of the depression on minorities and the poor, see "Job Loss Common in State, Poll Says," *Houston Post*, 6 December 1987, sec. A, p. 23.

16. See Harold Seneker, "A Wealth of Billionaires," *Forbes* 144 (24 July 1989): 117–19 (listing is on p. 119), which lists seven individual Texans and one Texas family in the billionaire class; and Harold Seneker et al., eds., "The Four Hundred Richest People in America," *Forbes* 142 (24 October 1988): 142–347, which lists sixteen Texans worth $500 million or more and another twelve worth at least $250 million. An August 1989 article in *Texas Monthly* claimed to have located one hundred individual Texans worth at least $100 million. (The ninety-nine richest Texans on my list circa 1980 qualified if their net worth was at least $50 million.) Thirty-eight on the *Texas Monthly* list were on my earlier list of the ninety-nine. Many of the latter not listed in the 1989 article had died in the interim. See John Anderson, "The Texas One Hundred," *Texas Monthly* 17 (August 1989): 111–71.

17. See "Williams Criticizes 'Liberals, Socialists' in Legislature," *Houston Post*, 9 September 1989, sec. A, p. 24.

18. Joe Conason, "Robert Mosbacher's Grand Scheme," *Texas Observer* 80 (28 April 1989): 11.

19. For details of the gift see "Criswell College gets $3 Million," *Houston Post*, 23 September 1989, sec. A, p. 24.

20. For details on Bass's contributions, see Richard L. Berke, "$100,000 Gifts Went to G.O.P. from Big Givers," *New York Times*, 17 November 1988, sec. B, p. 13; the Dawkins race is chronicled in Joseph F. Sullivan, "American Dreams Are on Display in Jersey Race," ibid., 6 March 1988, sec. 4, p. 6.

21. See Paul Burka, "Power," *Texas Monthly* 15 (December 1987): 118–24, 216–26 (especially p. 216); and Neal Tannahill and Wendell M. Bedichek, *Texas Government: Policy and Politics*, 3d ed. (Glenview, Ill., and London: Scott, Foresman & Company, 1989), 131.

22. Jim Henderson, "New Coalitions in Dallas Transform City Politics," *Dallas Times Herald*, 15 November 1987, special sec. H, p. 2.

23. For Jordan's criticism, see Maralee Schwartz and Lloyd Grove, "Barbara Jordan Lashes Jackson for Tepid Support of Ticket," *Washington Post*, sec. A, p. 4. For a perceptive account of Jackson's campaign, see Juan Williams, "Divided We Fell: Race and the '88 Election," *American Visions* 4 (February 1989): 31–37 (see p. 37 for Barbara Jordan's attitude toward Jackson).

24. For the *Texas Monthly*'s ranking of Edwards as well as a summary of his career, see Ken Herman and John Gravois, "Observers See Several Weak Links," *Houston Post*, 17 September 1989, sec. J, pp. 1, 3.

25. For percentages of Mexican American voters, see the *Southwest Voter Research Notes* 2 (May 1988): 1; for percentages in Houston's black precincts—usually a reliable indicator of black votes statewide, see tables (with their percentages) headed "How Harris County Democrats Voted Tuesday" and "How Harris County Republicans Voted Tuesday," in the *Houston Post*, 10 March 1988, sec. A, p. 19.

26. Andrew Rosenthal, "Foes Accuse Bush Campaign of Inflaming Racial Tension," *New York Times*, 24 October 1988, sec. A, pp. 1, 10 (quotation on p. 10). The Willie Horton ad—featuring a mug shot of the black murderer—was run by a group independent of the Bush campaign, Americans for Bush. The question remains whether there was contact between the group and the Bush campaign, which would have been illegal. The campaign did not run ads showing Horton's picture. Bush, however, frequently mentioned Horton in his attacks on Dukakis. And his campaign did not ask for the ad to be pulled until three days before its scheduled expiration date, after it had run for twenty-five days. Before then, Bush had told reporters, "I stand fully behind these ads." See Martin Schram, "The Making of Willie Horton," *New Republic* 202 (28 May 1990): 17–19; and Maureen Dowd, "Bush Denies Racism in Campaign, Saying Democrats Are Desperate," *New York Times* (national edition), 25 October 1988, sec. A, pp. 1, 11 (quotation on p. 11).

27. Peter Applebome, "The Battle for Texas," *New York Times Magazine*, 30 October 1988, pp. 34–37, 66–69, 100–101 (first quotation on p. 36, second quotation on pp. 36 and 66).

28. See Ken Herman, "Democrats: Clements Nixed Furlough Powers," *Houston Post*, 22 October 1988, sec. A, pp. 1, 17; and Rosenthal, "Foes Accuse Bush Campaign of Inflaming Racial Tensions," for details of the Bush campaign's use of Willie Horton as a racial issue.

29. See Applebome, "The Battle for Texas," 100.

30. See Ken Jackson, "Winning the South," *Southern Changes* 11 (March/April 1989): 1, 3–4 (all figures and percentages are on p. 3). This pattern—a modest upswing in Democratic voting among whites being eroded by black nonvoting—apparently existed statewide.

31. See Fred Bonavita, "Conservatives Savor High Court Win," *Houston Post*, 10 November 1988, sec. A, pp. 1, 18.

32. See *Fiscal Notes* (of Texas) 89 (June 1989): 6 and 7 (comparisons of Texas's expenditures to rest of the country); and Felton West, "Don't Call Our Legislators Big Spenders," *Houston Post*, 8 January 1989, sec. C, p. 3 (this article lists rankings for Texas's alcohol and drug abuse programs, community mental health funding, and community mental retardation services).

33. For a summary of statistics on Texas's needy and the paucity of social services, see Lorwen Connie Harris, *Children, Choices, and Change: An Adaptation of the Darker Side of Childhood* (Austin: Hogg Foundation for Mental Health, University of Texas, 1988).

Index

Abernethy, Byron R., 165, 208
Adams, Tod R., 224
AFL-CIO, 122–24, 126–27, 149, 164, 169, 187, 194, 303n.58
African Americans: attitudes toward illegal immigrants, 115, 300n.22; and Democratic conventions, 162–63, 166, 170–72, 174, 177, 188, 191, 194–96, 311n.19; and importance of percentage in population, 5, 9–10; and labor unions, 124, 126; in manual work force, 114–16; in 1988 presidential campaign, 266–70; nonvoting by, 56–58; officeholders among, 249–50; in Republican party, 226, 229, 232, 234, 237, 323n.77; voting behavior of, 14, 19–20, 43–44, 46, 268–69; voting of, monitored by Republicans, 235–36, 238–39. *See also* disfranchisement; poll tax as voting requirement; white primary system
Aid to Families with Dependent Children, 253
Alexander, Herbert E., 149
Alger, Bruce, 207
Alinsky, Saul, 254–55
Allegro Club, in Houston, 88, 90, 91
Allen, Robert H., 144, 305n.15
Allen, Ruth, 11
Allred, James V., 47, 105–6
American Association of University Professors, 208
American Civil Liberties Union, 78
American Federation of Labor (AFL), 124, 127–28
American party, George Wallace and, 45, 76, 206, 231. *See also* Wallace, George C.
Americans for Democratic Action (ADA), 220, 245
Anderson, James E., 137
Anderson, John, 176
Anderson Clayton, 77, 101, 139
Applebome, Peter, 268
Archer, Bill, 93
Armstrong, Anne, 95–96, 201
Armstrong, Bob, 191–92
Associated Research Group (ARG), 147–48

Association of Manufacturers, 103
Aston, James, 91
Atlas, Scott, 98

Bainbridge, John, 63, 88
Baker, Howard, 78, 102
Baker, James III, xviii, 100, 201
Baker, Robin, 118
Baker & Botts, 95–103
Baker v. Carr (1962), 247
Baptists. *See* Southern Baptists
bar associations, state and local, 296n.60
Barker, Bernard L., 144
Barnes, Ben, 54, 104, 140–41, 149, 263
Barrera, Roy, Jr., 237
Bartley, Numan V., 248
Bass, Harry, 139
Bass, Perry Richardson, 66, 73
Bass, Rita, 74
Bass, Robert M., 265–66
Bass, Sid Richardson, 66
Bass Brothers Political Action Committee, 73
Benton, Wilbourn E., 161
Bentsen, Beryl, 164, 308n.23
Bentsen, Lloyd, Jr., xvi, 27, 164, 192, 243, 310n.4; campaign against Jim Collins (1982), 76, 218; campaign against Ralph Yarborough (1970), 31, 138, 178, 180, 237; 1970 campaign expenditures, 281n.41; presidential campaign (1976), 182–90, 311–12n.19; vice presidential campaign (1988), 269. *See also* "Bentsen bill"
Bentsen, Lloyd, Sr., 198
"Bentsen bill" (creating the "Bentsen presidential primary" of 1976), 156, 175–76, 182–90; compared to unit rule, 311n.8
Berg, Larry, 150
Big 50 PAC, 146
Big Thicket National Preserve, 30
Big Three (Houston law firms), 95–103, 295n.39
bilingual education bill, 32
Billington, Monroe Lee, 24
Bishop, Jim, 86

black belt, southern, 5, 9, 11
blacks. *See* African Americans
Blakley, William, 166
Bluhdorn, Charlie, 85
Boatright, Mody C., 34–35
Bookout, John, 89
Boone, Pat, 210, 212
Bork, Robert, 266–67
Bourbons (conservatives), 5, 9; Democrats as, 20–21, 23
Bracewell, Searcy, 100, 106, 149, 298n.94
Bracewell & Patterson, 106
Bright, Harvey R. ("Bum"), 73, 146
Briscoe, Dolph, Jr., 29, 67, 173–74, 183, 190–91; and campaign in 1972, 50, 140; and Carter campaign, 192; as conservative, 243; and Crow, 74; defeat of, in 1978, 178; expenditures of, 80, 138, 141; friendly appointments for labor by, 194; and Guest, 176, 182, 195, 310n.62; and Ray Lee Hunt, 77; minority appointments by, 237; and membership in the ninety-nine, 73; signs "Bentsen bill," 184
Broder, David, 168
Brown, George Rufus: anti-union activities of, 105, 128–29; and Ed Clark, 105; financial empire of, 68–69; and Oveta Hobby and son Bill, 76, 91; and LBJ, 68, 105; and membership in ninety-nine, 73; as philanthropist with brother Herman, 129. *See also* Brown, Herman; Brown & Root
Brown, H. S. ("Hank"), 167, 169
Brown, Herman, 68, 73, 105, 128, 129, 139. *See also* Brown, George
Brown, Lee, 250
Brown & Root, 68, 94, 110, 128, 139, 145, 146
Brown Foundation, 73
Brown v. Board of Education (1954), 205, 213, 224, 247
Brunson, John, 195–96
Buckley, William F., 202, 210–11, 228
Budge, Hamer, 86
Bullington, Orville, 256
Bullock, Bob, 192
Bunche, Ralph, 3
Bureau of Labor Statistics, U.S., 122
Burka, Paul, 217, 266, 311–12n.19
Bush, George, xviii, 74; attacks Ralph Yarborough's civil rights and labor stance in 1964 contest, 228; backs open housing bill

of 1968, 202; conservative voting record in Congress, 202; in country club faction of Republican party, 201; defeated by Ralph Yarborough in 1964, 137–38, 202; endorsed by Criswell in 1986, 216; endorsed by Falwell, 202, 313n.12; expenditures in 1970 campaign, 281n.41; as Goldwaterite, 166, 202; and Horton ad in 1988 campaign, 267–69, 328n.26; and Robert Mosbacher, Sr., 78, 265; opposed to 1964 Civil Rights Act, 202, 267; in 1988 campaign, 265–70
Butt, Charles C., 71

Calaway, Jim, 142
Campbell, Thomas, 23
camps, summer, and Texas rich, 90
Campus Crusade for Christ, 76, 212
Cancer Act of 1971, 30
Carl, Colin, 182
Carleton, Don, 126
Caro, Robert, 105
Carr, Billie, 177, 263; background of, 180–82; and "Bentsen bill," 156, 163, 184–191; on Democratic National Committee, 175, 180–81, 195; and liberals' struggle for control of Democratic party machine (1976), 180–97; and Randolph, 180; refuses LBJ delegate slate (1968), 169; and Robert Strauss, 181; support for Tatum, 191–94
Carr, Waggoner, 138
Carswell, Harrold G., 31
Carter, Jimmy, 44–46, 60, 115, 176, 214, 255, 324; presidential campaign (1975–1976), 186–92, 196
Carter, Margaret, 114, 308n.23
Casdorph, Paul, 228
Castillo, Leonel, 115, 194, 195, 310n.62
Catholicism, and John F. Kennedy, 213–14
Chambers, Jim, 87
Chiles, Eddie, 64, 151
Chiles, Fran, 64
Christian, George, 106–7
Christian Americans, 126
CIO Political Action Committee, 127
Cisneros, Henry, 119, 250
Citizens for a Sales Tax, 106
Citizens for Goldwater, Goldwater's disapproval of campaign film, 319n.17

Citizens' Research Foundation (CRF), 80, 145, 149

Civil Rights Act of 1957, 30; LBJ and Ralph Yarborough's support for, 234, 248

Civil Rights Act of 1960, 31, 248, 251–52; LBJ and Yarborough's support for, 234

Civil Rights Act of 1964, 31, 124, 202, 205, 227; Bork opposed to, 266; Bush opposed to, 228, 267; and Compromise of 1877, 251; Goldwater opposed to, 227; LBJ's support for, 234, 248; Texas Republicans opposed to, 228–29; Tower opposed to, 31, 228–29, 234; Ralph Yarborough's support for, 31, 234

Civil War, 15, 18; rural poverty after, xxiv, 5

Clark, Ed, 100, 104–6

Clark, Lee, 104, 297n.80

Clark, Tom, 99

classes, Key's implicit definition of, 13. See also manual workers; upper class

Clayton, Billy, 107, 184–85, 189, 190, 266

Clayton, Will, 77

Clements, William P. (Bill), Jr., 29, 50–51, 95, 101, 122–23, 265; and Bright, 73; campaign expenditures (1982), 136; contributes to Helms campaign, 147; and Criswell, 214–15; defeats John Hill (1978), 176; and Horton issue in 1988 campaign, 268–69; as member of the ninety-nine, 74; and Perot, 78–79; and tax fight in legislature, 264; vetoes farm workers measure, 117; and Mark White, 57, 177, 199

Coastal States Gas Corp., 93

Cogburn, Ed, 182, 190

Cold War GI Bill, 32

Coleman, Lynn, 102

Coles, Robert, 129, 293n.10

Collie, Marvin, 91

Collins, Carr P., 213; and Jim Collins, 217

Collins, James (Jim), 201; and Carr P. Collins, 213; and Bentsen, 218; gives party for Dallas Republicans, 217; and Nelson Bunker Hunt, 76; opposes extension of Voting Rights Act, 234; defeated by Annette Strauss, 250

Commission on Party Structure and Delegate Selection (Democratic party), 172

Common Cause, 12, 145

Communist party, in America, 206

Communities Organized for Public Services (COPS), 255

Community Mental Health Centers Act, 30

"Compact of Fifth Avenue," Republican party and, 225

Comparative State Elections Project (CSEP), 36–38

Compromise of 1877, 251

Conaway, James, 17

Congress of Industrial Organizations (CIO), 124, 126–27, 278

Connally, John B., xvi, 91, 102, 195, 243; attempt while governor to change election years, 54; and bankruptcy, 263–64; and Barnes, 54, 263; and Bentsen, 182, 310n.4; and Christian, 106; as conservative paragon, 29; as coordinator of Texas Democrats for Nixon, 107; and Nelson Bunker Hunt, 76; and Johnson machine in Texas, 166; 1980 campaign of, 136; at 1988 Democratic convention, 169–72; 311–12n.19; and Religious Right, 218; as Republican, 203; and Robert Strauss, 174, 310n.4; and unit rule, 169–72; and Vinson & Elkins law firm, 100; and voter registration law, 51; and Don Yarborough, 1962 contest with, 27, 137–38

Connally, Tom, 86

conservatives, 17–39; advantaged in election campaigns by large donors, 137–43, 149, 151; basis of support for, 42–49; John Connally and Shivers as leaders of, 29; definition of, 29; within Democratic party, 7–8, 11, 13–14, 25–32, 158–79; higher proportion of in electorate than in population, 49–60, 65, 80–84; loss of Democratic control by, 159–61, 176–77, 180–97; and reaction to the 1960s, 205; and realignment, as described by Kevin Phillips, 233; in Republican party, 201, 254–59; and upper class, 65, 80–84. See also Bourbons; folk conservatism

Constitutional Convention of 1875, Texas, 21

Converse, Philip, 226, 229–31

Cookson, Peter, 89

Cooter, Al, 89

Coronado Club, in Houston, 91

corporate elite, 69–72; and corporations in politics, 92–95; definition of, 69–70; and political cohesion within upper class, 80; and super rich, 70. See also money in politics; upper class

corporate law firms, 95–103
corporations: and campaign donations, 144–
    50; and corporate law firms, 95–103; poli-
    tics of, 85–88, 92–95; recruitment of
    minorities and women by, 97. *See also*
    corporate elite; super rich
Cortes, Ernesto, Jr. (Ernie), 253, 255
Cosman, Bernard, 230
Cowdrey, Joe, 87
Cox, Jack, 166, 228
Cranfill, J. B., xxiii, xxiv, xxvii, 261
Creager, R. B., 198
Criswell, W. A., 207, 256, 265, 316–17n.53;
    Southern Baptists and, 212–16
Crow, Trammell, 65, 74, 151, 265
Cullen, Hugh Roy, 66
Cullen, Roy H., 126
Cullinan, Joseph ("Buckskin Joe"), 142
Cullinan, Nina, 142
Cullum, Charles, 71
Cullum, Robert, 71

Dallas Citizens Council, 77, 83, 249, 266
Dallas Junior League, 91
Daniel, Price, 29, 164–66
David, Paul T., 168
Davis, Cullen, 314n.16
Davis, Will D., 172
Dawkins, Pete, 266
Day, James C. (Jimmy), Jr., 104, 297n.80
Dean, Kris Wayne, 110
death rate, high agricultural, 300n.30; occu-
    pational, 120
Debs, Eugene V., xxvii
debutantes, Texas rich and, 90–91
De Leon, Diaz, 144
De Menil, Dominique, 81, 142
De Menil, John, 81, 142
Democratic National Committee (DNC),
    160, 168, 174–75, 180–82, 186, 190, 192,
    195
Democratic Organizing Committee (1950s),
    162
Democratic party: conservatives in, 17, 243;
    convention system's importance in, 155–
    58; defections to Wallace from, 59–60; and
    disfranchisement, 21; ethnic composition
    of, 323n.77; factionalism in, 7–8, 11, 13–
    14, 23–32, 158–79; funding for headquar-
    ters of, 313n.4; group support for liberal
    primary candidates in, 46–49; liberals'

struggle for control of, 155–79, 180–97;
    and opposition to Populists, xxiv, 19–20;
    in presidential campaign of 1988, 266–70;
    and registration law reforms, 51–55; and
    rules reforms, 169–76; and unit rule, 160–
    61, 169–72; and upper class, 80–83, 139–
    42, 144–46. *See also* Bourbons; white pri-
    mary system
Democratic presidential candidates, group
    support for, 42–46, 269–70
Democrats of Texas (DOT), 162, 164–65
DeNardo, James, 57–58; critics of, 285n.31
depression of 1980s, 262–66
desegregation, school: in Houston, 89, 224;
    U.S. Supreme Court and, 106
Dewey, Thomas, 80, 200
Dies, Martin, xvi, 126
discrimination, racial, by labor, 302–3n.58
disfranchisement, xxiii, 21–24, 50–55; in
    Key's theory, 8–9; and Populists as targets
    of, 277n.11
Dixie, Chris, 128
Dixiecrat party, 139, 206
Dixon, John, 71–72
Doggett, Lloyd, 26, 47, 179
Dole, Robert, 236
Dos Passos, John R., 99
Dubose, Danny Allen, 109–10, 116
Dugger, Ronnie, 40, 163, 173
Dukakis, Michael, 263, 267–69

Eastland, James, 76
Eckhardt, Bob, xiv, 54, 103, 125, 127
Edwards, Al, 267, 269
Eggers, Paul, 235
Eisenhower, Dwight D., xviii, 32, 73, 101,
    139, 164, 198, 214, 227; and black voters
    in 1956, 226; and civil rights plank at 1964
    Republican convention, 229; and Oveta
    Hobby, 75–76; and Sid Richardson, friend
    of, 73; as seen by Birch Society, 206; and
    Shivers machine, supported by, 162, 180
Elazar, Daniel J., 33
Electronic Data Systems Corp. (EDS), 78,
    145
Elementary and Secondary Education Act,
    32
Elkins, James ("Jim"), Jr., 91, 99–100, 101
Elkins, James ("Judge"), Sr., 98–100, 102
Ellis, Virginia, 147
Ely, Jane, 218

Endangered Species Act, 30
Engler, Robert, 83
Environmental Protection Agency (EPA), 118, 144, 247
Erwin, Frank C., Jr., 171
Eymard, David, 115

Facts Forum, H. L. Hunt and, 209–11
Fair Employment Practices Committee, 126
Falwell, Jerry, 29, 202, 215, 217
Farah Manufacturing Co., in El Paso, 131
Farb, Harold, 65
Farenthold, Frances ("Sissy"), 26, 41, 47, 103, 179, 186, 191; campaign funds in 1972 primary race, 141; in 1972 primary, 50, 140–41; in 1974 primary, 178
Farley, Jim, 207
Farm Bureau, 118
farm workers, 116–18
Farmers Alliance and Industrial Union, xxiv, 19
Fath, Creekmore, 164–65
Faulk, Henry, xxvii, 274n.24
Faulk, John Henry, 41, 274n.24
Fay, Albert, 226
Federal Deposit Insurance Corporation (FDIC), 263
Federal Election Campaign Act of 1971, 80, 305n.15
Federal Election Commission, 146, 188
Federal Energy Administration, 102
Federal Loan Agency, xvi
Federal Power Commission, 102
Fehrenbach, T. R., 33, 277n.5
Ferguson, James ("Farmer Jim"), 23, 278n.19
Ferguson, Miriam, 24
Ferraro, Geraldine, 229
Field, John Osgood, xviii
Fields, Wilmer C., 216
Fifteenth Amendment, 21
Figg, Harold, 193
Finance Committee to Re-elect the President (FCRP), 144–45
First City Bancorporation, 69, 98, 146
folk conservatism, as defined by Fehrenbach, 32–36, 281n.42
Ford, Gerald, 75, 78, 183, 188–89, 202, 214
Ford, Jon, 140, 149
Foy, Joe, 106
Francis, Jim, 146

Fraser, Donald, 172
fraud: 1896 Democratic, 19, 277n.12; savings and loan, 263; Texas Populists and, 20
Freeman, Richard B., 128–29
frontier ethic, Turner's, in Texas, 33–36
Fulbright & Jaworski, 95–103
fund-raising. See money in politics

Garner, John Nance, xvi, 104
Garwood, Ellen St. John, 77, 314n.16
Gibson, James, 160
Gladden, Don, 171
Glenn, John, 191
Glover, Robert W., 131
Goldberg, Billy, 142, 176, 196, 253
Golden Triangle (Texas), 124
Goldwater, Barry, 44, 73, 138, 171, 201, 204, 208; and Birch Society, 207, 315n.28; Bush's support for, 202; denounces "Compact of Fifth Avenue," 225; excites Texas conservatives, 189; and Haley, 209; opposed to Civil Rights Act of 1964, 227; pursues a white-oriented "southern strategy," 226–31, 319–20n.17; and racial polarization in 1964 electorate, 252; and rise of Texas Republicanism, 198; supported by Wallace, Tower, and Texas Republicans, 228
Gompers, Samuel, 127
Gonzalez, Henry B., xvii, 26, 40, 52–53
Good Government League, in San Antonio, 249, 266
Goodwyn, Lawrence (Larry), xxiv, 106, 276n.3
Gottlieb, David, 35
Graham, Billy, 76, 213
Graham, Donald Ralph, 277n.11
Gramm, Phil, 73, 244; anti-homosexual campaign of, 216, 218, 256; and Clements, 74; and Doggett, 179; as former Democrat, 199; and Rob Mosbacher, 78; supporters among the ninety-nine, 74
Gramm, Wendy, 244
Graves, Curtis, 171
Graves, Ruth, 117
Great Depression, xvi, 24, 125, 158, 264
Great Society, 137, 199, 217, 248
Green, George Norris, 206–7
Greenhill, Joe, 101
Grenier, John, 226
Griffith, Lanny, 236

Grover, Henry, 136, 140–41, 201
Guadalupe Mountains National Park, 30
Guest, Calvin, 176, 182–83, 190–96, 253,
    310n.62
Gulf Oil Co., 92, 94, 148
Gulf Resources and Chemical Co., 144
Gulf States Utilities, 150

Haden, Cecil R., 136
Hagstrom, Jerry, 103
Halbouty, Michel T., 75, 263
Haley, J. Evetts, 207–9, 214, 235
Hall, Anthony, 184, 188
Hall, Walter G., 140–41, 143, 159–60, 169,
    307n.7
Hamilton, G. G., xxvii
Hamilton, Richard F., xviii, 276n.36,
    284n.4
Hamon, Jake, 139
Hance, Kent, 73
Harlan, Doug, 218
Harris, Fred, 172, 186, 188
Harris, Louis, 35
Harris, Roy V., 59
Harris County, Texas, 101
Harris County (Texas) Democrats, 180
Harrison, Cecile, 191
Hart, Milledge A., III, 145
Harvin, William, 101
"have-nots," 12, 14, 55. See also poverty
Hay, Jess, 190, 192
Hayes, Rutherford B., 251
Haynsworth, Clement F., Jr., 31
Hazelton, Jared, 257
Head Start program, 30
Health, Education, and Welfare, U.S.
    Dept. of: Oveta Culp Hobby and, xviii,
    75–76
Heard, Alexander, 3, 307n.6
Helms, Jesse: campaign support from rich
    Texas Republicans, 147, 202–3; and Nel-
    son Bunker Hunt, 76, 212; and Religious
    Roundtable function in Dallas, 217; and
    Tower, 234
Henderson, Jim, 266
Herblock, 40
Herring, Pendleton, 157
Heston, Charlton, 212
Hicks, Joshua L., xxiii, xxiv–xxviii, 3, 261,
    271
Hightower, Jim, 29, 35, 40, 118–19, 253, 268

Hill, David B., 255
Hill, John, 98, 138, 176, 178–79, 196, 199,
    227
Hinajosa, Juan, 45
Hobby, Oveta Culp, xvii–viii, 91, 139; as
    member of the ninety-nine, 75–76
Hobby, William P. (Bill), Jr., 76; and
    Bentsen primary, 182; and leadership in
    legislative tax fight, 264; as lieutenant
    governor, 265
Hobby, William P., Sr., 75–76, 124, 139
Hofheinz, Fred, 249–50
Hofheinz, Roy, 249–50
Hofstadter, Richard, 205
Hogg, James S., 277
Holleman, Jerry, 164
Hollowell, Bill, 54
homeless population, in San Antonio 264
Hope, Bob, 212
Horton, Willie, 267–68, 328n.26
House, Edward M., xvi, xxv
Housing and Urban Development, U.S.
    Dept. of, 261
Houston, Sam, 18
Houston Independent School District
    (HISD), 95
Houston Lighting & Power Co., 94, 294n.32
Hubbard, Harry, 123–24, 187, 192, 194,
    303n.58
Hughes, Charles, 122
Humphrey, Hubert, 37, 59, 81, 167, 169,
    189
Hunt, H. L.: as big campaign contributor in
    1944; and children as members of the
    ninety-nine, 66; and Democratic ticket in
    1960, 316n.49; and family empire ca.
    1980, 67; influence of, 211; and Radical
    Right, 207, 209–14, 217; and Robison,
    217; ties to Shivers, Wayne, McCarthy,
    Robert H. Stewart III, and Criswell, 162,
    210, 213–14. See also Hunt, Nelson Bun-
    ker
Hunt, Lamar, 212
Hunt, Lyda, 66
Hunt, Nelson Bunker, 209; and Bright, 73;
    financial difficulties, 264; financial empire
    of, 67; Kennedy assassination and, 210;
    Radical Right and, 76–77, 206, 211; Wal-
    lace campaign and, 212
Hunt, Ray Lee, 66, 77, 151
Hunt, Ruth Ray, 66

Hunt, William, 67, 264
Hurt, Harry III, 40, 91, 210–11, 293–94n.24
Hutchinson, Everett, 102

ideological proclivities in Texas: distribution of, 26, 36–39; and voter preferences, 40–60; and voter turnout, 49–60. *See also* conservatives; liberals; moderates
illegal immigrants, 114, 299n.19
Illuminati, 203, 314n.16
Immigration and Naturalization Service (INS), U.S., 115, 195
immigration reform, Texas minorities' views on, 300n.22
International Committee for the Defense of Christian Culture, 76
Ivins, Molly, 40, 106, 261

Jackson, Henry, 81, 189
Jackson, Jesse, 267–69
Jackson, Shelby Stephen, 110
Janeway, Eliot, 225
Jasso, Sonia, 118
Javits, Jacob, 232
Jaworski, Leon, 97, 100–102
Jester, Beauford, 25, 29, 46, 161
Jim Crow system, 6, 28, 60, 205, 225, 227, 242, 251, 277n.11
job safety measures, 117–23
jobs, blue-collar. *See* manual workers
John Birch Society, 76, 203–4, 206–7, 211–12, 218, 228, 314n.16, 315n.25
Johnson, Eddie Bernice, 188, 195, 261
Johnson, Lady Bird, 210
Johnson, Lyndon B., xvi, 30, 137; and George R. Brown, 68, 73, 129; civil rights efforts of, 234, 248; and Dallas jostling incident, 210; and Democratic party organizational decline, 167; Great Society of, 199, 217; and Haley book, 209; liberals in 1956 and, 163–65; liberalism and, 25, 32, 279n.26; lobbyists and, 104–6; and 1964 election, 44, 54, 59, 82, 138, 204, 230; pursues Senate seat and vice presidency simultaneously (1960), 184, 198; Senate seat of won by Tower, 203; and Texas Democratic party control over, 165–66, 180; and Tower challenge in 1960, 225
Joiner, "Dad," 67
Jones, Jesse H., xvi, 92
Jones, Lee, 100–101

Jonsson, J. Erik, 77, 88, 145
Jordan, Barbara, xvii, 195–96, 262; and Jesse Jackson, 267; on LBJ's delegate slate in 1968, 169; Leland succeeds, 125; on Ralph Yarborough, 261
Justice, William Wayne, 257–58

Kahn, Herman, 87
Keeton, Richard, 100
Kemp, Jack, 210
Kempner family, of Galveston, Texas, 67
Kennedy, Edward, 30, 176, 261
Kennedy, John F., xvi, 30, 32, 51, 166, 226; assassination of, 73, 77, 170, 210, 250; civil rights stance, compared to Nixon's, 225; Democratic party disorganization encouraged by, 167; Tower opposes program of, 29; voter support for, 43–44
Kennedy, Robert, 169, 171
Key, V. O., Jr.: background of, 3; precursors of, 275n.5; and theory of southern politics, 3–10; and theory of Texas politics, 10–15 (explained), 240–59 (evidence for summarized)
Kilgarlin, William W., 305n.13
Kilgore, Joe, 100
King, Allan G., 131
King, Martin Luther, Jr., 209, 226, 234
King Ranch family, 67, 139
King Ranch fortune, 104
Kirby, John Henry, 92
Kleberg, Dick, 104
Klineberg, Stephen, 257
Knaggs, John, 236
Knights of Labor, 19
Kousser, J. Morgan, 19–22, 278nn.14 and 17
Ku Klux Klan, 24, 207

labor union precincts, voting returns from, 43, 48
labor unions: and anti-union laws, 105, 128; campaign donations by, 149; civil rights support for, 124, 249; communist influence in, 126; in Democratic conventions, 162, 166, 169, 187, 194–95; in Key's theory, 10; and manual workers, 123–28; and manual workers' willingness to join, 131; membership in, 128–30; in nineteenth century, 19; opposed to poll tax, 22; racial discrimination in, 123–24, 302–3n.58; sources of hostility to, 128–32; and sup-

port for Campbell, 23; women in, 124. *See also* AFL-CIO

Landrum-Griffin Act, 128

La Raza Unida party, 134, 140–41, 251

LaRouche, Lyndon, 218

Law, Theodore N., 136, 202

law firms. *See* corporate law firms

League of Women Voters, 51

Lee, Frania Tye, 288

Leeper, John, 88

Leland, Mickey, 124–25, 176, 194, 196, 235, 254, 267

LeMay, Curtis, 76, 212

Levison, Andrew, 111

Levy, Gus, 85

Lewellen, Wilbur, 72

Lewinson, Paul, 275n.5

Lewis, Arthur M., 287

Lewis, Gib, 17

liberalism in Texas: bases of support, 40–60; defined generally, 27–29, 279n.22; in the 1980s, 253

liberals: basis of support for, 40–49; campaign donations from the wealthy, 137–43, 149, 151, 305n.13; in the Democratic party, 7–8, 11, 13–14, 25–32, 158–79, 243–46; and LBJ, 279n.26; in Key's theory, 10–39; and labor unions, 123–28; nonvoting of, 49–58; in Republican party, 201; statewide candidates' victories in 1982, 253; takeover of Democratic machine, 159–61, 176–77, 180–97; in Texas, compared to selected states and the U.S., 38–39; and the upper class, 79, 81–82, 107–8; in voting-age population, 37; and Wallace, 59–60

Liddy, G. Gordon, 144

Liedtke, William, Jr., 144

LIFE LINE, H. L. Hunt and, 210–11, 213

Lindsay, Jon, 294n.32

Ling, Jim, 85–88

Ling-Temco-Vought Corp. *See* LTV Corporation

lobbyists, 103–7, 264, 266; defined, 296n.71

Locke, Eugene, 138

Long, Stuart, 158–59

Love, Ben, 94–95

Love, George, 87

Lowenstein, Allard, 169

LTV Corporation, 70, 85–88, 92, 146

lynching: of Jesse Washington in Waco, xxvii–xxviii; liberal opposition to, 28

Lyon, James, 203

McAshan, S. M., Jr., 77

McAshan, Susan, 77

McCarthy, Eugene, 31, 169–70, 180

McCarthy, Glenn, 139, 264

McCarthy, Joseph, 28, 30, 199; and homosexual-baiting, 256, 326n.17; H. L. Hunt and, 209; Shivers and, 76; Wayne and, 210

McClendon, Gordon, 137–38

McClesky, Clifton, 121, 137, 155

McGovern, George, xvii, 45, 80–82, 172, 174–75, 180, 183, 190

McGovern-Fraser Commission, 172, 174

Mackin, B. John, 71

Mackintosh, Prudence, 91

McWilliams, Carey, 114

Manges, Clinton, 80, 137; and liberals, 305n.13

Manion Forum, 76

Mann, Ted, 86

manual workers, 109–32; dangerous working conditions of, 109–12, 116–23; defined, 111–12, 298n.12; distribution in Texas work force, 112–13; ethnic minorities among, 114–16; and labor unions, 124–32; political disorganization of, 112–16

Marcus, Stanley, 139

Marek, Ann, 194

Marshall, F. Ray, 115

Martin, James, 227

Martin, Roscoe, 19, 274n.2

Mather, Russ, 236

Mattox, Jim, 40, 237, 253–54; and Manges, 305n.13

Mauro, Gary, 253; and Manges, 305n.13

Mauzy, Oscar, 54, 188

Maverick, Maury, Jr., xvii, 40, 171

Maverick, Maury, Sr., xvi, 162, 274

Mayer, Johnny, 87

Mazorra, Maria, 118

Medicaid, 246, 248

Medicare, 246, 248

Medoff, James L., 128–29

Meitzen, E. O., 274n.24

Meitzen, E. R., xxvii, 274n.24

Mengden, Walter, 203

Meredith, James, 227
Metropolitan Organization, The (TMO), 255
Mexican Americans: and Democratic conventions, 162, 166, 170–72, 174, 177, 187–88, 191, 193–96; and illegal immigrants, 114–15, 300n.22; and labor unions, 124, 130–31; in manual work force, 114–16; and nonvoting, 26, 53, 56–58; officeholding among, 249–50; and Republicans, 234, 237–38; 323n.77; voting patterns of, 14, 43–44. *See also* disfranchisement
Mexican American Democrats (MAD), 194
Mikulski, Barbara, 175
Mikulski Commission, 175
Milburn, Beryl Buckley, 202
Miller, Roy, 104
Mills, C. Wright, 65, 83, 113, 287–88n.7
Mills, Wilbur, 81, 145
minorities, ethnic. *See* African Americans; Mexican Americans
"Minute Women," 208, 314n.21
Mischer, Walter, 151
Mississippi Freedom Democratic Party, 169
Mitchell, John, 78, 231, 322n.46
Mitchell, Stephen, 162
moderates: as defined by Kevin Phillips, 233; in Democratic conventions, 176; distribution in Texas of, 36–39; and Eggers campaign of 1972, 235; in Republican party, 201; in 1980s, 253
Moncrief, Mike, 77
Moncrief, W. A. ("Monty"), Sr., 77–78
Moncrief, W. A. ("Tex"), Jr., 77–78
Mondale, Walter, 191, 239; minority vote for in Texas, 43, 46; minority vote for nationally, 282n.50
money in politics, 133–51; and big donors, 136–37, 139–46, 305n.13; and corporations, 144–49; influence on candidates and officials, 149–51; influence on elections, 133–35, 304n.2
Montford, John, 137
Moody family, of Galveston, 67
Moore, Frank, 192
Moral Majority, 29, 76, 215
Mosbacher, Robert (Rob), Jr., 75, 78, 265
Mosbacher, Robert, Sr., 75, 265; as member of the ninety-nine, 78
Muñiz, Ramsey, 81, 140–41
Murchison, Clint, Jr., 68, 145, 264

Murchison, John, 68, 145, 212, 264
Murray, Richard, 304n.2
Muse, Vance, 126
Muskie, Edmund, 81, 191
Myrdal, Gunnar, 3, 224

National Conservative Political Action Committee (NCPAC), 76–77, 212
National Defense Education Act of 1958, 32, 281
National Institute for Occupational Safety and Health, 120
National Labor Relations Board, 131
National Maritime Union, 126
National Occupational Hazard Survey, 121
National Petroleum Council, 78
National Rifle Association, 219, 257
neighborhoods, Texas rich and their, 88–89
Newberry, Robert, 40
New Deal, in Texas, 11, 12, 16, 123, 124; great causes of, 28
New Religious Right, 215. *See also* Radical Right; religious issues; Southern Baptists
newspapers, socialist, xxv
night riders, in East Texas, 19
"ninety-nine" (richest Texans). *See* super rich
Nixon, Richard M., xvi, 37, 45, 81, 85, 226, 232; big businessmen's unhappiness with, 87; and busing issue in Texas, 236; and Clements, 74; coattails of, in Texas, 199; and "Compact of Fifth Avenue," 224–25; and Jaworski, 97; and McGovern, 80; and OSHA, 30, 302n.49; and Perot, 78; Kevin Phillips's book dedicated to, 321–22n.46; super rich give money to, 145; Supreme Court nominees of, 31; southern support for in 1960, 229–30; and Tower support for, 202
Nolan, Joe, 235
Northcott, Kaye, 40
Novak, Robert, 229

Occupational Safety and Health Act of 1970 (OSHA), 30, 120–21, 280n.29
Occupational Safety and Health Administration (OSHA), 95, 110, 121–22, 301–2n.48
O'Connor family, of Victoria, Texas, 67
O'Daniel, W. Lee ("Pappy"), 47, 208, 213, 256
O'Donnell, Peter, 88, 202, 226

O'Neill, Thomas ("Tip"), xvii
Oil, Chemical, and Atomic Workers Union (OCAW), 120
oil industry. *See* petroleum industry
Olds, Greg, 167, 169
one-partyism: Creager on, 198; Key's theory of, 6–8; in Texas, 11, 112. *See also* two-partyism
open housing bill of 1968: Bush support for, 202; Ralph Yarborough support for, 31
organized labor. *See* labor unions
Orwell, George, 115
Osmond Brothers, 212

Padre Island National Seashore, 30
Palm, Nancy, 201
Palmer, Bruce, 20, 22
Park, Milton, 22
Parmet, Herbert, 172
Parten, Jubal R., 47, 142
Passel, Jeffrey S., 299n.19
Patman, Carrin, 188, 191
Patman, Wright, xvi, 89
Patterson, Paige, 215
Peale, Norman Vincent, 210
Peirce, Neal R., xx, 103, 273n.4
Peña, Albert, 171
Pennzoil Corp., 144, 266
People's party, 1890s. *See* Populism
Perot, H. Ross, 78–79, 145, 265–66
Perry, Robert J., 137
Persell, Caroline, 89
petroleum industry, xv, 35–36; links to other industries, 67–69; and politics, xvi, 64, 66–68, 73–79, 93–95, 105–6, 139, 142, 144–51, 162, 209–12; as source of wealth for super rich, 67
Phillips, Howard, 212
Phillips, Kevin, and strategy for Republicans, 231–35, 259, 321n.46, 322n.51
Phillips Petroleum, 148
phosgene gas, and industrial accidents, 109–11
Pickens, T. Boone, 78, 95, 151
Pigg, Robert, 237
Pittsburgh Corning Company, industrial accidents at, 119–20
political action committees (PACs): and Big Three Houston law firms, 100; and business corporations, 136–40, 145–49; and labor unions, 149

political culture, defined by Elazar, 33
poll tax, as voting requirement: abolished, 51, 278n.17; established, 21–24; in Key's theory, 8; and Terrell Election Law, 21–23; and turnout decline, 24, 51–52, 54
"poor whites": low turnout of, 51, 53, 57–58; as target of poll tax, 22; voting behavior of, 43–49, 60. *See also* "have nots"; poverty
Populism, xxiv–xxv, 4, 5–7, 18–22, 25, 274n.24, 275n.3, 276n.3, 277n.11, 277–78n.14
Post, Troy, 86
Pouland, John, 187
poverty, 114–16, 264; Texas expenditures on, 270–71. *See also* "have-nots"; "poor whites"
Powell, Adam Clayton, Jr., 252
Powers, Pike, 102
presidential campaign of 1988, 266–70
Pressler, Paul, 215
Prindle, David, 134
Prohibitionists, 4

racial polarization: and Phillips's thesis, 233; in presidential campaigns, 230–31 (1964), 239 (1968), 238–39 (1984), 269 (1988); between Republican and Democratic parties, 238; sources of, 252
Radical Right: and beliefs of various activists in, 314n.16, n.21; defined, 205–6; in Democratic party, 206; and labor union bashing, 126; and racism, 126, 206–7, 209, 213–14; religious component, 212–18; in Republican party, 201–220; and respectable Right, 201–3, 216–20, 238
Radnofsky, Barbara, 98
Rainey, Homer P., 25–27, 46–47, 127, 160; support for compared with that of LBJ and Ralph Yarborough, 279n.26
Ramada Club, in Houston, 91
Ramsey, Ben, 105
Randolph, Frankie, 142, 162–66, 180, 308n.23
Rapoport, Bernard, 140, 193–94; election year donations by, 305n.10
Ray, C. L., 100
Ray, DeWitt, 3d, 90
Ray, Ruth, 66
Rayburn, Sam, xvi, 161–63, 165, 180
Reagan, Ronald, 136, 177, 183, 201; appoints Texas fundraiser to head OSHA,

121; and Anne Armstrong, 96; coattails of, in Texas, 199; and Crow, 78; Evangelical support for, 255, 324n.2; Gerald Ford challenged by, 189, 235; and Halbouty, 263; Robert Mosbacher as fund-raiser for, 78; opposes open housing law, 227; and Religious Right, 215–18; and Tower, xviii, 202; and Vinson & Elkins, 101–2; and Wallace voters, 60

"Reaganomics," public disenchantment with, 253

realignment of parties, 6–15, 43–49, 199–201; and class, 230; defined, 319n.12; and factions within Democratic party, 155–79; impact of, 243–46; and race, 221–39

Reavis, Dick J., 316–17n.53

Reconstruction, 5, 18–19, 74

Reconstruction Finance Corporation, xvi

Reed, Tom, 50

registration laws, Texas voting, 50–54

Reinhard, David W., 205, 216

religion: of corporate elite, 70–71; of super rich, 66; of U.S. presidents, 213–14

religious issues: absence of in Key's theory, 244; Evangelical support of presidential candidates in 1976, 1980, and 1984, 324n.2; and Radical Right, 212–18

Republican National Committee (RNC), xviii, 236, 265

Republican National Finance Committee, 78

Republican party: basis of, 199–205; and busing issue, 236; in campaigns of 1988, 266–70; and convention delegates' income, 174–75; and ethnic minorities, 226, 229, 232, 234–39, 256–57; and ethnic minority turnout, 57, 177; Goldwater movement's significance for, 198, 201; growth of, following liberal takeover of Democratic machine, 197; headquarters and staff of, 313n.4; and homosexual issue, 216–18, 256–57; in Key's theory, 10, 14; 1988 ethnic composition of, 323n.77; in nineteenth century, 20; opposition to national health insurance, 176–77; opposition to poll tax in 1902 by, 22; PAC support for, 147; prospects for the future of, 257–59; pursuit of Wallace voters by, 60; and race issue, 221–39, 251–52; and Radical Right, 201–20; rise of since 1961, 198–239; and "Shivercrats" in 1952, 161–62,

180; and southern voter support for in 1964, 44; Tower election's significance for, 198; and upper class, 44, 46, 73–81, 139–41, 144–46

Reyes, Ben, 124, 195, 256

Reynolds v. Sims (1964), 247

Rice, Lawrence, 278n.16

Rice University, 90, 295n.43

Richards, Ann, 40–41, 253

Richardson, Rupert N., 19

Richardson, Sid, xvi, 73

"rim states," and blacks, 9, 11

Ripon Society, 232

Robertson, Corbin J., 63, 66

Robertson, Pat, 76, 217, 267

Robison, James, 217–18

Rockefeller, Nelson, 200, 224–26, 232

Roe v. Wade (1973), 173, 247

Rogers, Adrian, 215

Roosevelt, Franklin Delano, xvi–xvii, 24, 139, 159–60, 207, 214, 217

Roosevelt, Theodore, xxv; Bull Moose party and, xxvii

Rosenstone, Steven J., 49

Rottenberg, Dan, 287–88n.7

Rowland, Robert, 121

Ruiz v. Estelle (1980), 257

Rusher, William A., 231

Sadat, Anwar, 78

salaries, of Texas corporate elite, 71–72; in Big Three law firms, 97

Sanford, Marion ("Sandy"), 106

Sanford, Terry, 81

Sargent, Ben, 40

Sayers, Joseph, xxv

Scarlett, Harold, 109–11

Schieffer, Tom, 184

Schlafly, Phyllis, 217, 226

Schmidt, Fred, 122

Schoellkopf, Wilson, 87

Scholz Beer Garten, liberals' meeting at, 185

schools, preferred by Texas rich, 89–90

Schwartz, A. R. ("Babe"), 54, 150, 188

Scranton, William, 228

Sealy, Tom, 100

Seay, Harry L., 160, 307n.6

secession referendum, 18

Securities and Exchange Commission, 102

Shell Oil Co., 70, 89, 92, 120

Shinn, Allen, 52
"Shivercrats," 161, 166
Shivers, Allan, 161, 177; appointments phi-
    losophy of, 149, 151; and Billie Carr, con-
    frontation with, 180; as conservative
    leader, 29, 243; establishment connec-
    tions of, 91, 99; and Oveta Culp Hobby,
    76; and politics in 1952, 27, 162, 180; Rad-
    ical Right connections with, 25, 76, 210;
    school desegregation and, 224; Ralph Yar-
    borough's challenge of, 163
Shriver, Sargent, 81, 187–88
Skeen, Clyde, 86
Slagle, Bob, 196, 253
slavery, 6
Sloan, Hugh W., Jr., 144
Smith, Adam, 65, 92
Smith, Frank, on Goldwater's campaign in
    South, 319–20n.17
Smith, Griffin, 97
Smith, Preston, 29, 138, 140–41, 235
Smith, Richard Austin, 287
Smith v. Allwright (1944), 26, 159, 246
social directories, Texas cities, 71
social expenditures in Texas, 270–71
Social Security, 28, 246
socialism, xxiv–xxvii, 274n.15; and Popu-
    lism, 274n.24
Soukup, James R., 64, 80, 94
Southern Baptists: and corporate rich, 71;
    and Criswell, 212–16; and homosexual
    issue, 215–16, 218; and race issue, 213–
    14; and Radical Right, 212–18, 311n.14
Southern Christian Leadership Conference,
    226
Southern Methodist University, 71, 90, 208
"southern strategy": of conservatives, 60; of
    Goldwater, 226–31, 319n.17; of Key, 60,
    224; and Kevin Phillips's thesis, 231–34
Southwest Open Shop Association, 124
Southwest Voter Research Institute, 58
Southwestern Bell Telephone Co., 94
Spradling, Kenneth Wayne, 109
Spradling, Lynda Faye, 109
Spradling, Robert Avery, 109
Stanley, Charles, 215
State Federation of Labor (Texas), 22
Stauffer, Mervin L., 145
Stern, Andy, 95
Stevenson, Adlai, 75, 162, 164, 210, 226
Stewart, James, 97

Stewart, Robert III, 91, 210
Strake, George, 151, 217, 237
Strauss, Annette, 250, 266
Strauss, Robert: and Billie Carr, 175, 181;
    corporate law firm of, 102–3; as DNC
    chair, xviii, 100, 174, 182; as DNC treas-
    urer, 310n.4; friendship with Connally,
    xvii, 182; Annette Strauss and, 250; sup-
    ports loophole primaries, 191
strike, 1920 Texas longshoremen's, 124–25
Strong, Donald S., 3, 44, 227, 230
Sundquist, James, 251
super rich (ninety-nine richest Texans ca.
    1980), 65–69; and corporate elite, 70; and
    depression of 1980s, 264–65, 327n.16;
    politics of, 72–79, 81, 139, 145–46, 265–66
"Super-American," John Bainbridge de-
    fines, 63
Supreme Court, U.S.: Bork nominated to,
    266; Carswell nominated to, 31; Hayns-
    worth nominated to, 31; Roe v. Wade and,
    173; school desegregation decision by,
    106, 205; Smith v. Allwright and, 26, 159,
    205; Texas all-white primary declared un-
    consititutional by, 25, 46, 51, 238
Sweezy, Paul M., 88

Taft, Robert, 75
Taft-Hartley Act, 74, 128
Tarrance, V. Lance, 255
Tatum, John Henry, 182, 191–95
Tawney, R. H., 64
Tedin, Kent L., 304n.2
Tejeda, Frank, 255
Temple, Arthur, Jr., 79
Temple, Arthur ("Buddy") III, 79
Tenneco Oil Co., 69–70, 92, 145, 147
Terrell, Alexander Watkins, 21
Terrell Election Law, Texas passes, 21–23,
    51, 277n.14. See also white primary sys-
    tem; poll tax, as voting requirement
Texas: demographic characteristics of, xv–
    xvi; political importance of, xvi–xx; poli-
    tics, Key's theory of, 10–15
Texas, University of. See University of Texas
    at Austin
Texas Association of Realtors, 147
Texas Association of Taxpayers, 106
Texas Automobile Dealers Association, 147
Texas Chemical Council, 104
Texas Civil Liberties Union, 117

Texas Democrats for Eisenhower, 162
Texas Democrats for Nixon, 107
Texas Eastern Gas Transmission Company, 68, 145
Texas Good Roads / Transportation Association, 106
Texas House Elections Committee, 182
Texas Industrial Areas Foundation Network, 253–54
Texas Instruments, 72, 77, 88, 145
Texas Manufacturers Association (TMA), 80, 121
Texas Medical Association, 147
Texas Observer, 119, 163
Texas Occupational Safety Act, 121
Texas Railroad Commission, 79, 134
Texas Regulars, 159, 307n.6
Texas Research League, 83, 103
Texas Society of Certified Public Accountants, 106
Texas State Democratic Executive Committee (SDEC), 158–61, 164–67, 174, 176–77, 180, 182–83, 189–90, 193, 195–96
Texas Supreme Court, 179, 270
Texas Technological College, 165, 208
Thayer, George, 143
Thompson, Senfronia, 184, 188
Thurmond, Strom, 76, 206, 213, 227, 229, 231
Tower, John, xviii, 16, 203, 216; and civil rights, 228, 236; and Ed Clark, 105–6; Dallas establishment honors, 87; Goldwater backed by, 318n.7; Gramm succeeds, 179; JFK opposed by, 29; 1961 Senate victory, 166; opposes Civil Rights Act of 1964, 229; Reaganites opposed to, 209, 234–35; as Secretary of Defense nominee, 270; segregationist position of, 224; and Texas GOP, 198–220
Transportation, U.S. Department of, 102, 145
Truan, Carlos, 45, 261
Truman, Harry, 77, 160–61, 214
Tucker, Harvey J., 285n.31
Turner, Frederick Jackson, 33–34
Twenty-fourth Amendment, 51
two-partyism, in Key's theory, 6–8, 14. See also one-partyism

Udall, Morris, 186
United Farm Workers, 117

United States Industrial Council, 95
University of Texas at Austin: Rainey fired by regents of, 25, 46–47; upper-class attendance at, 90
Upham, Chet, 201
Upjohn Chemical Plant, industrial accidents at, 109–11, 116, 118
upper class: background of corporate elite, 69–72; background of super rich, 66–67; as Bourbon Democrats, 19–23; campaign donations by, 136–37, 139–51; cohesion of, 65, 80–84, 139–42; competition within, 64; and corporate law firms, 95–103; and corporate links, 67–69, 92–103; defined, 65, 286–88nn.5, 6, and 7; Democratic convention and, 159–60, 162, 168; in depression of 1980s, 263–66, 327n.16; and disfranchisement, 19–23; institutions of, 85–108; in Key's theory, 5–15; and lobby, 103–7; political strength of, 82–84; politics of, 80–84; and Republican party, 198, 201–4; and separation of ownership and control, 65; as a status group, 88–92; and wealth of corporate elite; 71–72. See also corporate elite; super rich
urbanism, in Key's theory, 9, 11
Uribe, Hector, 45, 117

Valley Interfaith, 255
Vance, Cyrus, 78
Vedlitz, Arnold, 285n.31
Velasquez, Willie, 58
Vietnam War, 28, 30, 45, 169; Brown & Root's involvement in, 68; opposed by Ralph Yarborough, 31
Viguerie, Richard, 215
Vinson & Elkins, 95–103
voter turnout: determinants of, 49–55; following disfranchisement, 23–24; effects of, 49–58; in Key's theory, 6, 8–9; by minorities, 57; since 1944, 54–57
Voting Rights Act of 1965, 17, 31, 53, 205, 231, 234, 247; and Compromise of 1877, 251; and growth of Republican party, 233; impact of on election of minority officials, 249–50; LBJ's role in passage of, 248

Walker, Charlie, 87
Walker, Tom, 86
Wallace, George C., 81, 182, 185; backs Goldwater campaign, 228; Briscoe's initial

1972 support for, 174; and Bush, 202;
  Democratic delegates in 1972 for, 183;
  and Houston corporate law firms, 101;
  and Nelson Bunker Hunt, 76, 211–12; and
  racial code words, 320n.19; strategy of
  based on race issues, 59; support for in
  Texas, 37, 45, 59, 173, 188; supporters of
  join Republican ranks, 204, 238, 255,
  314n.17; threat to Nixon in 1968, 231
Warren, Earl, 224
Washington, Craig, 40, 45, 236, 254
Washington, Jesse, lynching of, xxvii–
  xxviii
Watergate Hotel, 1972 break-in at, 144–45
Watson, Albert, 320
Watson, Marvin, Jr., 168
Watts, Ray, 91
Wayne, John, 210
Weddington, Sarah, 173, 247
Weeks, O. Douglas, 162, 166
Weinstein, James, 274n.15
Welch, Louie, 101, 256
Welch, Robert, 206, 211, 314n.16
Wells, Jim, 22
West, Felton, 79
West, Jim, 139
West, John, 320n.19
West, Wesley, 139
Westwood, Jean, 174
White, Danny, 212
White, Mark, 177, 196; appointees of, 79,
  151, 238; Bass family and, 73; Clements
  and, 57, 74; corporate law firms and, 102;
  expenditures in 1982 of, 136; group basis
  for support of, 157; minority support for,
  57, 177
White, Theodore, 223, 225
White Citizens' Council, 320n.19
white primary system: as voting barrier, 8,
  21, 25–26, 28, 46, 51, 159, 205, 238; and
  Terrell Election Law, 21; in Texas, de-
  clared unconstitutional, 25
Whitmire, Kathy, 249–50, 256
Whittenburg, Edward, 138
Whitworth, Harry, 104
Wiess, Harry, 139
Wiess, Margaret, 101
Wild, Claude, Jr., 148, 306n.31
Willeford, George, 236
Williams, Clayton, 265
Williams, Esther, 182
Williamson, Billy, 119–120

Wilson, Woodrow, xvi
Windsor, Duane, 92–93
"winner-take-all" Democratic primaries,
  183–86. See also "Bentsen bill"
Wirtz, Alvin, 104–5
Wirtz, Willard W., 121
Wolfe, Kris, 236
Wolfinger, Raymond E., xviii, 49
women: Big Three law firms' recruitment of,
  97; in Democratic convention politics,
  162–64, 166, 172, 174, 177, 183, 190,
  308n.23
Women's Army Auxiliary Corp., Oveta Culp
  Hobby and, xviii, 76
women's rights movement, 247–48
women's suffrage, xxvii
Wood, Robert E., 210
Woodrow, Sharon, 118
Woods, Stanley C., 26
Woodward, C. Vann, 3, 8, 20, 251, 275n.3,
  276n.3
Wooley, Bryan, 281n.41
Workers Compensation Act, 117
workers' compensation system, 110
working class. See manual workers
Works Progress Administration, 28
Wortham, Gus, 99
Wright, Charles Alan, 229
Wright, Clymer, 201
Wright, Jim, xvii, xix, 76, 78, 270
Wyatt, Oscar, Jr., 203

Yarborough, Don, 26–27, 47, 137–38, 142,
  166, 282
Yarborough, Ralph W., xvii, 27, 162, 177,
  180, 185–87, 191, 199, 258; Bentsen defeats, 178, 237, 281n.41; and Ed Clark,
  106; and education reform, xvi; group
  basis of support for, 47–48; group support
  for, compared to LBJ's and Rainey's,
  279n.26; Walter Hall backs, 143; and LBJ
  in 1964, 54; as liberal leader, 25, 29–32; in
  1964 election, 137–38, 167; and race
  issue, 224, 237; and Shivers, 76; sponsors
  major national legislation, 30–32,
  302n.49; statewide campaigns of, 29; sup-
  ports civil rights measures, 30–31, 228,
  234; Texas Observer fund-raiser for, 261;
  underfunding of 1970 election, 281n.41;
  votes received by, 26
Young Men for Bush, 77
Young Men for James Collins, 77